CASE STUDIES IN CONSUMER BEHAVIOUR

CASE STUDIES IN CONSUMER BEHAVIOUR

Edited by
S. Ramesh Kumar
Professor of Marketing
Indian Institute of Management Bangalore
Bangalore

PEARSON
Chennai • Delhi • Chandigarh

Published by Dorling Kindersley (India) Pvt. Ltd, Licensees of Pearson Education in South Asia.

ISBN 978-81-317-7448-9

First Impression

Head Office: 7th Floor, Knowledge Boulevard, A-8(A), Sector 62, Noida 201 309, UP, India.
Registered Office: 11 Community Centre, Panchsheel Park, New Delhi 110 017, India.

Compositor: White Lotus Infotech Pvt. Ltd, Puducherry.
Printer: India Binding House.

CONTENTS

PREFACE

After the launch of "Cases in Marketing Management" in collaboration with Ivey Business School and Pearson education, I thought the case collection needs to be furthered into one of the sub-areas of Marketing—Consumer Behaviour. With its interface with various other areas of marketing such as brand management, advertising and internet marketing, Consumer Behaviour seemed to be a good domain for a set of cases that cover a wide range of issues associated with the subject. Students who pursue Consumer Behaviour course after an exposure to the basic principles of marketing require systematic inputs on consumer behaviour and cases that reflect related issues that are important in an emerging context like the Indian marketplace.

There are several objectives associated with learning consumer behaviour. Firstly, students who are prospective managers should not only know about working out marketing strategies but also use the knowledge to emphasize the linkages between consumer behaviour and marketing strategies. A good collection of cases that enable students to understand how concepts of consumer behaviour connect with marketing strategies is one of the ways to strengthen the consumer behaviour course. Secondly, students of consumer behaviour need to be exposed to the unique challenges that are associated with marketing in an emerging market like India. A compilation of Cases on consumer behaviour could serve as a vital channel through which unique decision making scenarios can be taught. Finally the differences in applying the concepts of consumer behaviour across different product categories provide valuable insights to students and also supplement the learning that they derive out of regular textbooks with Indian examples.

The emerging Indian marketing scenario requires a specific mention whenever cases are presented to students. The Indian context has certain unique aspects: The huge market at the lower economic strata that runs to millions of households for fast moving consumer goods, the large youth population that makes the market especially attractive to several multinational brands, the growth of luxury markets in categories like watches, jewelry, holiday travel, apparel and accessories, and beauty care, the emergence of modern retail outlets in an environment that is still characterized by kirana shops and the enhanced rural consumption across several categories are just some of the important factors that make the Indian context significantly different from the Western markets.

Cases in Consumer Behaviour add value to the understanding of these context specific challenges.

The cases presented in this book require the student to read up the concepts in any textbook on consumer behaviour (after brushing up the fundamentals on the basic principles of marketing). This would ensure that the objective of providing these cases is well served. There needs to be an effort on the part of the student to apply the concepts of consumer behaviour to connect with the case information without treating the cases as strategy cases.

I trust that this collection of consumer behaviour cases will provide incremental value and augment the methodology of learning consumer behaviour in Indian business schools.

ACKNOWLEDGEMENTS

New ventures and attempts are a part of any environment and, more specifically, such endeavours are important for academics in an emerging academic environment like India. Every step taken towards academic experimentation, however incremental it may be, adds value, in my view, to the academic context. Prof. Paul Beamish's (Director, Engaging Emerging Markets Research Centre, Ivey Business School) suggestions on having a case book to suit the Indian context was indeed the basic motivational trigger that set me working on this project. His grasp of the Indian environment and the need for a conceptual book on marketing cases to address the environment opened up a dialogue between us on a host of important issues that were important to such a proposition in the Indian context. I thank him for triggering the project into action.

Amber Thomson (Ivey Publishing) provided the support I needed to have a complete grasp of the Ivey cases related to the area. She was also instrumental in handling several legal issues that had to be sorted out before the contract was signed. I thank her for all her efforts and focus that was critical to the endeavour.

Raza Khan, Editorial Director – B&E and HSS, Pearson Education, was highly excited about the project. He ensured that the various points of coordination were taken care of without any barriers to the completion of this project. I thank him for encouraging the project and being open to such "new to the environment" proposition. I would like to thank A. Maran for the help he has provided in this project. I also thank M. R. Ramesh and Sethurajan for their timely interventions to ensure that the contents published were in order.

I thank Dr. Pankaj Chandra of Indian Institute of Management Bangalore, India, for the facilities that were provided to me during this project.

Finally, I thank my parents who have always had a word of encouragement to any endeavour of mine and my wife Amrith Ramesh and daughter Sahana for providing a conducive environment that enabled me to focus on the work. Last but not the least, I would like to recall with gratitude, my association with Dr. B. Ilango, former Vice Chancellor of Bharathiar University, who had extended unflinching support to my initial academic endeavours.

S. Ramesh Kumar
Professor of Marketing
Indian Institute of Management Bangalore
rkumar@iimb.ernet.in

ABOUT THE EDITOR

Dr. S. Ramesh Kumar is Professor of Marketing, Indian Institute of Management Bangalore, India, for the last sixteen years. He has a diverse mix of industrial, academic and research experience spanning thirty years. His areas of interests include branding, consumer behaviour interface, cultural values, relationship marketing and combining online and offline marketing strategies. He has a PhD with an MBA and a basic degree in Engineering.

Awarded the ICFAI Best Teacher Award by Association for Indian Management Schools (AIMS), S. Ramesh Kumar specializes in applying marketing and behavioural concepts to the Indian marketing context. His co-authored papers/cases have appeared in *Journal of Integrated Marketing Communication*, *Journal of Brand Management*, *Ivey Business Journal*, *Marketing Review*, *Journal of Customer Behavior* and *Asia Pacific Journal on Economics & Business*. In addition, he has contributed several case titles to Richard Ivey Business School's case collection, Ivey's collection on marketing cases) and IIMB–Harvard Business School collaborative cases.

His book publications are *Marketing and Branding–The Indian Scenario*; *Marketing Nuggets—Conceptual Dimensions in Marketing*, which won the first prize awarded by The Federation of Educational Publishers in India; *Application Exercises in Marketing*; *Managing Indian Brands—Marketing Concepts and Strategies*; *Conceptual Issues In Consumer Behavior–The Indian Context*; and *Consumer Behaviour and Branding: Concepts, Readings and Cases–The Indian Context*. He has also co-authored a text book *Consumer Behavior* with Leon Schiffman and Lezlie Kanuk in collaboration with Joseph Wisenblit.

He has participated and presented papers at international conferences conducted by American Marketing Association at Vanderbilt University U.S.; Maastricht University, Netherlands; University of Queensland, Australia; Academy of Marketing Conference at U.K; Asian Business Case Writing Conference conducted by National University of Singapore at Singapore and International Congress of Psychology conducted by Swedish Psychological Association at Stockholm. He has been an invited speaker/Visiting Scholar at universities abroad for delivering specialized lectures on marketing in the Indian context.

Ramesh Kumar is on the editorial board of *Journal of Asian Business Studies* along with academics drawn from the best of business schools in the world.

Ramesh Kumar has conducted a number of training programs for corporate executives in Indian and multinational organizations.

1

Romantic Rides or Fiery Thrills: Positioning a Motorcycle Brand in the Indian Context[1]

Dr. S. Ramesh Kumar and Dr. M. Geetha.

Rajesh, who had just turned 50, saw the several brands of motorcycles parked at the theatre complex. They ranged from the rugged models that were about 10 years old to the dazzling ones that could set the heart pounding among the yuppies. Rajesh wondered if all these motorcycles were being used fully for their functionality (as a means of personal transport) or if there were symbolic reasons for the purchase of these motorcycles. These thoughts brought back to him the nostalgic memories of how the Yezdis and the Jawas, the brands of the yesteryears, were always considered the "in thing" during his college days. The thoughts, of course, triggered memories of the film *Andaz* of the early seventies, which dramatised romance with its symbolic motorcycle association (through its ever popular *"Zindagi Ek Safar . . ."* song that can be heard even today in several radio stations targeting the youth). The film launched all over the country reinforced the fact that films, as a medium, are instrumental in dishing out products that may have a special significance on the psyche of consumers—a reality that is true even to this day.

Rajesh was brought back to the realities of his current challenges when he noticed Kiran coming over to meet him. Rajesh, after his basic degree, had worked in the motorcycle industry for more than two decades, of which eight years had been with sales and marketing job profiles. His commitment and passion to work enabled him to move up to positions that involved branding and product management challenges that were normally the preserve of management graduates. His busy consultancy work relating to the marketing of durable product categories showcased his penchant for achieving success in a crowded marketplace. Among his assignments was probably the greatest challenge he had

---

[1] This case was prepared by Dr. S. Ramesh Kumar and Dr. M. Geetha, Assistant Professor, MBA Department, SSN School of Management and Computer Applications, Chennai, for class discussion.

faced in his career: to launch a new brand in the motorcycle industry. Kiran was the product manager of a new company and he had about 6 years of experience in both FMCG (fast-moving consumer goods) and durable product categories. Kiran's educational background in management, his conceptual and analytical abilities, and his thirst to succeed by fighting against the odds were the primary reasons for Windy Bikes Company to recruit him a few months back. The hardcore practical insight of Rajesh, in combination with the marketing intellect of Kiran, was probably the prerequisite to succeed in the Indian market, which had several complexities and nuances that reflected its developing nature. They had to meet the Chief Executive Officer of Windy Bikes in about two weeks to finalize the positioning strategy for their brand.

"The motorcycle industry has been catching up over the years and with our factory capacity, there will be no problems in catering to the demand; but the crucial aspect is going to be our positioning related to our brands" said Kiran. "What about finding the right brand name?" asked Rajesh more out of his enthusiasm than out of a disciplined conceptual thought. "Brand name is the last of our priorities, in my opinion" quipped Kiran, confident that this topic would not surface again until they had made strategic progress with the issue on hand. "What I fail to read is a specific pattern in the positioning of motorcycles. There were only a few brands in the eighties, and by default they had positioned themselves in different ways to ensure that they entered the consumers' psyche. There were just one or two bikes for style, one associated with adventure and probably one more for ruggedness. Today, the leading brands seem to have exhausted various positioning platforms" said Rajesh mirroring Kiran's views on the selection of the brand.

"There are already several models positioned on functional features and psychological aspects. There are also celebrity endorsements. I wonder how a brand can break this kind of clutter in the market" said Kiran. Rajesh was reminded of the ways in which companies have changed their strategies in tune with the environmental changes and competitive moves. Rajesh made an interesting observation that was applicable to the leading company, Hero Honda. "Yamaha, the Japanese brand that has just around 5% in the Indian market (the brand was doing well in Japan and several other parts of Asia with a significant market share), had RX 100 brand with a strong image as a two-stroke offering before Hero Honda entered the Indian market with a four-stroke engine. Yamaha failed to convert and sustain its image in the four-stroke engine category. Yamaha today, is attempting to focus on higher-end offerings instead of being present in all the segments. It has launched Gladiator, a 125 cc bike, to attract the urban youth segment, and priced it aggressively. Hero Honda had the first mover's advantage in the four-stroke engine category in the eighties. The company has managed its product-line without getting complacent with its initial success, and its brands have done well over the last two decades. It has created and dropped several sub-brands without losing its focus on the respective segment." Kiran agreed and added "Feature combination and price points form an effective appeal. For instance models with and without self-starters, provide a choice to the consumers—those who can afford the feature and those who would like to own the brand and also make a saving."

Rajesh continued, "TVS's Victor brand was positioned initially on multiple benefits and it was also backed up by a hot celebrity. 125 cc bikes seem to promise a huge potential." Kiran, turning his attention toward the rural market, remarked "Let us not forget the growing rural market. There are also bikes being created for the rural market."

The broad segments that were interested in bikes were students, government employees, private company executives, and businessmen. The segments in terms of the category of bikes were the economy segment, executive segment, and the premium segment. The executive segment had grown to about 51% of the market and this was in the price range of over ₹40,000. The economy segment that accounted for about 38% was in the range of about ₹30,000 to ₹40,000, while the premium segment was priced over ₹50,000 (Glamour and Karizma belong to this segment). Rajesh's observation that bikes were bought for style and prestige was confirmed by the launch of Apache by TVS. This bike was launched keeping in mind the growing personal aspirations reflected through style, looks, and riding comfort. Validating the observation of Rajesh is also the fact that bikes, especially the higher-end models, are bought not for just symbolic style. The design of brands at the higher end appears to be not restricted to a few features; it includes engine, transmission, brakes, fuel tank capacity, suspension, tyres and every aspect that contributes both to the internal functioning of the bike and its external appearance. Rajesh took out a report from his briefcase and handed it over to Kiran saying that they should meet again after Kiran had gone through it. The report was an overview of the motorcycle industry that Rajesh had prepared, showing market shares of brands and specifically what he considered was competition to map the mind-space of the consumer—perceptual maps indicating the approach of different brands drawn on specific dimensions. Crucial to the report and also to the strategy of Windy Bikes, were the results of a consumer and dealer survey that was commissioned by the company. Rajesh and Kiran had to finalize on several aspects relating to the launching of the new bike.

Exhibits 1 and 2 provide information about the motorcycle categories. Exhibits 3 to 6 refer to the attribute preferences/rankings, interest patterns, favorite pastimes/hobbies and occupations of urban motorcycle owners, respectively. Exhibits 7 to10 contain data on the factors associated with purchase, ranking of attributes, favorite pastimes/hobbies/recreation and occupations of prospective owners in urban markets. Exhibits 11 to 14 contain data on the preferences of attributes and other details concerning the demographics and psychographics of respondents of the segment belonging to owners of motorcycles in semi-urban markets. Exhibits 15 to 17 contain information about the preferences of attributes and other details concerning the demographics and psychographics of respondents of the segment belonging to prospective semi-urban consumers for the purchase of motorcycles.

EXHIBIT 1 Segmentation of Motorcycles

	Target Income Groups	Price Range (₹'000)	Fuel Efficiency	Margins
Economy	Low	Up to 38	High	Low
Executive	Medium	38–50	High	Moderate
Premium	High	50–60	Moderate	High

Source: CRISINFAC, www.crisil.com.

EXHIBIT 2 Market Share Comparison of Key Players (2003–04 and 2004–05) in the Motorcycle Segment

	2003–04	2004–05
Bajaj	24%	28%
Hero Honda	48%	50%
TVS	16%	13%

	2003–04	2004–05
HMSI	–	1%
Yamaha	6%	5%

Source: CRIS INFAC, www.crisil.com.

URBAN MOTORCYCLE OWNERS

The data was collected from 200 samples of a metropolitan city. The results are summarized in Exhibit 3.

EXHIBIT 3 Factors Associated with Purchase/Ranking Intended to Purchase

(a) Responses with Purchase of Motorcycle

	1	2	3	4	5	6	7	8	9	Total
Price	45	48	39	21	15	8	7	9	8	200
Looks	46	34	23	17	13	16	33	13	5	200
Mileage	47	67	36	18	11	9	8	4	0	200
After-sales service	5	9	19	44	36	26	18	21	22	200
Technology	17	15	26	17	33	37	37	11	7	200
Driving pleasure	19	16	14	34	26	39	23	20	9	200
Maintenance costs	12	9	31	23	28	28	32	20	17	200
Features	9	10	9	20	17	23	30	50	26	200
Fun	1	4	5	10	11	10	10	50	99	200
Others										

(b) Ranking of Attributes

Options	Weighted Average	Ranking
Price	6.71	II
Looks	6.04	III
Mileage	7.21	I
After-sales service	4.58	VII
Technology	5.05	IV
Driving pleasure	5.02	V

Options	Weighted Average	Ranking
Maintenance costs	4.7	VI
Features	3.68	VIII
Fun	2.3	IX

EXHIBIT 4 Information About Interest Patterns of Respondents

Interests	Yes	No	Yes Percentage	No Percentage
Buy designer/Branded shirts/Apparel	100	100	50	50
Music	140	60	70	30
Fashion with clothes/watches, etc.	123	77	61.5	38.5
Reading sports magazines	94	106	47	53
Current affairs/politics	92	108	46	54
Food/Liquor	91	109	40.5	20.6
Parties with friends	125	75	62.5	37.5
Traveling abroad	122	78	61	39
Sports/Film-based celebrities	85	115	42.5	57.5

EXHIBIT 5 Favorite Pastimes/Hobbies/Recreation

Pastimes/ Hobbies	Sports	Films	Television	Pubs	Resorts	Friends	Books	Magazines	Internet
Number of respondents	17	10	19	1	0	5	0	0	0
Percentage	32.69	19.23	36.53	1.92	0	9.6	0	0	0

EXHIBIT 6 Occupations of the Respondents

Occupations	Number of Respondents	Percentage
Student	61	30.5
Executive	87	43.5
Government employed	14	7

Occupations	Number of Respondents	Percentage
Professional (Doctor/Engineer/CA, etc.)	35	17.5
Others	3	1.5

PROSPECTIVE URBAN CONSUMERS FOR THE PURCHASE OF MOTORCYCLE

The data was collected from 116 samples of a metropolitan city. The results are summarized in the following exhibits.

EXHIBIT 7 Factors Associated with Purchase/Ranking Intended to Purchase

(a) Responses with Purchase of Motorcycle

	1	2	3	4	5	6	7	8	9	Total
Price	27	25	27	12	5	15	2	1	2	116
Looks	23	10	16	17	12	11	17	6	4	116
Mileage	34	46	19	8	5	1	3	1	0	116
After-sales service	0	1	12	11	20	24	21	14	13	116
Technology	9	16	16	12	14	13	16	16	4	116
Driving pleasure	13	16	5	15	17	16	12	13	9	116
Maintenance costs	4	3	6	27	23	18	13	16	6	116
Features	6	3	7	11	18	15	25	26	5	116
Fun	2	1	3	8	3	4	8	19	68	116

(b) Ranking of Attributes

Options	Weighted Average	Ranking
Price	6.89	II
Looks	5.79	III
Mileage	7.72	I
After-sales service	3.95	VIII
Technology	5.16	IV
Driving pleasure	5.086	V

Options	Weighted Average	Ranking
Maintenance costs	4.55	VI
Features	4.09	VII
Fun	2.21	IX

EXHIBIT 8 Information About Interest Patterns of Respondents

Interested in	Yes	No	Yes Percentage	No Percentage
Buying Designer/Branded shirts/Apparel	82	34	70.7	29.3
Music	105	11	90.5	9.5
Fashion with clothes/watches, etc.	98	18	84.5	15.5
Reading sports magazines	62	54	53.4	46.6
Current affairs/politics	80	36	69	31
Food/Liquor	52	64	45	55
Parties with friends	81	35	69.8	30.2
Traveling abroad	95	21	82	18
Sports/Film-based celebrities	68	48	58.6	41.4

EXHIBIT 9 Favorite Pastimes/Hobbies/Recreation

Pastimes/ Hobbies	Sports	Films	Television	Pubs	Resorts	Friends	Books	Magazines	Internet
Number of respondents	39	18	21	3	1	23	9	2	0
Percentage	3.6	15.5	18.1	2.6	0.9	19.8	7.8	1.7	0

EXHIBIT 10 Occupations of the Respondents

Occupations	Number of Respondents	Percentage
Student	79	68
Executive	11	9.5
Government employed	6	5
Professional (Doctor/Engineer/CA, etc.)	20	17

SEMI-URBAN MOTORCYCLE OWNERS

The data was collected from 50 samples of a semi-urban area. The results are summarized in the following exhibits.

EXHIBIT 11 Factors Associated with Purchase/Ranking Intended to Purchase

(a) Responses with Purchase of Motorcycle

	1	2	3	4	5	6	7	8	9	Total
Price	2	10	12	3	6	1	3	6	2	50
Looks	14	9	5	3	3	8	4	2	2	50
Mileage	21	12	5	5	2	2	0	3	0	50
After-sales service	0	3	4	8	13	6	10	3	3	50
Technology	4	3		6	9	12	5	7	1	50
Driving pleasure	3	6	9	6	6	3	12	3	2	50
Maintenance costs	0	4	6	4	9	10	9	5	3	50
Features	3	2	3	10	2	5	8	15	7	50
Fun	1	1	3	4	0	1	3	6	31	50
Others										

(b) Ranking of Attributes

Options	Weighted Average	Ranking
Price	5.14	III
Looks	6.32	II
Mileage	7.48	I
After-sales service	4.56	VI
Technology	4.8	V
Driving pleasure	5.02	IV
Maintenance costs	4.46	VII
Features	4.3	VIII
Fun	2.36	IX

EXHIBIT 12 Information About Interest Patterns

Interests	Yes	No	Yes Percentage	No Percentage
Buying Designer/Branded Shirts/Apparel	30	20	60	40
Music	40	10	80	20
Fashion with clothes/watches, etc.	32	18	64	36
Reading sports magazines	14	36	28	72
Current affairs/politics	29	21	58	42
Food/Liquor	26	24	52	48
Parties with friends	40	10	80	20
Traveling abroad	40	10	80	20
Sports/Film-based celebrities	29	21	58	42

EXHIBIT 13 Favourite Pastimes/Hobbies/Recreation

Pastimes/ Hobbies	Sports	Films	Television	Pubs	Resorts	Friends	Books	Magazines	Internet
Number of respondents	13	15	11	2	1	5	2	0	1
Percentage	26	30	22	4	2	10	4	0	2

EXHIBIT 14 Occupations of the Respondents

Occupations	Number of Respondents	Percentage
Student	27	54
Executive	3	6
Government employed	0	0
Professional (Doctor/Engineer/CA, etc.)	20	40

PROSPECTIVE SEMI-URBAN CONSUMERS FOR THE PURCHASE OF MOTORCYCLE

The data was collected from 50 samples of a semi-urban area. The results are summarized in the following.

EXHIBIT 15 Factors Associated with Purchase/Ranking Intended to Purchase

(a) Responses with Purchase of Motorcycle

	1	2	3	4	5	6	7	8	9
Price	1	25	9	3	2	8	2	2	0
Looks	10	2	7	5	3	6	6	11	2
Mileage	37	3	3	2	7	0	0	0	0
After-sales service	0	2	7	15	9	0	10	0	0
Technology	1	14	10	3	10	7	2	5	0
Driving pleasure	1	1	10	13	7	16	2	1	1
Maintenance Costs	2	6	5	3	12	2	14	8	0
Features	0	0	1	6	5	13	2	22	3
Fun	0	0	0	0	0	0	11	5	36

(b) Ranking of Attributes

Options	Weighted Average	Ranking
Price	6.58	II
Looks	5.17	V
Mileage	8.17	I
After-sales service	4.59	VII
Technology	5.82	III
Driving pleasure	5.25	IV
Maintenance costs	4.71	VI
Features	3.33	VIII
Fun	1.52	IX

EXHIBIT 16 Information About Interest Patterns of Respondents

Interests	Yes	No	Yes Percentage	No Percentage
Buying Designer/Branded Shirts/Apparel	17	35	32.7	67.3

Music	44	8	84.5	15.5
Fashion with clothes/watches, etc.	12	40	23.1	76.9
Reading sports magazines	32	20	61.5	38.5
Current affairs/politics	24	28	46.2	53.8
Food/Liquor	18	34	34.6	65.4
Parties with friends	28	24	53.8	46.2
Traveling abroad	23	29	44.2	55.8
Sports/Film-based celebrities	22	30	42.3	57.7

EXHIBIT 17 Occupations of the Respondents

Occupations	Number of Respondents	Percentage
Student	15	28.8
Executive	24	46.2
Government employed	8	15.4
Professional (Doctor/Engineer/CA, etc.)	5	9.6

APPENDIX 1

(Sample calculation on how rankings were arrived at) factors associated with purchase/ranking intended to purchase.

Ranking for Price

Ranks	Number of Respondents	Weights	Weighted Score
I	45	9	405
II	48	8	384
III	39	7	273
IV	21	6	126
V	15	5	75
VI	8	4	32
VII	7	3	21

Ranks	Number of Respondents	Weights	Weighted Score
VIII	9	2	18
IX	8	1	8
	Total	1,342	
	Weighted average	1,342/200 = 6.71	

Note: The ranking was calculated similarly for other attributes.

APPENDIX 2

(Authors' weightages for various brands).

Motorcycle Brands—A Comparison of Attributes/Appeals

Motorcycles	Price (INR)	Fuel Efficiency (km)	Features	Trendy Appeal
CD Dawn	34,835	65	1	1
CD Deluxe	37,890	60	1	1
Centra	38,390	53	0	1
Boss 115	38,660	62	1	1
Yamaha Crux S	39,010	91	0	2
Victor GX	39,390	68	0	2
CT 100 DX	40,180	69	0	1
Super Splendor	43,047	65	4	4
CD 100 SS	43,520	65	–	–
Victor GLX	43,850	53	2	4
Velocity	44,730	62	1	3
Gladiator	44,990	67	5	3
Shine	45,200	65	2	1
Libero G5	46,780	65	1	2
Splendor+ Disc	48,001	65	2	2
Passion Plus Disc	49,592	65	5	3
Fiero F2 Disc	49,630	53	4	2
Fiero FX Disc	50,520	53	2	2

Motorcycles	Price (INR)	Fuel Efficiency (km)	Features	Trendy Appeal
Discover (ES)	50,710	63	1	3
GF170 Disc	51,680	42	3	4
Unicorn (KS)	51,993	54	3	2
Achiever	52,646	52	3	4
Pulsar 150 (ES)	61,070	51	5	5
Pulsar 180 (ES)	65,450	42	5	5
Bullet 350	72,490	40	0	2
Karizma	76,303	34	6	6
Bullet Machismo	81,080	40	3	2
Electra	81,480	40	2	3
Bullet 500	98,000	35	2	2
Bajaj Platina	36,000	67	4	4

Sources: Top Throttle Positioning. *Auto Times, The Times of India*, May 25, 2006.
Pankaj Sukhija, Riding High on Style, *The New Sunday Express*, May 28, 2006.
S. Muralidhar, Yamaha Gladiator: Into the Colosseum for 125 cc Fight, *The Hindu Business Line*, May 28, 2006.
*www.tvsmotor.in/www.bajajauto.com/www.herohonda.com/www.yamaha-motor-india.com/www.royalenfield.com/ www.honda2wheelersindia.com/*Delhi Auto Expo., Bajaj Auto Displays, 2006, Model Lineup, *http://www.indiainfo-line.com/news/news.asp?dat=73969.* TVS Motor Records 25 pc Growth in Motorcycles Sales, *http://www.blonnet.com/2006/02/03/stories/2006020301030200.htm.* Suzuki Motorcycle Plans Indian Launch in Oct with 125-cc Bike, *http://www.blonnet.com/2005/07/14/stories/20050714-02530200.htm*
Mobike Makers Rev Up Launches in Entry-level Segment, *http://www.blonnet.com/2006/06/03/stories/2006060300670500.htm*
Question N Auto, *www.blonnet.com/iw/2006/01/01/stories/2006010100451500.htm*
Muralidhar, S., Lining up the 150 cc bikes, *The Hindu Business line*, May 14, 2006.
Cooper, S., Platinum Edge, *The Hindu*, June 14, 2006.
Glad to meet you, *The Hindu*, May 31, 2006.

Note on lifestyle positioning: Most brands of premium motorcycles have a strong lifestyle positioning. Executive segment brands and economy segment brands too have several shades of lifestyle orientation in their positioning. Other than the advertisements associated with the respective brand, these aspects were also observed in some of the Web sites of the respective brand/company. Fuel efficiency in the appendix is in kilometres, while trendy appeal and features have been assigned weightages based on authors' perception of these factors (higher number indicates a higher weightage).

2

Xylys: Exploring Consumer Perception About Premium Watches in the Indian Context[1]

Dr. S. Ramesh Kumar and Kasturi Baral.

INTRODUCTION

Manoj Chakravarti, Senior Advisor, Titan Industries, reflected about his twenty-eight years in the watch industry both in India and abroad, and contemplated about Xylys, Titan's premium watch brand, and its foray into the Indian market. He had formulated several aspects of marketing mix strategies in the past to face diverse kinds of challenges. For Chakravarti, any challenge in the watch industry, especially in an emerging market like India, was something he looked forward to, as it gave him immense satisfaction when he was able to find some insights. Xylys was a premium watch brand launched by Titan a few years ago; the brand was aimed at creating a unique perception among consumers. The challenge was to create and shape a perception unique to the brand, since premium watches in India were associated with the Swiss brands Omega and Rolex, or Tag Heuer and the like, which were more contemporary in nature. There were several interesting possibilities for Chakravarti to consider. Would a conventional positioning approach be sufficient? Was it necessary to obtain some insights regarding the application of the uniqueness aspect to the self-perception of consumers? How were such aspects of uniqueness related to other established brands? How important was the "Swiss-made" label? Did the buyers and prospective buyers of premium watches hold any specific stereotypical images of such watches? The case delved into several aspects of the perceptual fields

[1] This case was written by Dr. S. Ramesh Kumar and Kasturi Baral, Assistant Brand Manager, Proctor&Gamble, Singapore.

associated with consumer behaviour with the objective of finding the most appropriate approach to further the prospects of the Xylys brand.

BACKGROUND

The liberalization of markets, the rising disposable income, the exposure to western lifestyles, and the need for the new generation to establish an identity for itself are some of the reasons for the growth of the luxury watch category in India. Consumers were buying not only durable categories that were useful to them, but also categories and brands that reflected their personality. India had 28 states and seven union territories with a population of 77.42 million urban households. The income levels were categorized as follows: 62.7 million households earned up to INR 1,50,000 (Indian Rupees) per annum (1 USD was equivalent to about 45 INR), 11.6 million households earned between INR 1,50,000 to INR 3,00,000 per annum, and 3.1 million households earned more than INR 3,00,000 per annum.[2] With respect to the spending of households on top ten necessities across all classes of consumers, watches figured at the eighth position, on average.[3] The latest McKinsey report on India's consumer market pegged spending on personal products and service necessities (watches were included as the eighth most required item, as described above) at 8 per cent share-of-wallet (SOW) in 2005; this was expected to climb up to 9 per cent SOW by 2015, and to 11 per cent SOW by 2020.[4]

THE WATCH INDUSTRY TODAY

Global

A significant decline in the production of watches was witnessed globally in 2005–2009, with the volumes in 2009 at a fifth of the expected numbers.[5] This was attributed to the plummeting demand in the recession-hit markets of the U. S., Japan, and Europe, among others. The premium segment suffered the worst, with the exports of Swiss watches dropping by 22 per cent in 2009, despite having risen to an unprecedented high the previous year.[6] However, what was inexplicable was that while the rest of the world found even regular watches unaffordable, the developing markets of China and India were experiencing growth in consumer demand for luxury and premium watch products.

India

Over the last five years, the Indian watch market had been growing at an average rate of 8 per cent per annum.[7] The recession during 2008–2009 hindered the sector's growth, with a drop in the sales of luxury and premium watches, which was compensated by the growth of volume in the economy segment.[8] Thus, despite the global trends, the value and volume figures for 2009 stood at 40.6 billion

[2] "The Marketing White Book 2010–11: One Stop Guide for Marketers," *BusinessWorld*, New Delhi, 2010, pp. 52–54.
[3] Ibid., p. 63.
[4] "The 'bird of gold': The rise of India's consumer market," *McKinsey Global Institute*, May 2007, http://www.mckinsey.com/mgi/publications/india_consumer_market/images/India_Interactive1.swf, accessed on April 11, 2011.
[5] "Watches in India," Country report, http://www.euromonitor.com/watches-in-india/report, accessed on July 22, 2011.
[6] Ibid.
[7] Ibid.
[8] Ibid.

units and INR 54.6 billion, with a growth of 8.5 per cent and 15.4 per cent in volume and value, respectively.[9]

In terms of category sales, the highest share, as per value, involved watches priced between INR 500 and 3000. The premium segment—retailed between INR 4000 and 15000—had been growing at an exponential rate of 20 per cent annually.[10]

Low per capita consumption on the one hand and the growing demand for luxury watches on the other constituted the factors that forecast the compounded annual growth rates of 7.3 per cent and 13.7 per cent in volume and value, respectively, for the period 2009–2014.[11]

INDIAN WATCH INDUSTRY

Historical Perspective

The Indian watch industry had its origins in the 1960s, with HMT's Janata being launched in 1962. Before HMT, watches were sourced exclusively from imports, and could be afforded by only a small number of consumers. HMT was the first major watch manufacturer in India, and the sole indigenous player, until Titan Industries Limited—a Tata and TIDCO joint venture—was formed in 1984, and started retailing watches in 1987. Titan, with its focus on satisfying the customer's unspoken needs, gradually wrested market power and shares from HMT and became the undisputed leader in the wrist-watch segment over the past three decades. The only other major Indian player is P. A. Time, with its brand Maxima, which managed to survive despite fierce competition. Other indigenous brands such as Allwyn, Shivaki, and SITCO failed to keep up with Titan and languished, with marginal to negligible market shares.

In 1992, liberalization opened up the Indian market to foreign players, and Timex was the first on the scene. It was soon followed by Casio, Rolex, Citizen, Tissot, Omega, Rado, and TAG Heuer (the new export-import policy introduced in 1999 relaxed the hitherto stiff upper bar on imports of luxury wristwatch brands). After the foreign direct regulations were changed by the Government to allow for up to 51 per cent of foreign direct investment in single-brand retail operations, global brands set up subsidiaries in India, with apparel brands such as Esprit, Tommy Hilfiger, Benetton, and Levi's also launching brands of their own.

Growth of Industry

The Indian watch industry began in the 1960s with the public sector enterprise HMT, which was the government's initiative to start the indigenous manufacture of watches. The import industry brought in the more fashionable watches, but the basic need for timekeeping was satisfied by the sturdy and reliable mechanical wristwatch models manufactured by HMT. In the absence of other brands, HMT could afford to retain goodwill despite offering limited styling and choices to its customers. A few decades back (when HMT held a monopoly in the category), a watch was a product that anyone who had taken up a job aspired for. Traditionally, the penetration levels were quite low during this time; the notion of a "watch for the masses" was diffused in the psyche of consumers only after the late eighties,

[9] Ibid.

[10] Ibid.

[11] Ibid.

when the country witnessed major lifestyle changes. The nineties enhanced this perception as many brands entered the market following the liberalization of governmental policies.

The Tata group introduced the quartz watch in the 1980s under the Titan brand, and differentiated themselves on the basis of accuracy, style, choice, presentation, and vigorous push-marketing.[12] Timex, in collaboration with Titan, launched its range in India in the nineties, with a mutual understanding that the former would keep to the low price plastic segment, while the latter would manage the high price metal segment. Timex positioned itself with the tagline "You don't have to be rich to afford a Timex," and was well accepted by the market. After a few years, Timex became an independent brand and set up its own distribution channels, and emerged as a brand associated with the sports and casual wear segment.

Early in the twentieth century, many multinational players entered the market, which was made possible by the EXIM policies that raised the bar on the import of luxury watches in India.

An Overview of the Competition

The single largest player was Titan, with a brand share of 20.6 per cent in 2009.[13] The next player worth mentioning was Swatch, with a relatively small share of 5.9 per cent.[14] Timex was a relatively strong multinational brand in the market. Rolex, PA Time, Citizen, and Casio had small significant shares, and HMT was also in the Indian market.

Despite the presence of many brands, the market was still primarily controlled by the unorganized sector (to the tune of 65 per cent) even in 2009. The present competition arose from the increasing foray of multinational players into the lucrative luxury segment; however, the real challenge was to tackle the spurious imports being sold by the unorganized sector.

Watches transformed from time keeping instruments to fashion accessories during the eighties and nineties due to significant lifestyle changes; this was reflected in some of Titan's advertisements. Watches, as fashion accessories, were in completion with a variety of other products such as apparel and fashion handbags; hence, watches had to have a clearly differentiated element of perceived utility apart from fashion.[15]

Segmentation of the Watch Market

The watch industry could be segmented according to various criteria: technology, benefit, and price.

Watches could be classified into three kinds based on technology: mechanical, quartz analog, and quartz digital. The first went out of vogue since the bulky mechanical format did not allow for elegant design; it dropped in volume shares from 7.2 per cent in 2004 to 4.6 per cent in 2009. The second kind was the largest in both value and volume, and was expected to remain the market driver for growth in 2009–2014. Digital watches suffered from the consumer perception of being low cost and lacking in style, and hence, the market for them had not yet picked up. The sales figures by value for these subsectors for 2009 were INR 3,000, 46,000, and 6,000 million, respectively. The major market players in these three sectors were HMT, Titan, and Casio, respectively.

---

[12] "The Titan Story," http://www.titanworld.com/titan_stories, accessed on November 29, 2010.

[13] "Watches in India," Country report, http://www.euromonitor.com/watches-in-india/report, accessed on July 22, 2011.

[14] Ibid.

[15] Ibid.

The second basis of classification was benefit, and the market could be divided based on use, namely, casual, formal, and sports. Many of the brands offered some options in all three segments, but most catered only to the first two segments; the sports segment remained a largely untapped segment. Nearly 35 per cent of all watches retailed were casual, 60 per cent were formal, and a mere 5 per cent belonged to the sports segment.

The watch market could be classified into economy, standard, premium, and luxury segments.[16] The mass market (i.e., the economy segment) accounted for nearly 67 per cent of volume and 50 per cent of value shares, and was catered to almost entirely by the unorganized sector. Popular (standard), with prices ranging from INR 500 to 1200, was the lowest range offered by the organized sector (Titan and Timex, primarily). The premium segment consisted of watches in the INR 1500–5000 range, offered by almost all the indigenous and multinational brands. The demand from the middle and upper income groups promised to be the growth driver for this segment in 2009–2014.

A better explanation in terms of consumer behaviour was the third basis of segmentation as defined by Yankelovich (1964).[17] He presented a scheme for the non-demographic segmentation of various product categories, including watches. Segmentation by value was considered to be particularly apt for this market. Thus, the authors arrived at three distinct segments, each offering the customer a different benefit and value than the others. As was stated earlier, the watch had always been a product that appealed to people, but the nature of the appeal and the associations related to watches changed with the changing environment. A watch or a specific brand in particular, became a symbol of several associations that were in tune with the changing environment. These associations were generally glamour, fashion, sports, and fun, and the intensity of these associations became pronounced depending on the respective segment towards which a brand was positioned. Lifecycle stages also mattered—a school student would celebrate his/her first watch with neighbors and friends, a college student would garner attention among his/her friends with a recently bought watch, and a young executive who had been successful in his job might reward himself with a premium watch after a few years of hard work, and also "announce his arrival into a world of success" to the outside world.

Symbolic and lifestyle categories that were created in the last twenty years or so included apparel, watches, mobile phones, portable music players such as iPods, cars, televisions, two-wheelers, and spectacles, to name a few socially conspicuous product categories; brands made use of such psychological needs of consumers to position themselves, with one category often competing with another. For example, a typical middle class household in India that had bought a TV (it is a well-observed fact that a TV is generally high on the purchase agenda of a middle class family) on installment basis (the installment plan allows a consumer to pay for the purchased product over a period of time through monthly payments to the seller/retailer) might postpone buying a new watch for a student in the family who was entering college, due to financial pressures. Such instances would be rare in a developed market, especially with regard to the purchase of a watch. It was interesting to note that the lower end offerings (relatively lower end to be precise, when compared to the price of luxury watch brands) from brands like Titan also used glamour, romance, and celebrity orientation for the positioning strategies of several of its brands (such as Titan, Fastrack, Sonata, and Ragaa). Titan was a leader in the organized quartz analog watch segment, and millions of pieces had been sold over the years.

---

[16] Ibid.

[17] Yankelovich, D., "New Criteria for Market Segmentation," *Harvard Business Review*, March/April 1964.

Using the Yankelovich scheme, the watch market may be segmented as follows:

- *Value for money*: Low/regular-priced watches that were accurate and sturdy. Owners tended to replace these when they failed.
- *Premium watches*: High-priced watches, with assured longevity, excellent workmanship, and good styling. Owners were ready to pay a premium for the benefits that accompanied these brands.
- *Special watches*: Extra benefits like fine styling, brand name, and accessories (such as gold casings) were desired by potential customers. The watch, apart from being a fashion accessory, was part of a ritual gifting ceremony, and needed to encapsulate the emotional benefits required to succeed.

It was interesting to note that regardless of the price range or the benefit, watches held a symbolic appeal in the Indian context—an appeal that could be associated with the self-perception or the personality/style a consumer would like to project to the outside world. Luxury watches had a special appeal with regard to such an orientation among consumers.

The watch market in India was divided into three broad segments: mass market (price below INR 1,000), mid market (price between INR 1,000 and INR 10,000), and premium market (price starting at INR 10,000).

Luxury watches, in turn, were categorized into three sub-segments:

1. Premium watches: INR 10,000–50,000. This is the space where Xylys operated. The other prominent brands in this space were Tissot, Seiko, and Citizen, in addition to fashion brands such as Emporio Armani and Hugo Boss.
2. Accessible Luxury: INR 50,000–3,00,000. The biggest Swiss brands such as Rolex, Omega, Longines, and Tag Heuer operated in this space.
3. Exclusive Luxury: INR 3,00,000 and above. Very high-end brands such as Breguet, Patek Philippe, Audemars Piguet, Breitling, and Hublot populated this segment.

From the point of view of look, there were four philosophies from which brands tend to choose and occupy, namely, dress, classical, fashion, and sport. For example, among sporty watches, Tissot, Tag Heuer, and Breitling were the brands in the premium, accessible, and exclusive luxury sub-segments, respectively.

Luxury Brands

The market for luxury watches was estimated to be 3 per cent of watch retail and was growing at almost 20 per cent annually, which was more than twice the growth rate of the entire market.[18] Luxury brands were priced above INR 15,000, and primarily included imported brands offered by multinational players, such as Omega, Rado, Longines, Tag Heuer, and Tissot. Titan was the only Indian brand in this sector currently, with Xylys at the luxury end of its portfolio. Personal interviews with some managers at retail outlets suggested that the competition to the Xylys brand was from established brands like Seiko and Tissot.[19]

The main consumer of luxury brands was the new generation executive, who was set to move towards the prime of his career, and who had a keen sense of brand consciousness. These included

[18] "Watch industry in India to grow at 9%," *India Infoline News Service*, Feb 5, 2010.

[19] Interviews with Mr. Viraj, Branch Manager, World of Titan at Brigade Road, Bangalore and Ms. Saumya, Branch In-charge, Titan (multi-brand outlet) outlet at Jayanagar 4th Block, Bangalore.

an increasing number of young and middle-aged professionals in the upper strata of management in corporate houses, and also Indians who belonged to the higher socio-economic strata and had a penchant for luxury products. The major consumers of watches in the luxury segment included CEOs and senior professionals in their thirties and forties, new generation entrepreneurs, and young working professionals.

Successful brands sold because they positioned themselves based on the benefits they offered to those who possessed them; such benefits could be functional, symbolic, or experiential.[20] Brand concept management (BCM)[21] stated that for long-term success, the brand image needed to be based on a brand-specific abstract concept. The authors felt that such an orientation would help the long-term plans of luxury watch brands.

Functional brands provided tangible and practical benefits, and satisfied the real need for the product. Brands needed to necessarily satisfy functional needs, since these were the hygiene factors for acceptance in this category. Symbolic brands, on the other hand, catered to the consumers' preference for brands that matched their own "self concept"[22] and their symbolic needs for self-expression, prestige, and the enhancement of self-image and sense of belonging. Experiential brands satisfied the owner's need to experience sensory pleasure, variety, or cognitive simulation.

Luxury watches were bought for their symbolic and experiential benefits as opposed to their functional ones. The selling points were the status and sophistication that the brand denoted when worn by the owner; though aesthetic appeal and durability were important, precision and price were not.

Hence, the positioning diagrams for luxury watches would need to be based on factors such as status, prestige, and ego gratification.

The symbolism dimensions used in the study were derived from the work on the positioning of brands.[23] Three sets of questionnaires were used to record the respondents' opinions on brands, adjectives and phrases related to brand symbolism, and in-depth queries regarding the characteristics of brands and their users.

Methodology

The objective of the study was to analyze and link several aspects of consumer behaviour, and to compare users and non-users of premium watches. Three sets of questions were prepared. One set of questions dealt with the self concepts of consumers, another was about the brand personality aspects of their watches, and the last set of questions was related to the psychographics of individual respondents. Non-users were respondents who were potential buyers of premium watches in the near future. Scales were drawn from several resources available in the extant literature.[24]

---

[20] Park, C. W., Jaworski, B. J., & MacInnis, D. J., "Strategic Brand Concept Image Management," *Journal of Marketing*, Vol. 50, October 1986, pp. 135–145.

[21] Ibid.

[22] Malhotra N. K., "Self Concept and Product Choice: An Integrated Perspective," *Journal of Economic Psychology*, Vol. 9, 1988, pp. 1–28.

[23] Bhat, S., & Reddy, S. K., "Symbolic and Functional Positioning of Brands," *Journal of Consumer Marketing*, Vol.15, No. 1, 1998, pp. 32–43.

[24] Tian, K. T., Bearden, W. O., & Hunter, G. L., "Consumers' Need for Uniqueness: Scale Development and Validation," *Journal of Consumer Research*, June 28, 2001, pp. 50–66; Netemeyer R. G., Burton, S., & Lichtenstein, D. R., "Trait aspects of Vanity: Measurement and Relevance to Consumer Behavior," *Journal of Consumer*, Pearson Education, p. 143.

Forty current users of premium watches and forty potential users (prospective buyers) of premium watches were administered the questionnaire in April 2011, in Bangalore, India.

Exhibits 1, 2, and 3 were associated with self concept, brand preferences along with personality traits, and the Activities, Interests, and Opinions (AIO) of potential users of premium watch brands.

Exhibits 4, 5, and 6 dealt with the same factors of present users of premium watch brands (self concept, brand preferences along with personality traits, and AIO).

The description of the positioning strategies of the various brands presented below was based on the authors' perception of the advertisements of the respective brands.

Xylys

Xylys was a premium Swiss-made watch brand from the house of Titan in India. Priced between INR 10000 and INR 33000, the Xylys range of watches came in three collections—Contemporary, Classic, and Sport—and offered over sixty distinctive models. Xylys was available at select World of Titan showrooms, key multi-brand outlets, and at exclusive flagship boutiques in select cities.

Xylys targeted the lower spectrum of the luxury watch segment. Titan, which was the market leader in the mid-price segment in India, felt that the upper end of their target customers was moving towards iconic global premium brands.

The designs were created in collaboration with renowned Swiss designer Laurent Rufenacht, and Titan's own design advisor, Michael Foley. It was manufactured in a state-of-the-art factory in Switzerland, which had a heritage of over eighty years in the art of watch-making. All Xylys watches were created with exquisite craftsmanship and impeccable detailing, painstakingly made from carefully selected materials, and were crafted with a passion for detail.

While carefully analyzing the consumer behaviour of customers of premium watch brands, Titan found that consumers were highly influenced by the "country of origin" association. Consumers loved the "Swiss-made" tag, and there was a huge association of quality, precision, premium, etc with this tag. The insight was that it would be difficult for an "Indian-made" tag to impress the target segment.

The name Xylys was designed to have only two syllables, a distinctive name in itself. The brand charter aimed to convey style, attitude, and power. Xylys was created for new generation achievers who went beyond the obvious. Xylys reflected their values, attitudes, and unique personal identities. The brand was targeted at today's people who were supremely confident and conscious of the image they projected. These individuals actively sought new and unconventional experiences. Xylys, with its unique positioning of the "Power of X," underlined the power of one's attitude. This attitude stemmed from a person's self-belief, which enabled one to achieve success through a passionate pursuit of one's dreams. Xylys was launched as a contemporary brand targeting upwardly mobile, successful men and women. The brand segmented the market based on psychographic profiles. Xylys defined its customers as contemporary, dynamic, successful people who had attitude and confidence. The brand wanted to celebrate their success with them. The customers of Xylys were highly individualistic persons who did what they loved. These people would love to express themselves and to show their success to the world.

The three brand ambassadors of Xylys came from varied fields and represented the attitude of the new generation achievers. Actor Rahul Bose (ad), international supermodel Saira Mohan (ad), and tennis star Carlos Moya embodied the attitude of living life fearlessly on their own terms, with a passion to pursue their dreams. Speaking at the launch, brand ambassador Rahul Bose said, "Like every movie I choose to be a part of, I have chosen to endorse this brand after careful thought. I can only support those products that I am fully convinced about. It is an exciting new brand from India's leading watchmaker with an identity that reflects the attitude and values that I consider important—bold, unconventional, and distinctive."

In 2010, the brand changed its positioning from "Symbol of Success" to "Feeling of Love." The brand talked about falling in love with Xylys. Xylys ran a campaign reflecting the new positioning, which was a significant deviation from the core positioning of the brand. The entire brand personality of Xylys was changed in the current campaign.

The new identity reflected the attitude, lifestyle, and personality of the new generation consumer. "You don't possess a Xylys, it possesses you": this reflected irrational desirability of the brand. The new creative expression was carefully designed to reflect the effect Xylys watches had on their consumers. It was this aspect that created an "irrational" desire to own the watch, strongly backed by the "rational" reasons, namely, that Xylys came from the house of Titan and was Swiss-made.

Post the launch in 2006, the brand saw the volume of sales doubling between 2006–2007 and 2007–2008, and sales grew at about 33 per cent since then. In terms of value, Xylys grew at a CAGR of 54 per cent. Exhibit 7 presented one advertisement for Xylys.

Tissot

Tissot, with its signature "Innovators by Tradition," pioneered craftsmanship and innovation since its foundation in 1853. Tissot was a member of the Swatch Group, the world's largest watch producer and distributor. For over 155 years, the company had its home in the Swiss watch-making town of Le Locle in the Jura Mountains, and now has a presence in over 150 countries.

As official timekeeper and partner of the International Basketball Federation (FIBA), the Australian Football League, the Chinese Basketball Association, the MotoGP, and the World Championships of cycling, fencing, and ice hockey, Tissot was committed to respecting tradition, underlining its core values of performance, precision, and setting new standards.

The different collections of Tissot included Touch, Sport, Trend, Classic, Gold, Pocket, and Heritage, and the price spectrum was much wider than that of Xylys, covering both the affordable luxury and the premium luxury segment with ease.

The Indian brand ambassador for Tissot was movie star Deepika Padukone, daughter of a former badminton world champion. Her Tissot watch was projected as a symbol of luxury and glamour complementing her multi-faceted lifestyle. The similarities between her personality and the Tissot brand were captured in the brand's advertisements: "We are both adventurous, sophisticated and classy, yet very approachable."

Tissot's subsequent advertising campaign revolved around the theme "In Touch With Your Time." In its revolutionary new global campaign based on this theme, Tissot used a series of executions featuring brand ambassadors who presented luxury, as being accessible rather than exclusive. The brand attributed its success to the trust customers all over the world had in the quality and pleasure offered by Tissot timepieces. Millions of wearers evidently refused to compromise, and the campaign specifically congratulated them on their discerning selection of a stylish Swiss-made watch. The campaign's approach focused on the idea of "substance" (the unquestionable quality attached to traditional Swiss craftsmanship) and "style" (a truly appealing watch design).

The new global Tissot campaign captured real moments in the lives of its ambassadors where reality seamlessly merged with glamour. A variety of locations that were local to the ambassadors (e.g., Deepika Padukone in Mumbai, India) were used for the shoots, which enhanced the campaign's integral authenticity.

Seiko

SEIKO Watch India Private Limited is a 100% subsidiary of SEIKO Watch Corporation, Japan, set up in 2007; it is headquartered in Bangalore. Over the years SEIKO has established leadership position in a number of countries. Backed by such experiences and with India being one of the prioritized markets, the brand is expected to bring its " Total SEIKO brand experience" through its "Flagship stores" that will also provide good customer service.[25] The brand is available at several higher end multi-branded watch outlets in the country. SEIKO's technological development is focused on the creation of "emotional technologies"[26]. While the brand may be positioned below Tissot or Xylys (based on the observation of price points at retail outlets by one of the authors), the brand is likely to be perceived as a brand with strong value, given its heritage of technology and innovation.

EXHIBIT 1 Self Concept (Potential Users of Premium Watch Brands)

I would feel embarrassed if I was around people and did not look my best.	3.775
It is important that I always look good.	3.275
People notice how attractive I am.	3.675
My looks are very appealing to others.	3.075
I want others to look up to me because of my accomplishments.	3.075
I am more concerned about professional success than most people I know.	4.15
Achieving greater success than my peers is important to me.	3.475
I want my achievements to be recognized by others.	3.575
In a professional sense, I am a very successful person.	3.825
My achievements are highly regarded by others.	3.4
Others wish they were as successful as me.	3.675
I am a good example of professional success.	3.25
I often look for unique products or brands so that I create a style that is all my own.	3.225
The products and brands that I like best are the ones that express my individuality.	3
I rarely act according to what others think are the right things to buy.	3.375
I enjoy challenging the prevailing taste of people I know by buying something radical.	2.95
I often think of the things I buy and do in terms of how I can use them to shape a more unusual personal image.	3.05

[25] www.seiko.in/corporate/india.html accessed on October 26, 2011.

[26] www.seikowatches.com/story/index.html accessed on October 26, 2011.

When a product I own becomes popular among the general population, I use it less.	2.625
Concern for being out of place does not prevent me from wearing what I want to.	2.85

Source: The results were based on the questionnaires administered to users and non-users of premium watch brands.

Note: The statements were measured on a Likert scale ranging from Strongly Agree to Strongly Disagree for each respondent, and the values were coded as Strongly Agree = 5, Agree = 4, Neither Agree nor Disagree = 3, Disagree = 2, and Strongly Disagree = 1. The mean values were the average of the same across all the respondents.

EXHIBIT 2 Brand and User Personality (Potential Users of Premium Watch Brands)

Brand Factors		User Factors	
Up-to-date	3.525	Up-to-date	3.525
Reliable	4.075	Reliable	4.125
Down-to-earth	3.65	Down-to-earth	4
Honest	3.8	Honest	3.85
Daring	3.125	Daring	3.8
Spirited	3.775	Spirited	3.675
Exciting	3.625	Exciting	4.05
Imaginative	3.7	Imaginative	3.975
Successful	3.825	Successful	3.625
Upper class	3.325	Upper class	3.5
Tough	3.2	Tough	3.5

Source: The results were based on the questionnaires administered to users and non-users of premium watch brands.

Note: The statements were measured on a Likert scale ranging from Strongly Agree (5) to Strongly Disagree (1) for each respondent. The mean values were the average of the same across all the respondents.

EXHIBIT 3 Activities, Interests, and Opinions (Potential Users of Premium Watch Brands)

When I must choose between the two, I usually dress for fashion, not for comfort.	3.25
I try to arrange my home for my children's convenience.	2.975
I take a lot of time and effort to teach my children good habits.	2.85
I like parties where there is lots of music and conversation.	3.075
I would rather go to a sporting event than a movie.	3.425

I like to work on community projects.	3.4
I have personally worked in a political campaign, or for a candidate, or for an issue.	3.7
I think I have more self-confidence than most people.	2.55
I am more independent than most people.	3.725
I think I have a lot of personal ability.	3.8
I like to be considered a leader.	3.95
My friends or neighbors often come to me for advice.	3.7
I sometimes influence what my friends buy.	3.85
People come to me more often than I go to them for information about brands.	3.5
I often seek the advice of my friends regarding which brand to buy.	3.25
I spend a lot of time talking with my friends about products and brands.	3.575
I would like to spend a year in London or Paris.	3.175
I would like to take a trip around the world.	3.825
I will have more money to spend next year than I have now.	4.375
I spend more than an hour everyday reading the newspaper or watching the news.	4.025
I like to meticulously plan for future savings and expenditures.	3.175

Source: The results were based on the questionnaires administered to users and non-users of premium watch brands.

Note: The statements were measured on a Likert scale ranging from Strongly Agree (5) to Strongly Disagree (1) for each respondent. The mean values were the average of the same across all the respondents.

EXHIBIT 4 Self Concept (Present Users of Premium Watch Brands)

I would feel embarrassed if I was around people and did not look my best.	3.325
It is important that I always look good.	3.75
People notice how attractive I am.	3.45
My looks are very appealing to others.	3.425
I want others to look up to me because of my accomplishments.	3.65
I am more concerned about professional success than most people I know.	3.75
Achieving greater success than my peers is important to me.	3.925
I want my achievements to be recognized by others.	4.225
In a professional sense, I am a very successful person.	3.65
My achievements are highly regarded by others.	3.6

Others wish they were as successful as me.	3.4
I am a good example of professional success.	3.7
I often look for unique products or brands so that I create a style that is all my own.	3.225
The products and brands that I like best are the ones that express my individuality.	3.325
I rarely act according to what others think are the right things to buy.	2.75
I enjoy challenging the prevailing taste of people I know by buying something radical.	2.925
I often think of the things I buy and do in terms of how I can use them to shape a more unusual personal image.	3
When a product I own becomes popular among the general population, I use it less.	2.825
Concern for being out of place doesn't prevent me from wearing what I want to.	3.2

Source: The results were based on the questionnaires administered to users and non-users of premium watch brands.

Note: The statements were measured on a Likert scale ranging from Strongly Agree (5) to Strongly Disagree (1) for each respondent. The mean values were the average of the same across all the respondents.

EXHIBIT 5 Brand and User Personality (Present Users of Premium Watch Brands)

Brand Factors	
Up-to-date	3.775
Reliable	4.275
Down-to-earth	3.35
Honest	3.95
Daring	3.6
Spirited	3.75
Exciting	3.95
Imaginative	3.925
Successful	4.125
Upper class	3.975
Tough	3.975

User Factors	
Up-to-date	3.8
Reliable	4.025
Down-to-earth	3.65
Honest	3.925
Daring	3.675
Spirited	3.875
Exciting	3.9
Imaginative	3.6
Successful	3.725
Upper class	3.7
Tough	3.625

Source: The results were based on the questionnaires administered to users and non-users of premium watch brands.

Note: The statements were measured on a Likert scale ranging from Strongly Agree (5) to Strongly Disagree (1) for each respondent. The mean values were the average of the same across all the respondents.

EXHIBIT 6 Attitudes, Interests, and Opinions (Present Users of Premium Watch Brands)

Statement	Mean
When I must choose between the two, I usually dress for fashion, not for comfort.	2.775
I try to arrange my home for my children's convenience.	3.725
I take a lot of time and effort to teach my children good habits.	3.95
I like parties where there is lots of music and conversation.	3.075
I would rather go to a sporting event than a movie.	3.225
I like to work on community projects.	3.325
I have personally worked in a political campaign, or for a candidate, or for an issue.	1.725
I think I have more self-confidence than most people.	3.625
I am more independent than most people.	3.975
I think I have a lot of personal ability.	3.775
I like to be considered a leader.	4.125
My friends or neighbors often come to me for advice.	3.75
I sometimes influence what my friends buy.	3.325
People come to me more often than I go to them for information about brands.	3.3
I often seek the advice of my friends regarding which brand to buy.	2.95
I spend a lot of time talking with my friends about products and brands.	2.875
I would like to spend a year in London or Paris.	3.175
I would like to take a trip around the world.	4.2
I will have more money to spend next year than I have now.	3.925
I spend more than an hour everyday reading the newspaper or watching the news.	3.75
I like to meticulously plan for future savings and expenditures.	3.65

Source: The results were based on the questionnaires administered to users and non-users of premium watch brands.

Note: The statements were measured on a Likert scale ranging from Strongly Agree (5) to Strongly Disagree (1) for each respondent. The mean values were the average of the same across all the respondents.

EXHIBIT 7 Advertisement for Xylys

The authors would like to thank Mr. Manoj Chakravarti, Senior Advisor, Ms. Superna Mitra, Head, Global Marketing, Titan Industries Limited, and Prof Dinesh Kumar, Chairperson, Research & Publications, IIM, Bangalore, for the support provided to this case-study initiative.

3

Super Shampoo Products and the Indian Mass Market

In 2010, Suresh Venkataraman, following a successful period of marketing industrial products in the city of Coimbatore in the Southern part of India (a city known for its textile industries and entrepreneurs), became interested in consumer products. He had always been fascinated with single use packaging, and wondered how shampoo as a category was transformed from an unaffordable product to an affordable one with the invention of sachets (single use packs that had about six to eight millilitres (ml) of shampoo costing about $US 0.10). Venkataraman also had a firm belief that the lower economic strata of consumers, especially in the rural markets, offered a huge potential for consumer products. Though he did not have a management background, he had asked various people why several brands of shampoos (though quite successful in lower price segments and in the rural areas of the country) did not have a brand name that was simple to understand. His aspirations took shape when he decided to launch a product called Super Shampoo for this target segment. He selected the name "Super" as it was easy to pronounce and had an English overtone that was considered a part of the aspirations of rural consumers (who were influenced by the globalized urban markets); more specifically, he chose it because the word "super" was amplified by the media to celebrate film stars by projecting them as "superstars" (India ranks very high on the production of films, and films are a part of the Indian psyche). The word "super" triggered a superior image amongst whatever it was competing against in a specific context. Venkataraman had adequate business experience to know that a name alone cannot create a superior brand: the challenges were indeed quite confounding. How could established brands of shampoos be addressed? Super Shampoo would not have the financial muscle to compete against the advertising blitzkrieg of the megabrands. Were there ways to compete in the war of marketing communication when communication held much sway in such a competitive and glamour-ridden category? Venkataraman decided to consider such issues through a market survey set in a rural market in the Indian context to help analyze marketing communications and its impact on consumer behaviour.

THE INDIAN CONTEXT

In 2010, India contained a diverse array of product categories, brands, prices, lifestyles and cultures.[1] While marketers were upbeat about the consumption of categories and brands stretching from unbranded edible oil to prestigious brands of watches, there were unique challenges to marketers. These unique challenges included the management of marketing mix elements, understanding the diversity of cultures, development of appropriate product lines, localizing global communication and, more specifically, understanding the consumer psyche in a changing environment. While there were quite a few studies undertaken on several aspects of consumer behaviour, one of the most important facets of the Indian cultural environment was the aspiration-based appeals of marketing communication and brands that triggered such marketing communication. This was especially important given the fact that just 14 percent of the world's population lived in countries with a per capita GNP of greater than US$10,000. India was characterized by the unorganized sector[2] in a number of product categories.[3] The mindset of the "have not" with reference to the aspirations created by categories and brands has been largely explored. The shampoo category contained products in single use packs as well as regular packaging. Approximately 60 to 65 per cent of the market was accounted for by such packets, with significant volumes being sold to consumers in lower economic situations. In several fast-moving consumer goods, these lower-level consumers contributed to a significant amount of sales. This begs the questions, how do the non-users perceive the category of shampoos? Are they only influenced by functional attributes? Do they attach symbolic benefits to shampoos?

The high penetration yet low per capita consumption of shampoos in the Indian market was indicative of the available opportunity in the category, as there was a large segment of low frequency users (and non-users) for the category. What attitudes are developed in category non-users or low frequency users in the shampoo category in these low income markets where the key usage barrier is affordability? Which variables—such as their psychographics and lifestyle, media consumption, purchasing power and the brand communication of key players in this category—influence these attitudes? What would it take for a new shampoo entrant to use these attitudes to generate likeability and persuade consumers to try the brand?

[1] S. Ramesh Kumar, "Addressing Diversity: The Marketing Challenge in India," *Wall Street Journal*, October 20, 2010.

[2] A term used commonly to denote a sector of labour where production units are a subset of unincorporated enterprises owned by households, i.e., not constituted as separate legal entities independently of the households, and for which no complete sets of accounts (including balance sheets of assets and liabilities) are available, which would permit a clear distinction of production activities of the enterprises from other activities of their owners and the identification of any flows of income and capital between the enterprises and the owners.

[3] S. Ramesh Kumar, *Consumer Behavior and Branding: Concepts, Readings and Cases*, Pearson, New Delhi, 2009, p. 9.

INTRODUCTION AND BACKGROUND TO MARKET—BOTTOM OF THE PYRAMID

In 2010, there were about two billion middle-class consumers (annually earning US$13,500 to 113,000) in twelve countries (including the BRIC countries) that spent US$6.9 trillion.[4] The bottom of the pyramid (BoP) in India concerning income classification is defined as the bottom two classes of less than Rs 75,000 and between Rs 75,000 to Rs 150,000 per year.[5] This comprised roughly 150 million households across India, with 25 per cent of this coming from urban India and the remaining 75 per cent from rural (see Exhibit 1).

The rural Indian market has had a slower pace of change in the percentage of households that fall under the BoP classification, and it was expected to take at least 25 years from 2009–10 for rural India to get to the same salience as urban India with respect to the number of BoP households within the total households. Urban BoPs contributed to only 15 per cent of urban income despite comprising almost 40 per cent of the population, and this segment was expected to move upwards very fast. On the other hand, despite being such a large percentage of total rural households (82 per cent), the rural BoPs contributed to about half the total income of rural India.[6]

RURAL INDIA

The rural Indian consumer market consisted of between 720 and 790 million consumers with around 160 million households, and comprised 12.2 per cent of the world's population. The market grew 25 per cent in 2008 and was projected to be around US$425 million in 2010–11: double what it was in 2004–05.[7]

THE FMCG MARKET IN RURAL INDIA

The fast moving consumer goods (FMCG) category can be broadly split into household care, personal care and food and beverages (see Exhibit 2). The FMCG market in India was estimated at between US$15 billion to $18 billion and likely to grow to US$33 billion by 2015. Of the first figures, 57 per cent was contributed by rural India. The growth of rural India in the contribution to FMCG is evident from the fact that urban markets were once 50 per cent of total FMCG, and had reduced to 29 per cent (the rest coming from semi-urban), as of 2010.[8]

The BoP market had been seeing a lot of traction with big brands rushing to cash in on the huge opportunities to sell branded products to the estimated 350 million low-income consumers in the

---

[4] David Court and Laxman Narasimhan, "Capturing the world's emerging middle class," *McKinsey Quarterly*, Issue 3, 2010, pp. 12–17.

[5] "Section Title/Report Name," Indicus Analytics, www.indicus.net/blog/index.php/indian_economy/amit/the-bottom-of-the-indian-pyramid, accessed September 25, 2010.

[6] Ibid.

[7] "Rural Market," *India Brand Equity Foundation*, www.ibef.org/economy/ruralmarket.aspx, accessed on September 25, 2010.

[8] "Fast Moving Consumer Goods," *India Brand Equity Foundation Report*, www.ibef.org/download/fmcg_sectoral.pdf, accessed on September 25, 2010.

country. Below are some examples of how FMCG companies were responding to the traction in the rural markets[9]:

- According to published sources, several brands were conscious of the market for low priced offerings in India. Horlicks Asha, a low cost milk food, Coca Cola's Vittigo, a powder based beverage, Pepsi Co's ongoing work on low priced snacks, and Unilever India's Shaktimaan initiative to cover 150,000 villages that had a population of less than 2,000 through cycle vendors (as a low cost distribution alternative for rural Indian villages or hamlets) were examples of introducing priced cost offerings to rural segments or reaching out to rural segments.[10]

MEDIA TRENDS IN RURAL INDIA[11]

Unlike urban India, rural India was what one might call a significantly dark media market in terms of the most penetrated urban media; for example, television was the media with the highest reach, yet it penetrated only 38 per cent of rural India. Interestingly, radio was ahead of print in terms of reach, likely owing to literacy barriers: it reached 18 per cent while print reached 15 per cent. Cinema had a mere five per cent reach.

Some touchpoints that were used successfully by brands that have penetrated this market were the *melas*, *haats* or *mandis*, which were places where the entire population of a village congregated on a periodic basis to purchase a multitude of essential goods while also seeking a day's entertainment for the family. Outdoor media, such as wall paintings, folk media and fairs, had also been effective in reaching out to a large number of consumers at a time. Influencers were also an important medium of disbursing information and educating the consumer. This could be in the form of individuals such as the educated youth of the village, the local retail store owner, the key decision makers such as the chiefs and landlords or even a collective influence worked by women of similar background like through various self-help groups.

THE RURAL INDIAN CONSUMER

Rural India was a highly heterogeneous consumer market, making it impossible to look at it as a single consumer market. However, within a region, the homogeneity of the consumers was bounded by the traditions, customs and values of that region. Rural India had a lower level of traditional education; however, their awareness levels were going up with the increasing penetration of various media, as well as education of the youth and their migration to urban India. Rural Indian consumers were historically believed to be conservative, implying a high-value consciousness. Owing to the comparatively low per capita income levels, the rural consumer was more risk averse to spending when she did not see value clearly. The increasing influx of branded goods indicated that the consumer was willing to

---

[9] Ratna Bhushan, "Nestle exploring low-cost infant milk market," *Economic Times*, August 12, 2010, http://economictimes.indiatimes.com/news/news-by-industry/cons-products/food/Nestle-exploring-low-cost-infant-milk-market/articleshow/6296113.cms, accessed on September 25, 2010.

[10] Namrata Singh, "Shaktimaans to Power Rural Reach," *Times of India*, August 16, 2010, http://timesofindia.indiatimes.com/business/india-business/Shaktimaans-To-Power-Rural-Reach-/articleshow/6316529.cms, accessed on September 25, 2010.

[11] "Lintas Media Guide 2008: Urban and rural reach of advertising media," *afaqs!*, January 21, 2008, www.afaqs.com/perl/news/story.html?sid=20191, accessed September 25, 2010.

spend a little extra for quality and satisfaction, and was not conservative about the absolute outlay per se.

SHAMPOO MARKET IN INDIA—KEY BRANDS, SKUS AND SALIENCES

In 2010, the total hair care market in India was approximately Rs 70 billion in value,[12] of which the shampoo category was estimated to be around Rs 30 billion. There was a high awareness of the category in both the urban (90 per cent) and rural (80 per cent) markets. The overall shampoo market was growing at 14 per cent a year, and had taken penetration to more than 90 per cent in urban and 80 per cent in rural as well. Consumption, however, was still low for India as an index to other countries; for example, per annum consumption in India was 13 ml per capita, while in other parts of Asia it was much higher (160 ml in Indonesia and 330 ml in Thailand) [13].

The key national players in this category were Hindustan Unilever Ltd. (46 per cent share with brands such as Clinic Plus, Clinic All Clear, Sunsilk and Dove), Procter & Gamble (24 per cent share with brands such as Pantene and Head & Shoulders), Cavin Kare (18 per cent share with brands such as Chik) and Dabur (seven per cent with brands such as Vatika)[14].

The primary stock-keeping units (SKUs) in the shampoo category were bottles and sachets. Bottles ranged from 25 ml to 500 ml, whereas sachets usually contained around five to eight and were priced between 50p and Rs 3 depending on the segment. In urban India, the salience split between bottles and sachets was 60:40, whereas in rural India 90 per cent of the shampoo sales occurred as sachets.[15] There was a geographical skew in this too, with the southern market being a strong sachet hold: roughly 70 per cent of the sachet volumes came from the South. The North, on the other hand, contributed to 50 per cent of bottle volumes.[16]

BENEFIT-BASED SEGMENTATION OF THE SHAMPOO MARKET

The biggest consumer hair problem in India was hair fall. However, the fastest growing segment at 12 to 15 per cent growth year-on-year was the anti-dandruff segment, which was around 15 to 20 per cent of the market[17]. The key benefit segments were cosmetic (which refers to shine, strength and lustre), anti-dandruff and herbal (see Exhibit 3).

---

[12] "Hair Care in India," *Euromonitor*, www.euromonitor.com/Hair_Care_in_India, July 2010, accessed on September 25, 2010.

[13] Rupall Mukherjee, "Turf war: HUL losing share in toothpaste, shampoo market," *Times of India*, August 3, 2009, http://timesofindia.indiatimes.com/business/india-business/Turf-war-HUL-losing-share-in-toothpaste-shampoo-market/articleshow/4849829.cms, accessed on September 25, 2010.

[14] "Dabur, CavinKare see growth bubbling in shampoos," *The Hindu Business Line*, March 13, 2010, www.thehindubusinessline.com/2010/03/13/stories/2010031352130500.htm, accessed on September 25, 2010.

[15] "2nd strike P&G cuts shampoo prices," www.dnaindia.com/money/report_2nd-strike-p-and-g-cuts-shampoo-prices_1369108, accessed on September 25, 2010.

[16] "Shampoo Industry," http://sify.com/advertise/industry-shampoo.ppt, accessed on September 25, 2010.

[17] "Preity Zinta to endorse Dabur's anti-dandruff range" The Hindu Business Line, March 24, 2009, www.thehindubusinessline.com/2009/03/24/stories/2009032451681500.htm, accessed on September 25, 2010.

SHAMPOO MARKET IN RURAL SOUTH INDIA

The top three shampoo brands in rural South India (total region encompassing Tamil Nadu, Kerala, Karnataka and Andhra Pradesh) were Clinic Plus, Head & Shoulders and Chik. Below is a summary of each of these players along with an understanding of their consumer segment and positioning.

Clinic Plus—Background

Clinic Plus was a cosmetic shampoo brand of Unilever. It was in the popular/economy tier in terms of pricing and targeted at the low-income consumer (semi-urban and rural). The brand was sold in bottles ranging from 25 ml to 300 ml, sachets of 7.5 ml (Rs 2) and value packs or multi-sachet bundles. The brand's place in the company's shampoo portfolio seemed to be a "Family Value and Health Foundation" brand.[18] On viewing the Clinic Plus Indian ads, it was possible to establish an understanding regarding its target segment and positioning (see Exhibit 4).

Head & Shoulders—Background

Head and Shoulders was an anti-dandruff shampoo brand of Procter & Gamble. It was in the premium tier in terms of pricing and targeted at consumers who sought a chemically mild yet effective anti-dandruff solution. The brand was sold in bottles ranging from 100 ml to 400 ml, sachets of 7.5 ml (Rs 3) and value packs or multi-sachet bundles. The brand's place in the company's shampoo portfolio seemed to be the lead anti-dandruff shampoo, which was endorsed by experts.[19] On viewing the Head and Shoulders Indian ads, it was possible to establish an understanding regarding its target segment and positioning (see Exhibit 5).

Chik—Background

Chik was a cosmetic shampoo brand of Cavin Kare. It was in the popular/economy tier in terms of pricing and targeted at the low-income consumer (semi-urban and rural). The brand was sold in bottles ranging from 25 ml to 100 ml and sachets of 7.5 ml (50p to Rs 1). The brand's place in the company's shampoo portfolio seemed to be the flagship brand that promised soft, nourished, beautiful hair for the confident Indian woman.[20] On viewing the Chik Indian ads, it was possible to establish an understanding regarding its target segment and positioning (see Exhibit 6).

CONCLUSION

Venkatraman decided to commission a survey to obtain some insights related to the several attitudinal aspects of consumers towards the shampoo category as well as towards the brands. He thought this would enable him to decide on the marketing strategy for his brand. The following details provide the overview of his approach to the survey.

---

[18] Michel Dallemagne, "Unilever Asia Hair Care," *Unilever*, November 14, 2007, www.unilever.com/Images/ir_Hair-in-Asia_tcm13-114446.pdf, accessed on September 25, 2010.

[19] "Head & Shoulders," *Procter & Gamble*, www.pg-india.com/hp/hs.htm, accessed on September 25, 2010.

[20] "Chik Shampoo," *CavinKare*, www.cavinkare.com/chikshampoo.html?reload, accessed on September 25, 2010.

Before launching Super Shampoo, Venkataraman conducted a market survey. For the purposes of sampling, the target population was defined in terms of elements, sampling units, extent and time. The element was as below:

- Females aged 18 to 50, belonging to rural or semi-urban household basis income classification (annual household income of less than Rs 75,000 or between Rs 75,000 and Rs 150,000);
- Category (shampoo) non-users or low frequency users, yet aware of the top three shampoo brands in the market;
- Significant television media consumption and enjoys watching advertisements.

The sampling unit was households, since the income parameter was used at the household level. The second level included individuals fitting the demographics and consumption characteristics above. With regard to sampling frame, the basis of selection of representative elements of the target population were taken as gender, age group, household income, category consumption and media consumption as detailed above.

The extent was rural Karnataka, a state in South India; specifically, two towns (Bidadi and Hoskote) which are part of the Bangalore Rural District and a cluster of adjoining villages (Jigani) were selected for the study. An external agency was used to gather data. The questionnaires formulated in English as well as the brand communication material were translated into the local language of the consumer (i.e. Kannada) while it was administered. The time factor was the period of the survey (i.e. September 2010).

The selection of the towns, which could be treated as the strata, was performed based on the judgment of rural household penetration and category awareness. Within these geographies, probability sampling was the chosen technique, in which simple random sampling was performed to select the elements. The individuals were tested through the filter questionnaire to ensure that they met the demographic and category criteria that was required for the study. Seventy-five respondents were chosen based on the above criteria.

Exhibits 4, 5 and 6 capture the storyboards of the three brands (Clinic Plus, Head & Shoulders and Chik) along with the author's description of the storyboards. Also captured are some print ads that the consumers were exposed to as part of the study.

Exhibit 7 contains the respondent profile. A summary of the respondents' background, lifestyle and aspirations, media consumption and FMCG habits is captured here based on the in-depth interviews mentioned in Exhibit 8. The Attitudes, Interests and Opinions section is captured in a quantitative Likert scale, with mean values summarized in Exhibit 8. Exhibit 9 is the shampoo category questionnaire, whereas Exhibits 10, 11 and 12 are the brand-specific questionnaires for Clinic Plus, Head & Shoulders and Chik respectively. The values on the statements in Exhibits 9 to 12 are mean values of the agreement levels with the statement coded from a Likert scale.

The authors would like to thank Professor Dinesh Kumar, Chairperson, Research and Publications, Indian Institute of Management, Bangalore for funding the field survey associated with the study.

EXHIBIT 1 Emerging India

Income per year	Households in millions
Less than Rs 90,000	101.1 (Deprived)
Rs 90,000 – Rs 200,000	91.3 (Aspirers)
Rs 200,000 – Rs 500,000	10.8 (Seekers)
Rs 500,000 – Rs 1,000,000	2.4 (Strivers)
More than Rs 1,000,000	1.2 (Global Indians)

Source: "The Marketing Whitebook," *Businessworld*, 2007–2008, p. 33.

EXHIBIT 2 FMCG Categories

Category	Products
Household care	Laundry soaps and detergents, floor cleaners, dish cleaners, mosquito repellents, etc.
Personal care	Oral care (toothpaste/toothpowder and toothbrushes), hair care (hair oil, shampoo), skin care (soaps), etc.
Food & beverages	Cereals, bakery products, tea, coffee, vegetables, dairy products.

EXHIBIT 3 Shampoo Market Benefit Segments

Classification	Prominent brands
Cosmetic (shine, strength, health, lustre, anti-breakage, etc.)	Sunsilk, Pantene, Clinic Plus, Chik
Anti-dandruff	Clinic All Clear, Head and Shoulders
Herbal	Vatika, Nyle, Meera

EXHIBIT 4 Clinic Plus Sample Storyboards from TV Advertisements

*Clinic Plus Ad Understanding Summary	
Central character	Young girl, typically between 8 to 14 years old, school-going.
Personality and attributes of central character	Strong-willed, go-getter, sporty and playful, outdoorsy, will match up to young boys of her age, cherishes her long hair but does not want to be inhibited by the same when it comes to being free.
Setting	Problem-solving approach
Influencer	Mother
Drama	The drama focuses around a situation in which the need for the young girl to get out and be free is inhibited by the dirt and grime that impacts her hair from being clean, healthy and strong. The mother steps in here as a protector and advisor who introduces Clinic Plus to her daughter and gives her back her freedom, while her shampoo takes care of keeping her hair nourished and strong.
Inferred consumer segment	Clinic Plus is aimed at the entire family in low-income households and targets them through the mother who is the decision-maker or key influencer in this category.
Inferred benefit statement	Clinic Plus helps you keep your family's hair healthy and strong and lets them be uninhibited to do what they want.

Storyboard 1

A mother and daughter enter the sports-master's room in school. The mother requests that her daughter be a part of the cricket team, to which the sports-master says that it is for the boys. The mother argues that her daughter is as good or better than the boys, to which he expresses concern over how she will handle all the exposure to dirt and grime that will follow her clothes and her lustrous long hair in the outdoors. The mother requests that he let her on the team and leave the rest for her to worry about. Cuts to scene advocating Clinic Plus and its benefit of keeping hair healthy and strong due to features such as milk protein, so that one need not worry about their hair and can be free in the outdoors. Cuts back to scene where daughter plays for the team and drives them to victory in front of a proud mother.

Storyboard 2

A young girl asks the boys in her playground if she can join them. She is taunted by them when one of them pulls off her hair band and she loses some hair in the same. She goes home to her mother who then consoles her and gives her Clinic Plus, which keeps her long hair lustrous and strong, and encourages her to go out and take on the boys in the field. The daughter does so and enjoys herself uninhibitedly.

Sample Print Advertisements of Clinic Plus

*Authors have used their perception to describe the storyboard of the respective brand.

Source: Advertisements reproduced with the permission of Mukesh Pawar, Senior Brand Manager, Clinic Plus, Hindustan Unilever Ltd., India.

EXHIBIT 5 Head & Shoulders Sample Storyboards from TV Advertisements

*Head & Shoulders Ad Understanding Summary	
Central character	Young male or female, typically between 18 to 25 years old, attractive and smart. Has used celebrity faces such as Kareena Kapoor and Saif Ali Khan.
Setting	The ads are clinical and pristine in their setting, which is augmented by use of foreign models, lab settings and experts such as dermatologists.
Influencer	Expert (dermatologist) or celebrity
Drama	The drama focuses around a dandruff-related problem like hair fall and explains how Head and Shoulders is superior in dandruff-fighting capability. It explains the problem of dandruff with cause and effect using graphics and explains scientific components in the product (e.g. VitaZinc). It is accompanied by the use of a superiority claim like "95 per cent hair fall reduction" or "9/10 dermatologists recommend H&S." Some ads include an angle of attractiveness to the opposite sex or the courage to get closer without worrying about dandruff showing in some television commercials.
Inferred consumer segment	Targeted at both male and female audiences, aged 18 to 44 and suffering from dandruff problems.
Inferred benefit statement	Head and Shoulders is the expert-recommended brand for dandruff-free healthy hair.

Storyboard 1

A young woman is shown examining distastefully the hair that comes off on her hairbrush when she combs. The celebrity star explains to her that one of the causes of hair fall is dandruff and that is why you need Head & Shoulders. A voiceover goes on to explain how H&S removes dandruff and allows oil to permeate, allowing hair to grow stronger and reduce breakage. It closes with a "95 per cent less hair fall" claim and an endorsement from an "American testing centre."

Storyboard 2

An expert in a white coat says that he will demonstrate how Head & Shoulders is more effective than ordinary anti-dandruff shampoos in dandruff removal. There is the use of a dandruff-testing strip and

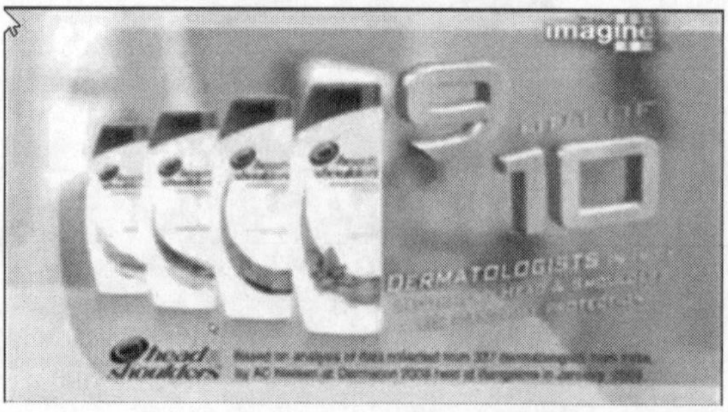

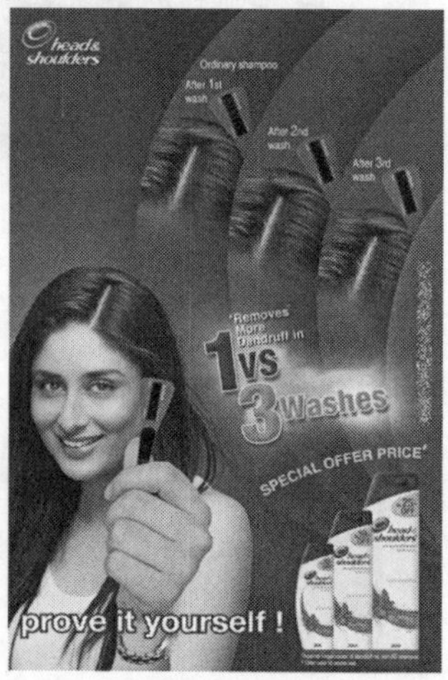

*Authors have used their perception to describe the storyboard of the respective brand.

Source: Advertisements reproduced with the permission of Anupam Chaudhury, Assistant Brand Manager, Head & Shoulders, Procter & Gamble, India.

a side-by-side comparison of scalp washed with ordinary anti-dandruff shampoo and with Head & Shoulders, and it says that while ordinary shampoos takes three washes to remove dandruff, Head & Shoulders does it in one. It uses the strip to compare the residual dandruff and show the difference. It ends with a claim that Head & Shoulders is endorsed by experts.

EXHIBIT 6 Chik Sample Storyboards from TV Advertisements

***Chik Ad Understanding Summary**	
Central character	Young woman, typically between 18 to 25 years old.
Personality and attributes of central character	Beautiful, assured of herself, pays attention to her looks, feels comfortable letting her hair down, progressive and outgoing.
Setting	Problem-solving approach
Influencer	Mother
Drama	The drama focuses around a situation in which the woman is out in the open and her hair gets tangled due to a natural circumstance. However, owing to the double conditioners in Chik shampoo, she simply smoothes her hair out and it is back to looking perfectly detangled and healthy with shine. Furthermore, Chik also has variants in different fragrances, such as jasmine, that appeal strongly to markets like the South, and trade up variants, such as satin for existing Chik consumers, which have an even more modern feel to the ad and the central character.
Inferred consumer segment	Chik is aimed at women in the age range of 18–44 in semi-urban and rural areas.
Inferred benefit statement	Chik keeps your hair soft, nourished and beautiful all the time so you do not have to worry about tangles and can look and feel your confident best.

Storyboard 1

Two young women dressed for the occasion enter a wedding hall. As the table fan next to them blows their hair, one of the women is concerned and distressed about her hairstyle being impacted and not looking her best with her hair tangled. The other woman, a Chik consumer, waits to pass the fan and smoothes out her hair with her hand, only for it to be perfectly set and looking soft and healthy. The product attribute of double conditioners is explained to establish the benefit.

Storyboard 2

A young attractive woman heading to work is standing on a railway platform and there is a young man watching her from the other side. As a train passes by, it blows through her hair and disturbs it completely, making it unruly as the young man watches in consternation. The young woman seems unconcerned and simply smoothes her hair back into shape. This benefit is then explained with the active double conditioners in Chik shampoo.

*Authors have used their perception to describe the storyboard of the respective brand.

Source: Advertisements reproduced with the permission of C. K. Ranganathan, Managing Director, Cavinkare Pvt. Ltd., India.

EXHIBIT 7 Respondent Profile

Respondent Background

The respondents were typically from families of four to five members in which the husband was predominantly the earning member of the household. The other members were usually one to two children or aged parents. Occupations of the main income provider included farming, sales jobs and working in a factory (manufacturing unit) on the job floor. The respondent was usually the wife, in the age group of 25–40, for the purpose of the depth interviews.

Identity, Aspirations and Dreams

Almost all of the respondents, when asked about themselves, described themselves with respect to the roles they play in the household and their relationships with each member of the family. Their identities were ingrained with their family.

These respondents belonged to the low-income households and a lot of their aspirations and dreams were on the lines of a better position in terms of wealth. However, equally important was to earn societal respect for their family, and their need to be seen as people-in-the-know among their friends and neighbours. They associated this with owning their own businesses or working for large corporations. They foresaw themselves as setting an example for others, and defining lifestyles for people of their kind. Some of these women aspired to work themselves and add to the household income, and they even had clear careers of their choice in mind. They saw the route to achieving their dreams as hard work, saving and compromising on current non-essential things in life.

Media Habits

TV viewing: The respondents were unanimously regular TV viewers. Typical TV viewing occurred in mid-morning when the household chores were done, and in the night with the rest of the family. A significant proportion of the programs watched were entertainment-related, including serials, movies and cinema-related shows. However, there was some information-seeking related viewing, primarily of the categories of shows that were women-specific and gave advice and lifestyle tips (i.e. cooking programs and the regional news channels). Health was another category of active information gathering as these respondents watched programs that provided advice on taking care of themselves and their family's health and fitness.

Advertisement involvement: Advertisements were watched and enjoyed by all these respondents with heightened levels of attention to certain categories, such as detergents, fairness creams and mobile phones. The reasons quoted for greater attention for certain categories of advertising was communication which addressed a current problem (e.g. detergents), use of celebrities (e.g. soap and fairness creams) and distinctiveness of communication (e.g. mobile phones and service providers).

Celebrity influence: Celebrities were seen as adding trust to an ad or product; however, it was not necessarily a reason to buy. Some regional movie celebrities were looked up to as role models, and this was explained with awareness of their associations with some social causes.

Other media: Radio was also a fairly popular media in two slots. The first was the early morning slot in which the program content was primarily devotional music. The second was morning to mid-morning, when the respondents said that cinema music would play on radio accompanying their household chores. Select radio show hosts were remembered by name and were liked for their styles and the kind of information they provided on their shows. Newspapers and magazines, however, were less popular forms of media. On occasion, coupons in newspapers were noticed and retained for promotional offers, and the classified section was an area of interest for jobs, depending on the life-cycle stage of the respondent; otherwise, it was a low-involvement media for women.

FMCG Buying Patterns

Categories and purchase behaviour: The monthly expenditure of these respondent households was primarily across the categories of groceries and cosmetics as the two broad heads. The food and beverages expenditure was around Rs 2,000 to 2,500 per month, whereas the personal products and cosmetics would add up to Rs 500. Purchase frequency was usually weekly. The standard place of purchase was the kirana stores close to home or sometimes ration shops.

Source of awareness: The shopper in the household was typically the one with more time, and hence the wife. She also usually decided what brands were to be bought on most household categories, unless asked specifically for something by the family members. She got her knowledge of new brands from three key sources. The first and most common was TV advertisements. They also remembered some brands due to program sponsorships, wherein the brand name was tied to the program name. In-store was another source of awareness of new brands and products. The third was through friends, neighbours and relatives. Although in-store created more awareness of brand, it was word of mouth that generated more trial.

New brand trials: Some of the most recent trials of new brands were initiated through word of mouth; for example, sensitive toothpaste because of a similar oral care problem affecting a relative. Products like hair oils (which were perceived as low risk) were tried out in small-sized bottles after having seen them on TV. Mobile phone was another category in which a new brand was tried; however, this was after TV awareness and retailer guidance. The retailer was usually asked for advice on medical products or new cosmetics regarding side effects of usage, but most other categories were not enquired about at the kirana.

Source: Based on actual respondents in field who were interviewed. Criteria for selection was provided by the authors.

EXHIBIT 8 Respondent Interview Questionnaire

Introduction

We'd like to know more about you. Could you please tell us the following details about yourself?

- Name
- Age
- How many members in the family and what do they do
- Occupation of main income earner
- Occupation of respondent (if different from above)
- Please tell us more about your daily routine. What is a typical weekday like? What is a typical weekend like?

Aspirations and Ambitions

- If you had to tell someone who doesn't know you about yourself, how would you describe yourself?
- What are your aspirations and dreams?
- If you were given a chance to look into the future, what do you see yourself as?
- What do you want to achieve? Why is that important? How different is that from the state you are in now?
- What do you think you need to do to achieve your dreams?

Media Habits and Attitudes

- Do you watch TV regularly? How often do you watch TV and when in the day do you watch?
- What do you watch on TV and why?
- What information do you seek from TV?
- Do you consider any TV celebrities as role models?
- Do you like watching advertisements? Can you tell us any advertisement you liked recently? Why did you like it?
- Do you listen to the radio? When in the day and how often do you listen to radio?
- What programs do you listen to and why?
- Do you read any newspaper or magazine regularly? Which ones? When in the day do you read?
- What kind of information do you seek from a newspaper/magazine?
- What sections of the newspaper/magazine do you read? Which is your favorite section in the newspaper? What do you like about it?
- Do you recall any advertisements in the newspaper/magazine? Do you spend time reading advertisements?

FMCG Buying Patterns

- What products do you buy for your household? How often do you buy them?
- Where do you buy these products?

- How much of your monthly expenditure is spent on food and beverages like rice, dal, milk, tea, coffee, etc., and how much is spent on personal care products like soap, detergent, toothpaste, shampoo, etc.?
- Who goes to buy these products?
- Who decides what brands to buy?
- Where do you learn about different brands?
- When did you last buy a new product or new brand? Why did you decide to try the new brand?
- Have you tried something new after seeing it on TV?
- Have you tried something new because you heard from a friend or relative?
- Have you asked the retailer's advice on what to buy?

Attitudes, Interests and Opinions

For each of the statements below, express your agreement or disagreement by marking the appropriate box on the side.

Statement	Mean Value
I enjoy watching TV	4.5
I enjoy spending time talking to my friends and neighbours	4.2
I do the shopping for my family's daily needs	4.2
I spend time every day on taking care of my hair and skin	3.1
I try out new products when I see them advertised on TV	3.2
I am interested in new products that come in the market	3.0
I always try new products in small quantities first	3.8
I always try to find out more information on beauty tips	2.3
I always look out for offers or promotions while shopping	3.8
I ask my retailer for his opinion when I am trying something new	3.4
I don't mind paying a little extra for branded goods	3.4
I ask my friends and neighbours before buying something new	4.0
I am the decision-maker for household products for the family	3.7
I believe it is important to be well-groomed all the time	4.0
If celebrities are endorsing a product, then it must be good	4.0

Mean value explanation: The above set of statements were measured on a Likert scale for each respondent ranging from Strongly Agree to Strongly Disagree, and the values were coded as Strongly Agree – 5, Agree – 4, Neither Agree nor Disagree – 3, Disagree – 2, Strongly Disagree – 1. The mean values are the average of the same across all respondents.

Source: Questions were created by the authors. Results are based on actual field interviews.

EXHIBIT 9 Shampoo Category Questionnaire

1. How often do you wash your hair?
   - Once in 2 weeks – **7 per cent**
   - Once a week – **48 per cent**
   - Twice a week – **43 per cent**
   - Thrice a week – **3 per cent**
   - Daily – **0 per cent**
2. What do you use to wash your hair? (can be a combination of more than one product)
   - Soap – **37 per cent**
   - Shampoo – **24 per cent**
   - Shikakai – **67 per cent**
   - Others (please specify)
3. Where did you learn about shampoos?
   - TV – **96 per cent**
   - Radio – **4 per cent**
   - Newspapers or magazines – **4 per cent**
   - Friends or relatives – **32 per cent**
   - Store – **31 per cent**
   - Others (please specify)
4. Please name some of the shampoo brand names you have heard of ________________________________

Top unaided awareness brands:

Unaided awareness (in per cent)	
Clinic Plus	93
Chik	76
Head & Shoulders	53
Sunsilk	37
Clinic All Clear	20

5. How often do you use shampoo to wash your hair?
   - Every time – **0 per cent**
   - Mostly use other products, occasionally use shampoo – **71 per cent**
   - Have used shampoo once or twice – **16 per cent**
   - Never – **12 per cent**
6. What brands of shampoo have you used?
   - Clinic Plus – **61 per cent**
   - Head and Shoulders – **35 per cent**
   - Chik – **49 per cent**
   - Sunsilk – **5 per cent**
   - Pantene – **1 per cent**
   - Rejoice – **0 per cent**
   - Meera – **2 per cent**

- Clinic All Clear – **5 per cent**
- Nyle – **0 per cent**
- Ayur – **0 per cent**
- Vatika – **0 per cent**
- Dove – **0 per cent**
- Any other (please specify)

7. Have you seen advertisements of any of the below brands?
   - Clinic Plus – **75 per cent**
   - Head and Shoulders – **47 per cent**
   - Chik – **59 per cent**
   - Sunsilk – **12 per cent**
   - Pantene – **5 per cent**
   - Rejoice – **0 per cent**
   - Meera – **1 per cent**
   - Clinic All Clear – **10 per cent**
   - Nyle – **0 per cent**
   - Ayur – **0 per cent**
   - Vatika – **0 per cent**
   - Dove – **0 per cent**
   - Any other (please specify)

   If so, please describe in brief for any 2 brands remembered
   Brand 1 - <brand name> <description> ________________
   Brand 2 - <brand name> <description> ________________
8. What pack type of shampoo have you used?
   - Bottle – **1 per cent**
   - Sachet – **99 per cent**
9. How did you choose the brand of shampoo?
   - Saw on TV and liked – **51 per cent**
   - Saw in store and liked – **4 per cent**
   - Recommended by friend/neighbour – **37 per cent**
   - Recommended by retailer – **8 per cent**

   For each of the statements, express your agreement or disagreement by marking the appropriate box on the side

Statement	Mean Value
Shampoos are not good for my hair since they have chemicals	3.2
Shampoo can be used for occasional wash but not for daily wash	3.2
I try out a shampoo that my friend or relative has recommended	3.7
Shampoo cleans my hair better than soap	3.9
Washing with shampoo makes my hair look beautiful	4.1
I feel more confident when I use shampoo	3.9
I use shampoo only when I have to wash oil from my hair	4.0
Shampoo is very expensive	2.5

Statement	Mean Value
Shampoo is a luxury that I use only for special occasions	2.6
I always buy shampoo in sachets only	4.1
Shampoo makes my hair strong and healthy	4.0

Mean value explanation: The above set of statements were measured on a Likert scale for each respondent ranging from Strongly Agree to Strongly Disagree, and the values were coded as Strongly Agree – 5, Agree – 4, Neither Agree nor Disagree – 3, Disagree – 2, Strongly Disagree – 1. The mean values are the average of the same across all respondents.

Source: Questions were created by the authors. Results are based on actual field interviews.

EXHIBIT 10 Clinic Plus Shampoo Questionnaire

For each of the statements, express your agreement or disagreement for the statement with respect to **CLINIC PLUS SHAMPOO** by marking the appropriate box on the side.

Statement	Mean Value
It has a lot of chemicals in it	3.1
It prevents my hair from getting dandruff	3.8
It makes my hair smell fresh	3.9
It keeps my hair healthy and strong	4.0
It has a great fragrance	3.9
It is not different from any other shampoo	3.2
It is an expensive shampoo	2.3
It is recommended by hair experts	3.2
It is for people with long hair	2.4
It keeps hair untangled and smooth	3.3
It is used by celebrities	3.2
It is a brand for my family	3.6
It is a shampoo I can trust for my hair	3.7
It makes me look beautiful	4.1
It makes me feel confident	3.4
It is a brand for those who are in the outdoors	2.6
It allows me to feel free and unworried	3.4
It is a brand for the youngsters	2.6
It is a shampoo for special occasions	2.5
It reminds me of my childhood	2.7
It makes me feel in control	3.4
The person in this advertisement reminds me of myself	3.5
It will make me refreshed and revived	3.5
It will make me feel like everyone's eyes are on me	3.4
It makes me feel taken care of by an expert	3.2
I will ask my friends or neighbours about this brand	3.9

Which of these statements best describes the chance that you will buy **CLINIC PLUS SHAMPOO** next time? – **3.9**

- I will definitely buy it
- I will probably buy it
- I am uncertain if I will buy it
- I will probably not buy it
- I will definitely not buy it

If the answer to above is "definitely buy" or "probably buy," then continue with below table, else move to next section.

Statement	Mean Value
I will search for this brand when I go shopping next time	4.5
I will buy shampoo only if I find this brand, else I will not buy	3.3
I will compare prices of different brands before I buy	3.3
I will buy the brand because I like its advertisement	3.9
I will buy the brand only if I like its packaging	3.4
I will buy the shampoo in sachet only	4.1
I will ask the retailer about it before buying	4.1
I will tell my friends and neighbours about my experience with the brand	4.1

Mean value explanation: The above set of statements were measured on a Likert scale for each respondent ranging from Strongly Agree to Strongly Disagree, and the values were coded as Strongly Agree – 5, Agree – 4, Neither Agree nor Disagree – 3, Disagree – 2, Strongly Disagree – 1. The coding for the likelihood to buy assessment was similar with "definitely buy" being 5 and "definitely not buy" being 1. The mean values are the average of the same across all respondents.

Source: Questions were created by the authors. Results are based on actual field interviews.

EXHIBIT 11 Head & Shoulders Shampoo Questionnaire

For each of the statements, express your agreement or disagreement for the statement with respect to **HEAD AND SHOULDERS SHAMPOO** by marking the appropriate box on the side.

Statement	Mean Value
It has a lot of chemicals in it	3.2
It prevents my hair from getting dandruff	3.9
It makes my hair smell fresh	3.9
It keeps my hair healthy and strong	3.8
It has a great fragrance	3.9
It is not different from any other shampoo	3.0
It is an expensive shampoo	2.5
It is recommended by hair experts	3.8
It is for people with long hair	2.5
It keeps hair untangled and smooth	3.1
It is used by celebrities	3.1

Statement	Mean Value
It is a brand for my family	2.6
It is a shampoo I can trust for my hair	3.1
It makes me look beautiful	3.2
It makes me feel confident	3.1
It is a brand for those who are in the outdoors	2.5
It allows me to feel free and unworried	3.0
It is a brand for the youngsters	2.4
It is a shampoo for special occasions	2.4
It reminds me of my childhood	2.4
It makes me feel in control	3.2
The person in this advertisement reminds me of myself	3.3
It will make me refreshed and revived	3.4
It will make me feel like everyone's eyes are on me	3.3
It makes me feel taken care of by an expert	3.8
I will ask my friends or neighbours about this brand	3.7

Which of these statements best describes the chance that you will buy **HEAD AND SHOULDERS SHAMPOO** next time? – **2.7**

- I will definitely buy it
- I will probably buy it
- I am uncertain if I will buy it
- I will probably not buy it
- I will definitely not buy it

If the answer to above is "definitely buy" or "probably buy," then continue with below table, else move to next section.

Statement	Mean Value
I will search for this brand when I go shopping next time	4.2
I will buy shampoo only if I find this brand, else I will not buy	3.1
I will compare prices of different brands before I buy	3.9
I will buy the brand because I like its advertisement	3.9
I will buy the brand only if I like its packaging	3.8
I will buy the shampoo in sachet only	4.1
I will ask the retailer about it before buying	4.0
I will tell my friends and neighbours about my experience with the brand	4.0

Mean value explanation: The above set of statements were measured on a Likert scale for each respondent ranging from Strongly Agree to Strongly Disagree, and the values were coded as Strongly Agree – 5, Agree – 4, Neither Agree nor Disagree – 3, Disagree – 2, Strongly Disagree – 1. The coding for the likelihood to buy assessment was similar with "definitely buy" being 5 and "definitely not buy" being 1. The mean values are the average of the same across all respondents.

Source: Questions were created by the authors. Results are based on actual field interviews.

EXHIBIT 12 Chik Shampoo Questionnaire

For each of the statements, express your agreement or disagreement for the statement with respect to **CHIK SHAMPOO** by marking the appropriate box on the side.

Statement	Mean Value
It has a lot of chemicals in it	3.1
It prevents my hair from getting dandruff	3.3
It makes my hair smell fresh	3.9
It keeps my hair healthy and strong	3.8
It has a great fragrance	3.8
It is not different from any other shampoo	3.2
It is an expensive shampoo	2.1
It is recommended by hair experts	3.5
It is for people with long hair	2.4
It keeps hair untangled and smooth	3.8
It is used by celebrities	3.0
It is a brand for my family	2.6
It is a shampoo I can trust for my hair	3.3
It makes me look beautiful	3.3
It makes me feel confident	3.2
It is a brand for those who are in the outdoors	2.9
It allows me to feel free and unworried	3.2
It is a brand for the youngsters	2.2
It is a shampoo for special occasions	2.6
It reminds me of my childhood	2.2
It makes me feel in control	3.3
The person in this advertisement reminds me of myself	3.3
It will make me refreshed and revived	3.4
It will make me feel like everyone's eyes are on me	3.2
It makes me feel taken care of by an expert	3.4
I will ask my friends or neighbours about this brand	3.8

Which of these statements best describes the chance that you will buy **CHIK SHAMPOO** next time? – **3.0**

- I will definitely buy it
- I will probably buy it
- I am uncertain if I will buy it
- I will probably not buy it
- I will definitely not buy it

If the answer to above is "definitely buy" or "probably buy," then continue with below table, else move to next section.

Statement	Mean Value
I will search for this brand when I go shopping next time	4.5
I will buy shampoo only if I find this brand, else I will not buy	3.3
I will compare prices of different brands before I buy	3.9
I will buy the brand because I like its advertisement	3.7
I will buy the brand only if I like its packaging	3.4
I will buy the shampoo in sachet only	4.4
I will ask the retailer about it before buying	4.2
I will tell my friends and neighbours about my experience with the brand	4.2

Mean value explanation: The above set of statements were measured on a Likert scale for each respondent ranging from Strongly Agree to Strongly Disagree, and the values were coded as Strongly Agree – 5, Agree – 4, Neither Agree nor Disagree – 3, Disagree – 2, Strongly Disagree – 1. The coding for the likelihood to buy assessment was similar with "definitely buy" being 5 and "definitely not buy" being 1. The mean values are the average of the same across all respondents.

Source: Questions were created by the authors. Results are based on actual field interviews.

4

Himalaya Herbal Toothpaste: Category and Brand Involvement in an Emerging Market

Dr. S. Ramesh Kumar and Nitya Guruvayurappan wrote this case solely to provide material for class discussion. The authors do not intend to illustrate either effective or ineffective handling of a managerial situation. The authors may have disguised certain names and other identifying information to protect confidentiality.

Ramesh Kumar had been teaching for the last twenty-five years, after spending a few years in the corporate sector. In addition to the satisfaction involved in the profession, he found that teaching presented many exciting opportunities to link concepts with practice. In January 2011, an executive of the Himalaya Drug Company attended his training program, and a discussion sparked off some interesting thoughts. Himalaya was a brand that had herbal offerings in health supplements and personal care products. The use of herbal remedies and products had been an integral part of Indian culture, and Himalaya's unique proposition was the scientific rigor associated with the testing of its herbal offerings. Historically, the brand had not advertised like a typical health care company; however, to build market share in the highly competitive personal care market, it had begun to advertise its face wash and toothpaste brands. Its offerings were exported to several countries, and the brand had a positive perception among consumers (www.himalayahealthcare.com).

Kumar was curious to find out whether consumers were really loyal to the brands in this category. He was interested in the toothpaste category, and Himalaya had herbal offerings in the retail and prescriptive segments. Were consumers involved in the category? Did they remember the functional brand benefits? Were consumers buying brands due to the social benefits reflected in the ads? Did consumers continue to buy particular brands without switching, due to inertia? Were consumers interested in herbal offerings? How should Himalaya be perceived by consumers? This medley of issues presented yet another opportunity to an academic to conceptualize the situation, one that was perhaps unique to the Indian context.

The concept of product involvement differentiated consumer segments based on the degrees of personal interest expressed by consumers with regard to specific products and services. High-involvement categories required consumers to be involved in extensive buying behavior that led to one or more of the following aspects: risk reduction, enhancement of self-image, and a greater degree of gratification in having achieved an optimal choice after examining the various alternatives in the category. Low-involvement categories were those that were bought in a routine manner by the consumer, with a degree of personal interest that was lower than that associated with the high-involvement categories. Marketers always had to face competitive challenges in enhancing the degree of involvement even in low-involvement categories through appropriate branding initiatives. The toothpaste category was one such category in the Indian context.

ORAL CARE INDUSTRY

The fast moving consumer goods (FMCG) category was broadly split into household care, personal care, and food and beverages. The FMCG market in India was projected to be around US$15–18 billion in 2010, and was likely to grow to US$33 billion by 2015. The average Indian consumer spent around eight per cent of his or her income on personal care (oral care, hair care, and skin care) products.[1] The increasing levels of discretionary spending, greater attention to personal hygiene, and proliferation of new media channels and distribution contributed to the growth of the personal care segment.[2]

The oral care category comprised toothpaste, toothbrushes, tooth powder, mouthwash, dental floss and whitening products. In 2010, the oral care market in India was around US$980 million (calculated at the rate of US$1 per Rs. 45). The growth trend of toothpastes over the past three years (11 per cent) was relatively slower than that of several other key FMCG categories. The growth of the toothbrush category was even lower, at around nine per cent.[3]

Some studies were undertaken on the perception of consumers regarding the toothpaste category. One study reported that 68 per cent of the Indian consumers who participated in the survey believed that using the right toothpaste was more important than using the right toothbrush. However, the consumers did not give much importance to the category itself, as most of them believed that oral care was not as important for personal grooming as hair care or skin care.[4] Another study revealed that only 28 per cent of the respondents brushed twice a day.[5] Yet another study indicated that 68 per cent

---

[1] "Fast Moving Consumer Goods," IBEF, www.ibef.org/download/fmcg_sectoral.pdf, accessed March 31, 2011.

[2] "Beauty and Personal Care in India," www.euromonitor.com/beauty-and-personal-care-in-india/report, accessed August 23, 2011.

[3] "Analyst Report," Colgate-Palmolive (India) Limited, www.colgate.co.in/Colgate/IN/Corp/InvestorRelations/Introduction/AnalystPresentation2010.pdf, accessed March 31, 2011.

[4] "The Tooth is Out There and It's Not Much to Smile About," *The Hindu*, www.hindu.com/2010/11/23/stories/2010112357 990200.htm, accessed March 31, 2011.

[5] "49 Per cent Indians Do Not Use Toothbrush: Survey," *Top News Health*, www.topnews.in/healthcare/content/2133849-percent-indians-do-not-use-toothbrush-survey, accessed March 31, 2011.

of the respondents had never visited a dentist, and 87 per cent would not consider visiting a dentist as a preventive measure.[6] The World Health Organization (WHO) reported that 98 per cent of the Indian population suffered from oral health problems.[7] The ratio of dentists to patients in India was dismally low, with just one dentist for 10,000 people in urban areas, and one for about 0.25 million people in rural areas.[8] Hence, it could be inferred that there was significant scope for marketers to enhance the involvement level associated with the toothpaste category among consumers.

TOOTHPASTE INDUSTRY: BRANDS AND SEGMENTS

The toothpaste market in India had a penetration rate as low as 60 per cent. Urban penetration was around 76 per cent, whereas rural penetration was 40 per cent.[9] The average consumption of toothpaste in rural households was significantly lower than in urban households.[10] The per capita consumption of toothpaste in grams per year in India was around 115, whereas it was 255 in China, and 542 in the United States.[11]

The key brands in the Indian oral care industry were Colgate-Palmolive India and Hindustan Unilever Limited. Colgate was one of the flagship brands for oral care, with the category contributing to 96 per cent of Colgate-Palmolive India's annual company sales, and it was the market leader in the toothpaste, toothbrush and tooth powder categories. It led the toothpaste market with a 52 per cent market share. Hindustan Unilever was second in the oral care market, and had a 25 per cent share in the toothpaste category.[12]

The toothpaste category was segmented into three price tiers, namely, economy, popular, and premium.[13] The toothpaste category existed in two product variant types: paste and gel formats. The definition of the price tiers and the classification of the key brands according to pricing and product variant type are summarized in Exhibit 1.

After reviewing the key benefits and the propositions of the various brands in the oral care market,[14] Kumar concluded that there were four benefit-based segments in the market. A detailed description of the key brands in each segment, along with the storyboard of a recent advertisement for each brand, is

---

6 "Free Dental Camp in October," *The Hindu*, www.hindu.com/2010/09/29/stories/2010092950160200.htm, accessed March 31, 2011.

7 "It Pays to Take Care of Your Teeth," *The Hindu*, www.hindu.com/2010/10/30/stories/2010103060180500.htm, accessed March 31, 2011.

8 "Indian Oral Care Market: Low Penetration Offers Growth Opportunities," Pharmaceutical Market Research, www.pharmaceutical-market-research.com/publications/treatments/indian_oral_care_market_low_penetration_offers_growth_opportunities.html, accessed March 31, 2011.

9 "Market Survey of India," diehardindian.com, www.diehardindian.com/overview/market.htm, accessed March 31, 2011.

10 "Fast Moving Consumer Goods," IBEF, www.ibef.org/download/fmcg_sectoral.pdf, accessed March 31, 2011.

11 "Analyst Report," Colgate-Palmolive (India) Limited, www.colgate.co.in/Colgate/IN/Corp/InvestorRelations/Introduction/AnalystPresentation2010.pdf, accessed March 31, 2011.

12 "Colgate Presentation," www.scribd.com/doc/29515992/Colgate-Toothpaste-Advertisement-on-Consumers, accessed March 31, 2011.

13 "Glaxo Sets Teeth on Dental Opening," *Rediff Business*, www.rediff.com/business/report/glaxo-sets-teeth-on-dental-opening/20110106.htm, accessed March 31, 2011.

14 "Colgate World of Care: Oral Care Center," Colgate, www.colgate.co.in/app/Colgate/IN/OralCare/ToothPastes.cvsp, accessed March 31, 2011; "Hindustan Unilever Limited: Our Brands," Hindustan Unilever Limited, www.hul.co.in/brands/?WT.GNAV=Our_brands, accessed March 31, 2011; "Dabur: Oral Care, the Natural Way," Dabur, www.dabur.com/Products-Health%20Care-Oral%20Care, accessed March 31, 2011; "Dental cream," Himalaya Herbal Healthcare, www.himalayahealthcare.com/products/dental_cream.htm, accessed March 31, 2011; Anchor,

provided in Exhibit 2 (Exhibit 3 presents the same for the Himalaya brand). The classification of the brands based on target segments and individual propositions is summarized in Exhibit 4.

Category Segments

Freshness

Key Benefit: The proposition for this segment was built around the concept of "Freshness that fills you with confidence."

Herbal

Key Benefit: This segment offered complete oral care with the help of natural/herbal or Ayurvedic ingredients.

Overall Oral Health

Key Benefit: This segment offered healthy teeth and strong gums for the entire family through protection from germs.

Niche: Problem Solving

Key Benefit: This segment offered specific solutions to oral health problems for consumers with higher involvement in oral care. The benefits included addressing sensitivity of gums and teeth, satisfying whitening requirements, and so on.

A fifth segment in this category was the children's toothpaste segment; however, it was not as significant in size as the others were. Children's toothpastes were flavored such that children would find them appealing, and included cartoon characters on the tubes or freebies. Colgate and Pepsodent both had variants in this segment, priced in the popular price tier. A detailed listing of all the brands is presented in Exhibit 1, and a positioning diagram in Exhibit 4 compares the pricing and proposition of the brands.

HIMALAYA: COMPANY PROFILE

The Himalaya Drug Company[15] had been in the pharmaceutical field for several decades.[16] In order to enter the consumer markets with wellness and personal care offerings, the company had launched Ayurvedic Concepts, which offered health supplements, skin care products and pain ointments. Ayurveda was a popular form of alternative medicine in India that was based on herbal ingredients.

Initially, in the late nineties, Ayurvedic Concepts targeted the young urban professional population, in an attempt to create awareness of the brand. In the early years of the twenty-first century,[17] in order to

---

www.anchorglobal.net, accessed March 31, 2011; "New Sensodyne Repair & Protect: A Breakthrough Formulation in Dental Care," www.gsk.com/products/consumer-healthcare/sensodyne-repair-protect.htm, accessed March 31, 2011.

[15] Himalaya Herbal Healthcare, www.himalayahealthcare.com/index.htm, accessed March 31, 2011.

[16] "Company Profile," Himalaya Herbal Healthcare, www.himalayahealthcare.com/abouthimalaya/cprofile.htm, accessed March 31, 2011.

[17] "Himalayan Odyssey," *Business Line*, www.thehindubusinessline.in/catalyst/2010/04/08/stories/2010040850100300.htm, accessed March 31, 2011.

head towards being a global brand, Ayurvedic Concepts was brought under the Himalaya umbrella brand for several categories such as soaps, shampoos face washes, health supplements, baby products, etc. In 2010, 40 per cent of Himalaya's turnover was from consumer products. It had several exclusive outlets throughout the country, and had shop-in-shop counters in modern retail outlets.[18] Himalaya did not advertise as much as other FMCG manufacturers, and brand associations were nurtured by word of mouth.

Himalaya's lead offering in the toothpaste category was Himalaya Dental Cream, with natural ingredients like neem, extracts of Toothache Tree, pomegranate, etc. It was priced in the premium tier. It offered several benefits including tightening and reducing swelling of gums, stopping gum bleeding, preventing toothache and decay and controlling bad breath.[19] Himalaya started advertising this toothpaste in above-the-line media with its concept "Indulge like a child, brush like an adult." Apart from this, Himalaya advertised in several top metropolitan cities through outdoor advertising, mainly through billboards. However, it had a relatively smaller presence in television advertising compared to the brands it competed with, such as Colgate and Pepsodent. The print advertisement for this brand of toothpaste and Kumar's interpretation of its storyboard are presented in Exhibit 3.

Following this, Himalaya went on to launch a range of herbal prescription-based oral care products — the HiOra range — which included a toothpaste, two mouthwashes, an ulcer gel, a gum astringent, and a whitening agent. HiOra was expected to compete with brands operating in the prescription oral care segment (prescribed by doctors) and not in the FMCG oral care segment. Although the doctor-prescribed oral care market was just five per cent in 2010, it was showing a growth of 21 per cent annually, indicating an increase in the awareness about oral care.[20]

METHODOLOGY

For sampling purposes, the target population was defined as:

- Females aged 25-55, belonging to urban households with an SEC socioeconomic classification (a classification of households in India commonly used as a market segmentation tool based on the educational level and occupation of the chief wage earner of the household that influenced the consumption pattern of the household).[21]

The geographical area was urban Karnataka, a state in South India. An external marketing research agency was used to collect data in April 2011. The questionnaires that had been formulated in English were translated into Kannada, the local language of the consumers. Based on the above criteria, 100 respondents were chosen, with twenty-five respondents from each benefit segment. The scales were designed to capture consumer involvement,[22] brand attitude, and brand attachment.[23]

---

[18] "South India's Largest Market for Us: Himalaya," *The Economic Times*, http://articles.economictimes.indiatimes.com/2010-05-14/news/27621681_1_consumer-products-retail-outlets-umbrella-brand, accessed March 31, 2011.

[19] "Dental Cream," Himalaya Herbal Healthcare, www.himalayahealthcare.com/products/dental_cream.htm, accessed March 31, 2011.

[20] "Himalaya Rolls in New Oral Range HiOra," *Business Line*, www.thehindubusinessline.in/2010/12/17/stories/2010121751480500.htm, accessed March 31, 2011.

[21] R. Bijapurkar, *We are Like That Only: Understanding the Logic of Consumer India*, Penguin Books India, 2007, p. 130.

[22] J. L. Zaichkowsky, "Measuring the Involvement Construct," *Journal of Consumer Research*, 12, 1985, pp. 341–352.

[23] C. W. Park, D. J. MacInnis, J. Priester, A. B. Eisingerich, and D. Iacobucci, "Brand Attachment and Brand Attitude Strength: Conceptual and Empirical Differentiation of Two Critical Brand Equity Drivers," *Journal of Marketing*, 74, 2010, pp. 1–17.

Exhibit 2 presents samples of brand communication of a key brand in each of the four segments. Exhibit 3 presents a sample of Himalaya's brand communication. Exhibit 5 presents the questionnaire that was deployed along with the mean values for the scale items by category and segment across the 100 consumers interviewed. Exhibit 6 presents other aspects of the consumer study as percentages.

Kumar had to process the data that the agency had collected.

The authors would like to thank Prof. Dinesh Kumar, chairperson of research and publications, for sponsoring the field study that was required for this case study. They would also like to thank Ms. Antaash Sheikh, manager of corporate communications at The Himalaya Drug Company, and Dr. Srikanth, national manager of scientific services of the pharmaceutical division at The Himalaya Drug Company, for their support during the creation of this case study. The authors would like to thank Mr. Atul Sinha and Mr. Madhurjya Banerjee of Unilever India Limited for their assistance in procuring one of the advertisements for publication in this case study.

EXHIBIT 1 Snapshot of All Key Brands

Company	Brand	Type	Price Tier*	Target Consumer	Brand Proposition
HUL	Closeup	Gel	Popular	Young adults, mostly urban	Freshness that gives you the confidence to get closer to someone
	Pepsodent	Paste	Popular	Family (strong children imagery)	Fights germs and prevents cavities for healthy teeth and gums
Colgate	Dental Cream	Paste	Popular	Family (strong children imagery)	All-round decay protection, even where a toothbrush cannot reach
	Total 12	Paste	Premium	Involved oral care consumers: Adults	Complete germ protection for a full range of oral health problems
	Sensitive	Paste	Premium	Niche: Consumers with dental sensitivity	Relief from pain and protection from tooth sensitivity
	Maxfresh	Gel	Popular	Young adults, mostly urban	Maximum freshness for maximum impact
	Fresh Energy Gel	Gel	Popular	Young adults	Fresh breath for confidence to seize every moment
	Herbal	Paste	Popular	Family	Strong teeth and healthy gums, naturally
	Cibaca	Paste	Economy	Family (some children imagery)	Strong teeth and fresh breath for your family
	Active Salt	Paste	Popular	Niche: Consumers with sensitive teeth	Fights germs for healthy gums and teeth
	Maxwhite	Gel	Premium	Niche: Consumers with whitening requirements	Whitens teeth to reveal a sparkling smile
Himalaya	Dental Cream	Paste	Premium	Adults	Indulge like a child, brush like an adult

Company	Brand	Type	Price Tier*	Target Consumer	Brand Proposition
	Babool Mint Fresh	Gel	Economy	Family (some children imagery)	Helps you start the day with a pleasant, fresh feeling
	Babool	Paste	Economy	Family (some children imagery)	A natural way to begin a great day
Dabur	Red	Paste	Popular	Family (strong children imagery)	Keeps your dental problems away with the power of Ayurveda
	Meswak	Paste	Premium	Family	Incredible herbal Meswak for complete oral care
	Promise	Paste	Popular	Family (some children imagery)	Fights cavities with the strength of natural clove oil
Anchor	Anchor White	Paste	Economy	Family (strong children imagery)	All-round protection to keep your teeth fit and life fit
	Anchor Gel	Gel	Economy	Young adults	Fights germs and keeps mouth fresh
GSK	Sensodyne	Paste	Premium	Niche: Consumers with sensitive teeth	World's number 1 toothpaste for sensitive teeth
Ajanta	Ajanta	Paste	Economy	Family (strong children imagery)	For healthy and sparkling white teeth

*Price tier definitions: Economy tier = less than Rs. 20; popular tier = between Rs. 25 and Rs. 35; premium tier = above Rs. 35.
Source: Authors' analysis of the advertisements of the respective brands.

EXHIBIT 2 Examples of Brand Communication from Various Benefit Segments

Freshness Segment

Storyboard Interpretation: Closeup[24]

The ad opened with a young, attractive couple sitting next to each other in a car. As they smiled at each other, their fresh breath attracted one another, and they came closer to kiss. The woman stopped and pointed coyly at something in the distance, where a flower vendor sat in view, surrounded by baskets of roses. The focus then shifted to a different scene, where another young and attractive couple entered an elevator. Once again, as they prepared to kiss, the girl pointed at the camera inside the elevator. The man pulled out a couple of rosebuds from her

[24] "Closeup Clever Couple," www.youtube.com/watch?v=nM6_YduDI6s&NR=1, accessed March 31, 2011.

hat and as she blew on them gently, the rosebuds bloomed into roses. Both scenes concluded with the couples kissing, which was hidden from view by strategically placing the roses in front of their faces. The "Paas Aao" (come closer) jingle played in the background through the advertisement; this had been a common theme across all the ads for Closeup over the past few years. The advertisement ended with a voiceover describing the active mouthwash present in Closeup that "makes one want to kiss."

Overall Oral Health Segment

Storyboard Interpretation: Colgate Dental Cream[25]
The latest advertisement for Colgate Dental Cream showed a dentist who found her young daughter examining her doll's teeth, pretending to ask the doll how many chocolates she had had. The mother asked her what was going on and her daughter explained that she was trying to find decay in her doll's teeth. Her mother explained that decay was not that easy to locate, given that it was usually hidden in between teeth and not visible, which was why they used Colgate. She went on to explain the product's benefits, and said that the calcium and minerals present in Colgate worked in hard-to-reach places, giving complete protection against decay; hence, there would be no hidden decay. The advertisement stated that the toothpaste offered the benefit of "all-round protection from decay," and closed with the claim that "Colgate is the No. 1 brand recommended by dentists."

Storyboard Interpretation: Pepsodent[26]
Pepsodent Germicheck had a campaign known as "Pappu and Pappa" (Pappu being the name of a child, and Pappa referring to his father), in which a popular celebrity played the role of the father. The campaign had multiple ads set in the washroom, with Pappu and his father brushing their teeth, and the drama enacted therein. In the first ad of the series, Pappu asked his father what would happen if they did not brush. His father replied with a dramatic story narrating how evil cavities and germs would affect all their teeth. In the second ad, Pappu's father pretended to refuse to brush, and then acted as if cavities within his mouth were hurting him. He then told a curious Pappu how this could be avoided and that his teeth could be protected in just two minutes with the help of Pepsodent Germicheck. The advertisement ended with the claim that Pepsodent Germicheck "removes 95% of germs in just two minutes."

Herbal Segment

Storyboard Interpretation: Dabur Red Toothpaste[27]
The Dabur Red advertisement opened onto the scene of a school elocution competition, where the topic was announced as "My toothpaste." A young boy started speaking about how despite brushing every day, people tended to have various tooth problems. He said that was why he used Dabur Red toothpaste. He explained that scientists had identified that this toothpaste had thirteen Ayurvedic ingredients, such as clove and mint leaves; the scene then shifted to a dentist who explained this to a group of children gathered around him. The dentist said that Dabur Red's advanced formula was unique in its composition and ingredients. The scene cut back to the young boy in the elocution competition who said that the brand kept teeth healthy from within. The

---

[25] "Colgate," www.youtube.com/watch?v=KFWCKvSVZlg&feature=fvsr, accessed March 31, 2011.

[26] "Second New Pepsodent Commercial: Pappu & Pappa," www.youtube.com/watch?v=EnavjlcxoyE&feature=related, accessed March 31, 2011.

[27] "Dabur Red Toothpaste Ad," www.youtube.com/watch?v=KgEH7gzJ9Zk, accessed March 31, 2011.

advertisement ended with a group of children coming together to deliver the punch line "Let's drive away dental problems."

Niche Segment

Storyboard Interpretation: Colgate ActiveSalt[28]

The ActiveSalt campaign had a consistent storyboard across multiple settings. The advertisement opened with the protagonist, who had just chewed on something and cried out in pain. The setting for this situation was different in different ads: in an airplane, at a cafe, at the checkout counter in a mall, and in the bathroom while brushing his teeth. As soon as the person cried out in agony, the door opened and a camera crew walked in, led by a young woman with a microphone in her hand. The setting resembled a typical media crew, with the young woman being the journalist. She pushed the microphone towards the man who had just cried out in pain, and asked whether his gums hurt and troubled him. He said yes, and then she asked whether his toothpaste had salt in it. He looked puzzled and she brought out the Colgate ActiveSalt pack and handed it to him, saying that it had salt in it. The voiceover described how the unique formulation of ActiveSalt killed germs to make gums strong and healthy.

Note: The descriptions of the various advertisements presented in Exhibit 2 are based on the authors' interpretation of the sources that have been cited.

EXHIBIT 3 Himalaya's Brand Communication

Storyboard Interpretation: Himalaya Dental Cream[29]

The advertisement rolled out backwards in time, and opened with a young, modern woman in bed at midnight. The next frames (all in reverse timeline) showed that just before going to bed, she had eaten a huge slice of pastry from her refrigerator. Before that, earlier in the evening, she had been at a social gathering where she had piled up her plate with a variety of food. The story continued backward, indicating that on her way back from work, she had enjoyed a bar of chocolate ice cream, and earlier at work, she had a helping from a colleague's birthday cake. Even earlier, on her way to work, she had stopped to treat herself to something sweet. At this point, the voiceover stated, "If you want to indulge like a child, first brush like an adult." The ad continued in reverse timeline, to show the woman brushing with Himalaya Dental Cream first thing in the morning. The advertisement ended with the statement that Himalaya was the only adult toothpaste with ingredients like neem, pomegranate, miswak, etc. that kept away adult dental problems.

Note: The description of the advertisement presented in Exhibit 3 is based on the authors' interpretation of the cited source.

---

[28] "Colgate Active Salt Ad," www.youtube.com/watch?v=cgP-O31j0MY, accessed March 31, 2011.

[29] "Himalaya toothpaste," www.youtube.com/watch?v=cW0oEFIWsOo&feature=related, accessed March 31, 2011.

EXHIBIT 4 Positioning Map of Brands

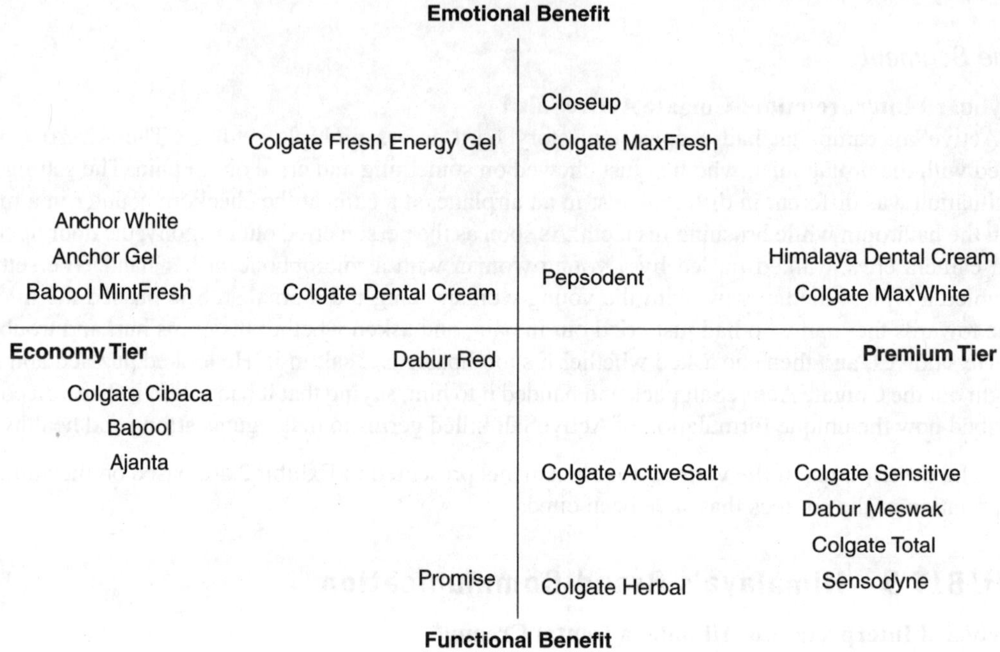

Source: Authors' perception of how individual brands are positioned based on their analysis of the advertisements of the respective brands.

EXHIBIT 5 Mean Values of Consumer Responses

For each of the statements below, the mean value is summarized, which is calculated by assigning values to the Likert scale responses of the consumers such that strongly disagree = 1 and strongly agree = 5.

Table 1 Involvement Levels with Respect to Toothpaste

Mean Values by Segment	Freshness	Herbal	Overall Oral Care	Niche: Problem Solving	Total Category
Toothpaste is valuable to me	3.63	3.32	3.38	3.90	3.56
Toothpaste is beneficial to me	3.60	3.42	3.32	3.90	3.56
Toothpaste is appealing to me	3.69	3.48	3.45	4.07	3.67
Toothpaste is essential for me	3.63	3.32	3.45	4.00	3.60
Toothpaste is of no concern to me	2.24	2.37	2.68	2.08	2.34
Toothpaste is irrelevant to me	2.28	2.37	2.68	1.96	2.32
Toothpaste is useless to me	1.28	1.68	1.56	1.28	1.45
Toothpaste is trivial to me	1.24	1.56	1.48	1.44	1.43
Toothpaste is boring to me	1.32	1.48	1.64	1.24	1.42
Toothpaste is unexciting to me	1.24	1.80	1.48	1.32	1.46

Mean Values by Segment	Freshness	Herbal	Overall Oral Care	Niche: Problem Solving	Total Category
Toothpaste is mundane to me	3.60	3.26	3.26	3.97	3.52
Toothpaste is undesirable to me	1.48	1.76	1.64	1.56	1.61
Toothpaste is not necessary for me	1.32	1.76	1.64	1.24	1.49
It is important to me that my toothpaste has gel	3.08	3.11	3.11	3.73	3.26
It is important to me that my toothpaste tastes good	3.42	3.26	3.35	3.83	3.47
It is important to me that my toothpaste freshens my breath	3.14	3.23	3.29	3.83	3.37
It is important to me that my toothpaste gives me confidence to get close to people	3.23	3.32	3.20	3.87	3.41
It is important to me that my toothpaste fights germs	3.32	3.20	3.23	3.83	3.40
It is important to me that my toothpaste prevents cavities	3.51	3.35	3.48	4.00	3.59
It is important to me that my toothpaste gives me healthy teeth	3.45	3.51	3.42	4.10	3.62
It is important to me that my toothpaste keeps my gums healthy	3.42	3.42	3.38	3.97	3.55
It is important to me that my toothpaste protects my teeth from decay	3.48	3.17	3.26	3.70	3.40
It is important to me that my toothpaste protects me from all oral health problems	3.35	3.17	3.26	3.77	3.39
It is important to me that my toothpaste protects my teeth from pain when I eat hot or cold things	3.38	3.45	3.42	4.10	3.59
It is important to me that my toothpaste has herbal ingredients	3.35	3.35	3.29	3.73	3.43
It is important to me that my toothpaste is made of natural ingredients only	3.54	3.51	3.45	3.83	3.58
It is important to me that my toothpaste keeps my children's teeth healthy	3.48	3.35	3.32	4.07	3.56
It is important to me that my toothpaste gives me a dazzling smile	3.48	3.42	3.45	3.87	3.56
It is important to me that my toothpaste makes my teeth whiter	3.42	3.29	3.29	3.93	3.48
It is important to me that my toothpaste has Ayurvedic ingredients	3.32	3.26	3.23	3.83	3.41
It is important to me that my toothpaste is recommended by dentists	3.35	3.35	3.35	3.73	3.45

Table 2 Attitude Towards Brand

Mean Values by Segment	Freshness	Herbal	Overall Oral Care	Niche: Problem Solving	Total Category
It makes my breath fresh	3.51	3.45	3.38	3.87	3.55
It has a great flavor and taste	3.54	3.29	3.26	4.10	3.55
It keeps my teeth healthy	3.57	3.42	3.42	3.93	3.59
It fights cavities	3.57	3.45	3.42	4.00	3.61
It prevents germs from affecting my teeth	3.45	3.29	3.35	3.90	3.50
It keeps my gums healthy	3.38	3.32	3.26	3.80	3.44
It protects my teeth from decay	3.42	3.26	3.29	3.83	3.45
It reaches even where a toothbrush cannot reach	3.60	3.20	3.26	3.90	3.49
It takes care of all my oral health problems	3.48	3.29	3.35	3.90	3.51
It gives me relief from toothache	3.26	3.29	3.38	3.83	3.44
It has natural ingredients	3.32	3.32	3.11	3.87	3.41
It whitens my teeth	3.32	3.14	2.98	3.93	3.34
It is recommended by dentists	3.20	2.86	2.86	3.83	3.19
It is used by experts	3.42	2.95	3.23	3.83	3.36
It is not different from any other toothpaste	2.88	2.34	2.76	1.56	2.39
It is an expensive toothpaste	2.48	2.52	2.28	2.80	2.52
It is for people with oral health problems	3.14	3.20	3.32	3.90	3.39
It is used by celebrities	3.29	3.29	3.23	3.33	3.29
It is a brand for my family	3.17	3.26	3.17	3.87	3.37
It makes my teeth look healthy	3.17	3.17	3.20	3.87	3.35
It gives me a dazzling smile	3.29	3.35	3.32	3.93	3.47
It gives me the confidence to get close to people	3.26	3.29	3.38	3.87	3.45
It allows me to enjoy eating all types of food	3.20	3.32	3.17	3.93	3.41
It allows me to feel free and unworried	3.26	3.26	3.23	3.97	3.43
It makes me feel protected by an expert	3.23	3.20	3.20	3.87	3.38
It makes me feel in control	3.32	3.20	3.26	3.93	3.43
It gives me a great start to my day	3.29	3.17	3.23	3.90	3.40
The person in the advertisement reminds me of myself	3.29	3.08	3.23	3.83	3.36

Table 3 Brand Attachment
For each of the statements below, the mean value is summarized, which is calculated by assigning values to the response scale of the consumer such that very low extent = 1 and very large extent = 5.

Mean Values by Segment	Freshness	Herbal	Overall Oral Care	Niche: Problem Solving	Total Category
To what extent do you feel emotionally connected to your brand?	3.48	3.26	3.26	3.47	3.37
To what extent does your brand say something to others about who you are?	3.08	3.29	3.17	3.50	3.26
To what extent do thoughts and feelings for your brand come to your mind on their own?	3.48	3.32	3.38	3.80	3.50
To what extent do you think of your brand naturally and instantly?	3.23	3.14	3.08	3.47	3.23
To what extent would you be distressed if your brand were discontinued?	3.26	3.14	3.29	3.37	3.27
To what extent is it difficult to imagine life without your brand?	3.26	3.14	3.17	3.20	3.19

Source: Data obtained from the survey conducted by the authors (discussed in the Methodology section).

EXHIBIT 6 Summary of Findings

Table 1 Participants' Responses Regarding their Habits and Practices (By Segment)

Habits and Practices		Number of Consumers				
		Freshness	Herbal	Oral Health	Problem Solving	Total Category
Frequency of brushing (daily)	Once	20	22	14	8	64
	Twice	5	3	11	17	36
Frequency of visits to the dentist	Once in six months	5	1	3	4	13
	Once in a year	1	1	0	1	3
	Once in two or more years	1	2	2	4	9
	Never	17	21	20	16	74
Did the dentist recommend the toothpaste?	Yes	2	1	3	1	7
	No	6	2	3	7	18
Did you change the toothpaste on your dentist's recommendation?	Yes	2	0	3	1	6
	No	0	1	0	0	1
Did you have any oral health problems?	Yes	3	2	5	5	15
	No	21	23	20	20	84
Did you change your toothpaste to solve any problem?	Yes	2	0	2	1	5
	No	1	2	3	4	10

Table 2 Category Involvement

Segment	High-involvement Consumers
Freshness	28%
Herbal	40%
Overall oral care	32%
Niche: Problem solving	64%
Total category	41%

Note: Although high involvement was clearly distinguished in the consumer responses by strong agreement to involvement indicator statements, the rest of the consumers were mostly neutral and did not express strong disagreement, which indicates that they were all moderate- to low-involvement consumers rather than strongly low-involvement consumers. This could be a function of the fact that all the consumers regarded the category as essential to their daily grooming/health rituals; hence, they could not completely disregard the category, although they were relatively indifferent to the benefits and the propositions.

Table 3 Attitude Towards Category

Cognitive Beliefs by Segment		Affective Beliefs by Segment	
Segment	Strong Cognitive Belief Consumers	Segment	Strong Affective Belief Consumers
Freshness	64%	Freshness	60%
Herbal	64%	Herbal	44%
Overall oral care	56%	Overall oral care	36%
Niche: Problem solving	92%	Niche: Problem solving	72%
Total category	69%	Total category	53%

Note: The strengths of the cognitive and affective beliefs for each individual segment were calculated by scoring the consumer responses to the cognitive/affective statements relevant to that specific segment; these were derived by examining the advertising communications of all the brands in that category.

Table 4 Comparison of Consistency Between Cognitive and Affective Beliefs of Consumers

Segment	Consumers with Strong Cognitive and Strong Affective Beliefs	Consumers with Strong Cognitive and Weak Affective Beliefs	Consumers with Weak Cognitive and Strong Affective Beliefs	Consumers with Weak Cognitive and Weak Affective Beliefs
Freshness	44%	20%	16%	20%
Herbal	40%	24%	4%	32%
Overall oral care	32%	24%	4%	40%
Niche: Problem solving	68%	24%	4%	4%
Total	46%	23%	7%	24%

Table 5 Low-involvement and High-Attitude Consumers

Consumers with Low Category Involvement Who have Strong Cognitive or Affective Beliefs towards Brand	
Freshness	66%
Herbal	46%
Overall	46%
Niche	89%
Total	58%

Note: Table 5 is to be interpreted as "percentage of consumers who had low involvement with category and also had high attitude towards brand."

Table 6 Attitude Towards Category: Cognitive and Affective Belief Strength for Key Brands

Cognitive Beliefs		Affective Beliefs	
Leading Brand in Segment	**Consumers with Strong Cognitive Beliefs in Line with Brand's Communication**	**Leading Brand in Segment**	**Consumers with Strong Affective Beliefs in Line with Brand's Communication**
Closeup (Freshness)	80%	Closeup (Freshness)	60%
Dabur Red (Herbal)	38%	Dabur Red (Herbal)	38%
Colgate Dental Cream (Overall oral care)	60%	Colgate Dental Cream (Overall oral care)	20%
Colgate ActiveSalt (Niche: Problem solving)	100%	Colgate ActiveSalt (Niche: Problem solving)	92%

Source: Data obtained from the survey conducted by the authors (discussed in the Methodology section).

5

www.dhonuk.com—Marketing Art in an Emerging Market

Dr. S. Ramesh Kumar and Shamit Bagchi wrote this case solely to provide material for class discussion. The authors do not intend to illustrate either effective or ineffective handling of a managerial situation. The authors may have disguised certain names and other identifying information to protect confidentiality.

Version: 2011-06-07

It was January 1, 2011. Shamit Bagchi was in a contemplative mood. A software engineer, Bagchi had worked at Bharat Electronics Limited and Honeywell Technology Solutions (a multinational company) for approximately eight years after attaining his engineering degree. From a young age, Bagchi had been passionate about the arts. While doing his postgraduate work in management at Indian Institute of Management (IIM) Bangalore, the idea of combining consumer behavior and art inspired Bagchito resign from his job and start an online art firm, www.dhonuk.com. After recognizing that art in India was a niche market, Bagchi attempted to make use of psychographics and the self-concept of art buyers.

Bagchi's challenge was the positioning that was required for www.dhonuk.com. Would he be able to capture consumers' perceptions of art? What about consumers' level of involvement in art forms? Could consumers use art forms to reflect their personality? Did the lifestyle of consumers who associated with art differ from the lifestyle of other consumers? Bagchi thought that several aspects of consumer behavior would likely be useful in formulating a strategy for a category such as art, which was not a common place consumer item.

BACKGROUND

Post-liberalization, in the early 1990s, when India opened up its economy, the Indian consumer had been characterized by low income, social and political conservatism, and a lack of options. Since then, India had witnessed many changes: Indians had gradually embraced a more consumerist culture,[1] particularly over the past decade. The country's economic performance had been a major driver for this shift. Gross domestic product (GDP) growth had been strong and sustained in the recent times, which had led to an increase in consumer spending.

Annual disposable income in India had reached US$1,061 billion in 2010, against an annual gross income of US$1,119 billion.[2] The wealthiest five per cent of Indian households accounted for 23.1 per cent of national income. 50 per cent of the country's households from the lower end of the economic spectrum accounted for 18.7 per cent of the total income. However, 58.2 per cent of the total income was earned by 45 per cent of households.

When current consumer spending habits were compared with similar habits in 2002, the expenditure on entertainment was revealed to have increased significantly. Indians constituted one-fifth of the world's citizens younger than age 20. A youthful, gung-ho generation, ready to pursue success, was joining the ranks of Indian consumers—and with a vengeance! The desire of this generation to look and feel good was thus a major guiding factor when making their purchase decisions.[3]

INDIAN HIGH-NET-WORTH INDIVIDUALS AND LUXURY GOODS

Along with the aspiring middle class, another demographic segment had been growing for the past decade—the HNIs, or high-net-worth individuals. A HNI was defined as a person with net assets of at least US$1 million (roughly INR50 million), excluding that person's primary residence and consumables. An ultra-HNI was a person who had an investible income of US$30 million (roughly INR1.5 billion).[4]

The sub prime credit crisis that hit the United States in the latter half of 2007 and spilled over to other economies had eroded investor wealth among India's population of high-net-worth individuals by 31.6 per cent. The number of HNIs had again rebounded (see Exhibit 1), thanks to the economy recovering in 2010, which had led to resurgence in demand for luxury goods.

Although India made up just 0.4 per cent of global luxury good sales, the luxury industry in India had shown very promising growth over the last couple of years and was set to grow at a minimum

[1] Ashok Gopal and Rajesh Srinivasan, "The New Indian Consumer," *Harvard Business Review*, October 2006; http://hbr.org/2006/10/the-new-indian-consumer/ar/1, accessed December 17, 2010.

[2] "Country Fact File—India," *Euromonitor International 2011*; www.euromonitor.com/factfile.aspx?country=IN; accessed December 17, 2010.

[3] "A Note on Consumer Spending Habits in India," *IBS Center for Management Research*, 2007; www.icmrindia.org/case studies/catalogue/Business%20Reports/BREP047.htm; accessed December 17, 2010.

[4] "High Net Work Individuals," *Swiss Private Bank*, www.swissprivatebank.com/HNWI_high_net_worth_individuals.html, accessed March 1, 2011.

of 25 per cent per year[5] over the next few years. Sales of luxury goods worldwide—including art, apparel, jewelry and leather goods was approximately US$230 billion.[6]

Worldwide, art-related products were estimated to comprise approximately 16 per cent of all luxury goods. Among the luxury goods, private jets, custom yachts, high-end automobiles and other luxury collectibles accounted for 16.2 per cent of passion investments among HNIs as a whole, followed closely by fine art at 15.9 per cent. Jewelry held third place at 13.8 per cent, and luxury/experiential travel ranked fourth at 13.5 per cent.[7]

Luxury goods, alternately called passion investments, made up five to eight per cent of an HNI's investment portfolio. Like the luxury goods market, the art market was driven by supply and liquidity. As their disposable incomes increased, more and more HNIs were turning to passion investments to diversify their portfolio and satiate their tastes for the finer things in life. Indians invested mostly in jewelry, gems and watches, followed by art and luxury collectibles. Indian HNIs mostly restricted their passion investments to tangible assets as against sophisticated financial instruments and were thus more conservative in their investment strategies.[8]

THE INDIAN ART MARKET VIS-À-VIS THE GLOBAL ART MARKET

India's art market grew six per cent in 2009, over the previous year and was estimated to be worth between INR8 billion and 10 billion[9] (US$1 equals approximately 45 Indian rupees, or INR45) in 2010, although this market represented a meager 0.55 per cent of the world art market. The total sale value of arts globally was approximately US$375 million in 2008 and approximately US$250 million in 2009.[10]

Art and luxury goods were aspiration-based products that the Indian middle classes could not yet afford. In 2001/02, middle-class households constituted approximately six per cent of the total Indian population and were expected to grow to 13 per cent in 2009/10. The group classified as middle-class households had annual incomes of INR200,000 to INR1,000,000 (US$1 was equal to approximately INR45) at 2001/02 prices, equivalent to US$4,500 to US$22,000; although there were several variants of the numbers that comprised the Indian middle class.

The news had indicated a rise in the sales of art that was categorized as "affordable" and was in the range of INR20,000 to INR75,000.[11] This segment of buyers was probably expanding—and benefiting—the most.

---

[5] Priyanka Banerjee, "Indian Luxury Market to Grow, Upper Middle Class Income Surges," *Luxury & Brands*, October 2, 2010; www.ibtimes.com/articles/67909/20101002/luxury-brands-cii-cwg.htm, accessed December 24, 2010.

[6] "Bain & Company Projects 10% Surge in Worldwide Luxury Goods Sales in 2010, Erasing Recessionary Declines," *Bain & Company,* October 18, 2010; www.bain.com/bainweb/about/press_release_detail.asp?id=28017&menu_url=for_the_-media.asp, accessed December 24, 2010.

[7] Ibid.

[8] Ashley Coutinho, "Wealthy Indians Prefer Tangible Assets as Passion Investments," *Express India*, October 11, 2010; www.expressindia.com/latest-news/The-wealthy-prefer-passion-investments/695330/, accessed November 20, 2010.

[9] Ibid.

[10] Ritwik Mukherjee, "Indian Art Market to Rise Tenfold by '18," mydigitalfc.com, March 31, 2010; www.mydigitalfc.com/art-and-culture/indian-art-market-rise-tenfold-%E2%80%9818-023, accessed November 20, 2010.

[11] Nalini S. Malaviya, "Affordable Art Market Picks Up," *The Economic Times*, November 14, 2010; http://articles.economictimes.indiatimes.com/2010-11-14/news/27627355_1_art-market-contemporary-indian-art-saffronart, accessed November 20, 2010.

Although India was not a big market for the arts, to be diffused at a greater pace, the technological interventions such as Art Project by Google[12] would usually broaden the interest of anyone who had a dormant interest in the visual fine arts. Online art auctions had also seen a rise[13] in the Indian context.

MODES OF SELLING ART

Traditionally, apart from private sales, the two most prominent modes of the organized selling of art were through art galleries and through physical art auction houses (auctions). 10 years earlier, Saffron Art, an online store for lovers of art, was started. Art websites had since caught on, as they provided the benefit of increasing reach to a greater number of buyers. Art fairs such as the annual India Art Summit, which started in 2008, were a recent trend.

WEBSITES SELLING ART

Many world-famous auction houses had an online presence:

- **Sotheby's:** Sotheby's was a global company that engaged in art auctions, private sales and art-related financing activities. Founded in 1744, Sotheby's operated in 40 countries, with principal sales rooms located in New York, London, Hong Kong and Paris.
- **Christie's:** Christie's salerooms had been a popular showcase for unique and beautiful art forms since 1766. They provided a variety of services for art collectors, and their website had a good FAQs (frequently asked questions) page that discussed how to buy and sell at auction.
- deviantArt: This firm provided a connection and a communication medium between artists and fans on a massive scale. deviantArt represented a breakthrough for the promotion and exposure of otherwise stranded artists in all corners of the globe. This firm's website gets 20 per cent of the visitors directed from search engines and the visitors, on an average, view 10.7 unique pages on an average day[14].

DESCRIPTION OF DHONUK—INDIAN ART LEAGUE

Dhonuk—www.dhonuk.com—an online platform for art lovers, art enthusiasts and artists, featured an in-built online social network. Dhonuk provided an online space for creativity in the arts and a platform to connect the artist and the "artsumer" (the art consumer, either organizational or individual). Artists were able to share, showcase, interact, learn and collaborate with one another. The website acted as a repository of fresh, interesting art content available free of charge to consumers who could browse through several kinds of information relating to art. Customized or premium content was charged based on the customer's needs.

---

[12] "Art Project powered by Google," www.googleartproject.com/; "Art In the Age of Google: Virtual Museums," http://economictimes.indiatimes.com/tech/internet/art-in-the-age-of-google-virtual-museums/articleshow/7457515.cms; accessed February 22, 2011

[13] Radhika P. Nair, "Online Auction Emerges as New Buzzword for Art,"*The Economic Times*, January 14, 2011, http://economictimes.indiatimes.com/news/news-by-industry/et-cetera/online-auction-emerges-as-new-buzzword-for-art/article show/7280591.cms,accessed February 22. 2011.

[14] "deviantart.com,"www.alexa.com/siteinfo/deviantart.com, accessed on June 3, 2011.

Features on the website enabled registered artists to showcase their individual profiles and upload photos of their artwork. A rating system allowed other members to view and rate the works and to leave comments. The website also hosted discussion forums for consumers and artists to interact and discuss techniques, trends and other art matters. Art lovers and art connoisseurs could interact with the artists and other buyers and could buy artwork from the artists, who were mostly young, budding artists but also included a few established artists. Members could select specific types of product categories including the following:

- Framed contemporary artwork targeted for gifting purposes or for decorating home interiors
- Custom artwork or pre-made authentic art pieces available at a premium
- Reprints from digitally generated art content on the social network

Custom artwork could be ordered through a sales email or a telephone number available on the website. Affiliated artists from the company's network would create art according to the customer feedback or the specific requirements of customers. Such an online system provided convenience buying without consumers having to physically visit art galleries and included the added advantage of providing the buyer with art—related, updated information on the website once a member was registered.

ARTBUYERS

Although not completely inseparable, buyers of art could be broadly categorized. Some buyers were wealthy and passionate art collectors who referred to art by using such words as *beauty*, *attractive*, *pride* and *aesthetics* and *enhancing status.* These art collectors felt that associating with the finest creative minds increased their own self-worth and worth in society.

For others, buying art was an obsession (i.e. representing a hoarding behavior), which led to repeat purchases. Afford ability was another important factor, which led to buying of art for the purpose of decorating and thus beautifying one's home.

Some buyers both appreciated art and saw it as a lucrative investment option. Other buyers merely considered art as an investment option; they bought only works by specific artists because their market value would increase over a period of time.

Among the occasional buyers were a few who became emotionally attached after seeing some works: they loved the aesthetics of the artwork and purchased art,but they were not necessarily repeat buyers. Many of the buyers with lower budgets were occasional art buyers who predominantly bought art for home decoration or sometimes for gifting purposes. These buyers were increasing as disposable incomes rose and as residential complexes became a part of the changing lifestyles of consumers. As an extrapolation, India produced the largest number of movies in the world.[15] Cinema may be considered as the "art for the masses" and therefore art seemed to have a dormant potential. Bulk buyers were a separate category and their purchasing typically occurred through interior decorators or other people within an organization who had been assigned the task of making art purchases.

---

[15] "The Hollywood–Bollywood Partnership,"www.thehindu.com/news/the-india-cables/the-cables/article1716143.ece, accessed on June 3, 2011.

Art buyers often were interested in several other performance arts activities, such as viewing plays and music or dance recitals. Some of these buyers were very reclusive and introverted as they preferred to remain in solitude and contemplate. Many art lovers were the wives of wealthy industrialists,many of whom had diverse buying needs and indulged heavily in such activities as shopping or gardening at home. Some of these buyers had unique collecting habits and were connoisseurs of good things in life.

THE MAJOR FORMS OF ART AVAILABLE ON THE DHONUK PLATFORM

Given the extensive questionnaire that had been used on the website, and the difficulty in finding art lovers (relative to locating users of typical consumer products and brands) due to the niche market status for art forms, it was not possible to interview the art lovers (respondents) extensively. The questionnaire itself was demanding on the part of the respondents in terms of time and effort, despite one of the authors assisting respondents while they filled in the form. Hence, the authors felt that it could be useful to visualize the specific type of consumer (connected with each specific art form) in a setting that was not associated with art to understand the type of segment better. This strategy was referred to as "Authors' hypothetical view of the consumer in another domain" when three art types were being discussed.

Fine Art

Fine art referred to art that was created on aesthetic rather than decorative grounds, to be understood and responded to on its own, without relation to anything else.

Typical Buyers of Fine Art

Fine art was bought by home decorators, art collectors and wealthy HNIs. Some fine art by young artists was available at affordable rates. Fine art ranged from low-priced to very high-priced works. Some were worth a few hundred million rupees. The buyers were usually also enthusiasts of other art forms. Some buyers were connoisseurs of art who reflected greater appreciation by studying the nuances of art.

Lifestyle: Buyers of fine art were usually very active socially. They typically indulged in performing arts, either as audience members or as performers. They liked to travel in luxury cars and to stay in mansions and luxury apartments.

One female fine art buyer typically drank Darjeeling tea. She usually wore luxurious clothing and attended business meetings. She used a handbag from an Italian fashion accessory house. Her custom was to visit the nearest art gallery in the evening whenever an art exhibition was on. She would meet her friends there and they would chat about various aspects of life, including art. She was also accustomed to attending the theater whenever she found time.

Another fine art buyer was an elderly businessman. He was an art collector, and his house was like a museum, filled with books, artwork, rare documents and collections from the past. He was on the boards of several museums and cultural institutions. He liked to recite the poetry of his favorite poet, watched TV for news coverage and spent a lot of time with his collection of art. He reminisced often about the bygone days. He attended several performance arts (e.g. dance and music) events with his wife, and they also socialized a lot. He wrote and read about art and owned an impressive collection of books on art.

Abstract Art

Abstract art was art that did not represent reality as we see it, though it might be based on an actual individual, emotion or object. Abstract art took its inspiration from the real world and used lines, patterns, shapes, texture and color for expression.

Typical Buyers of Abstract Art

Buyers of abstract art were intent on understanding the deeper meaning behind the symbols of religion. They also had a deep aesthetic sense and were not very open in discussing their ideas. They liked to have interpretations, and they derived satisfaction from artwork; their personal beliefs and their way of thinking often differed, in general, from others' opinions. They were comfortable with ambiguity in art and may also like landscape art.

Lifestyle: Buyers of abstract art were typically contemplative persons,who enjoyed walks in parks and indulged in gardening. These art buyers would not discuss much about art and were often reclusive and solitary beings. These buyers liked to read a lot of books.

One consumer associated with abstract art taught in a reputable institute and owned a collection of abstract art. She taught classes, read all types of books and had worked internationally. Thus, she was familiar with cultures of most nations. She specifically preferred abstract art over figurative art. She had very good taste in cooking and literature and was a contemplative person, although she was also a good communicator. She liked to meet people but is also enjoyed visiting forests and hills and listening to world music.

Authors' hypothetical view of the consumer in another domain:

The consumer of abstract art may also be interested in reading occult literature and may have read all the religious texts, which, she felt, helped her to better understand the world and how people behaved.

Figurative Art

Figurative art referred to art that was inspired by the natural or visible world and used tangible forms and objects to convey the artist's message. The human form or figure was the most common subject.

Typical Buyers of Figurative Art

Buyers of figurative art were typically homeowners who liked to understand the clarity of art or liked the aesthetics of form, color and style. These consumers were both rational buyers in terms of understanding exactly what the artwork conveyed and cognitive buyers who enjoyed the detail of art, artists and techniques. They also enjoyed art that was based on movies or other literary sources. Buyers of figurative art had strong analytical skills. They normally had portraits of their ancestors in the drawing hall of their residence.

Lifestyle: Buyers of figurative art typically indulged in high levels of TV viewing, watched movies and purchased DVDs of their favorite films. They also liked to be active in the social aspects of their community and kept track of recent social happenings. They were in the habit of visiting family and friends.

One purchaser of figurative art was a woman who owned a house,which she enjoyed decorating. She was involved in teaching and was a very family-oriented person. Much of her time was spent on homemaking for her daughter and her husband, who worked in the information technology (IT) industry. She enjoyed watching movies and soap operas on television. Some of her favorite TV serials involved family-related contemporary themes. She liked to shop and preferred to buy jewelry and food items after a good search.

Another occasional buyer of figurative art worked in a leading IT industry and enjoyed spending weekends traveling to resorts or on treks. He also played the guitar and was interested in singing and music. Although the majority of his time was devoted to his office-related workload, his recreation time was spent with his family and his spouse and in travelling.

Authors' hypothetical view of the consumer in another domain:

This consumer has a habit of doing things himself. For example, he likes to dismantle a clock or a faulty pump and repair it himself. He had a very strong drive to learn and apply his learning to repair complex items.

Digital Art

Digital art referred to works that had either been created on a computer in digital form or had been significantly modified by a computing process.

Typical Buyers of Digital Art

The buyers of digital art tended to be more intellectual than other art consumers and enjoyed non-traditional, concept imaginary art. These consumers also loved to see their own interest and wit in artwork, appreciated strong themes or imagery and enjoyed artwork that was high on imagination and the usage of digital techniques. These consumers were interested in contemporary society.

Lifestyle: The buyers of digital art were typically young buyers, influenced by the West. They used computers and relied heavily on social networking websites to search for unusual imagery and digital prints to decorate their homes. They liked to indulge in fantastic imagery and often socialized at pubs and discos.

One typical buyer of digital art was a male, who was interested in digital imagery. He worked as a business executive or a marketing executive, owned a Swiss watch, watched Western television channels and played games using Ninten do Wii. He read detective and fantasy novels on his Kindle device and favoured pop culture and contemporary themes. He visited pubs with friends on weekends and liked to discuss a variety of topics at book release events.

Another buyer of digital art was an assistant editor at a publishing firm. He was interested in reading and writing, and his day usually included reading a lot of fiction and non-fiction. He often attended gatherings at book launches or gatherings with intellectuals on a weekly basis. He liked to interact with his staff and friends, and he was a good communicator.

Authors' hypothetical view of the consumer in another domain:

This consumer was interested in shopping, but in very unusual ways. For example, he might ask a person to find out everything about cameras, but would not believe this person's opinion. He would then ask another person to find out everything about cameras, but would also not go by what that person told him. Instead, he preferred to research cameras for himself on the Internet and then purchased a camera on the basis of a recommendation of a close relative.

COMPETITORS OF DHONUK

- **Saffron Art:** Saffron Art was one of the most comprehensive and definitive sources of modern and contemporary Indian art. Saffron Art provided a platform that enabled consumers to view and purchase Indian art and to become involved in the development of Indian art globally.
- **Indian Art Collectors:** Indian Art Collectors was a forum for collectors and creators of Indian contemporary art to buy and sell art online. It housed one of the largest collections of Indian contemporary art for sale online and was India's only online interactive art platform in 2011.
- **Artjini:** Artjini was India's largest online art store. It showcased more than 150,000 poster images, tapestries and canvas transfers. Artjini offered images of famous paintings by artists from all over the world and included custom framing options.
- **Artflute:** Artflute was an online creative community where a consumer could buy and sell original art. It was an ideal art platform ford is covering new talent. Artflute was an endeavor to build India's first Indian contemporary art community.
- **Indian Art Ideas:** Indian Art Ideas aimed to bring the color of art to everyone's life by use of the Internet. Indian Art Ideas was an aggregation of finest pieces of Indian art in its all-encompassing form. It was a collaborative platform where art lovers, art collectors and artists could share their experiences and collections with each other toward the overall development and growth of Indian Art.

Buyers of Competitor Brand A (One of the Above)

Buyers of Brand A were extremely affluent and were considered to be high-net-worth individuals. They were usually art collectors themselves or considered art to been active investment option. Most of the artwork they bought was sold through auctions and was priced at more than INR100,000 (US$2,000), as exhibited on Brand A's website. These buyers bought luxury products and artwork made by artists who were reputedly the finest in India and with whom they had personal contacts.

Lifestyle: These buyers frequently attended social gatherings and concerts. Typically, they had a luxurious lifestyle and had time to indulge in the best that life had to offer. They had strong opinions and actively pursued a hedonistic lifestyle.

Buyers of Competitor Brand B (One of the Above)

Brand B buyers could not be easily categorized although they were price-conscious buyers of artwork in the range of INR100,000 to INR1,000,000. These reasonably priced artworks were typically created by young and budding Indian artists. The buyers typically made impulsive purchases although their search for art was limited, and they did not have contact with the artists. They were typically buyers without much knowledge of art and were primarily interested in home decoration. They were online buyers as Brand B sold only through its website. Brand B's website and its buyers did not possess any distinct personality. These art buyers were also not very active in terms of buying at galleries as they were rare buyers, and the artwork offered was not distinctive.

Lifestyle: Brand B's purchasers were typically home decorators, whose corporate life did not allow much time for art buying. Many were first-time home buyers who wanted to decorate their homes. They were typically high users of the Internet at their workplace and were frequent television viewers; they did not necessarily indulge in reading, writing or other literary activities. Homemakers and housewives were also included as Brand B purchasers. These attributes are based on the perspective of one of the case writers.

INITIAL POSITIONING

A relative positioning of Dhonuk with respect to some of its competitors was shown on the basis of a variety of parameters (see Exhibit 2), including physical accessibility (a convenience function) and online social network features of the various companies' websites. More specifically, the following parameters were used to position the existing websites and their brands:

1. **Online interactivity**—Online interactivity related to user engagement. Features that enabled and involved users tended to add value and to increase repeat views, encouraging the user to return to the website again and again. Interest level also increased if the communication was not one-sided but members could and were encouraged to interact with each other, by exploring and sharing ideas, techniques and content. The intent of online interactivity was to offer a collaboratively based social networking orientation with discussions forums and profiles, as opposed to hosting a simple,"plain vanilla" e-commerce site.
2. **A distinct brand personality**—A distinct brand persona that was based on the personality of the target market helped the brand both to connect better with users of the website and to spread word about the brand. A clearly demarcated personality that was based on the target segment helped to communicate the brand and its benefits to users. Subcultures were formed on the basis of the persona or the distinct imagery used to depict a brand.
3. **Access/Convenience**—Accessibility referred to the buyer going to the store or the store going to the buyer's doorstep. Convenience referred to buying or ordering artwork via an online payment gateway and seamless delivery to the buyers. Art galleries in countries like India didn't attract the same amount of attention as shopping malls. It was a good idea to host art shows and exhibitions in high-traffic areas frequented by the target buyers. Thus, access and convenience was a matter of traveling physically to view and purchase artwork versus accessing and purchasing artwork online for delivery to the consumer's doorstep.
4. **An experiential feel**—An experience engaged multiple senses through various means. In the field of art, such an experience could be created through strong visual appeals and through a consumer's interactions with artists and other buyers of art. Such an appeal was hedonic in nature and contributed to the experiential feel or appeal.

For example, deviant Art positioned itself as a youth brand,and its imagery and language seemed to target consumers who were fun-loving, exciting and youthful, predominantly those highly creative and unique individuals who deviated from society's norms. Deviant Art hosted forums for discussions and also posted artist/member profiles, which included artists' photographs and their artwork, and enabled artists and members to comment on others' artwork and to rate the artwork on display. Art-derivative items, like caps and t-shirts with art images on them were sold in addition to artwork and art prints.

Saffron Art had an up-market, luxury orientation with a minimalist and understated look and feel, characterized by muted colors. Its website featured neatly placed images of the artwork, clear sections on art history, artist categorizations, artist genres and a glossary. Auction-related information and the mode of buying were explained in detail. Accessibility was high, enabling consumers to purchase goods online. A mobile auctioning feature was introduced to make the auctions buyer-friendly.

Dhonuk planned to commission a survey to research consumer insights that could be useful.

METHODOLOGY OF THE STUDY

The survey instrument comprised scales to measure primarily three categories of factors—namely, lifestyle, uniqueness and involvement. Lifestyle was captured from questions about activities, interests and opinions of the respondents. This standard method[16] of obtaining psychographics was adopted because it had been found to be useful in past surveys. In order to obtain information about the art buyers' self-concept and perceived sense of uniqueness, the survey asked several questions centred on the dimension of uniqueness and its associated factors.[17] Art buyers were unusual and unique in many ways, including their needs, behavior, possessions and interests. They would often buy art to showcase how they differed from others in their tastes. The third set of factors, purchase and consumption involvement investigated art consumers' degree of involvement that made prompted them to buy art. The idea is was to obtain degrees of classifications based on level of involvement. The objective of including these three factors was to examine the motivational aspects associated with the need for uniqueness among the buyers of art.

The third set of factors, purchase and consumption involvement[18] investigated art consumers' degree of involvement that prompted them to buy art. The idea was to obtain degrees of classifications based on level of involvement.

The survey was conducted among those consumers who had purchased at least one piece of art (e.g. a painting) or were planning to buy an art piece in the immediate future (i.e. within a month or so).

The surveys were conducted during January 2011, at the biggest art fair in New Delhi, India, the four-day India Art Summit,[19] attended by 85 galleries (including 13 foreign galleries), which generated revenues of close to INR260 million (equivalent to approximately US$5.7 million).

Responses were also collected from art lovers and art enthusiasts at the Indian Institute of Management, Bangalore, India, during the annual cultural festival, Unmaad,[20] where Dhonuk conducted its art exhibition (held January 25 and 26, 2011).

Responses were also collected at the annual art market at Bangalore, Chitra Santhe,[21] held on January 30, 2011. The average scores of each survey question were calculated across the 50 survey responses (see Exhibit 3, Exhibit 4 and Exhibit 5).

Bagchi wondered what input and in sights the survey would provide to Dhonuk for formulating a strategy that should also include several aspects of consumer perception.

---

[16] William D. Wells and Douglas J. Tigert, "Activities, Interests and Opinions," *Journal of Advertising Research*, August 1971, pp. 27—35.

[17] Kelly Tepper; and Rick H. Hoyle, (1996) "Latent Variable Models of Need for Uniqueness," Multivariate Behavioral Research, Volume 31, Number 3, 1532–7906, (4) pp. 467–494.

[18] Judith Lynne Zaichkowsky, "Measuring the Involvement Construct," *Journal of Consumer Research*, Volume 12, number 3, pp. 341–352.

[19] "IAS Art Fair," www.indiaartsummit.com/, accessed March 2, 2011.

[20] "Unmaad, therefore I am," www.unmaad.com/dhonuk.php, accessed March 2, 2011.

[21] "Chitra Santhe,"http://chitrasanthe.com/about.html, accessed March 2, 2011.

EXHIBIT 1 Number of High-net-worth Individuals in India, the Asia Pacific Region and the World

Year	India	Asia Pacific	World
2005	70,000	2.3 million	8.3 million
2006	83,000	2.4 million	8.7 million
2007	100,015	2.6 million	9.5 million
2008	123,000	2.8 million	10.1 million
2009	84,000	2.4 million	8.6 million
2010	128,700	3 million	10 million

Source: "Chindia to Lead Emerging Markets in HNI Growth Story," The Economic Times, June 24, 2010; available at http://economictimes.indiatimes.com/news/economy/indicators/Chindia-to-lead-emerging-markets-in-HNI-growth-story/articleshow/6084277.cms, accessed May 19, 2011.

EXHIBIT 2 Initial Positioning Diagrams

Interactivity versus Brand Personality

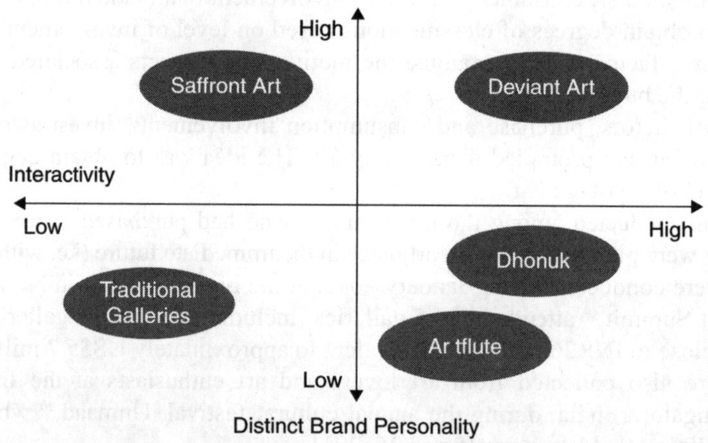

Accessibility versus Experientialism

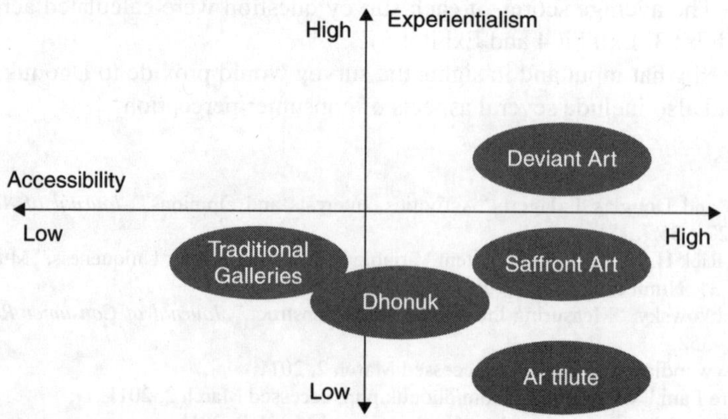

Source: Created by author.

EXHIBIT 3 Lifestyle Analysis

	Activities	Average Score
1	I often go to theatres	2.11
2	I read the newspaper everyday	4.50
3	I follow news on the arts	1.88
4	I use my credit card quite often	4.71
5	I buy art and often visit art galleries	3.62
6	I do a lot of shopping	2.91
7	I shop heavily online	1.92
8	I browse online social networks everyday	3.00
9	I browse through websites sometimes up to five hours per day	1.86
10	I search for information on areas of interest on the web	4.38
11	I often visit parties, social gatherings	3.13
12	I visit resorts and natural spots often	2.71
13	I think a lot about various topics	3.71
14	I read a lot of books, magazines	3.82
15	I go to the temple often	2.17
16	I discuss art and general topics a lot with friends	3.14
17	I go to the cinemas often or buy movie DVDs	3.08
	INTERESTS	
18	I am interested in learning about society	3.78
19	I like to keep myself updated on current affairs	4.00
20	I like to collect art works	3.94
21	I like to buy a variety of things	3.43
22	I am interesting in artistic things including fine arts	3.57
23	I like to shop in malls	3.00
24	I like to leave comments on products and read reviews to understand the product details	2.83
25	I like to converse and chat with people	4.00
26	I like to explore the online world once in a while	3.83
27	I like to meet new people all the time	3.50
28	I am a nature lover, love watching National Geographic and Discovery	3.73
29	I enjoy the intellectual exercise of analyzing, conceptualizing	4.13
30	I have a great hunger for knowledge	4.17
31	I want to understand the deeper things behind religion, etc.	4.00
32	I like to chat a lot with friends	3.00

	Activities	Average Score
33	I like to keep track of movies being released	2.67
34	I like to stay alone and prefer solitude often	2.71
35	I like to decorate my house	4.43
36	I like to gossip, chat with friends	3.00
37	I like bright vibrant colors in whatever I buy	3.29
	OPINIONS	
38	We should be updated with different aspects and issues in the society	4.33
39	It is important to be knowledgeable about society, country and international affairs	4.43
40	I feel emotionally involved with art as this makes me feel satisfied/pleasure	3.33
41	I think we should buy what we really like irrespective of the price	2.67
42	I think art is a very important thing due to the aesthetics and creativity involved	4.00
44	I think online buying is very convenient and quick	4.29
45	It is good to have a large social network of friends—online/offline	3.88
46	I think internet is an excellent tool to find new things and knowledge	4.71
47	I search for information on areas of interest on the web	4.63
48	I think contacts help me grow personally and professionally	4.00
49	I think environment needs to be kept clean and this is very important	4.83
50	I think man is a product of his mind	4.43
51	I think it is very important to understand the technical details of things	4.00
52	I am a very spiritual person	3.45
53	I think discussions help me gain knowledge	4.17
54	I think it is important to have some fun, entertainment in life	4.50
55	No two art pieces are similar in my view	4.29
56	It is important to meet important intellectuals, thinkers and artists	3.17
57	Artworks are very costly	2.63
58	Experts in every field are necessary	4.33
59	Too many people at a place, makes me uncomfortable	2.14
60	Abstract art is very confusing	2.00
61	I can interpret any piece of art	2.00
62	I prefer figurative art, things that I can clearly understand	3.33

Note: A 5-point Likert Scale was used with the following rating scale: Strongly Disagree = 1, Disagree = 2, Neither Agree nor Disagree = 3, Agree = 4, Strongly Agree = 5.

The scores noted above are averages of responses from questions that were posed to the survey takers.

Source: Created by author.

EXHIBIT 4 Analysis of Consumers' Uniqueness

	Self-concept Scales	Average Score
1	I collect unusual products as a way of telling people I'm different	2.41
2	I have sometimes purchased unusual products or brands as a way to create a more distinctive personal image	3.25
3	I often look for one-of-a-kind products or brands so that I create a style that is all my own	2.78
4	Often when buying merchandise, an important goal is to find something that communicates my uniqueness	3.00
5	I often combine possessions in such a way that I create a personal image for myself that can't be duplicated	2.50
6	I often try to find a more interesting version of run-of-the-mill products because I enjoy being original	3.17
7	I actively seek to develop my personal uniqueness by buying special products or brands	2.71
8	Having an eye for products that are interesting and unusual assists me in establishing a distinctive image	3.14
9	The products and brands that I like best are the ones that express my individuality	3.57
10	I often think of the things I buy and do in terms of how I can use them to shape a more unusual personal image	2.67
11	I'm often on the lookout for new products or brands that will add to my personal uniqueness	2.67
12	When dressing, I have sometimes dared to be different in ways that others are likely to disapprove	2.86
13	As far as I'm concerned, when it comes to the products I buy and the situations in which I use them, customs and rules are made to be broken	3.00
14	I often dress unconventionally even when it's likely to offend others	2.00
15	I rarely act in agreement with what others think are the right things to buy	3.00
16	Concern for being out of place doesn't prevent me from wearing what I want to wear	3.64
17	When it comes to the products I buy and the situations in which I use them, I have often broken customs and rules	2.83
18	I have often violated the understood rules of my social group regarding what to buy or own	2.00
19	I have often gone against the understood rules of my social group regarding when and how certain products are properly used	2.17
20	I enjoy challenging the prevailing taste of people I know by buying something they wouldn't seem to accept	2.00
21	If someone hinted that I had been dressing inappropriately for a social situation, I would continue dressing in the same manner	1.67
22	When I dress differently, I'm often aware that others think I'm peculiar, but I don't care	3.36
23	When products or brands I like become extremely popular, I lose interest in them	2.71
24	I avoid products or brands that have already been accepted and purchased by the average consumer	2.00

	Self-concept Scales	Average Score
25	When a product I own becomes popular among the general population, I begin using it less	2.33
26	I often try to avoid products or brands that I know are bought by the general population	2.33
27	As a rule, I dislike products or brands that are customarily purchased by everyone	2.00
28	I give up wearing fashions I've purchased once they become popular among the general public	2.00
29	The more commonplace a product or brand is among the general population, the less interested I am in buying it	2.57
30	Products don't seem to hold much value for me when they are purchased regularly by everyone	2.33
31	When a style of clothing I own becomes too commonplace, I usually quit wearing it	2.17

Note: A 5-point Likert Scale was used with the following rating scale: Strongly Disagree = 1, Disagree = 2, Neither Agree nor Disagree = 3, Agree = 4, Strongly Agree = 5.

The scores noted above are averages of responses from questions posed with regard to the survey takers' need for uniqueness.

Source: Created by author.

EXHIBIT 5 Analysis of Involvement

	Involvement Scales	Average Score
1	I would be interested in reading information about how the artwork is made	3.25
2	I would be interested in art journals or magazines	2.63
3	I have compared the art pieces across different art galleries	1.83
4	Which art gallery I buy from is important	1.71
5	The art gallery I go to treats me as a patron	1.33
6	The art gallery curator is very knowledgeable	2.29
7	I speak to a lot of curators before buying	1.17
8	I think there are a great deal of differences between different artists' worth	3.33
9	I have a most-preferred artist	1.50
10	I have a most-preferred art gallery	1.43
11	I do not doubt my preferred art gallery curator	2.17
12	Art is of no concern to me	1.63
13	I am neither interested in art nor in artists	1.69
14	Art info is beneficial to me	3.29
15	Art investment you feel is exciting—great scope there	2.86
16	Art gallery I feel is not much use to me	3.00
17	Online art websites are not needed	3.14
18	Online social networks are a waste of time	3.00
19	I buy artwork as a means of home decoration	4.14
20	I buy artwork because I feel emotionally attached to them	2.83
21	I buy art as an investment option	1.43
22	I buy art only if I like a particular piece of art	3.50
23	I buy art created by my favourite artist only	1.50
24	I buy art rarely and as an impulse buy	3.57

Note: A 5-point Likert Scale was used with the following rating scale: Strongly Disagree = 1, Disagree = 2, Neither Agree nor Disagree = 3, Agree = 4, Strongly Agree = 5.

The scores noted above are averages of responses from questions posed to understand survey takers' consumption and purchase involvement, including parameters that identify why they purchased art.

Source: Created by author.

Given the depth and diversity of the data, the data were presented with mutual exclusivity of the three dimensions of consumer behavior—namely, lifestyles, need for uniqueness and involvement levels. If these dimensions had been combined for specific respondents and then clustered into combinations, the data analysis would have become complicated. For example, the percentage of respondents who had scored high on specific items of lifestyle, low on some aspects of uniqueness and lower on their level of involvement could be combined into one cluster of responses. Such combinations would have led to a large number of clusters and would have also given rise to unpredictable patterns that would have been unusable due to lack of coherence. The case writers recognize that this direction, too, would have lent itself to some kind of analysis; however, because the focus of the case was to illustrate the impact of different dimensions of consumer behavior on the marketing of art, such a direction was not pursued by the case writers.

6

The Importance of Experiential Marketing in Marketing Communications[1]

Dr. S. Ramesh Kumar and Kavitha Murali.

INTRODUCTION

This case illustrates the importance of experiential marketing in the Indian context, which is cluttered with positioning and advertising communications. We have chosen the product category of shampoo, and for purposes of clarity, the case is confined to two basic sub-categories: "the overall benefit" category consisting of brands that are advertised on benefits other than "anti-dandruff"; and the "anti-dandruff" category, which covers brands that carry the "antidandruff" proposition. The case requires the student to apply certain concepts of consumer behaviour and to answer a few questions provided on the case.

Concepts associated with the case: Experiential marketing, attitudinal components, brand imagery, brand associations, brand personality.

INDUSTRY OVERVIEW

Hair shampoos and conditioners have been traditionally targeted at the upper middle-class. However, this category has recently expanded to include the middle class, housewives and upper-class rural consumers. Teenagers also form a major segment.

The shampoo market is segmented on benefit platforms as cosmetic (shine, health, strength), anti-dandruff and herbal.

---

[1] This case was written by Dr. S. Ramesh Kumar, and Kavitha Murali, Associate Consultant, KPMG Advisory Services Private Limited, Mumbai.

The southern market is predominantly a sachet market, accounting for 70 per cent of sachet volumes. In contrast, shampoo bottles are more popular in the northern markets with about 50 per cent of the shampoo bottles sold in the northern region alone. The size of the shampoo market in India is around 930 crores and per capita consumption of shampoo in India is 13ml. Further, shampoo penetration all over India has been 14 per cent with the urban and the rural areas accounting for 40 per cent and 10 per cent of the penetration respectively.

HLL has been the undisputed leader in the shampoo market from the early '90s. Sunsilk was launched in 1964 on the "general shampoo" platform. Clinic Plus was launched in 1971 as a family and health shampoo. Clinic All Clear, a therapeutic anti-dandruff shampoo, was launched in 1987. Sunsilk was re-launched in 1987 as a shampoo with conditioner on the beauty platform. Clinic Active with pro vitamin B was launched in 1991. Sunsilk was re-positioned and the brand re-launched its shampoo in 1994 for different types of hair – pink for dry hair, yellow for normal hair, green for oily hair and black for long hair. P&G entered India in November 1995, with the world's largest selling brand – Pantene. Colgate Palmolive launched Optima in November 1995 claiming to have made a breakthrough in keratin treatment. Nirma launched Nirma shampoo, which sailed into rough weather because it also had a detergent and a soap with the same name. The brand name also had low price connotations. In mid-1997, per capita consumption of shampoo increased. Of the Rs 350 crore shampoo market, the anti-dandruff segment accounted for a 20 per cent share. P&G launched its internationally acclaimed anti-dandruff shampoo, Head & Shoulders, in 1997 with zinc pyrithine (ZPT) – a unique anti-microbial agent. Sachet sale increased to 40 per cent of all shampoo consumption in the country. In 1998, HLL re-launched Clinic and Sunsilk brands. Sunsilk was re-launched with Fruitamins. HLL launched Dove in March 2006, and this opened up the premium shampoo segment. The high price, value for money and mildness connotations of the Dove soap have stuck on to the shampoo brand as well, and helped in boosting sales.

The sales curve for the shampoo market remained almost flat at Rs 1,500 crore in 2006–'07 and grew by just 6.6 per cent in terms of value. It grew by a more-than healthy 14.4 per cent in the three months prior to June 2007. However, Hindustan Unilever Ltd (HUL) and Procter & Gamble (P&G), India, do not seem to have significantly benefited from this growth. HUL's share in the shampoo market registered a marginal increase from 46.9 per cent (in terms of value) in the March quarter to 47.5 per cent in the June quarter, while rival P&G's share dipped from 25 per cent to 24.8 per cent in the same period.

While HUL's best-selling brand Clinic Plus continued to lead the segment with a 31.3 per cent market share, the share of Rejoice, a mass-market brand of P&G, slipped from 2.6 per cent to 2.3 per cent. P&G's Pantene, however, increased its share by 0.6 per centage points to 12 per cent in the June quarter over the previous quarter. Dabur India Ltd's Vatika had a share of 4.9 per cent while the share of smaller brands such as Nyle and Ayur stood at 1.6 per cent and 3.2 per cent, respectively. The positioning of leading shampoos in the market, as well as the imagery associated with them are given in Table 6.1.

Several companies are now eyeing the growing shampoo market and the existing players have to defend their turf by launching new products, reducing prices, and focusing on promotions. Companies are pushing rural penetration by focusing on the sale of sachets. Godrej Consumer Products Ltd recently made an aggressive entry into the market with the launch of its brand, Godrej No. 1, priced at 50 paise. The launch challenged the share of value-for-money products such as Chik, owned by Chennai-based CavinKare. The latter's share in the market fell by 0.4 per centage points to 12.7 per cent in the June quarter. Sachets account for around 70 per cent of the market. Premium brands such as Garnier have also started selling sachets to tap the growth opportunity. In the anti-dandruff shampoo market, P&G scored

Table 6.1 Brand positioning and imagery–Shampoo market in India

Si.	BrandName	Proposition/Positioning*	*Imagery of advertisement
1.	Sunsilk	Silky, shiny, voluminous, strong and black colored hair	a) Happy woman bouncing her great hair, showing off its smoothness and silkiness b) Not much emphasis on ingredients c) Tries to strike an emotional chord with the consumer rather than leverage on functional benefits
2.	Pantene	Smooth, silky, voluminous, full, lively, long, black hair	a) Functional benefits stressed through Pro-V amino acids b) Shiny black hair reinforced c) Monotonous advertisements making a functional point
3.	Dove	Daily care for hair, damage control and special shampoo targeting dry and frizzy hair	a) Clear focus on functional benefit b) Clear premium image comes across in the brand variants c) Use of ingredients – 1/4th moisturizing milk–to stress upon the functional benefit as well as emotional benefit viz. mildness
4.	Chik	Fragrance (rose and jasmine), strength (egg), keeps hair cool and black	a) Clear image of an economy brand b) Message sent across—beautiful hair in public c) Beautiful hair refers to hair being untangled, smooth and silky
5.	Head & Shoulders	Anti-dandruff shampoo that clears dandruff in one wash Vs three washes in other shampoos	a) Functional benefit specified clearly b) 7 out of 10 dermatologists recommend H&S—proof for functionality c) Boring and educational advertisement
6.	Clinic All Clear	Positioned as the first anti-dandruff shampoo exclusively for men	a) Soft romantic advertisement b) Sends across message on hair fall and dandruff control c) Strikes a cord with the consumer both on emotional as well as functional terms

* —as perceived by authors.

over HUL. P&G's Head & Shoulders brand, the market leader in the segment, saw its share increase by 3.3 per centage points to 54.8 per cent. HUL's Clinic All Clear saw its share fall by 2.4 per centage points to 39.6 per cent. HUL launched an anti-dandruff men's shampoo called Activsport in April–June. Recently, ITC has launched its premium shampoo, Fiama Di Wills, with extensive advertisement campaigns on frequently viewed entertainment and news channels such as Zee, CNN–IBN, NDTV etc.

POSITIONING MAPS

The following positioning maps have been drawn by the authors with available data about five brands of shampoo. For reasons of ease, these brands have been labeled as follows for reference in the maps:

S – Sunsilk
P – Pantene
D – Dove
H&S – Head and Shoulders
CAC – Clinic All Clear

(i) Price – Variety Relationship

Sunsilk is available in a whopping 23 varieties at the lowest price of Rs 40 per 100 ml. As opposed to this, Clinic All Clear is available only in two varieties, namely, Clinic All Clear Anti–Dandruff and Clinic All Clear Total. Hence, it has been plotted at the left-most end of the graph but at a price point slightly higher than that of Sunsilk as it is priced at Rs 55 per 100ml. Dove, which is the highest priced at Rs 65 per 100ml has very low number of varieties, Damage Therapy, Dry Therapy and Normal Therapy. Head & Shoulders is priced one rupee lower than Dove at Rs 64 and comes in four varieties. Pantene, which is priced at Rs 61, is available in the market in six different varieties. Considering these facts, the map has been drawn as shown in Figure 6.1.

(ii) Price – Quantity Relationship

Except Sunsilk, all brands of shampoos considered here, including Clinic All Clear, Pantene, Head & Shoulders and Dove, are priced per 100ml bottle. Hence, they fall on the same vertical line, with changes in price points—Rs 55 for Clinic All Clear, Rs 61 for Pantene, Rs 64 for Head & Shoulders and Rs 65 for Dove. Sunsilk alone comes in a 125 ml pack, which is priced at Rs 55, the same as Clinic All Clear's price at 100ml. (See Figure 6.2).

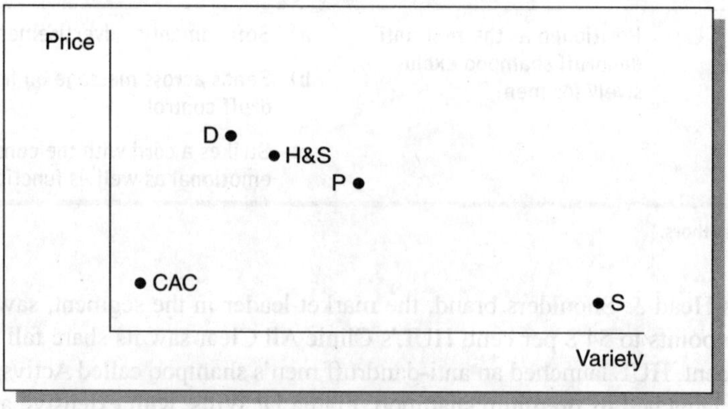

Figure 6.1 Price–Variety Relationship

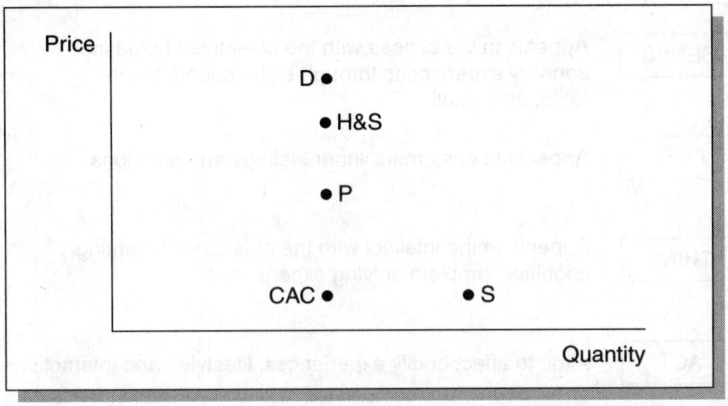

Figure 6.2 Price–Quantity Relationship

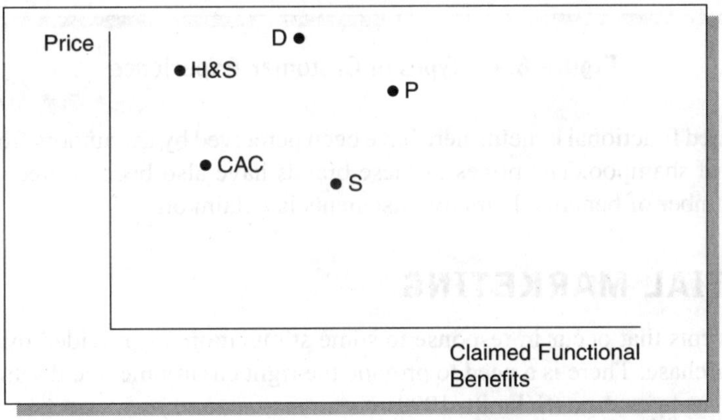

Figure 6.3 Price–Claimed Functional Benefits Relationship

(iii) Price – Claimed Functional Benefits Relationship

Sunsilk claims around five functional benefits including silky, shiny, voluminous, strong and black hair. Pantene's promised functional benefits are almost the same but include just one more, namely, long hair. But, there is a huge price gap between these two brands, which is adequately represented in Figure 6.3.

On the other hand, Head & Shoulders and Clinic All Clear being predominantly anti-dandruff shampoos, have clearly positioned themselves on the dandruff control platform, and hence, are understood to provide one functional benefit. The positions of these two brands form a vertical line towards the left end of the map as their number of functional benefits are the smallest and equal to one another while the difference lies only in the price, with Head & Shoulders being far higher priced than Clinic All Clear. As a contrast to all these brands, Dove is the most expensive of the lot, but does not provide too many functional benefits either. Its communication strategies suggest that it has positioned itself to provide three important functional benefits only and hence assumes the center point on the x-axis while being situated at the highest point on the y-axis in Figure 6.3.

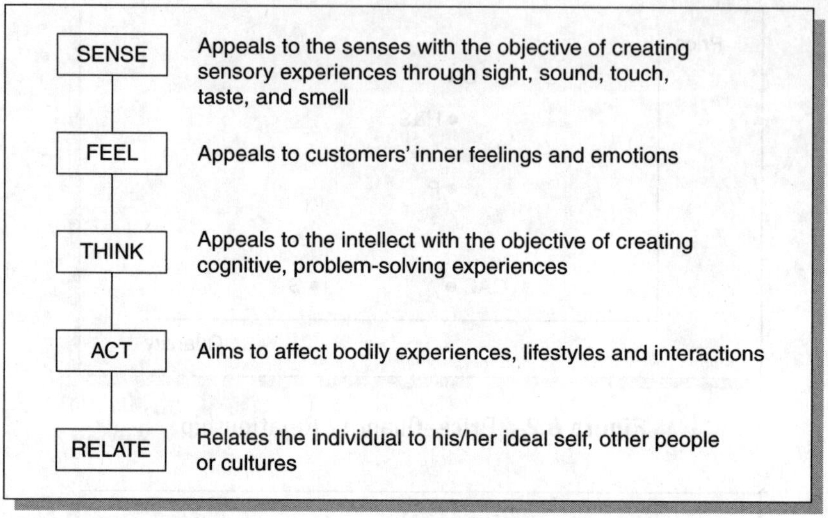

Figure 6.4 Types of Customer Experience

Note: The claimed functional benefits here have been perceived by the authors from advertisements of various brands of shampoo. The prices of these brands have also been plotted on the positioning map against the number of benefits their advertisements lay claim on.

EXPERIENTIAL MARKETING

Experiences are events that occur in response to some stimulation, as provided by marketing efforts before and after purchase. There is a need to provide the right environment and setting for the desired customer experiences to emerge (Schmitt, 1999).

The five types of customer experiences that form the basis of the experiential marketing framework are as shown in Figure 6.4

DETAILS OF METHODOLOGY USED IN THE CASE

Sampling Method and Process

The sampling design was chosen based on the probability sampling process. This was because, though operationally non-probability sampling is very simple, the estimates are not statistically projectable to the population; since there is no way of determining the probability of selecting any particular element for inclusion in the sample.

Further, the sample was to be chosen primarily based on a demographic characteristic, namely, age (18–30) in this case. Hence, stratified sampling was adopted.

Stratified sampling is a two-step process in which the population is partitioned into sub-populations or strata. The strata should be mutually exclusive and collectively exhaustive. Next, elements are selected from each stratum by the simple random sampling process (Malhotra, 2007).

In this case, a sampling frame of 200 people consisting only of women was selected. The segment of women was targeted in order to maintain uniformity across the brands in the two different sub-categories, which catered predominantly to the female population. The responses obtained were then segregated across two sub-categories and 50 responses each were chosen randomly, for each sub-category. The random choices were obtained through a simple random sampling method by assigning a unique number to each of the responses across the segregation and then generating random numbers through a computer program to choose the random sample. The sample size of 50 each for the two sub-categories is above the minimum requirement of 30 for a normal distribution, and hence, it would yield statistically significant results (Malhotra, 2007). This decision was taken after considering the time and logistical constraints.

Activities, Interests and Opinions as a Reflection of Lifestyle of Respondents

While the users of overall benefit shampoos are neutral towards indoor activities and are not involved in too many outdoor activities, the anti-dandruff shampoo users seem to be leaning more towards outdoor activities such as sports, shopping, rock shows and partying.

On the other hand, while the users of overall benefit shampoos seem to have neutral interests that lean neither towards indoor, reticent interests such as music, cooking and interior design nor towards gregarious interests such as keeping track of current affairs, the anti-dandruff shampoo users seem to have a diametrically opposite level of interest including music, cooking, interior design and reading. The interest levels of the anti-dandruff shampoo users seem to be in direct contrast to the activities of overall benefit users.

While the anti-dandruff shampoo users have an opinion of emulating the Western world in beauty care, an urge to try out new beauty care products and the willingness to spend money on hair care, the overall benefit shampoo users seem to be more reticent in this regard and are very neutral with regards to their opinions about beauty care, hair care and grooming.

The questionnaire used in the study and the responses obtained from the respondents on various aspects of experiential marketing are provided in Appendices 1 and 2.

QUESTIONS

1. Compare the positioning strategies of each of the brands provided in the industry overview with the results from respondents. Comment on the imagery of each of the brands with respect to the results obtained.
2. Analyze each of the brands from the viewpoint of each aspect of experiential marketing.
3. From 1 and 2,
   (a) how would you formulate an experiential advertisement for
      (i) the overall benefit category and
      (ii) for the anti-dandruff category.
   (b) point out clearly how your recommendation differentiates the new advertising imagery from the brands discussed in the industry overview.
4. Complete a positioning diagram that explains how your new experiential imagery differentiates itself from the other brands in
   (a) the overall benefit category and
   (b) the anti-dandruff category.

Use the data provided in the tables as appropriate.

State your assumptions, if any, for the above questions. You may categorize the brands into either of the sub-categories (overall benefit or anti-dandruff) based on information provided in the case or using any additional information, which you may find in secondary sources.

APPENDIX1: QUESTIONNAIRE USED IN THE STUDY

Sense

This part of the study measures what you think are the benefits that the shampoo you use provides to you. Please mark X on the blank that best indicates how accurately one or the other adjective describes what benefits you think you get from your shampoo.

1. Silky __________ Rough
2. Shiny __________ Dull
3. Voluminous __________ Scant
4. Strong __________ Weak
5. Soft on hair __________ Harsh on hair
6. Fragrance __________ No fragrance
7. Dandruff control __________ No dandruff control
8. Hair fall control __________ No hair fall control
9. Damage control __________ No damage control
10. Herbal __________ Non-herbal

Feel

This part of the study measures what emotions you feel because of using your shampoo. Please mark X on the blank that best indicates how accurately one or the other adjective describes what emotions you think you feel on the usage of your shampoo.

11. Like __________ Dislike
12. Good __________ Bad
13. Pleasing __________ Displeasing
14. Exciting __________ Dull
15. Enjoyable __________ Not enjoyable
16. Enthusiastic __________ Boring
17. Adore __________ Hate
18. Contented __________ Discontented
19. Passionate __________ Indifferent
20. Happy __________ Unhappy

Think

Listed below are different facts about your shampoo. Please indicate how strongly you agree or disagree with each by using the following scale:

1 —Strongly disagree
2 —Disagree
3 —Neither agree nor disagree
4 —Agree
5 —Strongly agree

21. Good value for money:
22. Effective on hair:
23. Gentle on hair:
24. Good variety:
25. Easily available:
26. Premium brand:
27. Augmented benefits beyond just cleansing of hair:
28. Frequency of usage needed is not high:
29. Ingredients are not harmful on hair:
30. Provides benefits as claimed on advertisements and package:

Act

This part of the study measures the reasons that make you buy the shampoo you currently use. Please mark X on the blank that best indicates how accurately one or the other adjective describes the reason why you buy your shampoo.

31. Good advertisements ______________ Not good advertisements
32. Attractive promotional offers ______________ Not attractive promotional offers
33. Attractive packaging ______________ Dull packaging
34. Measurable functional benefits ______________ Non-measurable emotional benefits
35. Natural ingredients ______________ Artificial ingredients
36. Rightly priced ______________ High priced
37. Belief in celebrity endorsements ______________ Not belief in celebrity endorsements
38. Easy availability of sachets ______________ Not easy availability of bottles
39. Fragrance ______________ Not fragrance
40. Ease of use ______________ Not ease of use

Relate

This part of the study measures the kind of adjectives that you associate with the brand of shampoo you use when you imagine the shampoo to be a person, and the reasons that make you buy the shampoo you currently use. Please mark X on the blank that best indicates how accurately one or the other adjective describes the personality of the shampoo you have in your mind.

41. Friend ______________ Mentor
42. Trustworthy ______________ Not trustworthy
43. Warm ______________ Cold
44. Caring ______________ Aloof

45. Sincere	____________________	Superfluous
46. Dependable	____________________	Not dependable
47. Non-traditional	____________________	Conservative
48. Gregarious	____________________	Introverted
49. Intimate	____________________	Professional
50. Confident	____________________	Insecure

Activities

Listed below, are different pastime activities that you may be associated with or like. Please indicate how strongly you agree or disagree with each as one of your favorite pastime activity by using the following scale:

1 —Strongly disagree
2 —Disagree
3 —Neither agree nor disagree
4 —Agree
5 —Strongly agree

51. Sports:
52. Shopping:
53. Partying:
54. Watching rock shows:
55. Indoor games:

Interests

Listed below, are interests that you may have in different sectors of life. Please indicate how strongly you agree or disagree with each as one of interest to you by using the following scale:

1 —Strongly disagree
2 —Disagree
3 —Neither agree nor disagree
4 —Agree
5 —Strongly agree

56. Music:
57. Reading:
58. Cooking:
59. Interior design:
60. Current affairs:

Opinions

Listed below, are different opinions you may have on hair care in specific, and beauty care in general. Please indicate how strongly you agree or disagree with each one of these opinions by using the following scale:

1 —Strongly disagree
2 —Disagree
3 —Neither agree nor disagree
4 —Agree
5 —Strongly agree

61. I like trying out new beauty care products:
62. I prefer natural hair care products over artificial shampoos:
63. I believe in celebrity endorsements of cosmetics:
64. I do not mind spending much on hair care:
65. I like the Western style of beauty and grooming more than the Indian style:

APPENDIX 2: SCORES OBTAINED FROM RESPONDENTS ON VARIOUS ASPECTS OF EXPERIENTIAL MARKETING*

Table A1 Sense—Means of overall benefit respondents across individual characteristics

Silk	Shine	Volume	Strength	Soft	Fragrant	Anti D.ruff	Hairfall control	Damage control	Herbal	Average
1.92	2.1	2.67	2.84	2.04	1.92	3.1	3.18	2.52	3.25	2.55

Table A2 Sense—Means of Anti-dandruff respondents across individual characteristics

Silk	Shine	Volume	Strength	Soft	Fragrant	Anti D.ruff	Hairfall control	Damage control	Herbal	Average
2.3	2.6	2.5	2.95	2.29	2	1.84	3.1	2.9	3.06	2.52

Table B1 Feel—Means of overall benefit respondents across individual characteristics

Like	Good	Please	Excite	Enjoy	Enthuse	Adore	Content	Passion	Happy	Average
1.7	1.8	1.9	2.6	2.5	2.8	2.82	2.4	2.68	2.4	2.33

Table B2 Feel—Means of anti-dandruff respondents across individual characteristics

Like	Good	Please	Excite	Enjoy	Enthuse	Adore	Content	Passion	Happy	Average
1.87	2.08	2.16	2.65	2.68	2.83	3.04	2.53	2.89	2.27	2.43

Table C1 Think—Means of overall benefit respondents across individual characteristics

Value	Effect	Gentle	Variety	Avail	Premium	Extra benefit	Usage	Harmless	Benefits as claimed	Average
2.27	2.28	2.2	2.22	2.18	1.84	2.34	2.92	2.68	2.81	2.37

Table C2 Think—Means of Anti-dandruff respondents across individual characteristics

Value	Effect	Gentle	Variety	Avail	Premium	Extra benefit	Usage	Harmless	Benefits as claimed	Average
2.45	2.33	2.35	1.8	1.79	1.89	2.57	2.65	2.7	2.78	2.26

Table D1 Act—Means of overall benefit respondents across individual characteristics

Ads	Promotion	Package	Function	Natural	Price	Celebrity	Sachet	Bottle	Use	Average
2.48	3.15	2.65	2.46	2.92	2.73	3.6	3.45	2.29	2.17	2.67

Table D2 Act—Means of anti-dandruff respondents across individual characteristics.

Ads	Promotion	Package	Function	Natural	Price	Celebrity	Sachet	Bottle	Use	Average
2.4	2.65	2.3	2.49	2.9	2.43	3.3	1.97	2.4	1.87	2.39

Table E1 Relate—Means of overall benefit respondents across individual characteristics

Friend	Trust	Warm	Caring	Sincere	Dependable	Non-traditional	Gregarious	Intimate	Confident	Average
2.6	2.36	2.65	2.5	2.68	2.39	2.68	2.83	2.98	2.44	2.5

Table E2 Relate—Means of Anti-dandruff respondents across individual characteristics

Friend	Trust	Warm	Caring	Sincere	Dependable	Non-traditional	Gregarious	Intimate	Confident	Average
2.25	2.31	2.82	2.17	2.37	2.53	3.13	3.02	3.21	2.1	2.47

Table F1 Overall Experience—Means of overall benefit and antidandruff categories of respondents

Overall Benefit	Anti-dandruff
2.486378	2.418725

Table G1 Activities—Means of anti-dandruff respondents across individual characteristics

Sports	Shopping	Partying	Rock shows	Outdoor games	Average
3.56	1.56	2.1	3.22	3.94	2.876

Table G2 Activities—Means of overall benefit respondents across individual characteristics

Sports	Shopping	Partying	Rock shows	Outdoor games	Average
1.53	2.16	1.78	1.98	1.93	1.876

Table G3 Interests—Means of overall benefit respondents across individual characteristics

Music	Reading	Cooking	Interior design	Not current affairs	Average
1.12	1.05	1.35	1.23	1.3	1.21

Table G4 Interests—Means of anti-dandruff respondents across individual characteristics

Music	Reading	Cooking	Interior design	Not current affairs	Average
4.175	3.21	3.42	3.78	4.21	3.759

Table G5 Opinions—Means of anti-dandruff respondents across individual characteristics

Like trying new beauty care products	Do not prefer natural products	Belief in endorsements	Do not mind spending on hair	Like Western style	Average
2.56	3.21	3.54	2.978	2.607	2.979

Table G6 Opinions—Means of overall benefit respondents across individual characteristics

Like trying new beauty care products	Do not prefer natural products	Belief in endorsements	Do not mind spending on hair	Like Western style	Average
1.12	2.32	2.21	1.054	1.011	1.543

7

Ethnic Consumers Consulting

Dr. S. Ramesh Kumar, Nitya Guruvayurappan and Madhurjya Banerjee wrote this case solely to provide material for class discussion. The authors do not intend to illustrate either effective or ineffective handling of a managerial situation. The authors may have disguised certain names and other identifying information to protect confidentiality.

It was a humid day in September 2010 in the historic city of Mumbai, where millions of people who barely made ends meet coexisted with a niche segment of consumers who led hedonistic lifestyles oriented towards consumption for pleasure, indulging in the best of brands from across the globe. Nitya Guruvayurappan was busy preparing a presentation for a multinational client on her first probable assignment in her consulting work. With her basic degree in engineering, she had never thought that she would develop so much passion towards consumer behaviour. It was her aspiration to start a consulting company that exclusively dealt with consumer behaviour issues that were unique to the Indian context. With a postgraduate degree from a premier institute and a few years of work experience in the marketing field in a multinational company, she thought it was time to address her aspirations. Guruvayurappan was meeting her first prospective client, a company that manufactured hair oil and fairness cream. She remembered a research publication that she had co-authored in 2007, and she wanted to make use of the data to build a case with a practical orientation that would result in interesting insights for the client on consumer values—an area lacking study in this emerging market (see Exhibits 1 and 2). Were emerging markets significantly different from developed markets in terms of their consumer values? Could brand differentiation transcend the usual generic symbolic benefit to accommodate brand symbolism associated with the deeper levels of values? Were existing brands connecting themselves with the diverse value bands associated with Indian consumers? Could values get associated with different socio-economic classes of consumers?

INDIAN CONTEXT—DEMOGRAPHICS, LIFESTYLE AND VALUES

In 2010, India contained a diverse array of product categories, brands, prices, lifestyles and cultures. While marketers were upbeat concerning the consumption of categories and brands stretching from unbranded edible oil to symbolism light-emitting diode (LED) watches, there were unique challenges to marketers: these included the management of marketing mix elements, understanding the diversity of cultures, development of appropriate product lines, localizing global communication and more specifically, understanding the consumer psyche in a changing environment.

As the economy grew between the years 2000 to 2010, so had the spending power of consumers. In 2010, real average household income in India had roughly doubled over the past two decades. Consumption had increased along with rising income, especially with the emergence of India's growing middle class.[1] According to the official definition, urban India consisted of 5,161 towns and cities and included nearly 30 per cent of the population; rural India consisted of more than 600,000 villages and included more than 70 per cent of the population.[2]

Across urban and rural India, the "emerging India" households in 2010 could be classified into five groups based on annual household income. The "deprived" (earning < Rs90,000) consisted of 103 million households (HHs) of mostly subsistence farmers and unskilled labourers. The "aspirers" (earning Rs90,000–Rs200,000) consisted of 91.3 million HHs and included small-scale shopkeepers, farmers—with small areas of owned land—or industrial workers; it was expected that this group would reduce from 41 per cent to around 35 per cent due to their moving into the middle class. The "seekers" (earning Rs200,000–Rs500,000) consisting of 11 million HHs and the "strivers" (earning Rs500,000–Rs1,000,000) consisting of 2.5 million HHs were developing into India's huge new middle class. "Seekers" included young college graduates, government employees at intermediate levels and owners of small- to medium-sized businesses. "Strivers," the upper end of the middle class, were senior government employees, owners or managers of large businesses, professionals and wealthy farmers. In 2010, the middle class numbered some 50 million individuals, but that was expected to grow 10 times and become approximately 41 per cent of the population between the years 2020 to 2025. The "global Indians" (earning > Rs1,000,000) were the other major spending force in India's new consumer market, comprising more than one million HHs: they were senior executives in large corporations, owners of large businesses, politicians and rich farmers with large landholdings.[3]

Changing Values and Lifestyles

In 2010, consumers were characterized by a rising income, aided by the increasing affordability of products. Urban consumers looked more for material success and understood the need to satisfy their desires, rather than practice restraint. They respected their traditions, but did not tie their

[1] "The Bird of Gold: India's Rising Consumer Market," chapter 1, www.mckinsey.com/mgi/reports/pdfs/india_consumer_market/MGI_india_consumer_chapter_1.pdf, accessed October 10, 2010

[2] "The Bird of Gold: India's Rising Consumer Market," chapter 2, www.mckinsey.com/mgi/reports/pdfs/india_consumer_market/MGI_india_consumer_chapter_2.pdf, accessed October 10, 2010.

[3] "Next Big Spenders: India's middle class," www.mckinsey.com/mgi/mginews/bigspenders.asp, accessed October 10, 2010.

lives to these traditions. The need for convenience and lack of time resulted in urban consumers becoming increasingly dependent on technology; therefore, technical competence was seen as a must for the urban youth. Urban consumers strove for success and were self-confident about their abilities. Preference for English education was a common factor across all urban consumers and was becoming increasingly important with semi-urban consumers.

As consumerism and media exposure increased, India also saw an evolution in its value systems and beliefs. Indian consumers traditionally saved their money. Contemporary consumers were not looking for cheap goods; rather, they were looking for value and were willing to pay extra for it. The fundamental values of conservatism and risk avoidance were gradually being replaced by an openness to experiment and to spend money on items beyond the essentials: in segments such as the "global Indian," this even translated to conspicuous consumption. This increasing risk appetite also extended to the mindset of Indians in terms of careers and lifestyles: they were willing to try out new career paths and were not bound by the same organization for their entire career lifetimes. Rural Indians saw a lot of migration to the cities and moved beyond their conventional forms of earning livelihood.

The Indian youth was also seeking individuality as opposed to the need for affiliation and social acceptance that was characteristic of older generations. Despite there being close family relationships, families were rapidly growing nuclear and very few parts of urban India still upheld the joint family model. The influence of the West could be seen in the changing lifestyle and trends of the Indian consumer: personal grooming had increased in importance, especially with more women stepping out and making careers for themselves. The work culture had also grown significantly, with more people having jobs in multinational corporations.

CATEGORY AND BRAND SUMMARY—FAIRNESS CREAMS AND HAIR OILS

Fairness Creams Market in India—Category and Key Brands Summary

In 2010, the personal care industry—which included bath and shower products, hair care, skin care, cosmetics and fragrances—in India was around US$4 billion.[4] Skin care comprised 16 per cent of this segment; the skin care segment consisted of everything from basic creams and moisturizers to specialized products such as anti-wrinkle and dark circle removing creams. The cosmetic industry was expected to grow at a compound annual growth rate (CAGR) of approximately 17 per cent by 2013, and within this industry skin care was one of the most attractive segments, with facial skin care (85 per cent of total skin care sales) outperforming the rest of the skin care segment.[5] Within facial care, facial moisturizers and cleansers accounted for the bulk of sales.

Traditionally, India was a country in which the population had a natural bias towards lighter skin; catering to this bias, skin care in India was flooded with facial moisturizers that either positioned themselves completely as fairness creams and skin-whitening products, or at least offered

[4] Pratik Kadakia, Abhishek Nigam and Ashwin Rao, "Outlook for Personal Care Industry: An Indian Perspective," *Chemical Weekly*, www.tsmg.com/download/article/Personal_Care_Chemicals.pdf, accessed October 10, 2010.

[5] "Indian Cosmetic Market Ready to Escalate," *PR Log*, www.prlog.org/10931927-indian-cosmetic-market-ready-to-escalate.html, accessed October 10, 2010.

fairness as an added benefit. Tapping into this huge demand for fairness in India, facial moisturizers were the biggest contributors to skin care in India, comprising almost 50 per cent of the skin care segment.

While Indians were likely to remain partial towards lighter skin, fairness alone was not expected to be the driving force of skin care sales in the near future; rather, exfoliation, nourishment and freshness were expected to become key selling points as almost all skin care products in India already offered fairness benefits. Anti-aging products, comprising just two per cent of the skin care segment, were set to grow as well with multiple brands entering this segment while also offering the whiteness benefit. Furthermore, taking a cue from more developed countries, skin care in India was set to undergo a metamorphosis from a one-product-fits-all mentality to providing separate solutions to suit each different skin type.[6]

Another trend seen in this industry was the introduction of multiple brands in the men's whitening segment. Men accounted for about 25 per cent of the fairness cream usage in the country and that figure was growing in "absolute terms."[7] This trend was even seen in the comparison of the growth rates of women's and men's fairness creams, which were seven to eight per cent and 25 per cent, respectively.

Penetration and consumption were still challenges in this category. Fairness creams penetrated only 25 per cent of the market, with the South being the largest market (36 per cent). The North and West contributed 23 per cent each and the East contributed approximately 18 per cent.[8] In comparison with China[9], despite India having a higher personal disposable income per household and an increasing population of women in the 25–44 age group (the key consumer segment), it spent only about one-tenth of what China spent on skin care. Pricing in the skin care market ranged from offerings as low as the Rs5 sachets of fairness creams in low income markets to Rs500-600 for the super-premium end of anti-aging creams.

The major players in the fairness cream market were Hindustan Unilever Ltd (HUL), with a market share between 50–70 per cent on its flagship brand Fair & Lovely which also enjoyed a high rural penetration, and CavinKare, which held about one-fifth of HUL's market share with its leading brand Fairever.[10]

HUL's Fair & Lovely fairness cream[11] had been the undisputed leader of skin care products in India for more than a quarter of a century. Fair & Lovely (F&L) was in the popular/economy tier of the market and was targeted at low and middle income Indian consumers across urban and rural India. F&L had a range of product offerings such as Multivitamin, Ayurvedic, AntiMarks and Menz Active. It was available in a range of stock-keeping units (SKUs) from nine gram sachets to 80 gram tubes. In the company's portfolio, it was the flagship skin care brand along with Ponds,

---

[6] Pratik Kadakia, Abhishek Nigam and Ashwin Rao, "Outlook for Personal Care Industry: An Indian Perspective," *Chemical Weekly*, www.tsmg.com/download/article/Personal_Care_Chemicals.pdf, accessed October 10, 2010.

[7] "The Regime of Fairness is Not Limited!" *oneIndia Living*, November 28, 2007, http://living.oneindia.in/men/for-him/men-cosmetics-fairness-creams.html, accessed October 10, 2010.

[8] Sravanthi Challapalli, "All's fair in this market," *The Hindu Business Line*, September 5, 2002, www.thehindubusinessline.com/catalyst/2002/09/05/stories/2002090500040300.htm, accessed October 10, 2010.

[9] Pratik Kadakia, Abhishek Nigam and Ashwin Rao, "Outlook for Personal Care Industry: An Indian Perspective," *Chemical Weekly*, www.tsmg.com/download/article/Personal_Care_Chemicals.pdf, accessed October 10, 2010.

[10] "How fair is Fair & Lovely?," *Rediff India Abroad*, March 9, 2007, www.rediff.com/money/2007/mar/09guest.htm, accessed October 10, 2010.

[11] "Fair & Lovely," *Hindustan Unilever Limited*, www.hul.co.in/brands/personalcarebrands/FairAndLovely.aspx, accessed October 10, 2010.

and was among their "Super Brands." (An example of F&L's advertising with the case authors' description of its storyboard, as well as the case authors' interpretation of F&L's communication is included in Exhibit 3.)

CavinKare's Fairever[12] managed to retain consumer interest and was the second-best selling brand in facial moisturizers with a 12 per cent value share backed by strong brand equity in South India and constant product innovation. Fairever was available in its base variant and a Fairever Fruit variant perched on the 'naturals' platform. (An example of Fairever's advertising with the case authors' description of its storyboard, as well as the case authors' interpretation of Fairever's communication is included in Exhibit 4.)

Hair Oil Market in India—Category and Key Brands Summary

Indian consumers were traditionally accustomed to using various natural forms of hair oil as a leave-on conditioning treatment. The most popular hair oil in the Indian context was coconut hair oil, which represented the bulk of sales. Although coconut oil had been the traditional hair oil variety, there were other segments in the market such as perfumed hair oils, light hair oils, cooling oils and tonics or hair gels. Even coconut hair oil was further segmented into plain coconut hair oil and added-value hair oil. In 2010, the $1.28 billion hair oil market in India was categorized into coconut hair oil (50 per cent), *amla* (18 per cent), light (17 per cent), cooling (10 per cent) and tonics and gels (five per cent).[13]

The coconut oil market had been witnessing a change in usage behaviour in both urban and rural markets. The rural consumer, who traditionally purchased unbranded oil, was expected to gradually shift to branded hair oil, given the resistance to adulteration. The penetration of hair oil was high at around 87 per cent and similar across the urban and rural areas.[14]

The use of hair oil had become a deeply ingrained habit in the consumer psyche: it was perceived to encompass multiple benefits such as nourishment, strengthening and revitalizing the hair. Moreover, hair oils also achieved cosmetic benefits as the hair remained soft and shiny after application.

In 2010, the hair oil category in India was slowly reaching saturation as this traditional hair care product was facing tough competition in the urban markets from foreign conditioners. The presence of a huge organized sector and proliferation from the edible oil segment made the hair oils easily accessible to different segments of society, being available at different price points. The market was expected to become such that any brand of hair oil could not charge a price premium based on traditional attributes, as most of them had become hygiene factors and were offered by almost all competing brands. As a result, when newer attributes such as 'cool' oils, herbal products, anti-dandruff and non-greasiness agents were added to traditional coconut hair oils or amla hair oils, this attracted a price premium.

The SKUs in this category ranged from three millilitre (ml) sachets to 300 ml bottles, with the sachet distribution being highly penetrated in the rural markets. The biggest segment was the popular

---

[12] "Fairever," *CavinKare*, www.cavinkare.com/fairever.html, accessed October 10, 2010.

[13] "Marico to move court on coconut oil excise notice," http://epaper.timesofindia.com/Repository/ml.asp?Ref=RVR-ELzIwMDkvMDcvMTQjQXIwMTgwMg==&Mode=HTML&Locale=english-skin-custom, accessed October 10, 2010.

[14] www.equitymaster.com/research-it/sector-info/consprds/consprds-products.html, accessed October 10, 2010.

tier with brands such as Parachute and Dabur Amla oil; the economy tier followed with brands such as Nihar, Shanti Amla and other regional brands. The premium tier consisted of brands such as Dabur Vatika and Hair and Care.

The leading company in this category was Marico, with its flagship brand Parachute holding almost 50 per cent of the coconut oils segment, which itself was 50 per cent of the total hair oil category[15]. Other big players were Dabur and Bajaj, with their respective brands Dabur Amla and Bajaj Almond leading the segments of the heavy amla and light oil segments.

Parachute[16] was a market leader in its category and positioned on the platform of purity. It was also available in pouch packs such as Parachute Mini, a Re1 SKU, and a 20 ml Parachute sold at Rs5 for the rural consumer. Although historically Parachute had positioned itself on the platform of purity, the communication had evolved over time to appeal to different consumer groups. The brand name extended to a range of variants such as Advansed and Jasmine, and to adjacencies such as shampoo and hair gels. (An example of Parachute's advertising with the case authors' description of its storyboard, as well as the case authors' interpretation of Parachute's communication is included in Exhibit 5.)

Dabur Amla[17] was a heavy amla oil with a composition of natural amla for enriching and strengthening hair; it was available in Re1 sachets as well as bottles. It had non-sticky variants based on flower fragrances. Dabur Amla was targeted at the middle and low income markets with its economy tier pricing, while Vatika from the same company had offerings in the premium end of this segment. (An example of Dabur Amla's advertising with the case authors' description of its storyboard, as well as the case authors' interpretation of Dabur Amla's communication is included in Exhibit 6.)

PREPARING THE PRESENTATION

Following an analysis of the relevant industries, Guruvayurappan conducted a consumer survey in order to understand the dominant cultural values among consumer groups of these categories across socio-economic classes (see Exhibit 7). Based on this data and an understanding of the communication of leading brands in these categories, Guruvayurappan seemed to have identified an area of differentiation based on cultural values and ritual experiences from which brands in an emerging market could benefit when they were pitched against one another. The challenge was to use some frameworks to understand how brands could differentiate themselves using values unique to the Indian context.

---

[15] "Marico to move court on coconut oil excise notice," http://epaper.timesofindia.com/Repository/ml.asp?Ref=RVR-ELzIwMDkvMDcvMTQjQXIwMTgwMg==&Mode=HTML&Locale=english-skin-custom, accessed October 10, 2010.

[16] "Parachute," *Marico*, www.marico.com/brands_n_business/parachute/index.html, accessed October 10, 2010.

[17] "Dabur Amla," *Dabur*, www.dabur.com/Products-Personal%20Care-Amla%20Hair%20Oil, accessed October 10, 2010.

EXHIBIT 1 Values Questionnaire

Each of the 32 values is defined by five statements which are to be rated on the five-point Likert Scale (strongly agree, agree, neutral, disagree, strongly disagree) by the side. In the final form of the questionnaire, all 160 statements will be mixed up to remove any bias. The defining value will not be shown to the respondents who were asked to mark one (1) against their level of agreement with each statement given below.

VALUES
Power Distance
I often seek opinions from people before making decisions
There are many distinctions between people in my locality
I believe that some people in my locality are clearly more influential than others
I don't think equality is a practical concept
I look up to some people in society as really knowledgeable
Uncertainty Avoidance
I don't like being uncertain about things
I search for a lot of information before I do or buy something
I don't like being in unfamiliar situations
It gives me a reassurance if other people are doing/buying the same thing as me
I generally do not experiment while buying things
Forward-looking
I often think about the future when I need to make a decision
I believe in saving money for a rainy day
When I earn some unexpected money, I don't generally spend it on myself
I don't expect immediate results for things I do
I engage in a lot of planning and don't believe in just living for the present
Conservatism
I do not like to stand out in a crowd
I am careful about the money I spend
I don't get too carried away when I am happy or successful at something
I am cautious about my dress and behaviour when I am with people
I don't think I can ever lead a flashy lifestyle
Need for Affiliation
It is important for me that others approve of what I do
When in a group, I often behave in a manner that makes me fit in
I often pay attention to others' reactions to my behaviour
In case of uncertainty, I look at others to get cues from them
I often feel bad if my peer group doesn't praise me for something worthy I've done
Family Bonding
I have a close relationship with my family
I feel it is very important to bond well with family
Family is the only long-lasting association that people have in life
I could leave an important career if it gave me no time with my family
I feel close to members of family even if there are physical distances

Utilitarianism
I generally buy products only if they are useful
I am not impressed by free offers unless I definitely need the product
I never buy items just because I liked its advertisement
I don't simply follow my heart while selecting products
I make most purchases with a lot of thought
Fatalism
I generally accept things that happen as fate
I don't think we have control over our destiny
If bad things are to happen, they will happen
I feel helpless in losing situations
I can achieve only what is in store for me
Nominalism
I am not sure what many rituals of my religion actually stand for
I sometimes follow practices without thinking much
I don't think I have tried to seek explanations of things that my parents tell me to follow
I am indifferent to most of the cultural practices I indulge in
With more time, I would try to learn about cultural aspects like weddings, etc.
Achievement Seeking
I am highly ambitious in my career
Being successful is the most important thing to me
I like finding solutions to challenging problems
I need to be acknowledged for my abilities by people around me
I keep seeking milestones even when I have conquered one
Respect for Age
I believe my parents know better than me
I always get up from my seat if I see an elderly person standing
It is very annoying to see old people being spoken to rudely
I believe that one can only get better with age as one gains experience
I feel comforted when there is someone older to take care of certain situations
Co-operation
I believe better work can be done by co-operating with peers
I sometimes feel that competing in things may lead to less work getting done
When there is a task to be done, I try to think of how well we can get together and do it
I enjoy donating things to charity
I like taking part in community service at work or in the neighbourhood
Nuclear Family
I think small family is a happy family
It's important for both parents to earn money as living costs rise up
I think both parents should share the work in the house
I do not think we have enough space to have both my parents and my children in the house
I have never lived in a joint family

Group Emphasis
I love to hang out with my friends
I'd rather go out for dinner with friends after work than go home alone
I do not like to go alone to have lunch in the office/college canteen
I am not dependent on one or two persons to make my weekend plans
I am in touch with my college/school group through regular meetings
Respect for Work
I think success comes through hard work alone
I believe that every field of work is equally appreciable
I always try to give 100 per cent to the task at hand
If my subordinates work hard, I never fail to compliment/reward them
I respect everyone who does his/her work well, even though their social status may not be the same
Seeking Prosperity
I want to have all the latest durables in my house
I want my children to have the best education
I think prosperity is related to social status
I would not mind swapping a job just for the salary hike
I want to earn enough for fulfilling all my adulthood desires
Hospitality
I always invite friends and relatives over for dinner
I love to have my relatives from other cities visiting me
It's great to have your colleagues come over for a chat
I am never put off by someone coming over without informing me
I love to have my children's friends dropping by even when my kids are not at home
Social Orientation
I am very particular about what I wear and whether it matches my personality
I like to think that what I own is unique to me in some ways
I try to develop an image based on the things I own
I think my lifestyle is an actual reflection of my personality
My friend circle and I have similar views towards life
Self Esteem
I seem to have a great deal of self respect
In almost every aspect, I am glad to be the person I am
I feel I have a number of good qualities
I take a positive attitude towards myself
I feel I am a person of worth, at least on an equal plane with others
Honour
I believe that the family name should be upheld
I believe in spending lavishly in accordance with my status in family functions
I would be exceedingly averse to borrowing money from people
My family prestige is of utmost importance to me
I'd rather give up durables than part with a family heirloom

Innovativeness
I like to experiment with my ideas
I would like a job that requires frequent changes from one kind of task to another
I like to try new and different things
I often try new brands before my friends and neighbours do
I am not afraid of failing with my creativity
Conspicuous westernized symbols
I Like to Party Regularly
I think social drinking is acceptable and at times necessary
I own several designer clothing items and accessories
I lead a hectic life where take-away food is a significant part of my routine
I feel it is a good thing to inculcate some western practices
Gifting Trends
Whenever I go to visit a friend or a relative, I carry a gift along
It's not the cost of the gift that matters to me, it's the thought
The more expensive the gifts are, the better people would think of my social standing
I take a lot of pains to choose the right thing for the right occasion
I feel honoured when people put an effort to buy gifts for me
Personal Grooming
I pay a lot of attention to how I look when I go out
I am conscious of my looks even when I am not going out for an occasion
I think first impression is very important and I need to appear well-groomed when meeting someone new
I occasionally indulge in a beauty salon or similar place to shape up my looks
I tend to make opinions about people who are shabbily attired or too casual in appearance
Family Hierarchy Orientation
It is the men in the family who purchase goods in my household
The main earner has an important say in selecting brands
The women of the house offer suggestions but the men make the decision
Even for toothpastes, soaps, hair oil, creams, etc., one person picks up brands for everyone
The youngsters in my house have become more independent in buying after they started earning
Ethnocentrism
I generally search for brands with Indian names or symbols
I don't think a foreign brand is necessarily better than an Indian brand
I feel an Indian brand is more suited to my needs
I buy regional or national brands due to a strong sense of loyalty
I feel we must buy more local products for helping Indian brands go global
Individualism
I prefer making most of my decisions myself
I generally buy or consume things which reflect my uniqueness
I like to be different from the crowd at times
I am not affected much by what other people do
It is important to me that people respect my individuality

Thriftiness
I am careful about the way I plan my finances
Price promotions in shops often attract me
I generally think low-priced goods can serve my needs well
I don't invest or spend money in ventures that I am uncertain about
I would like to save money for a rainy day
Celebrity Orientation
I would buy a product that is endorsed by a celebrity I like
I am attracted to advertisements that use celebrities
If a celebrity is endorsing a product, he or she must have tested the qualities
By using the brand of my favourite hero, I feel I am being like him
I change my brands based on my favourite sportsperson/film star's preference
Time Orientation (living in the past/present)
I often think about the good old days
I do not believe exciting days are coming ahead in my life
Life was much simpler and carefree during my parents' time
I wish I could have my old favourite brands back—they denoted quality
You cannot be sure about product quality any more these days
Emotional Decision Making
I often make my decisions from my heart
I feel it is healthy to express emotions
I don't like to always be rational
My opinions about people can be quite subjective
I am open about my feelings with my peers
Neo-mindset Orientation
I change habits and behaviour with time
I am often influenced by some of the new happenings around me
I cannot stick to the same old practices all my life
I don't mind breaking off from conventions
I could call myself rebellious to a certain extent

Source: S. Ramesh Kumar, Nitya Guruvayurappan and Madhurjya Banerjee, "Cultural Values and Branding in an Emerging Market—The Indian Context," *The Marketing Review*, 7 (2007), pp. 247–272, reproduced with the permission of the journal's editor.

EXHIBIT 2 Dominant Values Identification

Consumer Class: Middle		Consumer Class: Upper	
Category: Fairness Creams			
VALUES	**μ/σ***	**VALUES**	**μ/σ***
Power distance	7.199	Power distance	6.061
Uncertainty avoidance	5.901	Uncertainty avoidance	6.828
Forward-looking	6.734	Forward-looking	7.017
Conservatism	6.240	Conservatism	5.132
Need for affiliation	5.673	Need for affiliation	6.024
Family bonding	6.860	Family bonding	6.203
Utilitarianism	7.423	Utilitarianism	6.274
Fatalism	4.397	Fatalism	3.410
Nominalism	6.360	Nominalism	4.815
Achievement seeking	7.092	Achievement seeking	5.962
Respect for age	7.111	**Respect for Age**	**5.679**
Co-operation	**9.186**	Co-operation	7.217
Nuclear family	7.039	Nuclear family	6.952
Group emphasis	6.662	Group emphasis	6.623
Respect for work	8.250	Respect for work	8.574
Seeking prosperity	6.073	Seeking prosperity	6.638
Hospitality	5.837	Hospitality	6.676
Social orientation	5.516	Social orientation	6.821
Self Esteem	**8.288**	Self esteem	6.776
Honour	4.359	Honour	6.615
Innovativeness	7.020	**Innovativeness**	**7.241**
Conspicuous westernized symbols	4.236	Conspicuous westernized symbols	4.774
Gifting trends	7.645	**Gifting Trends**	**7.479**
Personal grooming	3.371	Personal grooming	4.640
Family hierarchy orientation	3.873	Family hierarchy orientation	4.851
Ethnocentrism	5.528	Ethnocentrism	5.962
Individualism	**8.700**	Individualism	6.010
Thriftiness	5.569	Thriftiness	6.676
Celebrity orientation	3.243	Celebrity orientation	2.391
Time orientation (living in the past/present)	5.012	Time orientation (living in the past/present)	4.573
Emotional decision making	6.181	Emotional decision making	4.165
Neo-mindset orientation	6.868	Neo-mindset orientation	7.201

Note: *μ/σ is the inverse of coefficient of variation where μ stands for the mean of the individual ratings and σ is the standard deviation.

Consumer Class: Middle		**Consumer Class: Upper**	
Category: Hair Oil			
VALUES	**μ/σ***	**VALUES**	**μ/σ***
Power distance	7.181	**Power Distance**	**7.331**
Uncertainty avoidance	6.916	Uncertainty avoidance	5.886
Forward-looking	6.930	Forward-looking	5.568
Conservatism	4.907	**Conservatism**	**7.301**
Need for affiliation	5.606	Need for affiliation	5.323
Family bonding	7.620	Family bonding	6.840
Utilitarianism	6.971	**Utilitarianism**	**8.029**
Fatalism	3.755	Fatalism	3.692
Nominalism	4.683	Nominalism	5.320
Achievement seeking	7.093	Achievement seeking	6.632
Respect for Age	**6.905**	Respect for age	5.994
Co-operation	7.968	Co-operation	6.384
Nuclear family	6.458	Nuclear family	5.976
Group emphasis	7.525	Group emphasis	4.645
Respect for work	9.359	Respect for work	6.417
Seeking prosperity	5.982	Seeking prosperity	5.675
Hospitality	6.170	Hospitality	4.869
Social orientation	6.101	Social orientation	4.847
Self Esteem	**9.148**	Self esteem	6.608
Honour	4.667	Honour	5.839
Innovativeness	7.463	Innovativeness	6.380
Conspicuous westernized symbols	4.371	Conspicuous westernized symbols	4.088
Gifting trends	7.524	Gifting trends	6.525
Personal grooming	4.287	Personal grooming	4.847
Family hierarchy orientation	4.045	Family hierarchy orientation	3.599
Ethnocentrism	4.662	Ethnocentrism	4.930
Individualism	**8.376**	Individualism	6.900
Thriftiness	5.581	Thriftiness	6.173
Celebrity orientation	3.218	Celebrity orientation	2.997
Time orientation (living in the past/present)	5.016	Time orientation (living in the past/present)	5.189
Emotional decision making	5.923	Emotional decision making	6.784
Neo-mindset orientation	6.403	Neo-mindset orientation	6.355

Note: *μ/σ is the inverse of coefficient of variation where μ stands for the mean of the individual ratings and σ is the standard deviation.

Note: The data can be interpreted as the values with the highest μ/σ are the most dominant in terms of having the highest mean while accounting for standard deviation as they are most clustered around the mean for the individual consumer responses. Higher score reflects higher intensity of the respective factor.

Source: S. Ramesh Kumar, Nitya Guruvayurappan and Madhurjya Banerjee, "Cultural Values and Branding in an Emerging Market—The Indian Context," The Marketing Review, 7 (2007), pp. 247-272, reproduced with the permission of the journal's editor. The authors thank Dr. Ann Foy, editor, Marketing Review for permitting the use of this data in the case study.

EXHIBIT 3 Communication of Fair & Lovely Brand

Fair & Lovely Sample Storyboard and Ad Interpretation

Storyboard 1: The ad starts in a household with an elderly couple where the husband asks for some more milk in his tea and the wife says there is not enough milk since it is just his pension that runs the household for three people. The husband comments that it would have been good to have a son, which his daughter overhears when walking in. She gets upset on hearing this and decides to do something to prove she can be as good as a son. She finds an advertisement in the newspaper for an airhostess job but is uncertain if she can get it owing to her dark skin. A Fair & Lovely ad plays on the TV and she realizes how it would help her achieve her dream. She walks into the interview confidently and does very well and gets the job. She shares her achievement by taking her parents out to eat, and they are proud of her success.

Storyboard 2: The ad shows snatches from a young girl's life where on every occasion she is seen acting as a commentator to a cricket game—sometimes to a game in her locality, sometimes to a match on TV—with a make-believe microphone in her hand. One day a friend of hers takes the microphone from her and gives her a tube of F&L instead. Consequently, the girl applies and is hired to perform commentary in a live cricket match, along with a famous Indian cricket commentator. Her co-commentator is awed by her presence and confidence and she is surrounded by a barrage of fans seeking her autograph after the game.

Authors' Interpretation: F&L has used the running theme of how fairness leads to self-confidence and success in most of their ads. It builds on the Indian mentality (typical to lower and middle classes) that fair skin gets you noticed and hence helps you go a long way in life. The central character is shown as a young woman in her twenties who is ambitious but does not pursue her dreams because she is kept back by her self-consciousness about her looks. She aspires to be in areas that are either dominated by men or which require her to be attractive and confident with a remarkable personality. Sometimes she also bears the brunt of criticism or humiliation from those around her—either family members or people in society who attach a lot of importance to appearance. As a consequence, it impacts her self-esteem and she is motivated into changing her life and proving a point to those people. She is introduced to F&L by a friend or relative or from some other source of information and her life changes—she achieves her dream and is treated with respect and awe by the very same people who earlier would have ignored her. The inferred benefit here is the confidence to achieve your dreams, because looking good leads to feeling good. F&L uses an approach of creating discomfort and negative emotion in order to magnify the victory and positive emotions as an outcome of using the product even more.

Source: Advertisement reproduced with the permission of Mohit Sud, Brand Manager–Skin Care, Hindustan Unliver Limited, India. The authors analyzed the advertisement for the brand based on their perception of the advertisements as consumers associated with the Indian context.

Storyboard 1: www.youtube.com/watch?v=2a1iXt1yPsk, accessed October 10, 2010.

Storyboard 2: www.youtube.com/watch?v=zRt8E8sfiSw, accessed October 10, 2010.

EXHIBIT 4 Communication of Fairever Brand

Fairever Sample Storyboard and Ad Interpretation

Storyboard 1: The ad shows a group of school girls on a bus going through a village. When the bus halts for a while, one of the girls sees a woman in labour riding on a bullock cart. She runs to help and offer her some water, and asks the man with her why they cannot take her to the nearest hospital soon. The man remarks that the nearest hospital is very far since they do not have one in the village. The girl goes back and sees a bookmark of Fairever packaging which says 'You can change your future.' She decides to study to become a doctor, despite facing opposition from her family who are unable to understand why she is wasting an expensive degree in the U.S. on a small village where she might not even make money; however, she is determined to do what she feels is right and goes to serve the village which was lacking in medical facilities, making her family proud and making herself loved by the villagers. The ad places emphasis on Fairever giving her the confidence to write her own destiny.

Storyboard 2: The ad shows a little girl exclaiming, "They've come," and shows that it is a house with festoons and decorations. A family comes with a beautiful girl (celebrity) and are invited in. It becomes evident that this is a ceremony where the girl meets a boy in an arranged marriage scenario, but the roles are reversed. Not only does the girl come to see the boy, but also the boy serves the families with tea and snacks, and performs music and dance in front of them. The voiceover (VO) says that when Fairever is making women so beautiful, shouldn't it be the men who have to do all this to win their heart. It ends with the girl saying that she likes the boy and the VO says "changing the colors of life."

Authors' Interpretation: Fairever's key benefit was to encourage young women with the thought that they can write their future. It suggested that Fairever gave women the confidence to write their destinies and become successful. In the above ad, Fairever touches on women's confidence and determination to do things without dwelling on the negative elements and stigma associated with being dark complexioned, unlike its competitor. The ad works on an overall positive approach like the first storyboard rather than showing a negative emotion and then overcoming the same. It also uses creative situations to indicate how powerful beauty and confidence can make a woman, as in the second storyboard. Certain campaign ads also took a dig at competition by declaring that the woman was equally powerful and supported the family, and one did not have to be a son to be the breadwinner. This was explicitly targeted at a competitor's campaigns to make women look empowered after they are shown as the weaker sex initially. Gradually, Fairever is using more celebrities and is also placing emphasis on product claims like "four tones lighter in four weeks" and "three times more protection from the sun." It also talks about product features like milk proteins and saffron white essences in the communication to enhance credibility of the claim. Fairever also uses the whiteness meter in its communication in order to establish that it is an equally effective product, given that it competes with a goliath market leader and hence first needs to establish that the functional benefit that leads up to the emotional benefits is actually strong in its product offering.

Source: The authors analyzed the advertisements for the brand based on their perception of the advertisements as consumers associated with the Indian context.
Storyboard 1: www.youtube.com/watch?v=_KljS8_6ofI, accessed October 10, 2010.
Storyboard 2: www.youtube.com/watch?v=vhp3KSOry5c, accessed October 10, 2010.

EXHIBIT 5 Communication of Parachute Brand

Parachute Sample Storyboard and Ad Interpretation

Storyboard 1: Three young women are out on a picnic and see a waterfall at a distance; one of the women says she is looking forward to taking a shower and shampooing her hair. One of the friends (a popular celebrity) says that first they need to oil their hair and leave it on for an hour, and takes out a Parachute bottle. On being asked why, she explains that hair tends to become dry and rough on shampoo alone and hence it is necessary to moisturize and nourish hair with oil prior to that. The ad closes with the "gorgeous hamesha" tagline and theme music, which is part of the campaign that Parachute women are always gorgeous and do not need to be made up in order to look beautiful.

Storyboard 2: The ad shows a celebrity experimenting with her hairstyle on different occasions. In the first, she has wavy hair, in the second situation it is her birthday and she has straight hair. On the third occasion, she colors her hair in streaks. She visits the hairstylist again and sits in the chair saying, "What shall we try new today?" To this, the hairstylist replies that the first thing they ought to do is an hour's soaking and massage of hot Parachute coconut oil. She explains that when you experiment with your hair and try new things, it tends to lack the nurture and care and becomes dry and lifeless. In order to rejuvenate her hair, she needs the good old coconut oil treatment. The celebrity gets the same done and is ready to try a new hairstyle all over again.

Authors' Interpretation: Parachute has moved out of the many years of mother-daughter related advertising to now appeal more to the youth, especially given that there are so many category substitutes like leave-on conditioners penetrating the youth market. The Parachute campaign is targeted at young women and seeks to assure them that real beauty does not have to dress up and the Parachute women are "gorgeous hamesha" (always gorgeous). The campaign has both functional and emotional elements, with the emotional campaign being the one in which it has captured beautiful women in different moods and settings and generated awareness for this campaign and tagline. It has subsequently leveraged this in its functional ads like the storyboard mentioned above to drive the benefit of nourishment and keeping hair from going dry. For this, it has built on the accepted consumer belief that a lot of its target audience practices the usage experience of a massage and one-hour leave-on of oil prior to shampoo. Parachute has used celebrities in their campaigns to depict the beauty concept while driving the functional need of oiling as their hair is often subjected to a lot of rough handling in their profession. The second ad is an example of the same. It also captures how Parachute as a brand sits on the border of innovation and tradition, as is true of the women it targets: although they want to try out new things and experiment with their hair and styles, coconut oil will still remain a part of their hair care and hence they are driving the concept of a hot oil massage before a shampoo.

Source: Advertisement reproduced with the permission of Sonal Krishen, HR Manager, Marico India.The authors analyzed the advertisements for the brand based on their perception of the advertisements as consumers associated with the Indian context.

Storyboard 1: www.youtube.com/watch?v=qGPLSvS23KI&feature=related, accessed October 10, 2010.
Storyboard 2: www.youtube.com/watch?v=w7I2cgOWmDs, accessed October 10, 2010.

EXHIBIT 6 Communication of Dabur Amla Brand

Dabur Amla Sample Storyboard and Ad Interpretation

Storyboard 1: The ad starts with the central character (a celebrity) walking past, waving her silky hair and the VO says "hair is meant to be shown off." The central character is then shown at a celebration where she urges her friend to come and join her on the dance floor. The friend refuses, due to awkwardness about her oily hair. The VO then says "hair is not meant to be hidden." The ad then goes on to say how other oils make hair sticky while Dabur Amla nourishes and makes hair stronger and shinier. The VO concludes with saying that "hair is meant to win hearts."

Storyboard 2: The celebrity (central character) sees a young girl trying to collect money for a charitable cause but no one on the streets seems to be paying her any attention. The celebrity immediately collects a group of young women and they put on a street dance to attract the crowd. They look attractive and happy as they dance uninhibited and letting their hair loose. The VO says that Dabur Amla adds zest to hair and hence fun to your life.

Authors' Interpretation: Dabur Amla has been using celebrities in their campaigns for both hair oil and shampoo. The central character, usually the celebrity, is shown as attractive, confident, willing to take on challenges and comfortable in her personality. The setting is usually one in which a situation requires two women, the protagonist and another character, to let their hair loose and enjoy, wherein the non-user is reluctant because her hair isn't attractive enough. The benefit communication explains the merits of *amla* in the hair oil and how it nourishes and strengthens hair, leaving it shiny and soft. It focuses on how women's crowning glory is their hair and hence insists that they shouldn't settle for anything less when it comes to taking care of their hair. Dabur has taken on competition explicitly with their other line extensions like Vatika, wherein they do comparative advertising in which they show packaging that looks identical to the immediate competition without naming them explicitly—like Parachute or Bajaj (almond category)—and compare superiority of their own brand versus those competitors. Amla on the other hand finds them as the market leaders by a significant margin and hence their communication is limited and targeted mainly at the middle-tier market.

Source: The authors analyzed the advertisements for the brand based on their perception of the advertisements as consumers associated with the Indian context.
Storyboard 1: www.youtube.com/watch?v=qyO6A4weVTk&feature=related, accessed on October 10, 2010.
Storyboard 2: www.youtube.com/watch?v=9apExNucf2M&feature=related, accessed on October 10, 2010.

EXHIBIT 7 Methodology Used for Data Collection

1. Two categories close to the Indian consumer and the prevalent cultural context—hair oil and facial creams—were selected in order to understand the effects/implications of cultural values on branding.
2. An industry analysis was performed and a perceptual map of available brands was developed in order to understand the parameters for brand differences and subsequent classification of those for the categories identified. This helped in understanding how different social class segments perceive the various brands and hence which are more likely to be consumed in specific segments.
3. A list of 32 core Indian values were generated based on literature, consumer reports and the authors' subjective judgment based on their experience in the Indian context as consumers. A measurement scale was composed for each of these values such that each value has five points of measurement in its scale and five levels from "strongly agree" to "strongly disagree." Respondents were expected to express their agreement or disagreement with the items in the scale for each value. Stratified sampling of the target population was performed—with appropriate representation obtained from each social class—and the above questionnaire (after randomization of the statements) was sent to them. Upper and middle socio-economic classes were covered for the categories chosen. Sixty-four respondents from each of the strata were selected for each of the categories. This would equal a total of 384 respondents (in two strata for each of three categories).
4. Coefficient of variation was used as the metric for dominant value identification to minimize variation and find the values in which the ratings congregate closer to the mean value.
5. Analysis of advertisements and communication of prominent brands in each category and for each social class was performed. Gaps in the values between those dominant in Step 4 and the ones reflected in the perception of advertisements (as perceived by the authors of this case) for each social class and the respective category were identified. The final recommendation was based on bridging this gap with the dominant cultural value in each class.

8

Kraft Foods: The Coffee Pod Launch (A)

Aleem Visram prepared this case under the supervision of Professor Robin Ritchie solely to provide material for class discussion. The authors do not intend to illustrate either effective or ineffective handling of a managerial situation. The authors may have disguised certain names and other identifying information to protect confidentiality.

INTRODUCTION

Geoff Herzog, product manager for coffee development at Kraft Foods Canada (Kraft), sat in his office after reviewing encouraging results for the single-serve coffee pod system in Europe. On a typical day, Herzog would have used the office coffee station for his morning cup of coffee, but today he had brewed his own cup using a single-serve coffee pod machine. It was July 6, 2004, and Herzog had just learned that Kraft Foods North America was planning an aggressive launch of coffee pods in the United States. He had less than a month to decide whether Kraft should proceed with a simultaneous launch in Canada, or await the U.S. results.

If Herzog went ahead with the launch, he would have to make several decisions. First, since Kraft owned two major coffee brands in Canada, Maxwell House and Nabob, a suitable branding strategy would be needed. Herzog would also have to set a wholesale and a suggested retail price for the coffee pods, choose which flavors to offer and decide whether Kraft should use traditional distribution channels or direct-to-store delivery (DSD). In addition, he would have to develop an effective advertising and promotion strategy on a relatively limited budget. Herzog knew that whatever recommendations he made, he would need to make a convincing case that his plan would help Kraft expand its share of the Canadian coffee market, while generating a satisfactory return on the company's marketing investment.

KRAFT FOODS INC.

Founded as a cheese manufacturer in 1903, Kraft Foods Inc. (Kraft Foods) had evolved into North America's largest food and beverage company and the number two player in the world. In 2004, Kraft Foods had operations in more than 155 countries. Although the company had previously been a division of Philip Morris Companies (since renamed Altria Group), it had become a public company in June 2001.

Kraft operations consisted of Kraft Foods North America and Kraft Foods International, and its business was divided into five product categories: beverages, convenience meals, cheese, grocery and snacks. The Kraft brand portfolio was among the strongest of the global consumer packaged goods players, with more than 50 $100-million brands and five $1-billion brands. Along with its size and impressive brand portfolio, Kraft Foods boasted a strong distribution network and a well-earned reputation for developing innovative new products and food applications. The company's mission was to achieve leadership in the markets it served, which it pursued by fostering innovation, achieving high product quality and keeping a close eye on profit margins. Five operational objectives had been established to achieve these goals:

1. Build superior brand value for consumers by delivering greater product benefits at the right price, compared to the competition.
2. Enhance product demand among consumers by building relationships with trade partners.
3. Constantly adjust the product portfolio to align with consumer trends, especially in fast-growing channels and demographic groups.
4. Expand global scale by increasing business internationally, especially in the world's fastest-growing developing countries.
5. Build a leaner cost structure through better use of assets to generate savings for reinvestment in brand building.

Kraft Foods was the world leader in coffee sales with 15 per cent of the global market. In Canada, Kraft's Maxwell House and Nabob brands enjoyed a combined 32 per cent share, followed by Nestlé at 17 per cent and Procter and Gamble with nine per cent. Private labels accounted for nearly 23 per cent of the market, with smaller companies making up the remaining 19 per cent.

The company's Maxwell House line was Canada's top retail brand of roast and ground coffee, while Nabob was the leader in Western Canada and number two nationally. Both were available in a variety of flavors, sizes and formats (see Exhibit 1). All beans used by Kraft were custom-roasted to deliver peak aroma, and had a fine grind to ensure a fresh, rich flavor.

SINGLE-SERVE COFFEE PODS

The single-serve coffee pod (SSP) machine was the first major innovation to hit the coffee-brewing industry since the introduction of the drip coffee maker in the 1950s. First conceived of in 1978 by Italy's Illy Caffé, which targeted it to office users, the pod had been redesigned for consumer use by Kraft Foods, which introduced its home version in Switzerland in 1982. By 2003, Kraft Foods marketed consumer coffee pods in 10 European countries. Kraft Foods' most serious competitor in Europe was Senseo, a partnership between Dutch electronics and appliance maker Philips and the Douwe Egberts division of U.S.-based Sara Lee Corporation, the world's second largest coffee roaster. Senseo had been launched in 2001, and some five million coffee makers and three billion pods were sold in the first three years.

By 2003, single-serve coffee pod units accounted for nearly 15 per cent of all coffee makers sold in Europe, and 5.8 per cent of coffee sales by value. By 2008, annual European sales were forecast to exceed both 82 million coffee pod machines and $150 million worth of coffee pods. By 2010, it was expected that SSP machines would account for 10 per cent of the European home coffee brewer market. Significantly, as much as 30 per cent of total coffee pod sales were expected to be incremental volume, drawn from individuals who would normally have bought their coffee out-of-home, or not consumed coffee at all.

The Technology

Similar to machines used by coffee houses to make specialty coffee, SSP machines used pre-packaged single servings to make high-quality coffee in less than a minute. Instead of percolating water through the ground coffee via gravity like conventional coffee makers, SSP machines forced hot water through the coffee pod at high pressure. The pods were similar to teabags in that the ground coffee was encapsulated in perforated paper, but, unlike tea, the coffee was packed tightly to ensure sufficient flavor. Each pod measured 59 to 62 millimetres in diameter, and contained between seven and 10 grams of ground coffee (see Exhibit 2).

Two types of SSP machines were available. So-called "open" systems used a standard-sized coffee pod that could be used interchangeably with pods from different manufacturers. Conversely, "closed" systems could only use a specific pod shape and size, and only accepted coffee pods compatible with these systems. In either case, the coffee produced was of similar quality to that available at cafés.

Although the cost per cup with SSP machines ($0.20 to $0.50 per cup) was higher than with traditional drip coffee machines ($0.05 to $0.15 per cup), SSP systems provided several advantages. First, an SSP machine took less than a minute to make a cup of coffee, compared to nearly 10 minutes from a traditional brewing machine. As well, SSP machines were easier to use than the drip machines since there was no need to measure the ground coffee or use a filter. They were also easier to clean, with no messy ground coffee left over to toss, no leftover coffee to pour down the sink and no pot to clean—users simply disposed of the coffee pod in a garbage or compost bin.

The pod system was most advantageous when a person wanted to make coffee in small batches, or cater to several different tastes at the same time. For instance, if one person wanted a decaffeinated coffee after dinner, a single cup could be prepared without having to make an entire pot. Similarly, if family members each liked a different kind of coffee, separate coffees could be brewed simply by using a different flavor pod for each cup. Bill VandenBygaart, director of coffee development for Kraft Canada, was confident about the value of the system to consumers: "We believe Canadians will see real value in the convenience, choice and quality that single-serve pod machines provide."

THE CANADIAN COFFEE MARKET

Because grocery stores carried a growing selection of coffee brands, flavors and formats, competition in the Canadian coffee market was intense. The past decade had also seen specialty retailers, such as Starbucks and Tim Hortons, enter the market in a serious way, selling their brands of ground coffee and coffee beans in grocery outlets as well as in their own stores. Brewed coffee from these restaurants and cafés was further cannibalizing grocery sales, with consumers willing to pay a substantial premium for the convenience, customization and variety they offered.

Retail sales of instant, ground and whole bean coffee in Canada topped $600 million in 2003, of which $425 million was sold by grocery, mass retail, and club stores. Sales of specialty coffees—a category that included espresso and cappuccino, flavored coffees and iced coffees—had dropped 12 per cent in dollar terms and 11 per cent by volume. Sales of instant coffee had increased two per cent by volume, but declined by two per cent in dollar terms, due to lower retail prices. This reflected the higher quality and availability of specialty coffee from coffee shops and cafes.

The home-prepared coffee category in Canada was also becoming increasingly polarized between premium and mainstream brands. The popularity of large-size containers of discount coffee had led to price wars between manufacturers of these brands in most mainstream retail channels, eroding margins and decreasing profitability. Conversely, at about 15 to 20 per cent of total sales volume, higher priced premium coffee was a much smaller business that was enjoying double-digit sales growth. Herzog believed there was an opportunity for higher-end products to capture an even larger portion of the category over time, with higher price points and greater profitability.

Coffee Consumption Behavior

Canadians were among the world's leading drinkers of coffee, consuming some 3.5 million cups of coffee daily in 2003—a number that had risen by an average of 4.5 per cent over each of the previous five years. After water, coffee was easily the most popular daily beverage of Canadian adults (see Exhibit 3), with an average consumption of 2.6 cups per day among coffee drinkers. Roughly 63 per cent of Canadians drank at least one cup daily, while 83 per cent enjoyed coffee at least occasionally. Half of all Canadians drank at least some specialty coffee (espresso, cappuccino or flavored coffee); these individuals tended to be younger than the average coffee drinker, with higher education and higher incomes. The percentage of regular coffee drinkers varied considerably across the country, from a high of 70 per cent in Quebec, to 67 per cent in the Prairies and the West, 60 per cent in Ontario and 53 per cent in the Atlantic region.

By volume, more than two-thirds of the coffee consumed in Canada was prepared at home. Four out of five Canadian households made at least one store trip to buy coffee: These coffee-buying households averaged seven such trips per year, bought 0.7 kilograms of coffee on each trip, and spent $9 per kilogram. Coffee sales were greatest among middle- to upper-income Canadians, particularly 25 to 40 year-olds and middle-aged childless couples, who purchased more than 10 kilograms of coffee per year at an average price of $7 per kilogram. Nearly 38 per cent of all coffee in Canada was purchased in bulk or on promotion.

COMPETITIVE LANDSCAPE

Based on the major brands available in Europe and the United States, Herzog had identified four likely SSP competitors for Kraft in Canada:

One-to-One

Germany's Melitta Group had joined with Salton, makers of the George Foreman Grill, to create the Melitta One-to-One SSP machine. The system was capable of brewing coffee in two sizes using a specially filtered system designed to deliver coffee-bar quality at home. The spout of the coffee machine could also be changed to make hot or iced tea. One-to-One machines were already available across Canada, and came with a six-flavor javapod sampler.

Melitta was the only SSP system to use 9.7 gram javapods, rather than the seven gram coffee pod sizes used by Home Café, Senseo and Bunn. As a result, while other coffee pods were all interchangeable across manufacturers, they could not be used in the Melitta One-to-One (and vice versa). Rumors were rampant, however, that Melitta was planning to switch to standard-sized coffee pods. Melitta javapods were sealed in oxygen-free foil packs to preserve flavor, and retailed for $4.99 for a package of 16 (see Exhibit 4). Three different varieties were available: 100% Arabica Medium Roast, 100% Colombian, and Light Roast. Pods were available from the same retailers where the Melitta One-to-One System was sold: Zellers, the Bay, Home Outfitters and Canadian Tire.

Home Café

The Home Café system was the result of a partnership between Procter and Gamble, and two leading makers of small appliances: Applica Inc. (owner of Black & Decker), and Jardine Corporation (owner of Mr. Coffee, Rival and Sunbeam). Home Café used a specialized pressure-brewing technology to deliver single servings of fresh coffee in less than a minute while bringing out the full flavor of the coffee bean. The machine could brew three different cup sizes, and featured a removable cup platform to prevent spilling as well as an easy-clean removable drip tray. The water reservoir was also removable and could be rotated for fast and accurate filling. In the United States, Home Café machines came with a free bag of Folgers coffee pods. It was widely expected that the system would be introduced to Canada in September 2004 through Wal-Mart.

Reliable sources had told Herzog that Home Café would launch with four different flavors of coffee pods under Procter and Gamble's Folgers brand: Classic Roast, Classic Decaf, 100% Colombian and French Vanilla. The pods were expected to be available in packages of 16 and retail for $4.99 (see Exhibit 4).

Senseo

Senseo was a partnership between Philips Electronics and Sara Lee Corporation, the world's second largest coffee roaster. The Senseo machine used balanced portions of coffee and water, mild pressure and a special spray head to produce an optimally balanced filtering process and a rich froth on top of each cup. The quick and easy one-touch system brewed a cup of coffee in 30 seconds, with auto shut-off after one hour. The machine was available in four colors and had dishwasher-safe removable parts for easy cleaning. As an added incentive, customers who registered their Senseo machine were sent a free bag of coffee pods and $2 off their next pod purchase. Senseo was expected to launch in Canada in early 2005.

Senseo coffee pods were marketed using Sara Lee's Douwe Egberts brand, using the slogan "one taste and you will know the extraordinary difference." They used premium-quality beans that had been carefully roasted and blended, and offered four flavors, including mild, medium, dark and decaffeinated roast. Senseo pods came in packages of 18 for a retail price of $4.99 (see Exhibit 4).

Bunn My Café

Bunn Home Brewers had announced plans to launch the My Café single-serve pod machine in Canada in November 2004. My Café claimed to offer great-tasting coffee quickly, simply and consistently. The system worked with a large array of pods and teabags, featured a removable easy-fill reservoir and patented spray head design for maximum flavor extraction, and could brew a cup of coffee in 30 seconds. The brew control had nine settings to alter coffee strength, and was made with dishwasher-safe parts. Bunn did not plan to manufacture its own coffee pods (see Exhibit 4).

MARKETING STRATEGY

With an annual budget of only $1 million for a potential launch, Herzog faced tight constraints on his ability to introduce Kraft coffee pods in Canada. If he proceeded with the launch, he would need to identify a cost-effective way to convince consumers that Kraft's pods delivered better value than competitors' pods. The goal was for 80 per cent of SSP machine owners to try the product, and for 60 per cent of those individuals to repeat purchase. Herzog was expected to at least break even by the end of 2006.

Target Market

Although SSP machines had only recently been introduced to Canada, Herzog had access to market research on current Canadian coffee pod users. These individuals were typically coffee lovers between the ages of 25 and 54, tended to be well educated and had an average household income of $91,000 (the Canadian average household income was $55,000). Nearly three-quarters were married, and 88 per cent lived in single-detached homes in urban areas, primarily in the population-rich provinces of Ontario, Quebec, British Columbia and Alberta. They were characterized by high levels of consumption, and their interests included exercising, entertaining at home, gourmet cooking, household decorating, gardening and taking exotic vacations.

Maxwell House and Nabob buyers had similar profiles to SSP machine owners, except that they were typically over the age of 45. They also tended to be a mix of maturing, established families and single professionals.

Buyer Behavior

Although most SSP machines used standard-sized coffee pods, experience in Europe had shown that consumers usually purchased pods of the same brand as the machine they bought (i.e. Folgers pods with Home Café machines, Senseo pods with Senseo machines, and Javapods with Melitta One-to-One machines). At the same time, focus group research suggested that SSP machine owners valued the flexibility of using different coffee brands in their brewers. Coffee quality was also critical, since it defined the entire coffee experience. Coffee drinkers were looking for a fresh, hot cup of coffee with peak flavor and aroma.

Market Share

Kraft expected that, of the roughly 12.5 million households in Canada, SSP machines would be adopted by six per cent by the end of 2004, and eight per cent by the end of 2006. Average household consumption of coffee pods among SSP machine owners varied from seven to 14 pods per week. To maintain Maxwell House and Nabob's share of the Canadian coffee market, Herzog estimated that Kraft would need to capture at least 35 per cent of the coffee pod segment. His actual goal was to obtain a 45 per cent market share by the end of 2006. Herzog knew this would require significant advertising and promotion to generate the necessary awareness and sales. He was uncertain whether he would be able to achieve his target and still break even.

Product

If he went ahead with the launch, Herzog would also need to decide on a flavor selection for Maxwell House and/or Nabob coffee pods. He felt that a variety of pod offerings would be critical for building market share and category growth. Kraft's manufacturing facility also had the ability to offer the product in a re-sealable bag with zip closure, which would help keep the product fresh.

Price

In the United States, Kraft planned to sell pods under the Maxwell House label at a lower price point than rival brands, retailing a pack of 18 pods for US$3.99. In contrast, Folgers charged US$3.99 for a pack of 16. This pricing would give retailers a 25 per cent margin on Maxwell House and, at $0.22 per cup, revenue that was more than four times the $0.05 per cup from canned ground coffee

Herzog was not sure whether to follow the U.S. lead on pricing. On one hand, a low price would serve to drive sales volume and establish Kraft as a market leader, but this strategy risked eroding brand image. Another consideration was the highly concentrated nature of the Canadian grocery sector and the relative power of retailers. Given the failure rate of new products, Herzog suspected that stores would only be willing to carry one or two brands of coffee pods. Canadian grocers typically enjoyed margins of 20 to 30 per cent, but Herzog believed margins of 35 per cent would be needed as an incentive to list Kraft's coffee pods. With an average production cost of $0.02 per pod, he was unsure of the best wholesale and retail selling price to recommend.

Distribution

Most of Kraft's products were delivered to retailers via warehouse distribution. Under this system, Kraft was responsible for delivering all merchandise to the customers' warehouses. From these warehouses, retailers then distributed the goods to individual stores. Retailers were responsible for stocking products, refilling shelf space, maintaining inventories and maintaining displays—services for which Kraft paid in excess of $200,000 for national listing fees. Such a system eliminated the need for Kraft to constantly monitor and track inventories, distribution and stock.

The alternative was to use direct-to-store-delivery (DSD). Under this system, Kraft would be responsible for delivering merchandise to individual stores, holding inventories and restocking shelves. This method was currently used by Kraft for its Mr. Christie cookie products. A joint DSD program with Mr. Christie would enable Kraft to lower the overall cost for coffee pod distribution to approximately $150,000 by reducing supply chain expenses and minimizing inventory holding costs. DSD would also allow Kraft to control product displays, ensure superior product freshness, improve customer service, collect insights from retailers and sidestep warehouse capacity restraints. Finally, since 40 per cent of all coffee makers were sold in November and December, DSD would also provide Kraft with speed to market during this period.

Despite these advantages, Herzog was not convinced that DSD made sense. There was a reasonable probability that Kraft would not be able to maintain a DSD approach if the coffee pod sales increased significantly in the future, as the company had both limited space in its distribution centre and a limited delivery truck fleet. Furthermore, with numerous retailers and thousands of stores spread across the country, he wondered whether Kraft had sufficient resources to adequately restock product shelves, update product displays and maintain inventory on a store-level basis. He also wondered how retailers would perceive the DSD system, instead of their preferred warehousing distribution system.

ADVERTISING AND PROMOTION

Herzog expected the makers of rival SSP machines to engage in heavy advertising and promotion to generate consumer awareness of SSP technology and to educate them on the benefits. If Kraft entered the segment, it would need to be serious about building awareness and trial of Maxwell House and/or Nabob coffee pods. Herzog needed to select the promotional vehicles that would generate the greatest number of loyal customers. He had identified several possibilities:

Print Advertising

Print offered a broad range of options. After meeting with his advertising agency, Herzog narrowed the choice to magazines in six categories: women's interest, decorating, gardening, food, travel, and regional and city magazines. Based on magazine features, readership, customer profiles and costs, Herzog would need to identify a specific set of publications for advertising inserts. He also had to determine the number of advertisement inserts for each magazine (see Exhibit 5).

TV Sponsorship

Kraft's ad agency had also recommended a television sponsorship program in Toronto, Vancouver and the province of Quebec to build awareness.

The Toronto and Vancouver initiatives would be conducted in partnership with CityTV, and would include coverage on popular local programs, such as Breakfast Television, CityLine, CityPulse News and CityOnline. Kraft's coffee pod logo would also appear on all-news channel CablePulse24 and the CityTV website.

The cornerstone of the Toronto/Vancouver TV sponsorship program was contests and giveaways. CityTV would air a 30-second promotional spot encouraging viewers to qualify for giveaways by watching CityPulse. During the telecast, viewers would be asked to e-mail the answer to a contest question, and CityTV would select one winner each night. To generate additional interest, CityTV would also offer smaller draw prizes via its website, and offer random product giveaways during its other programming. Total cost of the Toronto and Vancouver sponsorship programs was $52,300, for a total reach of more than 364,000 viewers (see Exhibit 6).

The TV sponsorship plan for Quebec consisted of a low-key effort to generate awareness and educate viewers about the product. Coffee pods would be featured on two French-language programs on the TQS network: Caféine (a morning talk/variety show), and La Roue Chanceuse (a French-language version of "Wheel of Fortune"). In exchange, Kraft would agree to provide coffee pod gift baskets and coffee pod machines, which the hosts of these shows would give away to viewers.

Consumer Shows

A third option was to introduce the product at high-traffic home and garden shows across the country. This promotion would entail an elaborate exhibit, featuring hands-on, shopping channel-style demonstrations, taste tests and a projection screen TV (see Exhibit 7). The message would emphasize the café quality of Maxwell House and/or Nabob coffee pods, and the variety of flavor choices. Bunn My Café had contacted Kraft and suggested splitting the cost through a jointly operated booth. Regardless of whether he accepted this partnership, Herzog had the option of selecting a 10 × 30 foot booth for $485,200 or a 10 × 20 foot booth for $361,450. In addition, he would need to decide which trade shows would provide the most value and highest reach to the prospective target market. If Kraft attended all the fall and spring trade shows, they would be able to reach more than 1.4 million attendees for a total cost of $147,377 (see Exhibit 8).

Direct Marketing

Herzog could also target existing Kraft customers through a direct mail campaign. Kraft had a database of more than one million subscribers, who voluntarily subscribed to receive its quarterly *What's Cooking* magazine. Herzog estimated that the cost of a direct mail insert, profiling the coffee pod product, would be $50,000.

An alternative was to target Kraft customers through an e-mail campaign. Customers that fit the profile of single-serve coffee machine purchasers could be sent an e-mail inviting them to visit a website and register to win a free year's supply of coffee pods. When customers visited the website, they would be given information about the SSP machines and the benefits of Maxwell House and/or Nabob coffee pods. Total cost for the website, e-mail campaign and giveaway was estimated at $30,000.

Merchandising

Finally, Herzog was contemplating a variety of in-store merchandising. Kraft had previous experience with three different kinds of display systems. Off-shelf display bins could hold 24 packs of coffee pods and consisted of a stand, a colorful reader card to attract attention, and space for coupons. Herzog felt that a "buy one, get one free" coupon would provide sufficient incentive for SSP machine owners to try Kraft's coffee pods. Another possibility was on-shelf racks, which would ensure that the product would always be neatly and tidily presented. These racks were capable of holding specific point-of-sale merchandise to ensure customer visibility, and would be held down using magnets so that they could be easily moved. An additional option was to use metal shelf strips, which held a coupon attachment and up to 12 bags of coffee pods, and could attach easily to any retail shelf. The display bins, on-shelf racks and shelf-strips would cost a total of $70,000 and the coupons $13,800 (see Exhibit 9). Together, these in-store displays and coupon offerings were forecast to increase product trial by an additional 250 per cent.

CONCLUSION

With the high growth potential of the single-serve coffee machines in Canada, pressure to go ahead with the launch was high. By launching immediately, Kraft would also have a better opportunity to defend against Procter and Gamble, whose Folgers brand was linked to the Home Café SSP system. If Folgers gained a dominant position in the coffee pod market, there was a reasonable chance that its success could also spill over into the standard roast and ground coffee business.

Conversely, there was a chance that coffee pods would not be well received in North America; by waiting for the results of the U.S. launch, Herzog could minimize risk. Waiting would also enable Kraft to determine which customers were buying the SSP machines, enabling them to target marketing efforts more effectively.

In any case, if Herzog decided to launch the Maxwell House and Nabob Coffee Pods, he would need to create a marketing plan that could break even by the end of 2006. With that firmly in mind, Herzog took a final sip of his coffee and went to work.

EXHIBIT 1 Maxwell House and Nabob Product Lines

	Brand Positioning	Current Products
Maxwell House	Maxwell House is "good to the last drop" • Canada's number one brand and favorite mainstream coffee • Roasted to deliver peak flavor and aroma	326g tin SKUs: • Original Roast • Mellow Roast • Rich Dark Roast • Decaffeinated • Half Caffeine
Nabob	Nabob delivers a better cup of coffee, every time • Canada's leading premium coffee • 100 per cent Arabica Colombian beans, carefully chosen by Nabob for taste and quality • Custom roasted by Nabob to ensure perfect flavor and aroma	350g "Nabob Tradition" SKUs: • Caffeinated—Regular Grind • Caffeinated—Fine Grind 326g "Nabob Tradition" SKUs: • Decaffeinated—Regular Grind • Decaffeinated—Fine Grind 326g "Nabob Blend" SKUs: • Full City Dark • Summit 100% Colombian • Summit Decaffeinated • Milano Espresso • Golden Java Sumatra • Carnival Brazil 1kg "Nabob Tradition" SKU: • Caffeinated— Regular Grind

Source: Company files.

EXHIBIT 2 Operation of the Single-serve Pod System

Single-serve pod systems use pre-heated water and high pressure to quickly extract the coffee from pre-ground coffee pods in less than a minute.

Step 1

First the water reservoir in the back is filled. The water is pre-heated so that it is dispensed hot without waiting. Most reservoirs hold between eight and 10 cups of water before needing to be refilled.

Step 2

The coffee pod is then inserted into the machine and the desired size selected. Most brewers give consumers the choice of more than one size of cup. Two pods can be inserted for a stronger coffee.

Step 3

The machine then brews the coffee directly into your cup in less than a minute. Coffee pods can be used only once per coffee serving to ensure optimal taste and freshness are maintained.

Step 4

Once the brewing is finished, the pod is thrown out and another inserted. There is no flavor transfer between pods during usage.

Source: Company files.

EXHIBIT 3 Canadian Coffee Consumption Data

Types of Beverage Consumed

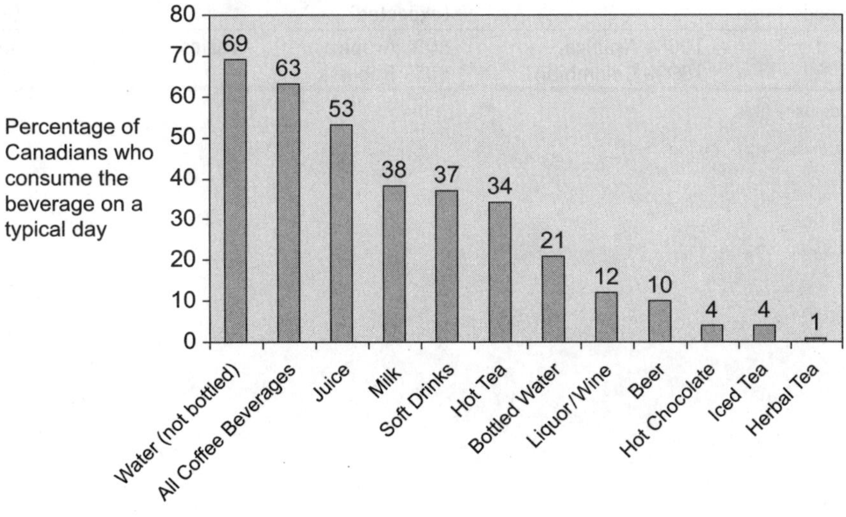

Timing of Coffee Consumption

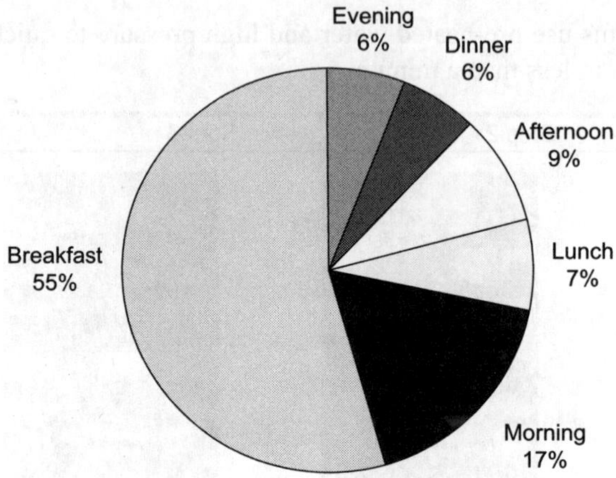

Source: Coffee Association of Canada.

EXHIBIT 4 Comparison of Coffee Pod Offerings

	Melitta One-to-One	Home Café	Bunn My Café	Senseo
Launch Date	In-Market	September 2004	November 2004	Early 2005
Machine manufacturer	Salton	Black & Decker	Bunn	Philips
Retail selling price for machine	\$60–\$75	\$75–\$89 (expected)	\$150+ (expected)	\$85–\$99 (expected)
System type	Closed	Open	Open	Open
Primary pod supplier	Melitta	Folgers & Millstone (P&G)	Various	Douwe Egberts (Sara Lee)
Retail selling price for pods	\$4.99 for 16	\$4.99 for 16 (expected)	Varies	\$4.99 for 18 (expected)
Beans used	100% Arabica, 100% Colombian	60% Arabica, 40% Robusta	Varies	To be confirmed

Source: Company files.

EXHIBIT 5A Print Ad Comparison—English language

Category	Magazine	Features	Readership (000s)	Coverage (%)	Insertions	Total Cost ($)
Women's interest	Chatelaine	• Reader profile that fits (High household income, well educated) • Appropriate environment with features on home and food	2,950	24.9	2	55,900
	Wish	• New launch (September issue on sale in August) • Targeting the busy, urban, upscale woman • Home and food comprise half the editorial content	1,100	n/a	1	14,900
Decorating	Style at Home	• Reader profile that fits (High household income, well educated) • Appropriate environment featuring modern decorating	1,600	14.0	1	9,300
	Cottage Life	• Appropriate environment featuring travel accessories, recipes and home design • Reader profile that fits (High household income, well educated) • Reach both males (53%) and females (47%) of the target market	574	n/a	1	6,200
	Canadian House & Home	• Appropriate environment that includes features on home, garden, food, wine, travel, technology and lifestyle trends	2,327	17.8	2	28,600

(Continued)

EXHIBIT 5A (Continued)

Category	Magazine	Features	Readership (000s)	Coverage (%)	Insertions	Total Cost ($)
Gardening	Gardening Life	• Reader profile that fits (High household income, white collar professionals) • Environment that is appropriate with the target including features such as food trends, entertaining, music and décor	1,700	8.6	1	9,700
	Canadian Gardening	• Appeals to both men (30+%) and women (60+%) • Profile readership that matches (children in HH, high household income, educated)	2,572	13.5	1	9,000
Food	Food & Drink	• Lifestyle magazine dedicated to the art of drink and entertainment • Appropriate environment that features ideas and news of food trends • Reaches both male (40%) and female (60%) of target market	1,631	16.3	1	14,100
Travel	enRoute	• #1 ranked publication in terms of composition • Targets frequent travelers with an above average disposable income • Reaches both males (51%) and females (49%) of the target market	863	17.2	2	42,000

Regional/ City	Vancouver Magazine	• Reader profile that fits (High household income, well educated) • Reaches both males (53%) and females (47%) of target market	351	2.3	2	15,500
	Toronto Life	• Reader profile that fits (High household income, well educated) • Reaches both males (53%) and females (47%) of target market • Appropriate environment that reaches the affluent, sophisticated consumer who is engaged in the City of Toronto	603	11.2	1	13,000
	Western Living	• Appropriate environment featuring travel tips, cuisine, home and garden • Reaches both the males (44%) and females (56%) of target market • Reader profile that fits (children>18 years, well educated)	810	11.2	2	29,200
	Ottawa City	• Upscale, urban publication targeting Ottawa's affluent consumer • Covers art, entertainment, food and drink	603	n/a	1	4,000

n/a = Data not available.

Source: Company files.

EXHIBIT 5B Print Ad Comparison—french Language

Category	Magazine	Features	Readership (000s)	Coverage (%)	Insertions	Total Cost ($)
Decorating	Décor Chez-Soi	• Appropriate environment that features high-quality home décor tips • Reader profile matches target (affluent women, well educated, high household income)	n/a	20.2	2	$ 5,700
Gardening	Les Idées de ma Maison	• Appropriate environment that features trends and designs	n/a	23.6	2	5,800
	Fleurs, Plantes, Jardins	• Reader profile that fits (High household income, well educated, children <18 years) • Appropriate environment that features gardening advice and new products for your home and garden	n/a	12.4	2	5,700
Women's interest	Châtelaine (French)	• Reader profile that fits (live in urban areas, have children <18 years, well educated, high household income)	n/a	21.3	2	9,300
	Clin d'Oeil	• Appropriate environment featuring money matters, fashion news and home • Reader profile that fits (live in urban areas, high household income, well educated)	833	16.9	2	14,100
	Plaisirs de Vivre	• Reader profile that fits (High household income, well educated, professionals) • Reaches both males (40%) and females (60%) of target market	191	n/a	2	6,000
	Coup de Pouce	• Ranked #1 in reach across the target market • Great publication to raise awareness of Maxwell House coffee pods	1,213	32.6	2	9,200
	Elle Québec	• Reader profile that fits (live in urban areas, well educated, high household income) • Appropriate environment featuring home ideas, health advice, music and entertainment news	830	13.5	2	16,900

n/a = data not available.

Source: Company files.

EXHIBIT 6 Television Sponsorship Campaign

Audience Size

Weekly Audience	Toronto	Vancouver	Total
CityPulse at Six (evening news)	65,000		65,000
Breakfast Television (morning news show)	105,000	3,000	108,000
CityLine (mid-morning variety show)	33,000	4,000	37,000
CityOnline (interactive viewer-driven show)	20,000		20,000
CityTV.com (website)	109,000	25,100	134,00
Total	332,000	32,100	364,100

Giveaways

Program	Week	# of Machines	Machine Costs	Misc. Basket Items	Total Cost
Breakfast Television (morning news show)	1	10	$1,000	$500	$1,500
CityLine (mid-morning variety show)	1	5	$500	$250	$750
City Online (interactive viewer-driven show)	1	1	$100	$50	$150
CityPulse News	2	5	$500	$250	$750
Caféine Talk (morning talk / variety show)	1	5	$500	$250	$750
La Roue Chanceuse (Wheel of Fortune)	2 3	10	$1,000	$500	$1,500
Total Costs					$5,400

Total Promotional Costs

Promotion	Cost
Production of a 30-second English-language contest spot	$10,000
Airtime to run English-language spot for one week	$15,000
Sponsorship of CityPulse Webtest news contest for one week	$16,900
Giveaways	$5,400
Promotional execution	$5,000
Total Cost	$52,300

Source: Company files.

EXHIBIT 7 Coffee Pod Demo Program Booth

Source: Company files.

Features

- Choice of 30-foot or 20-foot wide booth
- 12-foot to 14-foot towers and back wall
- Counters kept to side to maximize traffic flow
- Potential for Nabob and Maxwell House co-branding (see above)
- Premium look and feel

EXHIBIT 8 Consumer Show Information

Show	City	Date	# of Days	Attendance	Cost	Cost per Thousand
Barrie Fall Home Show	Barrie, ON	September	2	12,000	$3,002	$0.25
Ottawa Fall Home Show	Ottawa, ON	September	3	25,000	$3,436	$0.14
BC Fall Home Show	Vancouver, BC	October	4	45,000	$5,382	$0.12
Vancouver Home & Interior Design Show	Vancouver, BC	October	4	25,000	$5,054	$0.20

Show	City	Date	# of Days	Attendance	Cost	Cost per Thousand
Edmonton Fall Home Show	Edmonton, AB	October	3	20,000	$4,968	$0.25
Autumn Home Show	London, ON	October	2	50,000	$3,415	$0.07
Fall Home Show	Toronto, ON	October	4	75,000	$6,365	$0.08
Markham Home Show	Markham, ON	October	3	48,000	$4,468	$0.09
International Home Show	Mississauga, ON	October	4	60,000	$7,418	$0.12
Guelph Fall and Leisure Expo	Guelph, ON	October	3	25,000	$3,278	$0.13
Fall Home Show	Montreal, QC	October	5	45,000	$4,347	$0.10
Fall Ideal Home Show	Halifax, NS	October	3	20,000	$2,898	$0.14
Royal Winter Fair	Toronto, ON	November	8	100,000	$9,315	$0.09
Homexpo	Calgary, AB	January	4	24,000	$4,312	$0.18
Toronto Home Show	Toronto, ON	January	7	85,000	$6,037	$0.07
Metro Home Show	Toronto, ON	January	4	50,000	$6,279	$0.13
BC Home and Garden Show	Vancouver, BC	February	5	48,000	$4,122	$0.09
Calgary Home & Garden Show	Calgary, AB	February	5	55,000	$4,312	$0.08
Edmonton Home & Garden Show	Edmonton, AB	March	4	52,000	$4,778	$0.09
Home Expressions	Winnipeg, MB	March	5	12,000	$3,657	$0.30
Barrie Spring Home Show	Barrie, ON	March	2	20,000	$3,277	$0.16
Guelph Home Show & Leisure Expo	Guelph, ON	March	3	12,000	$3,888	$0.32
Hamilton Home & Garden Show	Hamilton, ON	March	3	20,000	$4,123	$0.21
The Home Show Designs for Living	Hamilton, ON	March	3	20,000	$2,967	$0.15
International Home & Garden Show	Mississauga, ON	March	4	126,000	$5,432	$0.04
Ottawa Home & Garden Show	Ottawa, ON	March	4	15,500	$6,210	$0.40
Montreal National Home Show	Montreal, QC	March	10	183,500	$7,762	$0.04
National Home Show	Toronto, ON	April	10	100,000	$6,727	$0.07
Hamilton Home Show	Hamilton, ON	April	3	18,000	$4,071	$0.23

Show	City	Date	# of Days	Attendance	Cost	Cost per Thousand
London Spring Home & Garden Show	London, ON	April	4	29,600	$3,070	$0.10
Nova Scotia Ideal Home Show	Halifax, NS	April	3	35,000	$3,001	$0.09

Source: Company files.

EXHIBIT 9 Coffee Pod Merchandising Tools

Shelf-Strips with Coupon AdPad	On-Shelf Racking	Branded Off-Shelf Bins

• Holds 12 bags • Includes coupon holder/ branding on top	• Holds seven bags per side (14 total) • Ensures neat and orderly product on shelf	• Holds 24 bags per side • Delivered pre-filled with product • Header card with coupon also available

Source: Company files.

9

Living Arts Centre of Mississauga: Condensed Version

Professor Michael R. Pearce prepared this case solely to provide material for class discussion. The author does not intend to illustrate either effective or ineffective handling of a managerial situation. The author may have disguised certain names and other identifying information to protect confidentiality.

INTRODUCTION

Mr. Warren Garrett, Marketing Director for the Living Arts Centre (LAC) of Mississauga, paused to look out his 11th floor office window. Directly across the street was the Mississauga City Hall, an imposing and unusual structure, while off to his left was an enormous parking lot for the huge Square One shopping centre. However, his focus was on the six acre construction site between these two landmarks where the three acre Living Arts Centre was under construction. (See Exhibit 1 for a map.) It was March 1996, just about a year away from the scheduled LAC opening. He watched the cranes and bulldozers for a moment, then returned his attention to the numerous significant questions which Mr. Garrett knew he'd be asked about. For example, how much of the LAC programming should be "popular" as opposed to "sophisticated"? How should LAC communicate with potential audiences? How should LAC approach the diverse ethnic groups, especially the one-third non-English speaking audience? Should an audience loyalty program be developed? What about the retail space, food and beverage, studio rentals and programs, tours, and so on? The biggest question of all in his opinion was how to prepare the LAC for its planned official opening in late 1997, especially since it appeared that most programs would begin half-way through a traditional annual season. He wanted to be able to provide opinions based on a thorough understanding of the

LAC market of today and in the years to come, which meant he needed to glean every possible insight from the research information available to him.

MISSISSAUGA

Located in the most populous area of Canada (the Greater Toronto Region), the City of Mississauga was located in a market of approximately six million people within a one-hour drive. Mississauga, a collection of seven towns that had amalgamated in 1974, had a population of 567,700 in 1996. Because the Mississauga area was spread out, reliance on the automobile for transportation was extensive. Five major highways passed through Mississauga. There was also an extensive public transportation system. In 1991 an estimated 162,000 people commuted to jobs in Mississauga from other communities. Twenty-five of Canada's top 500 corporations were headquartered in Mississauga in 1993. While there was a local newspaper, media readership studies indicated that most Mississauga residents relied instead on the Toronto media for most of their news.

In the Mississauga area in 1993, there were 163 schools serving 102,000 students. The Erindale campus of the University of Toronto had 7,000 students. Sheridan College, a community college, also had campuses in Mississauga.

The largest shopping centre in Mississauga was Square One, a 2.1 million square foot regional shopping centre with 350 stores which attracted 18 to 20 million visitors annually. This made Square One the second most visited shopping centre in Canada. Square One was expected to expand its size with Market Walk, a 500,000 square foot the med food and entertainment area due by 1998. Market Walk would be between the existing Square One building and LAC.

There were several Mississauga-area performing arts organizations, both amateur and professional, including: Mississauga Symphony Orchestra, Mississauga Choral Society, Opera Mississauga, Mississauga Concert Band, Mississauga Players, Spotlight Theatre, and the Credit Valley Dramatic Society. There were also several visual arts facilities and organizations in Mississauga, including the Art Gallery of Mississauga, the Erindale Campus Art Gallery (part of the University of Toronto), the Heritage Peel Complex in Brampton, the Springbank Visual Arts Centre (for exhibiting and teaching arts and crafts), and a variety of other spaces. Other than theatres contained within the individual high schools and a 400 seat proscenium theatre in northwest Mississauga called Meadowvale Theatre, no purpose-built, publicly owned performing arts facilities existed in Mississauga as of 1996.

Toronto, approximately a 45 minute drive from downtown to downtown, was regarded as a world-class centre for the arts, with facilities and events only exceeded by New York. Metropolitan Toronto had the following major performing arts venues:

O'Keefe Centre	3,167 seats
Massey Hall	2,765
Roy Thompson Hall	2,812
Pantages Theatre	2,200
Elgin Theatre	1,800
Royal Alexandra Theatre	1,500
Princess of Wales Theatre	1,800
Ford Centre for the Performing Arts (North York)	2,000/1,000
St. Lawrence Centre for the Arts	800/500

Major visual arts venues in the Toronto area included:

- The Art Gallery of Ontario
- The Royal Ontario Museum
- The Ontario Science Centre
- Harbourfront Centre
- McMichael Gallery

A BRIEF HISTORY OF LAC

The Mississauga Arts Council was established in 1981 to promote the arts and develop the cultural core of the City of Mississauga. In 1986, the Interim Steering Committee for a Mississauga Living Arts Centre was created. The original idea was a centre for all the visual arts primarily for artists and audiences within Mississauga. Over time, this concept was expanded to include a facility used by local performing arts organizations; touring performers and performing arts organizations; studio and exhibition space for all the visual arts; incorporation of multi-media and communications technology; facilities for meetings and other community functions; and other functions. Included would be a concert theatre with 1,315 seats, a second theatre with 384 seats and a third theatre with 110 seats.

In the fall of 1987, the Interim Steering Committee issued terms of reference for a study to determine if there was a need, demand, and support for an arts centre in Mississauga. A multi-firm team headed by Frank Wolman Associates was selected to examine the need, demand, and support for a performing and visual arts centre in Mississauga. In their report, dated January 1989, *need* was defined as follows: "The lack of community facilities and activities that the residents of Mississauga want or expect and which, if available, they would participate in or attend." *Demand*, on the other hand was defined differently, as follows: "By demand we mean the market that would be willing to pay to use or attend the proposed centre. Demand is not congruent with need; demand can come from outside Mississauga, from visitors to Mississauga and from persons who do not necessarily want or expect to have a centre."

Among its many other research activities, the feasibility study term reviewed general attendance and subscriber origin data of major organizations in Metro Toronto and areas close to Mississauga.

Excerpted from the Technical Report of the Feasibility Study, here are some quoted observations made about the Canadian arts audience in general:

- Education is the variable most consistently related to attendance (and frequency of attendance) of arts and culture in Canada. A large percentage of audiences are university educated.
- Participation tends to be highest among the young and middle-aged and lowest among older age groups. Older audiences are more common for music, opera and ballet whereas theatre and dance attract younger audiences.
- There is some positive relationship between higher disposable income, and arts participation, but studies have not confirmed that income is causally related to arts attendance.
- Women typically comprise 60 per cent of arts audiences in general.
- Single persons and those without children at home are disproportionately represented in arts audiences. Theatre attendance is highest for young and childless adults while much lower for parents and homemakers, whereas museum and art gallery attendance does not show many significant changes over the life cycle.

- People of an ethnic minority are less likely to participate in the arts, usually due to language barriers in addition to other real and perceived cultural barriers.

Here are some quoted excerpts from the Feasibility Study regarding their analysis of the resident market for LAC:

- Between 1961 and 1986, the population of Mississauga increased fivefold from 75,000 to just over 374,000. In 1986, Mississauga accounted for 11 per cent of the entire Toronto Census Metropolitan Area. Mississauga's rate of growth was greater than that of Toronto or Ontario as a whole. By 1996 the population is expected to reach over 500,000 and by 2006, over 600,000.
- Twenty-three per cent of Mississauga residents have some post secondary university education which is slightly higher than the Ontario average of just under 19 per cent. Comparatively, Oakville, Metro Toronto, and Burlington have higher levels than Mississauga.
- While aging, Mississauga's population is generally younger than the population of Ontario as a whole. Compared to Metro Toronto, Burlington, and Oakville, Mississauga has a relatively smaller percentage of residents 55 years of age and over and a larger percentage of population under 35 years of age.
- Mississauga residents have an average and median income close to $50,000 according to the 1986 census, which means that of the nearby areas, only Oakville had a higher level.
- Mississauga is a strongly family oriented community with 82 per cent of households in the 1986 census being family (two or more related persons). About 62 per cent of these husband–wife families were two income families in 1982 (no data available in 1986). By 1986 it was estimated that 10 per cent of families in Mississauga were single parent led.
- Those of English origin account for the largest portion (32 per cent) of the population of Mississauga, followed by Italian (nine per cent), Scottish, Irish and others. More than 40 other ethnic origins and 40 mother tongue languages are represented. About 76 per cent of the population had English as their mother tongue, followed by Italian, Portuguese and German. Over one-third of all Mississauga residents were born outside Canada.
- The school market is large and growing because of the relatively young population in Mississauga. Both public and private school boards were interviewed. It appears both systems are placing an increasing emphasis on the arts and its role in education. Both school boards have already active programs, but are limited by available facilities and budgets.

The Feasibility Team also examined the visitor market.[1] Among their observations were the following:

- Although Mississauga is not a tourist destination, there are still visitor markets for the proposed Living Arts Centre to tap into. According to the Tourism Strategy report, the primary tourist markets for Mississauga are the meeting and convention delegates, persons visiting friends and relatives (referred to as VFR), and persons attending special events.
- The VFR component of the tourism market represents 36 per cent of total Ontario travel visits.
- According to the Tourism Strategy report, Mississauga has a particularly strong convention and meeting market due to its proximity to the Toronto airport. According to the Metropolitan Toronto

[1] Mississauga did not have a tourism portfolio in its Economic Development Program. Tourism was regarded by the City Government as a private industry matter.

Convention and Visitors Association study, over 50 per cent of convention and meeting attendees participate in extra-curricular activities before or after meetings, and of these, 30 per cent visit attractions.

- Mississauga hosts a variety of over 150 special events each year such as outdoor sports tournaments, festivals, exhibitions, and shows. Many events are held at the International Centre, a facility that attracts over one million people annually. However, there are few well-known attractions in Mississauga. A recent study by the Metropolitan Toronto Convention and Visitors Association showed the most popular attractions in Metro Toronto were the Eaton Centre, the CN Tower, Harbourfront, Ontario Science Centre, and the Royal Ontario Museum. Unfortunately, Mississauga does not have an attraction of this calibre.

During August to September 1988, the Feasibility Team surveyed by telephone 509 randomly selected Mississauga residents and sent questionnaires to 48 local performing arts groups, 26 visual arts groups, and 132 non-arts community groups. Two surveys were developed: a main survey administered to the male/female head of household and a sub-survey administered to the same or other members of the household who participate in the arts. The respondents ranged in age from 18 to 78 (average age 39), were 48 per cent male, and most (71 per cent) owned their own home. Households on average had one child present who was under 18 years old.

Respondents were asked how many times in a typical year they attend seven different types of entertainment: ballet or dance theatre, pop music concerts, classical music concerts, theatre for plays and comedies, theatre for musical productions, art or craft exhibitions, and opera. With the exception of art or craft exhibitions, respondents attend each category of entertainment less than once a year in Mississauga and once a year or more outside Mississauga (the exception was opera which was very low inside and outside Mississauga). The majority of respondents who go outside Mississauga for their entertainment go to Toronto. They do not go to venues closer to Mississauga such as Oakville and Brampton in the numbers their population base would lead one to expect. Forty-four per cent of those who attend outside Mississauga said that they wanted to see performances not then available in Mississauga, while 36 per cent said Mississauga was inadequate in terms of comparable facilities and entertainment.

Respondents were asked:

> Some families like to attend events such as festivals, art exhibitions, concerts . . . that relate to their heritage or family background. Have you or your family attended any such events that relate to your heritage?

Twenty per cent said they had and two-thirds of those had done so in the past nine months and 40 per cent were participants. There was a great diversity in the types of events attended, with national festivals being most common.

Respondents who had children at home were asked about the kinds of activities their children were involved in. About 25 per cent of the children of respondents were involved in some related activity outside of school. The top ranked responses, in order of most frequent, included music (solo instrument), ballet/dance theatre, music (group), craft classes, and painting.

Respondents were also asked how many times in a year they would likely attend the same seven types of entertainment "if there were an arts and entertainment centre in Mississauga with interesting shows and a central location near Square One." Attendance patterns projected would on average be twice as high in Mississauga, as the following table from the study projects:

Type of Entertainment	Average Annual Projected Attendance
Theatre for plays and comedies	2.4
Art or craft exhibitions	2.2
Pop music concerts	1.8
Classical music concerts	1.7
Theatre for musical productions	2.6
Ballet or dance theatre	1.5
Opera	0.5

A study of statistical patterns showed that younger respondents were more likely to say they'd attend pop music concerts and older respondents to say they'd attend opera and classical music concerts. Respondents said they would go on an average of 7.2 times "if the facility were built to your liking," with no correlation between age and general attendance interest. Almost 60 per cent of the respondents indicated support for the Centre, with 37 per cent "no comment."

Respondents gave their views on the features and services they regarded as most important. Entertainment was highest rated, followed by parking and architecture. From a list of physical components, respondents placed a concert hall or theatre highest, followed by art gallery and exhibition space, then workshop space. A restaurant was rated as the most important service facility followed by a movie theatre for showing special films.

The sub-survey for those involved in artistic activities was administered to 45 respondents. Due to its small sample size, it is not reported here in detail. The Feasibility Team summarized it by saying:

> Respondents regard facilities and programming as the most important features . . . [they] rated an art gallery and exhibition space highest and then both concert hall or theatre and workshop space for artists and art students. A cafeteria, followed closely by a restaurant, were the service facility preferences.

The Feasibility Team interviewed local performing arts groups and reviewed existing performing arts facilities within the Mississauga area and concluded that they were all inadequate, with "deficiencies which cannot be overcome" and thus that Mississauga's performing arts groups could not develop further without a new facility. The survey findings indicated that all groups interviewed, regardless of whether they might use the new centre or not, believed there was a need for the new centre in Mississauga.

The Feasibility Team interviewed several professional performing arts groups and promoters (such as The National Ballet of Canada, Toronto Dance Theatre, The Toronto Symphony Orchestra, The Canadian Opera Company, Labatt's Promotions Group and many others). Their conclusion was as follows:

In summary, professional touring companies, concert promoters and independent producers were positive about a new arts centre in Mississauga. Most indicated that if the city had a new facility with the expected standards of a professional theatre today, they would likely include Mississauga on their touring schedule.

Non-arts groups contacted were also enthusiastic, although to varying degrees. Ethnocultural groups were most supportive, indicating their organization would consider using the centre for their activities and events.

The Feasibility Team also focused on visual arts. Visual arts facilities in the Mississauga region were compared and questionnaires were sent to 26 visual arts groups in Mississauga and residents were contacted by telephone to discuss visual arts. Here are some quoted excerpts from the Feasibility report:

- Arts and crafts organizations range in size from eight to 600 and are growing.
- Seventy per cent of the groups consider their members to be amateur or recreational artists; however, the largest sized groups consider themselves to be semi-professionals, with the result that approximately half of the represented population deemed themselves to be semi-professionals.
- The existing network of visual arts facilities is seen by the groups as meeting their basic needs but constraining to future growth.
- Visual arts organizations and visual arts audience rate highly the establishment of a central art gallery and exhibition space that would showcase the best work of Mississauga artists and provide workshop and studio space for artistic activities of outstanding interest.
- Among residents, attending arts or crafts exhibitions would be the second most popular form of entertainment at the proposed centre (the first being attending theatre for plays and comedies).
- On average, residents reported visiting arts and crafts exhibitions 1.2 times per year in Mississauga and 1.6 times outside Mississauga. They said they would likely attend 2.2 times per year in Mississauga if the proposed centre were built.

The Feasibility Team concluded in their January 1989 report:

> In our opinion, the ample evidence that we have researched points to a strong need, and also to demand and community support, for the proposed Living Arts Centre.

In 1993, an extensive business plan was prepared for LAC. According to the 1993 Business Plan:

> The City of Mississauga, one of the 10 largest and most rapidly growing cities in Canada, needs a cultural "heart" to enrich the experiences and understanding of its diverse population. Until now, there has been no single environment in which the over 200 cultural organizations and thousands of individuals who work and contribute to the artistic life of the region may develop their skills, exchange their opinions, and celebrate their accomplishments. There has been no "place to go"—to create, experience, explore. Neither has there been a facility with the physical or electronic capacity to open the arts to seniors, those with physical challenges, or others with special needs.

The purpose of the LAC was summarized as follows:

> It is the principal objective of the Centre that it be a place for people of all ages, cultures, and artistic interests to create, explore, and experience.

During the development of the project, many outside consultants were engaged to study and recommend on various topics. For example, in 1993 Ernst & Young developed an economic impact projection for LAC. This study calculated additional expenditures in Mississauga during construction of $38 million, 412 new jobs, and $320,000 additional city taxes generated. During the operation of LAC, they estimated $6 million in new expenditures, 79 new jobs, and $61,000 additional taxes for Mississauga.

The design of the building resulted from extensive consultations among artists in the community (visual and performing), educators, community representatives, and many professionals.

Central to the development of LAC was Bruce Heyland of Hammerson Canada Inc., a firm known for its shopping centres. He was Chairman of LAC. In the February 1993 LAC Business Plan, he wrote:

> The Centre must, and will, significantly help to meet the artistic needs of all those within its reach. It is designed to include, not exclude. So the programme development, physical design, and operating philosophy are based on continuous consultation with the many groups and interests within the community.

The groundbreaking ceremony was held in September 1994. At that time, LAC was only able to show the public a watercolour rendering of the building and site plan.

Mr. Garrett was hired in October 1994. Mr. Garrett's background in cultural management included sales and marketing positions with Orchestra London and the Hamilton Philharmonic Orchestra, as well as board memberships in the Association of Cultural Executives, the Ontario Choral Federation, the Festival County Travel Association, and the Hamilton and Region Arts Council. He was asked for a 1995 marketing plan outline as soon as possible. This plan was largely oriented to an initial communications program. The program objectives were as follows:

- Promote awareness of the $20 million Capital Campaign.
- Promote use of the Centre's space to programmers and artists.
- Build advance markets among travel trade, convention and meeting planners.
- Build local, regional and international interest in the Centre.
- Construct an audience direct marketing data-base.
- Conduct market research.

When Mr. Garrett undertook the LAC position, he was under the common impression that the traditional market for the arts in Mississauga was South of the Q.E.W. highway. He spoke with counterparts at other Mississauga arts organizations about their sense of the market. Most felt it was very difficult to get much response in this "cultural wasteland." Few of the major groups had done market surveys. Mr. Garrett decided LAC would have to undertake its own market research.

Mr. Garrett obtained summaries of the major markets in the Mississauga area from the City of Mississauga and The Financial Post Survey of Markets, an annual commercially available publication based on Statistics Canada information. He entered data from these summaries onto a spreadsheet to look for insights (see Exhibit 2).

Mr. Garrett developed a long list of community outreach activities ranging from membership in numerous arts groups to publicity events. All of the activities Mr. Garrett proposed in that initial marketing plan were undertaken during 1994 to 1995. Of the $407,000 budgeted for this program, approximately $40,000 was spent on market research.

In May 1994, Research Dimensions Limited, a Toronto-based research firm was contracted to conduct two triads and a focus group to test some ideas about a communications program for LAC. More specifically, the study objectives were as follows:

- Test four different positioning statements that explain the Living Arts Centre concept.
- Review how respondents become motivated or influenced to attend or become involved in the arts.
- Understand where respondents get their information about arts events.
- Assess the areas of community/individual "resistance" to becoming involved in the arts or the Living Arts Centre.

All participants were recruited from people in Toronto and Mississauga "with a broad background and ethnic mix." The first triad participants were 15 to 21 years of age and had attended some form of arts activity or arts related courses in the past year. The second triad was a group of parents who had attended some form of arts activity or arts related courses in the past year. The focus group was comprised of a group of parents who had been to an arts event or course in the past year and had undertaken an active involvement in a cultural or artistic activity during the past year. At least one half of the group was also recruited on the basis of familiarity with computers.

The researchers qualified their findings as follows:

- The limitations of qualitative research must be kept in mind. Respondents were selected on a non-random basis and their views cannot be regarded as quantifiably projectable to any specific population cohort or universe. The information obtained may be viewed as an indication of what attitudes exist but not of the extent to which these attitudes are represented in any defined population. Finally, the methods used are not "unreliable surveys." They are essentially idea generating vehicles where any avenue of information which appears to evoke useful ideas or problem solving suggestions is pursued and reported.
- In the first part of the research process, respondents were questioned about how they were influenced to become involved in the arts. The researchers reported that family was often instrumental in building and developing a child's experience in the arts as well as the important influences of school, friends, and peers. According to the researchers:
- Most respondents hear about events on the radio and get more detailed information from the local newspaper.

Other findings included:

- The cost of an art activity or course event plus parking charges was often seen as considerable. Most participants seem to be operating on a budget and as a result the costs associated with arts involvement limit the extent of participation and involvement.
- The inability to get to, or park at, an arts event often limit involvement. The accessibility of the proposed site by public transportation will be very important. This is true for both those living in Mississauga and those living further away who have to use public transportation.
- The availability of facilities and studios will be very important. An inability to book the use of facilities and space leads to a lack of involvement in arts activities.
- Those who live in Mississauga will tend not to use a new centre unless it provides them with unique activities that they cannot find in their local community centre.
- Those who live outside Mississauga will not use the Centre unless the Centre provides identifiable unique events, courses, or performances that cannot be found in their own communities.

Later in the interview, the LAC concept was presented in detail, and then four positioning statements were presented to each respondent. They were asked to assess individually how well each of the positioning statements matched the concept described. The four statements were as follows:

1. Where traditions of culture and arts embrace the educational and technological trends of tomorrow in a uniquely creative and stimulating environment.
2. Canada's centre for lifelong learning, creativity, and true innovation. From the techno-arts to the performing arts, the Living Arts Centre is a place where everyone can experience the leading edge in their field of interest, the place where possibility lives.

3. A Centre where what's possible in all aspects of the arts can be explored or enjoyed by everyone. The Living Arts Centre in Mississauga delivers on the promise for hands-on, lifelong learning, creativity, and innovation.
4. The Living Arts Centre will take us beyond the information age to the Innovation Age by blending art and technology with the desire to learn and the desire to create.

For the most part, participants did not like these positioning statements. On the whole, they were viewed as too wordy, too ambitious, too overwhelming, pretentious, vague and uninvolving. Of the four, number three was the most favoured. There was confusion among participants regarding who the target was for LAC. They were uncomfortable blending arts and technology. According to the researchers:

- Technology seems to mean dull, uncreative, boring, necessary, person-replacing, threatening, not fun. Education appears to mean boring, necessary, uninteresting, required, and definitely not fun.
- When asked what words they would include in a positioning statement, respondents offered the following: innovative, arts/crafts, entertainment, participation, fun, technology for now, computer, explore, for all ages, unique place.

The researchers also examined the name itself. They reported as follows:

> Overall, the Living Arts Centre is seen as a good name for the Centre. This name creates a positive action oriented image. This is a Centre where there is involvement and ongoing activity. The main negative response to the title is in the use of the word Centre. For many, "centre" creates an image of a local community centre, a place to swim, do sports, go to art classes, etc. Participants feel there is a danger in the Living Arts Centre not being perceived as a special unique place.

In late 1994, LAC management commissioned Taylor & Browning Design Associates Inc. to propose a positioning strategy for LAC. The agency report, received in January 1995, was based on an examination of five major competitive organizations relative to the LAC: The Banff Centre, Ford Centre, Harbourfront, Ontario Science Centre, and Roy Thompson Hall. These organizations were reviewed despite their wide geographic distance apart (for example, The Banff Centre is in Banff, Alberta) using the following dimensions: hands-on or participatory, entertainment or performance, learning or educational, broadcast, space rentals and corporate/conference events. Taylor & Browning recommended the following position strategy:

> Electronically "wired" for evolving technologies and artfully designed to meet the needs of talented people, the Living Arts Centre in Mississauga is North America's premier venue for inspiration. It is where students and families, neighbours and tourists, hobbyists and professionals, artists and performers, and many other people with wide-ranging interests—including Internet surfers and multi-media enthusiasts—can come together in one eclectic space to explore their creative capacities and enjoy the products of imagination.

Taylor & Browning went on to suggest four "slogans" to summarize the positioning strategy:

1. "Find your inspiration"
2. "For real inspiration"
3. "Get inspired"
4. "Inspired reality"

Taylor & Browning proposed a detailed $626,000 campaign for 1995 and $925,000 for 1996 based on their positioning strategy. LAC management rejected their recommendations.

Mr. Garrett was under some political pressure to seek more visibility for LAC in 1995 than he felt was appropriate since they had little to show the public in terms of actual building plans or programming commitments. In May 1995, there was an LAC "media event" to show more detailed plans, including the interior. A major colour booklet was prepared to show drawings and floor plans. A pamphlet was also prepared for "take-one" displays throughout the area. Exhibit 3 provides some excerpts from this pamphlet.

Also, in May 1995, another positioning study was conducted by Research Dimensions Inc. Three focus groups were interviewed in Toronto consisting of one group of seniors (over 55), one group of young people (15 to 24 years of age), and one group of parents with children under 15 at home. All respondents lived in Brampton, Mississauga or Etobicoke, were selected to 50/50 male/female, and said they took part sometimes or regularly in artistic or cultural activities.

Some of the key findings reported included:

- Word-of-mouth and local information outlets such as community newspapers and cable access stations are very important to all groups in gaining information about cultural activities.
- Consumers see cultural activities as primarily connected to the performing arts, but other areas which are important include crafts and community events.
- It is apparent that the Mississauga/Brampton area is seen to be a "wasteland" where cultural activities are concerned.
- Seniors and young people engage in cultural activities because they want to for themselves; parents engage in activities for their children's sakes.
- Availability of (free) parking and accessibility are of extremely high importance to seniors (and some young people) in participating in cultural activities.
- Cost and distance travelled are important barriers to participation to all groups, especially parents.

A central part of the research involved getting reactions to the LAC concept and to several positioning statements. According to the researchers:

- Respondents are uniformly positive about the LAC concept, and agree that they will attend shows/events there. Many mentioned similarities with the North York Centre for the Performing Arts. They are somewhat unsure about their participation in crafts/educational/hands-on activities, however.
- Respondents can easily visualize LAC's role as a performing arts facility, but they require a greater stretch of the imagination to understand the educational/studio/hands-on aspect of LAC.
- For the most part, respondents do not object to the idea of $50 million in public funds being spent on LAC, and they see it as a good investment. There are some lingering concerns, however, about LAC's ability to generate adequate operating revenues once it has been built.
- The Living Arts Centre name is well-liked by all respondents, although some question the need for including "in Mississauga" in the name. There are suggestions that this will limit LAC's appeal and send a message that LAC is only for Mississauga residents.
- Very powerful words to all groups are "accessible" "entertainment" "hands-on." "Multimedia" works with young people and parents, but not seniors. "High tech" "electronically wired" and "inspiration" were not liked by any group.

- The Board of Directors' positioning statement (of May 1994) is preferred two to one to the Gottschalk+Ash statement (designed for LAC just before this research in May 1995), although it was not regarded as perfect. The Board's statement was:

  > The Living Arts Centre is a place where everyone can explore and enjoy all aspects of the arts. This unique centre provides exciting opportunities for hands-on creativity, innovation, and excitement.

- Part of the research interviews focused on the corporate identity logo which had been developed by a public affairs committee and consultant to signify a "living L." Respondents did not see the logo this way and in fact, they characterized the logo as cold, corporate, unappealing, or for some, meaningless.

In the "blue sky" portion of the interview when respondents were asked to let their imaginations go concerning what could be done at LAC, the researchers reported that the youths and the seniors were most able to visualize exciting possibilities, whereas the mid-life adults were most interested in whether the LAC would be a good place for the family. For example, some seniors mentioned swing bands, barbershop quartets, world-wide electronic hookups for chess and bridge tournaments, whereas youth mentioned a virtual reality exhibit, state-of-the-art videogame arcades, laser shows, and other ideas. Parents mentioned day care, arts and crafts programs for their children, a shuttle bus to Square One, a zoo, and other ideas.

Because Mr. Garrett was not satisfied with the demographic statistics he had found, in November 1995, he hired Genovese Vanderhoof and Associates (GV&A), a Toronto-based arts consulting firm, to undertake a psychographic examination of the LAC market. They, in turn, worked with Compusearch, a marketing research company based in Toronto, to do an $8,500 geo-psychographic mapping of Mississauga.

The Compusearch approach was trademarked PSYTE. This approach segmented Canadian census enumeration areas (the smallest census grouping of households, typically about 200) into 60 clusters. Based on their statistical analysis of many data sets, Compusearch had constructed an extensive profile of each of these clusters, thus providing a portrait of a small geographic unit of the market without their client having to interview or survey those who lived in that area. According to Compusearch, their method offered a comfortably close, although not totally accurate picture of each household in that area. The major PSYTE segments identified in the LAC vicinity are listed in Exhibit 4 and mapped in Exhibit 5.

LAC was intrigued by the possibility of using the PSYTE research as a baseline for preparing predictive models for its marketing decision-making. For example, management hoped to be able to examine questions such as "If we offer this program, what per cent of the market would be likely to attend and which media should we use to advertise to them?" Mr. Garrett also foresaw shared box office systems among major arts organizations which would allow greater understanding of market responsiveness and potential audiences to seek.

After Compusearch had done the original mapping, further analysis was done. Genovese Vanderhoof and Associates then used 24 month ticket purchase information from several Southwestern Ontario and Toronto-based arts organizations to develop a matrix of arts participation in LAC's primary market area (Mississauga) and its secondary markets (Etobicoke, Oakville, and Brampton). Each of the co-operating organizations provided a download of its ticket purchasing audience members whose postal code address fell in the presumed LAC market area. Then GV&A developed a spreadsheet to show to what extent LAC prospective audience members were currently patronizing other organizations.

In other words, postal code information was mapped against the total number of households in each market to arrive at penetration. An index was developed to enable selection of key target areas for LAC marketing efforts. The following table provides a summary of GV&A's findings as reported in November 1995:

Type of Arts Activity Attendance	Primary Market % Penetration (173,000 Households)	Secondary Market % Penetration (198,372 Households)
Commercial theatre (Broadway Musical)	4.4	5.1
Classical theatre (Shaw and Stratford)	2.5	4.1
Symphony orchestra (TSO and MSO)	1.5	2.5
National Ballet (includes Nutcracker)	1.2	1.6
Meadowvale and Heritage (Brampton) theatres	0.7	1.5
Non-profit theatre (Canadian Stage Company)	0.5	0.9
Canadian Opera Company	0.5	0.8
Art Gallery of Ontario	0.2	0.5

Further Compusearch work was a possibility in Mr. Garrett's opinion.

Mr. Garrett wondered how best to use the Compusearch research. For example, he had several descriptive profiles of the PSYTE segments provided by Compusearch, as exemplified in Exhibits 6 and 7.

In early 1996, approximately two dozen arts organizations in the Halton-Peel region (which includes Mississauga) undertook a co-operative $68,000 arts audience research study. Mr. Garrett was encouraged by this co-operation because he was aware that several organizations were concerned that LAC would steal away their audiences or even their programming. Mr. Garrett was awaiting results from this group interviewing study which was focused on the question: "What issues get in the way of people coming to the arts?"

Business planning was proceeding. A number of strategic business units were established for LAC including: live entertainment, studio arts, education, facility rentals, retail, and food and beverage. Mr. Garrett would be involved in the marketing programs for these SBUs.

CONCLUSION

In March 1996, Ian Mccallum, President of LAC since 1995 and previously a successful management consultant, commented that while most cultural institutions are artist driven, he liked to characterize LAC as market driven:

I know this is heresy to many in our field, and I have encountered lots of resistance when I make statements like this. However, I think some organizations who get excited about being artist driven are merely lazy—it's hard work finding out what a market wants and then deciding whether to give it to them. We simply have to be market driven now, meaning we're for and about people so we make decisions knowing as much as we can about them. We're just getting started. Later I hope we can balance out a little more to have greater direction from the artistic side too. We'll see which of our assumptions and interpretations pan out and then we'll change.

EXHIBIT 1 Area Map

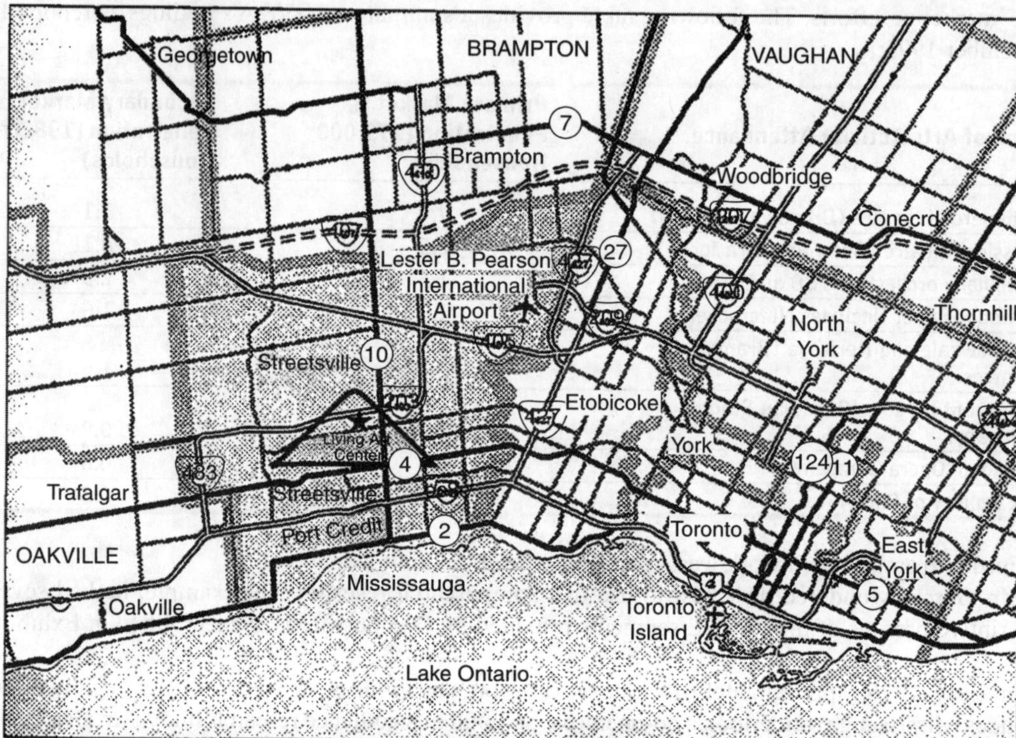

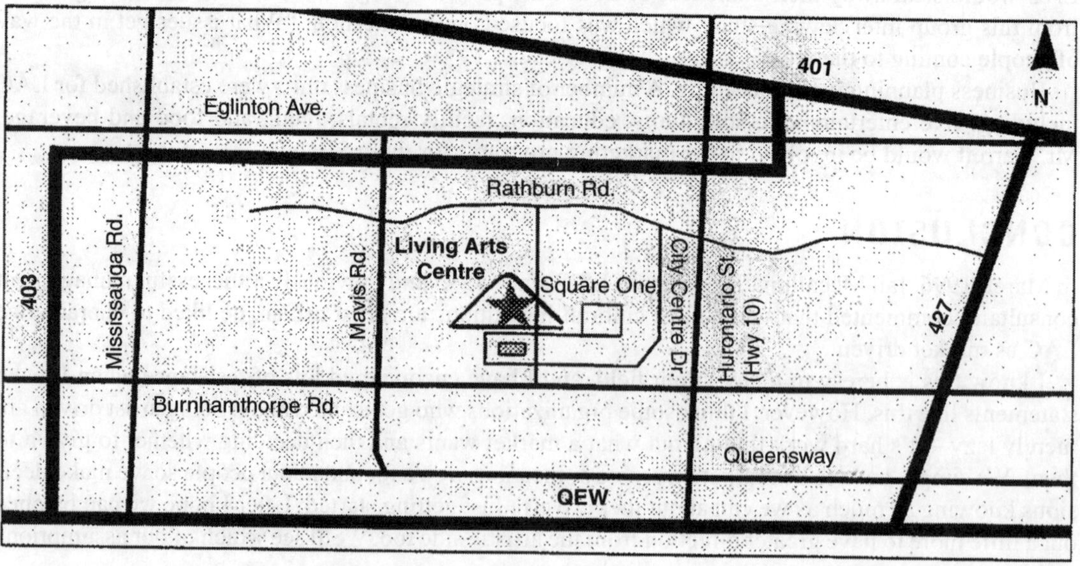

EXHIBIT 2 Spreadsheet of Market Information

Population		Mississauga	Burlington	Brampton	Caledon	Etobicoke	Halton Hills	Milton	Oakville	Orangeville	Totals		
Total		463,390	129,275	234,445	34,965	309,990	36,815	32,075	1114,670	17,920	1,373,845		
	M	230,030	63,430	117,485	17,700	150,630	18,710	16,270	56,675	8,860	679,790		
	F	233,355	66,145	116,960	17,260	159,365	18,110	15,805	57,995	9,060	694,055		
Age Group 0-4	M	18,305	4,405	9,995	1,355	9,805	1,415	1,140	4,435	855	51,710		
	F	17,325	4,305	9,360	1,270	9,155	1,245	1,075	4,095	775	48,605		
5-9	M	17,330	4,330	9,460	1,380	8,670	1,66	1,340	4,165	740	48,770		
	F	16,465	4,145	9,245	1,335	8,205	1,270	1,175	3,970	680	46,4690	195,575	13%
10-14	M	16,895	4,205	9,235	1,355	8,005	1,235	1,350	3,985	670	46,935		
	F	16,140	4,060	8,845	1,315	7,600	1,165	1,320	3,775	615	44,835		
15-19	M	17,015	4,615	9,280	1,385	8,875	1,445	1,335	4,370	685	49,005		
	F	16,155	4,395	8,745	1,265	8,425	1,335	1,225	3,900	615	46,060	186,835	14%
20–24	M	18,170	4,640	9,595	1,225	11,965	1,470	1,250	4,010	630	52,955		
	F	18,625	4,510	9,775	1,110	11,970	1,350	950	4,030	625	52,945		
25-29	M	22,520	5,290	11,970	1,190	14,935	1,605	1,280	4,125	920	63,835		
	F	22,945	5,365	11,705	1,180	14,410	1,565	1,185	4,410	970	63,735	233,470	17%
30-34	M	22,615	5,490	11,315	1,380	13,845	1,715	1,315	4,895	925	63,495		
	F	23,215	5,660	11,400	1,525	13,475	1,610	1,375	5,295	895	64,450		
35-39	M	20,020	4,925	9,830	1,480	11,470	1,495	1,385	4,785	705	56,095		
	F	21,260	5,345	10,350	1,595	12,085	1,455	1,505	5,260	735	59,590	243,630	18%
40-44	M	19,535	5,065	9,965	1,625	10,425	1,490	1,620	4,790	700	55,125		
	F	20,235	5,495	9,960	1,680	11,010	1,505	1,600	5,170	685	57,340		
45-49	M	15,285	4,525	7,950	1,460	8,305	1,370	1,180	4,190	495	44,760		
	F	14,715	4,705	7,315	1,370	9,020	1,345	1,085	4,175	470	44,200		
50-54	M	12,240	3,680	5,845	1,160	7,825	1,075	840	3,315	380	36,360		
	F	11,210	3,635	5,365	960	8,865	975	715	3,030	370	35,125	273,000	20%
55-59	M	9,570	3,230	4,505	850	8,595	910	630	2,815	300	31,405		
	F	9,025	3,265	4,140	730	9,340	795	560	2,690	275	30,820		
60-64	M	7,540	3,020	3,345	720	8,775	810	545	2,405	210	27,370		
	F	7,650	3,025	3,275	555	9,495	750	500	2,335	275	27,860		

Population		Mississauga	Burlington	Brampton	Caledon	Etobicoke	Halton Hills	Milton	Oakville	Orangeville	Totals		
65-74	M	9,025	4,110	3,565	755	13,140	895	700	2,990	360	35,540		
	F	11,045	4,930	4,520	815	15,790	1,105	805	3,475	530	43,015		
75+	M	3,965	1,910	1,635	370	6,000	430	365	1,395	275	16,345		
	F	7,355	3,300	2,970	560	10,525	645	730	2,385	545	29,015	241,370	18%

Source: 1994 FP Canadian Markets.

	Mississauga	Burlington	Brampton	Caledon	Etobicoke	Halton Hills	Milton	Oakville	Orangeville	Totals	
Mother Tongue											
English	306,185	1112,235	175,250	29,355	197,760	32,750	28,665	91,105	16,755	9990,0607	72%
French	6,820	2,395	3,275	300	3,260	645	345	1,945	165	19,150	1%
Arabic	3,680	255	735	20	1,815	15	35	305	5	6,865	0%
Athapaskan languages	5	0	0	0	0	0	0	0	0	5	0%
Chinese	12,600	590	2,495	25	4,265	80	50	1,330	30	21,465	2%
Cree	5	0	0	0	10	0	0	0	0	15	0%
Dutch	1,485	1,580	1,585	250	885	555	335	855	205	7,735	1%
German	5,245	1,745	2,470	850	4,780	575	560	2,015	165	18,405	1%
Greek	2,910	280	835	85	2,015	75	35	270	30	6,535	0%
Italian	17,350	1,215	7,670	1,855	17,770	230	695	2,460	95	49,340	4%
Micmac	5	0	5	0	0	0	0	0	0	10	0%
Polish	12,825	1,215	1,535	195	12,315	120	105	1,135	30	29,475	2%
Portuguese	14,120	535	8,165	165	4,180	260	100	2,920	45	30,500	2%
Punjabi	9,160	540	6,715	105	4,810	25	15	745	20	22,135	2%
Spanish	5,960	345	1,995	40	5,390	85	55	460	5	14,335	1%
Tagalog (Filipino)	6,175	120	1,645	45	7,495	100	80	570	15	13,080	1%
Ukrainian	3,510	700	465	145	7,495	100	80	570	15	13,080	1%
Other languages	55,350	5,825	19,605	1,530	41,165	1,275	985	8,110	345	134,190	10%

Source: 1994 FP Canadian Markets.

EXHIBIT 3 Living Arts Centre, Mississauga

A Welcoming Place—Atrium

The open and spacious layout of the Living Arts Centre announces its accessibility to all. The soaring, 60-foot glass-walled Atrium, suitable for public gatherings and catered events of up to 1,000 people, is connected to a glass-roofed Galleria with views to all three levels of the Centre's Studio Wing.

Public amenities include a restaurant, café, gift shop, an electronic InfoStudy, Image Shop and interactive Discovery Deck complete with a Virtual Reality suite. Underground parking for 450 cars provides visitors with secure, well-lit and weather protected access to all of the Centre's attractions.

A Communications Hub

The Living Arts Centre will serve as a major communications centre. Its theatres, studios, meeting spaces, instructional classrooms and conference rooms will be equipped with the latest in fibre-optic and digital technology permitting a variety of uses from video-conferencing to distance education. Central Communications will combine computing and broadcasting to permit the world-wide transmission of voice, video and data programs. A Media Wall on the exterior, front facade will be used for programming and promotion.

The Concert Theatre

The 1,300 seat Concert Theatre will offer superb acoustics and sight lines for the enjoyment of plays, concerts and major touring productions. Its seats are arranged in a u-shape lay-out on three levels. Conferences, product launches and corporate meetings can also take place here.

Digital, Music Recording and Dance Studios

The Centre's multi-faceted uses are evident in the number and variety of studio spaces it houses. The second level, digital, music and recording studios offer opportunities in graphic animation, multimedia development, composition and sound recording. The Dance Studio on the third level is fully equipped with a sprung floor, mirrors and barres. It can be used by choreographers, dancers and other performers or as a meeting/classroom space.

All of the Arts

The Living Arts Centre offers access to a complete range of artistic endeavours. Eight large studios are devoted to the production and display of glass, sculpture, wood, ceramics & pottery, jewellery, print making, photography, painting and drawing. Studio spaces will be used for instructional programs, and made available to artists on a rental basis.

Discovery Deck

The Discovery Deck, located on the Centre's third level, features an interactive display space and children's technology discovery area. Together with a fully equipped Virtual Reality Studio, these amenities will encourage creative adventure and exploration.

Theatres II and III

The 400-seat Theatre II and the 110-seat Theatre III add flexibility and capacity to the Centre's presentation and performance capabilities.

Theatre II's retractable, tiered seating system, sprung floor and full lighting grid enable a variety of uses, from theatre-in-the-round and chamber concerts to banquets, receptions and meetings.

Theatre III, with a film/video projection room, can be used for film screenings, music recitals and lectures. It is located near the west entrance of the Galleria, for convenient access by school and bus tour groups.

The Staging Room

The Staging Room on the second level has a large floor area. Its two-storey height and sprung floor permit full-scale productions to be pre-mounted before moving to the Concert Theatre or Theatre II. Meetings, classes, banquets and receptions may also be held in this space.

EXHIBIT 4 Compusearch Psyte Segments

Psytee Cluster	Primary Market			Secondary Market	
	Households	Market %	Cum. %	Households	Market %
Satellite Suburbs (S4) 14	22,409	12.95	13	27,790	14.01
Mortgaged in Suburbia (S1) 06	20,477	11.84	25	17,435	8.79
Technocrats & Bureaucrats (S1) 07	18,146	10.49	35	8,753	4.41
Young Urban Mix (U4) 29	17,358	10.03	45	21,289	10.73
Suburban Executives (S1) 03	11,353	6.56	52	9,741	4.91
Stable Suburban Families (S2) 08	10,874	6.29	58	11,802	5.95
High Rise Melting Pot (U2) 41	10,708	6.19	64	10,162	5.12
Boomers & Teens (S2) 05	10,329	5.97	70	14,104	7.11
Europa (U2) 21	6,688	3.87	74	4,512	2.27
Brie & Chablis (S3) 10	6,133	3.55	78	8,793	4.43
Suburban Nester (S3) 10	5,314	3.07	81	17,284	8.71
Young city Singles (U4)	4,887	2.82	84	1,218	0.61
Old Bungalow Burbs (S2) 16	4,817	2.78	86	6,932	3.49
The Affluentials (U1) 02	3,734	2.16	89	7,178	3.62
Asian Heights (S1) 09	3,487	2.02	91	198	0.10
Town Renters (T2) 35	3,182	1.84	92	665	0.34
Conservative Homebodies (U3) 28	3,098	1.79	94	7,033	3.55
Kindergarten Boom (S4) 23	2,950	1.71	96	1,601	0.81
Urban Gentry (U1) 04	2,191	1.27	97	9,615	4.85
High Rise Sunset (U3) 33	1,240	0.72	98	958	0.48
University Enclaves (U4) 40	1,031	0.60	98	958	0.48
Young Urban Intelligentsia (U4) 36	879	0.51	99	999	0.50
Struggling Downtowners (U6) 48	643	0.37	99	0	0.00
Aged Pensioners (U6) 58	466	0.27	100	748	0.38
Old Grey Towers (U6) 60	443	0.26	100	1,387	0.70
Old Towns' New Fringe (T1) 27	133	0.08	100	0	0.00
Aging Erudites (S3) 17	33	0.02	100	660	0.33
Big City Stress (U6) 59	0	0.00		1,437	0.72
Canadian Establishment (U1) 01	0	0.00		1,115	0.56
Young Urban Professionals (U4) 20	0	0.00		453	0.23
Blue Collar Winners (T1) 13	0	0.00		330	0.17
	173,003	100.0		198,372	100.0

EXHIBIT 5 Psyte Mapping

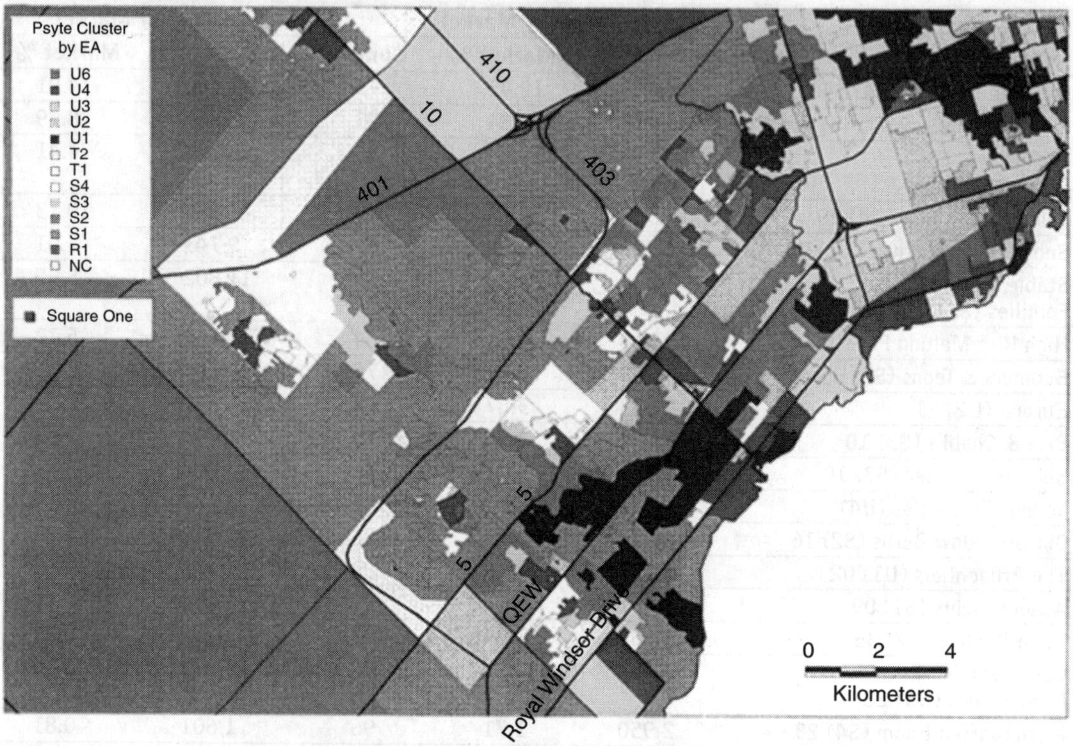

Source: Compusearch Micromarketing Data & Systems.

EXHIBIT 6 Additional Psyte Analysis

Activities	CMA Households	Comm. Theatre	ST & SH* Theatre Festivals	Symphony Buyers	Ballet Buyers	Area Theatre Buyers	Can Stage Buyers	Opera Buyers	AGO Member
Urban Elite (U1)									
The Affuentials 02	3,734	142	380	462	309	176	530	416	511
Urban Gentry 04	2,191	110	284	252	193	213	414	255	379
Total (U1)	5,925	130	345	385	266	190	487	357	462
Suburban Affluent (S1)									
Suburban Executives 03	11,353	147	178	197	196	124	196	206	197
Mortgaged in Suburbia 06	20,477	179	100	79	145	100	77	122	73
Technocrats & Bureaucrats	18,146	118	114	107	114	142	101	92	82
Asian Heights	3,487	104	56	32	88	47	30	65	48
Totals (S1)	53,463	146	118	110	142	116	107	126	101
Suburban Upscale Families (S2)									
Boomers & Teens 05	10,329	10	141	162	134	129	148	144	149
Stable Suburban Families 08	10,874	93	132	158	136	122	161	152	172
Old Bungalow Burbs 16	4,817	67	95	80	0	71	64	99	60
Total (S2)	26,020	93	129	145	129	115	138	139	142

Activities	CMA Households	Comm. Theatre	ST & SH* Theatre Festivals	Symphony Buyers	Ballet Buyers	Area Theatre Buyers	Can Stage Buyers	Opera Buyers	AGO Member
Suburban Older Singles and Couples (S3)									
Suburban Nesters 10	5,314	105	142	119	113	188	128	125	109
Brie & Chablis 12	6,133	101	153	146	46	177	134	74	135
Aging Erudites 17	33	0	0	0	0	0	0	0	123
Total (S3)	11,480	103	147	133	77	182	131	97	34
Suburban Younger Families (S4)									
Satellite Suburbs 14	22,409	84	49	57	61	95	52	45	37
Kindergarten Boom 23	2,950	67	27	26	40	93	35	56	14
Total (S4)	25,359	82	46	5.	58	95	50	47	34
Town Upscale (T1)									
Old Town's New Fringe 27	133	204	0	0	0	309	0	156	0
Total (T1)	133	204	0	0	0	309	0	156	0
Urban Ethnic (U2)									
Europa 21	6,688	63	41	26	47	43	37	46	31
High Rise Melting Pot 41	10,708	37	32	26	33	8	29	23	27
Total (U2)	17,396	47	35	26	38	21	32	32	29

Urban Older Singles and Couples (U3)									
Conservative Homebodies 28	3,098	61	102	95	68	111	80	74	174
High Rise Sunsets 33	1,240	53	179	177	34	122	33	33	167
Total (U3)	4,338	59	124	119	59	114	67	62	172
Urban Young Singles (U4)									
Young Urban Mix 29	17,358	59	60	49	60	51	57	58	69
Young Urban Intelligentsia 36	879	90	29	78	29	16	47	71	189
University Enclaves 40	1,031	50	99	93	99	120	60	80	80
Young City Singles 51	4,887	102	40	63	40	67	46	55	68
Total (U4)	3,182	53	29	28	29	26	32	46	26
Urban Downscale (U6)									
Struggling Downtowners 48	643	21	6	32	13	64	0	32	65
Aged Pensioners 48	466	68	35	59	91	59	88	89	0
Old Grey Towers 60	443	122	73	78	38	155	47	47	94
Total (U6)	1,552	64	34	53	44	88	40	53	53
Total Buyer Households	173,003	7,666	4,279	2,519	2,041	1,262	839	835	417

EXHIBIT 7 Compusearch Psyte Profile Examples—Suburban Executives (1.58 % of HHDS)

Demographics	Cluster Average %	Canadian Average %	Index	Preferences	Index
Education				CARS	
University Degree	32.9	14.0	235	Lexus LS 400	698
Some University	20.5	11.8	174	Nissan maxima	540
College	19.4	23.6	82	Cadillac Deville	478
High School	24.7	14.1	18	Toyota Previa	447
Less Than High School	2.6	14.1	18	Toyota Cammy	447
				Jeep Grand Wagoner	417
Occupation				PRODUCTS	
Managerial	24.4	11.0	222	Own Waste Disposal Unit	368
Other White Collar	38.7	24.9	156	Education	308
Blue Collar	21.1	32.0	66	Drink Liquor/scotch	289
Grey Collar	38.4	38.8	99	Home Security System	222
Unemployed	4.8	10.8	45	Drink Wine	205
Females in Labour force	69.2	58.7	118	Own Home Computer	203
Family Type				Self-Administered RRSP	200
1 Person Households	5.5	22.8	24	Out of Country Medical Ins.	185
Households with Children	64.1	37.3	172	3 or More Credit Cards	163
Children 0-5	21.0	25.4	83		
Children 6-14	38.3	36.0	107	MEDIA	
Children 15+	41.0	37.5	109	City & Country Home	372
Lone Parent Families	5.9	13.2	44	Saturday Night	370
Maintainer Age				Globe & Mail	366
15-24	0.6	4.6	13	Watch TV-Family Channel	173
25-34	12.1	21.8	56	Watch TV-Tennis	160
35-54	64.4	40.0	161	Watch TV-CN	152
55-64	14.5	14.1	103		
65+	8.4	19.3	44	ACTIVITIES	
Home Language				Downhill Skiing	225
English	83.0	69.6	119	Go to Club	182
French	9.7	22.4	43	Attend Tennis Matches	177
Other	7.2	7.7	94	Attend Live Theatre	177

Demographics	Cluster Average %	Canadian Average %	Index	Preferences	Index
Immigrant Population	22.4	15.2	147	Golfing	139
Percent Immigrants Post '81	12.4	10.1	122		
1991 Household Income					
<$20,000	3.2	19.3	17		
$20,000-$34,999	4.8	17.2	28		
$35,000-$49,999	8.4	15.5	54		
+ $50,000	78.1	29.2	267		
Avg. Income (1994) ($)	104605.0	46206.1	226		
Personal Income					
> $100,000	5.2	0.7	785	Source: Compusearch Micromarketing	
Dwelling Status				Blackburn/Polk Vehicle Information	
Single-detached	92.1	59.7	154	Services Print Measurement Bureau	
Apartments 5+ Storeys	0.3	9.5	3	Statistics Canada.	
Other Dwellings	7.5	28.0	27		
Rented	5.7	35.3	16		
Owner Occupied	94.3	63.5	148		
Mobility					
Moved Since 1990	12.6	16.8	75		

10

Molson Canadian—The Rant

INTRODUCTION

The marketing team on Molson Canadian had a difficult task ahead of them. They had to find the theme for the next advertising campaign for Molson's flagship brand and Canada's best selling beer, Canadian. The previous campaign, "The Rant" had been one of the most successful ads for Molson and Canadian in a long time. See Exhibit 1 for a storyboard of The Rant television commercial.

The Rant was an incredibly popular commercial that had won numerous international and domestic awards in the advertising industry. Introduced on March 26, 2000 with a single television spot during the Academy Awards telecast, The Rant featured Joe, a Canadian who is proud of what makes him different from Canada's neighbors to the south. "It's kind of an educational thing, telling Americans what we are and what we aren't," said Glen Hunt the writer of the ad.[1] Poking fun at the differences between Canadians and Americans tapped into the minds of Canadians from British Columbia to Newfoundland. Canadian's market share increased a reported two points after The Rant advertising campaign.

This was a critical time for Molson. Molson's overall market share had been slipping while its main competitor, Labatt, had been gaining share. Industry analysts estimated Molson experienced

[1] *Marketing News*, May 8, 2000, Tom Cohen.

approximately $100 million in lost profit as a result of market share losses since 1989, and with a net loss in 2000 of $44 million, there was no room for miscalculations. Molson had recently invested 10 per cent of revenue to revise its operations in an attempt to improve profitability and was now concentrated on beer production and marketing. Finally, new competition from micro breweries, imports and a regional Canadian brewer was making the fight for each point of market share more difficult. Dan O'Neill, Molson's new president, was watching closely and expecting results.

CANADIAN BEER INDUSTRY

The Canadian beer industry can trace its roots back to 1668 when Jean Talon established the first domestic brewery to avoid buying expensive alcohol from France. Since that time, the Canadian market evolved into a virtual duopoly. Two players, Molson and Labatt, dominated the industry. Between them, they controlled approximately 90 per cent of the $5 billion to $6 billion Canadian beer market while regional brewers, import beers and micro breweries fought for the remaining 10 per cent.

Facing increasing competition from other alcoholic beverages, beer sales had been flat in Canada, hovering around 20 million hectolitres (hl)[2] since 1989. Sales had increased marginally in 1999, moving from 20.5 million hl to an estimated 20.7 million hl in 2000.[3] Exhibit 2 provides detailed sales information for the Canadian beer market.

Between 1995 and 1999, the per capita consumption (based on total population) in Canada increased in all three alcoholic categories (beer, wine and spirits) (see Exhibit 3). Beer was growing the slowest and was losing ground each year to wine and spirits. Beer consumption by legal-age drinkers in Canada had decreased from 103.88 litres in 1989 to 89.89 litres in 1999. According to the Brewers Association of Canada, the total consumption on a per capita basis was 68 litres in 1999. The world's biggest beer drinkers were in the Czech Republic where they consumed 160 litres per person annually.

Sales in the beer industry in Canada were fragmented between brands and provinces. In 2000, the largest market was Ontario, followed by Quebec and British Columbia. As shown in Table A, Ontario and Quebec make up over 60 per cent of the total market, and the mix of sales by province had remained the same for the last 10 years.

Table A Beer Sales by Province in HL

	1996	1997	1998	1999	1999(%)
Ontario	7,186,365	7,131,366	7,410,873	7,529,057	36.3%
Quebec	5,428,362	5,471,431	5,581,622	5,724,050	27.6%
All others	4,593,589	4,683,832	4,888,310	4,975,694	24.0%
British Columbia	2,571,454	2,557,156	2,562,042	2,526,908	12.2%
Canada	19,779,770	19,843,785	20,442,847	20,755,709	100.0%

Brand sales and market share varied significantly depending on the province. For example, Molson Canadian, the market leader in Ontario, was not sold in the second largest market, Quebec. The top 10 brands in Ontario are listed in Exhibit 4.

With each market share point worth approximately $15 million in profit each year,[4] together Molson and Labatt spent an estimated $400 million on advertising and promotion to gain and defend their

[2] 100 litres = 1 hl = .839 U.S. barrels = 26.42 U.S. gallons and approximately 12 cases of 24 bottles.
[3] *Molson 2000 annual report* and *Brewers Association of Canada 1999 Annual Statistical Bulletin*.
[4] *Maclean's*, May 3, 1999.

market positions. For the large breweries, industry estimates on costs varied. The general breakdown was that for each dollar 37 cents was paid in tax, 20 cents was spent on marketing and 15 cents went to profit.

The amount of imported beer as a percentage of total beer sales increased from 2.5 per cent in 1993 to 6.8 per cent in 1999. Compared to the previous year, the import segment increased by 21 per cent to a total of 1.4 million hl and had been growing at more than 10 per cent per year since 1996.

The growth in the industry was in the imports and the Can-Am brands (Miller, Coors Light and Bud) Heineken and Corona. This presented major challenges for the future of the Canadian-based brands.

COMPETITION IN THE CANADIAN BEER INDUSTRY

The two dominant forces in Canadian brewing, Molson and Labatt, faced increased competition from small, regional breweries like Sleeman's and micro breweries. In 1988, there were 50 breweries in Canada and by 1999, that number had grown to over 75. There were 24 conventional breweries and 52 micro breweries according to the Brewer's Association of Canada. A micro brewery was classified as having sales of less than 60,000 hl and distribution mainly through on-site retail outlets, while a conventional brewery was classified as having sales greater than 60,000 hl and mass retail distribution.

Molson

Molson was founded in Montreal Quebec in 1786 and was the oldest beer brand in North America. The founder, John Molson, an immigrant from England, provided the basic philosophy of Molson: "An honest brew makes its own friends."

With wholesale sales in 2000 of just over $2.5 billion and a net loss of $44 million, Molson was one of two leading breweries in Canada. See Exhibit 5 for Molson's financial information. Molson employed 3,600 employees and operated six breweries across the country. Molson's overall market share had decreased from 52 per cent in 1989 to 45.0 per cent in 1999, a decline that cost Molson over $100 million in profits. In the past year, 2000, Molson's market share registered a slight increase from 45.0 per cent to 45.1 per cent.

Motivated by the significant loss of long-term market share and facing a serious efficiency disadvantage when compared to the competition, Molson had spent $200 million to strategically refocus its business on the core operations of the firm and on making and marketing beer.

In 2000, The Molson Company was divided into two divisions: brewing, and sports and entertainment. Molson's brewing division owned 100 per cent of Molson Breweries and was involved in two joint ventures with the Adolph Coors Company—Coors Canada and Molson USA. Molson distributed Coors Light in Canada under contract while Coors distributed Molson products in the United States.

The holdings of Molson's sports and entertainment division included the Montreal Canadiens and their newly constructed arena, The Molson Centre. The sports and entertainment division also coordinated promotional initiatives, including the House of Blues music series and the Toronto and Vancouver Molson Indy C.A.R.T. motor racing series.

Molson's strategy was to focus on existing markets, expand the Molson brand to new markets and position Molson as a participant in the international brewing industry. A new national strategic marketing group was formed in 2000 to direct the newly focused marketing of the Molson brands. New additions to Molson's marketing team in 2000 included Michael Downey, former president of

Toronto's Sky Dome sports stadium, who joined Molson as senior vice-president of marketing; Rob Guenette, who came to Molson from Lever Pond's where he was the director of the hair-care category; and Brett Marchand, who had come to Molson from the Campbell's Soup Company in the United States, where he had worked for Molson's new president and chief operating officer (COO), Dan O'Neill.

Headed by Downey, the strategic marketing group consolidated the brand portfolio into seven uniquely positioned brands, each with its own identity. Regional marketing teams helped guide the national programs and capitalized on local knowledge and relationships. The seven core brands were; Molson Canadian, Molson Dry, Molson Export, Coors Light, Rickard's Red, Corona and Heineken. Molson Canadian, Molson Dry, Molson Export, and Coors Light brands competed in the mainstream domestic segments. Rickard's Red was positioned in the specialty segment while Corona and Heineken competed in the premium import market. The non-core Molson brands would continue, but marketing support was significantly limited.

Molson's core brands were available across the country, with the exception of Canadian, while the regional brand and non-core brands were available in limited areas.

Labatt

Founded in 1847, in London Ontario by John Kinder Labatt, The John Labatt Brewery had a rich Canadian background, although the multi-billion-dollar international brewer Inter brew had purchased Labatt in June 1996 for $2.9 billion. With approximately 45 per cent of the total Canadian market, Labatt was very aggressive in its advertising and promotional strategies. The two companies often "traded" in-case and consumer promotions by matching each other's offers. The result was that many promotions were offset and market share remained the same.

Financially, Labatt had already restructured and refocused its operations in the mid-90s and was enjoying an estimated $100 million in additional profits when compared to Molson, even though the two firms were similar with respect to sales and employees. Since 1989, Labatt increased its market share and profits by two per cent and to $30 million respectively.

Labatt controlled 60 regional and national brands that covered almost every segment of the beer market (see Exhibit 6). Labatt Blue and Labatt Blue Light were its main products and in addition to its own brands, Labatt brewed, under licence, foreign beers including Budweiser, Bud Light, Carlsberg and Carlsberg Light. Budweiser was the most successful of the international beers that Labatt produced.

Sleeman Brewers Ltd.

Founded in 1834 when the Sleeman family started brewing beer in Guelph Ontario, Sleeman Brewers Ltd. has grown to become the number three brewer in Canada. John Sleeman, great-great grandson of the founder, revived the business in 1988, and by 2000, Sleeman operated five breweries across Canada, each producing and distributing the core Sleeman brands and a family of strong regional brands. As shown in Exhibit 5, Sleeman's 2000 sales were $141 million, up 47 per cent from the previous year while total production volume increased by 75 per cent to 943,000 hl in 2000.

Sleeman's success was, in part, a result of its positioning as a small, craft brewer and an alternative to the larger national brands. Sleeman maintained this image as it expanded operations to include brewing and marketing of the international premium brands Samuel Adams, Scottish and Newcastle, Beck's and value-priced Stroh brands. Exhibit 6 provides a listing of Sleeman brands.

Brand advertising by the smaller breweries was designed not to compete directly with the large players. John Sleeman, president of Sleeman Breweries Ltd., stated that his firm steered clear of competing head-to-head with the large breweries. The microbrewers and smaller brewers generally avoided expensive television advertising and used radio, outdoor and print to promote their brands. The product attribute positioning of the microbreweries was also different from Molson and Labatt. Rather than a lifestyle message, Sleeman's advertising focused on the history of the firm, the differences in production processes and the recipe book that originated with John Sleeman's great-great-grandfather.

Budweiser

Budweiser, marketed by Anheuser-Busch of the United States, was the number one selling beer in the world and number three in Canada.[5] As shown in Exhibit 5, total sales for Anheuser-Busch were US$14 billion in 2000 with a net income of US$1.5 billion.

With 10 per cent of the Canadian market, Budweiser was growing steadily across Canada and was unique because it was performing well in all areas of the country. Known as "the King of Beers," Budweiser had a very well-developed brand image in Canada as a result of Labatt's advertising programs and the impact of American advertising on Canadian media. Budweiser's advertising and promotions were tied heavily to NFL sponsorship and included a nationwide Super Bowl party.

Coors

The Adolph Coors Brewing Company, located in Golden Colorado, posted total sales of US$2.4 billion for 2000, an increase of eight per cent over the previous year. Coors' net income had increased by 18 per cent to almost US$110 million in 2000 (see Exhibit 5).

Coors Canada was a joint venture between the Adolph Coors Company and Molson, which owned 49.9 per cent. Coors Canada was responsible for the distribution and marketing of the Coors Light brand and had been showing very positive results. Market share for Coors Light had increased from 5.5 per cent of the national market to six per cent from 1999 to 2000, making it the fourth largest brand in Canada and one of the fastest growing.

Microbreweries and Brewpubs

The microbreweries and brewpubs were growing in popularity with the Canadian consumer, but they still held only a small fraction of the total market. A microbrewery produced a limited amount of beer that was distributed in local bars or from a store at the brewery. Limited to regional distribution, the microbrewers lacked the economies of scale to produce and distribute nationally. Often their small-scale production and attention to taste was what attracted customers to the microbreweries. Advertising and promotions were equally limited, and many microbreweries relied completely on word of mouth for promotion.

The brewpubs were very similar to the microbreweries, except they were a combination of brewery and beer pub. The beer was brewed and served in the same location. Like the microbreweries, advertising and promotion was minimal.

---

[5] *Anheuser-Busch company annual report*, 2000.

CONSUMER BEHAVIOR

In Canada, each province set its own legislation for the brewing, selling and transporting of beer and alcohol. This resulted in a complicated and awkward national market. In all provinces, beer was available in bars, restaurants and at some sporting events. In some provinces, consumers could purchase beer at grocery stores and corner stores, while in other provinces, beer could be purchased only in government-run or regulated stores.

The legal drinking age in Canada was 19, and the breweries were trying to reach the valuable 19-to-24-year-old segment before consumers had formed a strong brand preference. Beer consumption deceased after the age of 24 as people drank less, or switched to other alcoholic drinks such as wine or hard liquor. Research by the beer companies has shown that within the 19-to-24-year-old market, sports fans consumed twice as much beer as non-sports fans.

Advertising

Besides the automotive industry, the beer industry in Canada is one of the few that was still producing large budget, big production advertising domestically. Many other industries, including the package goods, were using internationally developed campaigns. The size of the budgets and the mostly cutting-edge positioning of the beer commercials made a beer account very appealing for an advertising agency. According to AC Neilson, Molson and Labatt each spent over $50 million in media purchases in 1998 and over $200 million each on total advertising and promotions.

With the amount of money that was being spent on advertising by the beer companies, there was a concern about return on investment. Michael Downey, explained that Molson was very concerned with the correlation between advertising and increased sales, "What is important to us now is that the advertising be pre-tested and proven to move incremental cases of beer."[6]

Advertising for the large, national brewers was very much tied to lifestyle, showing the product in a social setting, being enjoyed by young, energetic and healthy people. Robitaille feels that beer advertising is a mirror of society and that "it's not just about advertising, it's about being part of their life." To make their advertising stand out, beer companies often identified new trends and made them more popular by including them in the advertising.

The image created by advertising is critical to the success of a brand. Beer is sold in the same basic package, in the same bottle, at the same price, and many consumers can't tell the difference in blind taste tests. A 1998 study found that less than 50 per cent of Molson Canadian or Labatt Blue drinkers could identify their favorite brand when given unmarked glasses of both products. As a result, beer marketers focused on brand-level rather than attribute-level advertising.

Government regulations on beer advertising were very strict. There were 17 sections in the Canadian Radio and Television Commission Act that outlined the rules for beer advertising in Canada and included restrictions on what could be seen and heard in a beer commercial. Ads could not include the sounds or images of people drinking beer. Half-empty glasses or bottles could not be seen and people in the ads had to be over 19. The brewers were careful, however, to make sure that all actors in beer commercials were over 25 to avoid any concerns about marketing to young adults.

---

[6] *Selling Suds*, May 24, 2001.

Promotional Activity

To support the media advertising campaigns, breweries invested in many different promotional and sponsorship activities. Sponsorships were focused on but not limited to sporting events and included everything from motor racing and hockey to equestrian events. A well-planned promotion or sponsorship would often pick up the slack from an ineffective advertising campaign and keep the brand name in the minds of the consumer.

The range of promotional activities used by the brewers was extensive, covering almost every possible category and including in-store signage, logo clothing, mixed cases that had two different brands in one case, and prizes in each case. Tie-ins with advertising were common, and Labatt Blue customers, for example, would find a miniature Stanley Cup in specially marked cases as part of the "Out of the Blue" advertising.

Molson had been lucky with its "Blind Date" and "House Party in the Rockies" promotions that helped support Molson during lean advertising years. The Blind Date was based around a well-known band playing at a small club and only a few lucky Molson drinkers would qualify to win. The House Party in the Rockies promotion consisted of specially marketed bottles placed in cases of Molson Canadian. If you purchased the winning case, you would win a house party for yourself and your friends in the Rockies.

Molson Canadian Advertising

Molson Canadian was the number one brand in Canada with a reported 12 per cent to 14 per cent[7] market share; it was also the flagship brand for Molson. Canadian's market share had increased for each of the previous six years, and it was a priority for Molson to maintain this leadership position. The Canadian brand also maintained significant brand equity. Research by Molson showed that Canadian was the number two brand that young Canadian adults were most proud of, just ahead of the number three brand, Labatt's Blue and behind fashion retailer ROOTS.

Michael Downey defined the positing of Molson Canadian as:

> . . . a young male who is looking for a big popular brand that is a little safer, that is one that he knows what it's about, knows that a lot of other people are drinking it and is reinforcing something that is important to young males, as well as young females at this point in time . . . pride in Canada.[8]

In the 10 years since the early 1990s, Molson Canadian had utilized several different advertising campaigns. The "Taste That Will Stop You Cold" and "What Beer's All About" campaigns each ran successfully, but eventually became less effective. Under pressure to perform, Molson's advertising agency of 42 years, McLaren McCann of Toronto, developed "I Am Canadian," a campaign that was used from 1994 through 1998. The I Am Canadian spots were replaced by the "Monkeys" campaign that premiered in May of 1998, which was followed by "Here's Where We Get Canadian." Exhibit 7 provides an overview of Molson's advertising.

Rankin Carroll felt the I Am Canadian campaign was initially a strong campaign, "that was rooted in insights around youthful individuality." The message was primarily about being young and being an individual. Secondarily, it was about doing these two things in Canada. The emphasis was on the

---

[7] *Marketing Magazine*, October 4, 1999.

[8] *Selling Suds*, May 24, 2000.

I Am Canadian, not *We* are Canadian. After the campaign was launched, Canadian's market share soared up five full points.

As time went on, the creative for the I Am Canadian spots became watered down and the message was lost. Management started to look for a new angle on Canadiana, the stereotypical beaver and Mounties that would somehow bring them closer to Canada. Carroll reflects, "... we couldn't get our heads around the insights that bring us closer to Canada, so we started to go down this road of a new Canadian confidence."

Molson's competitor, Labatt, launched "Out of The Blue" in February of 1998 and caught Molson off guard. The Labatt advertising was clever and fun. The first ad showed a spontaneous street hockey game coming together on a city street. The tag line "A whole lot can happen out of the Blue" left the number of possible executions wide open. "Street Hockey" was followed by "Shopping Carts" and gave Labatt significant presence in the market.

In May of 1998, Molson unveiled the "Monkeys" campaign. The premise behind these spots was that if you placed infinite number of monkeys in a room with typewriters, they would eventually define what it is to be Canadian. Described by a Molson executive as horrendous and a flop, Monkeys was replaced the following year by "Here's Where We Get Canadian."

By considering questions such as, "How well does being Canadian fit the beer drinking experience?" Carroll's team started to relate the beer-drinking experience to the Canadian attributes that they perceived. Molson's promotional agency, Encore, came up with an idea called "Here's Where We Get Canadian" and it seemed to fit. The idea appeared to have legs, both in terms of brand advertising and also in terms of promotional breadth, "... Here's where we'll act Canadian, here's *us* getting together, at a Rock Show, a House Party or Hockey game ... that's where we really "get Canadian." We liked the idea because it had the brand in there. It was much more about here's where *WE* get Canadian" reflected Caroll. The campaign ran during the summer of 1999 and received some attention, but was not the answer for the Canadian brand.

A New Advertising Agency

The failure of the Monkeys advertising and a new management team at Molson led to the announcement on May 17, 1999, that Molson had fired MacLaren McCann and announced that it would be placing the Molson advertising account under review. The review team was headed by Molson executives at the time, Dan O'Neill, Richard Kelly, senior vice-president, strategic marketing; and David Perkins, Ontario/Atlantic region president.

Molson received approximately 30 responses from agencies across North America and Europe. The 30 agencies were short-listed to four, and the winner, Bensimon Byrne D'Arcy, was selected on September 20, 1999, after a summer of strategy meetings and presentations.

Molson did not treat the selection of a new agency lightly. A new agency would have to share the vision of Molson and particularly the Canadian brand. David Perkins felt that hiring a new agency, "is probably the most important decision that we will make this year."[9]

Canadian Patriotism

Molson conducted research in 2000 that indicated there might be a shift in the attitudes of its primary market segment, the young adults. Comparing results from previous studies, Molson discovered that

[9] *Marketing Magazine*, "The Canadian Way", October 4, 1999.

since 1994, young adults in Canada had become more driven and sophisticated in what they were trying to achieve. Respondents also had a stronger sense of belonging to Canada. The new research also showed that more than 75 per cent of young adults in English Canada believed that Canada was "better than the United States," because of less crime and a better quality of life. See Exhibit 8 for select results from the 2000 research.

Although the research results were very positive towards a patriotic theme, researchers noted that there was a correlation between the attitudes of young adults towards Canada and the general state of the economy. At the time the study was completed, the Canadian economy was relatively strong.

THE DECISION

The Rant was played in movie theatres, sports arenas and finally on television. By many accounts, the ad was a huge success, receiving media coverage on television, radio and newspapers; more than $1.5 million of free publicity was generated for Molson Canadian. Advertising awards, including a Clio, best of show at the Bessies, and Bronze from the Cannes-Lyons festival, rolled in and the Molson Canadian marketing team was feeling good.

When considering the creative that would replace the Here's Where We Get Canadian campaign, Molson reviewed the results that Labatt had posted from the Out of the Blue campaign. Consumer awareness and key messages rated very high for Out of the Blue, but the market share numbers had dropped. Some beer industry observers felt that Labatt had traded younger drinkers for older drinkers. Although the Out of the Blue campaign did not use a specifically patriotic theme, traditional Canadian images of hockey and curling played a significant role in the advertising. Industry experts wondered if a patriotic image could sell beer.

Research by Bensimon Byrne D'Arcy indicated that youth in Canada would respond well to a nationalistic message. "We [Molson] never wrapped ourselves in the flag, perhaps because we always assumed that it would be un-Canadian. The research helped us break through that."[10] The Rant went on to be a critical success, although the question of how much patriotism young Canadian adults would respond positively to had not yet been answered.

When asked, "Where do you go next?" Mr. Carroll did not have a definitive answer. How long could Molson execute off the patriotic theme of The Rant without people getting bored? How could Molson maintain the momentum of The Rant and keep the advertising fresh and interesting to the target? Should Canadian's advertising move towards more traditional beer advertising or maintain the non-traditional theme of The Rant?

With each point of market share worth $15 million, the stakes were high. At the very least the new advertising campaign had to ensure that Canadian maintained its market leadership position and ideally attracted new customers to the brand.

In addition to being very nationalistic, not a normal trait for Canadians, The Rant was unique among beer advertising in that it did not show a bottle of beer or people socializing. Downey noted: "While it is a great emotional ad and very positive, people both internally and externally said, 'That's not beer advertising. Where are the people socializing?'"[11]

---

[10] Personal interview, Rankin Carroll.

[11] *Marketing Magazine*, December 18/25, 2000.

EXHIBIT 1 Storyboard for "The Rant"

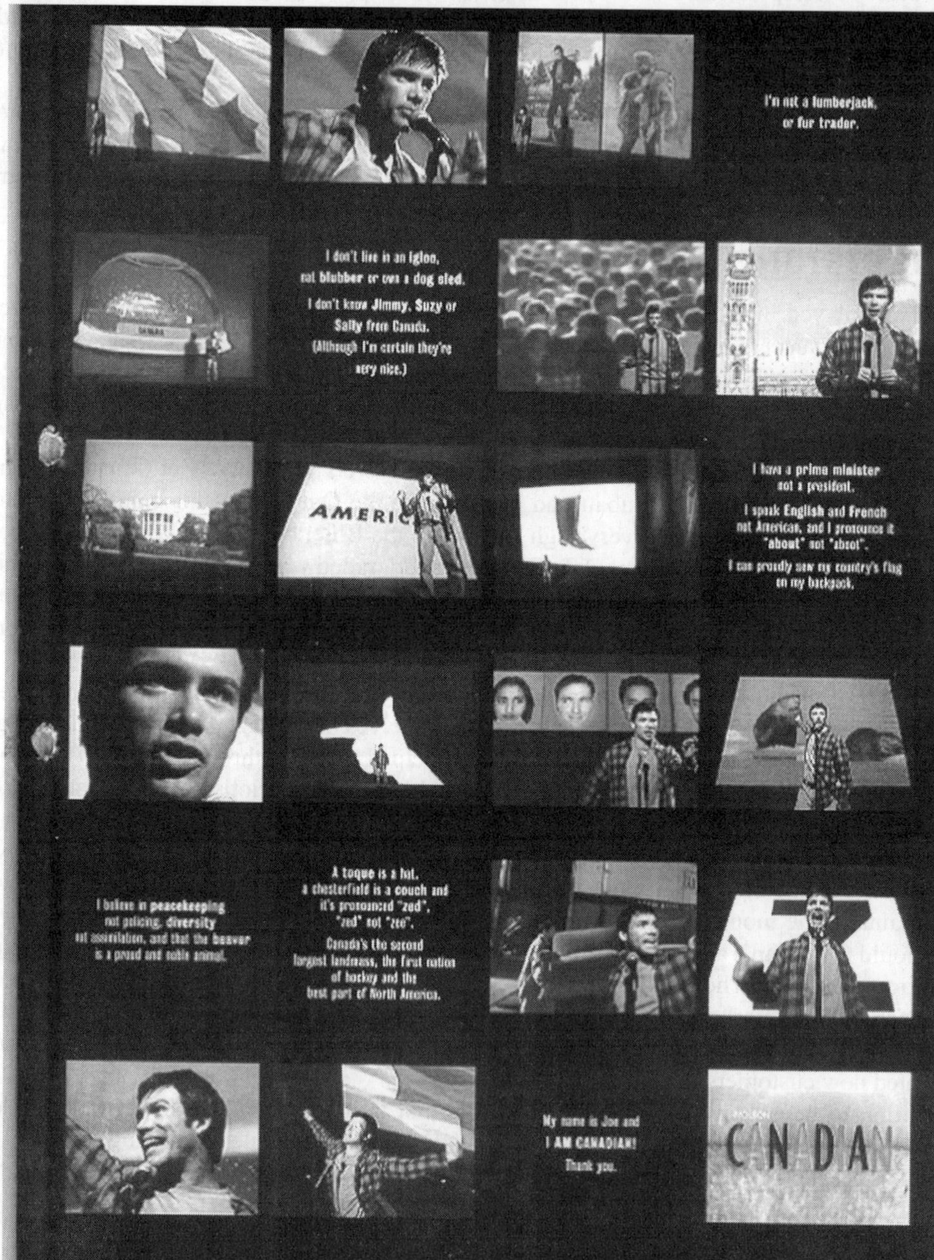

Source: Molson 2000 Annual Report.

EXHIBIT 2 Domestic and Imported Beer Sales in Hectolitres—Canada

Domestic	1989	1990	1991	1992	1993	1994	1995	1996	1997	1998(r)	1999
Bottles	14,842,658	14,430,319	13,848,677	13,819,975	14,080,041	13,928,402	13,414,855	12,941,587	12,920,120	13,224,306	13,404,886
Cans	3,442,175	3,713,359	3,813,770	3,098,953	2,831,294	3,132,919	3,611,792	3,719,668	3,661,775	3,795,901	3,677,006
	18,284,833	18,143,678	17,662,447	16,918,928	16,911,335	17,061,321	17,026,647	16,661,255	16,581,895	17,020,207	17,081,892
Draught	1,901,878	1,948,471	2,026,114	2,132,857	2,167,558	2,190,628	2,215,748	2,251,625	2,244,177	2,255,951	2,259,235
Sub-Total	20,186,711	20,092,149	19,688,561	19,051,785	19,078,893	19,251,949	19,242,395	18,912,880	18,826,072	19,276,158	19,341,127
Imported	849,403	686,201	663,941	604,623	497,411	578,654	659,447	866,890	1,017,713	1,166,689	1,414,582
Total Sales	21,036,114	20,778,350	20,352,502	19,656,408	19,576,304	19,830,603	19,901,842	19,779,770	19,843,785	20,442,847	20,755,709
Share of Domestic Beer Sales by Package Type											
Bottles (%)	73.5	71.8	70.3	72.5	73.8	72.3	69.7	68.4	68.6	68.6	69.3
Cans (%)	17.1	18.5	19.4	16.3	14.8	16.3	18.8	19.7	19.5	19.7	19.0
Draught (%)	9.4	9.7	10.3	11.2	11.4	11.4	11.5	11.9	11.9	11.7	11.7
Share of Domestic and Imported Beer Sales											
Domestic (%)	96.0	96.7	96.7	96.9	97.5	97.1	96.7	95.6	94.9	94.3	93.2
Imported (%)	4.0	3.3	3.3	3.1	2.5	2.9	3.3	4.4	5.1	5.7	6.8
United States (%)	78.8	74.8	75.8	64.7	58.0	53.0	49.3	57.1	58.4	53.4	44.1
Other Countries (%)	21.2	25.2	24.2	35.3	42.0	47.0	50.7	42.9	41.6	46.6	55.9
Per Capita Consumption of Domestic and Imported Beer Sales in Litres*											
Total	77.09	75.01	72.61	69.27	68.20	68.30	67.80	66.66	66.17	67.59	68.07
Adult	97.25	94.58	91.51	87.33	85.94	85.94	85.13	83.53	82.67	84.16	84.46
Legal Age	103.88	100.93	97.61	93.11	91.57	91.54	90.69	89.01	88.08	89.62	89.89

(r) - Domestic sales were revised.

* Statistics Canada revised population data for 1997 and 1998.

Note: Domestic beer sales are recorded consumption only, and do not include consumption arising from U-Brews or home brewing across Canada.

Source: Brewers Association of Canada, 1999 annual statistical bulletin.

EXHIBIT 3 Index of Per Capita Consumption of Beer, Wine and Spirits

Based on Total Population

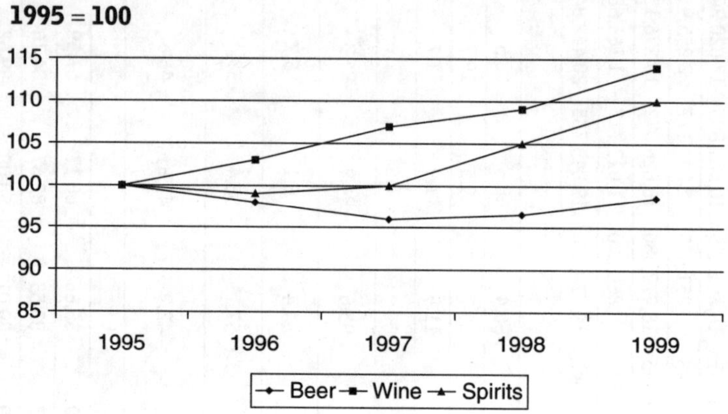

EXHIBIT 4 Rank of Brands in Ontario

Rank	Brand	Brewer
1	Molson Canadian	Molson
2	Labatt Blue	Labatt
3	Coors Light	Molson
4	Budweiser	Labatt
5	Molson Export	Molson
6	Blue Light	Labatt
7	Labatt Extra Dry	Labatt
8	Black Ice	Molson
9	Carling Light	Molson
10	Molson Dry	Molson

EXHIBIT 5 Financial Highlights

	Sleeman Breweries Ltd.[1]		Anheuser-Busch Companies[2]		Adolph Coors Company[3]		Molson Inc.[4]	
	2000	1999	2000	1999	2000	1999	2000	1999
Total volume (000's hl)	943	539	121,300	118,000	27,406	26,167	11,500	11,500
Net Revenue	141.5	96.1	12,261.8	11,703.7	2,414.0	2,237.0	2,517.1	2,129.1
Operating profit (EBIT)	20,092	14,627	2,494.7	2,302.3	N/a	N/a	102.4	209.6
Net income	8,969	6,549	1,551.6	1402.2	109,617	92,284	(44.0)	169.9
Earnings per share (fully diluted)	0.58	.039	1.69	1.47	2.93	2.96	(0.74)	2.88

In thousands of dollars except volumes and per share amounts.

Source: [1]Sleeman Breweries Ltd. 2000 Annual Report.

[2]Anheuser-Busch's Companies 2000 annual report, all dollar amounts U.S. dollars.

[3]Adolph Coors Company 2000 annual report, all dollar amounts in U.S. dollars.

[4]Molson Inc. 2000 annual report.

EXHIBIT 6 National and American Brands by Company

	Molson Inc.	Labatt	Sleeman Breweries Ltd.
National Brands	• Canadian • Molson Dry • Export • Rickard's Red • Corona • Heineken	• Labatt Blue • Labatt Blue Lite • John Labatt Classic • Labatt Select • Labatt Genuine Draft • Labatt Lite • Labatt Wildcat • Labatt ".5" • Labatt IceTM • Labatt Extra Dry • Labatt "50" • Boomerang • Carlsberg • Carlsberg Lite • Guinness Extra Stout • President's Choice family of brands	• Cream Ale • Honey Brown Lager • Silver Creek Lager • Original Dark • Steam Beer • Premium Light • Beck's • Beck's Non-alcoholic

	Molson Inc.	Labatt	Sleeman Breweries Ltd.
American Brands	• Coors Lite	• Budweiser • Bud Lite	• Stroh • Old Milwaukee • Rainier • Colt 45 • Red Bull • Bull Max • Olympia • Lone Star • Samuel Adams • Boston Lager

Source: Labatt Web site, May 31, 2000, *Molson Inc. 2000 annual report, Sleeman Breweries Ltd. 2000 annual report.*

EXHIBIT 7 Advertising Campaigns and Market Share

Molson Canadian Ads	Taste that will stop you cold	What beer's all about	I am Canadian	Monkeys	Here's where we get Canadian	The Rant

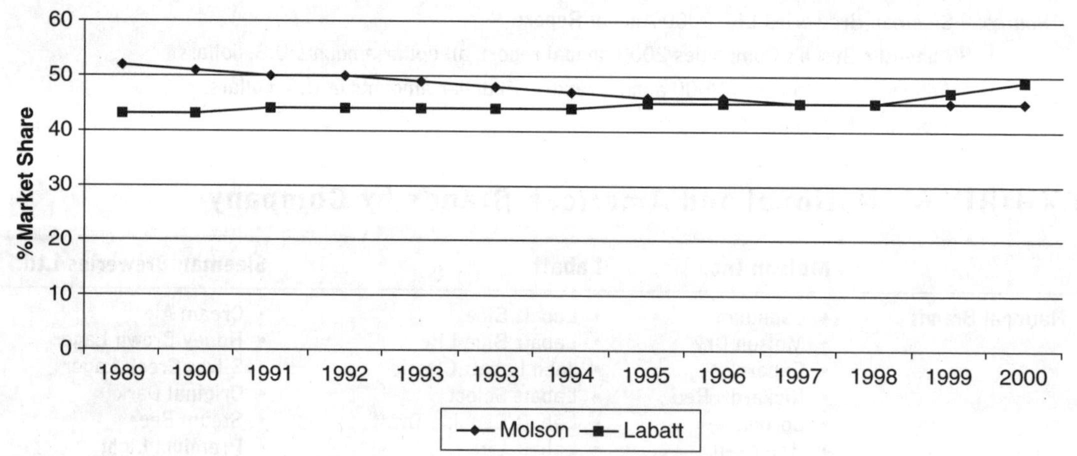

EXHIBIT 8 Molson Research Results[1]

How well does each of the following describe what it means for you to be Canadian?

% of Respondents Saying...	Very Well	Fairly Well	Not well at all
Having the freedom of choice to do what you want to do	70	26	5
Belonging to a multicultural society	57	37	7
Being considerate of others	57	37	7
Being accepted of no matter what your race or religion is	55	36	9
Being in control of your own destiny	53	40	8
Not being American	52	20	29
Having lots of opportunity	48	44	8
Being patient/understanding	49	42	9
Being boring/conservative	8	18	73

[1] Some data may be disguised.

11

Logitech: Launching a Digital Pen

Ken Mark prepared this case under the supervision of Professor Mark Vandenbosch solely to provide material for class discussion. The authors do not intend to illustrate either effective or ineffective handling of a managerial situation. The authors may have disguised certain names and other identifying information to protect confidentiality.

INTRODUCTION

Yves Karcher, retail pointing devices unit director at Logitech, held up his company's newest product, "Logitech io," a personal digital pen designed to electronically record a user's written notes and drawings. It was September 24, 2002, in Romanel-sur-Morges, Switzerland, and Karcher was discussing the future of Logitech io with Jean-Claude Etter, the project manager io product. The Logitech research and development team had spent months working on io and were eagerly awaiting its launch in November 2002. Even though development was complete on the original version of the product, research work was beginning on the second-generation version. There was still a need to identify potential users of the product and to decide which features and applications would be most valuable to those users.

HISTORY OF LOGITECH

Logitech designed, manufactured and marketed computer peripheral products that provided people with easy access to the digital world. Peripheral devices connected to the computer but were external in relation to the processing unit. These products included Internet video cameras, mice and trackballs, keyboards, audio and telephony products, interactive gaming devices and 3-D controllers.

Logitech was founded in October 1981 by Pierluigi Zappacosta and Daniel Borel in Switzerland. The two men had been developing a European word-processing/DTP package for Bobst Graphics when that company was sold and the new owners did not want to continue the project. Zappacosta had met Borel at Stanford University, while they were completing their computer science (MS) degrees. After an initial attempt to bring U.S. technology to Europe with their own software company, Borel and then Zappacosta had joined Bobst to gain industry contacts. They had then formed their own software company with Bobst as the major client. Giacomo Marini, a software manager at Olivetti and a friend of Zappacosta's from the time when they had both worked in Pisa, Italy, joined in founding Logitech together with a group of young engineers. Hardware and software development contracts with Ricoh and Swiss Timing set the stage for Logitech's initial growth and development. A major turning point in the strategic direction of the organization was its contract with Hewlett-Packard to supply mice under an original equipment manager (OEM) contract. Logitech redesigned the mouse for mass production and set up a manufacturing operation in Redwood City, California. Control over manufacturing and a commitment to quality led to rapid growth in the OEM mouse market with contracts from Apollo, Olivetti, AT& T and other key computer manufacturers in the late 1980s.[1]

In 2001, Logitech had market leadership in many different peripheral products. Two examples of its success were its 45 per cent share of the PC camera market after pushing rival Intel out of the Webcam business,[2] and its market leadership position in computer mice, a product line in which Logitech faced competitors such as Microsoft Corporation. During the past few years, Logitech had significantly broadened its product offering and increased its presence in the retail sector. As a result, Logitech's retail business in 2001 accounted for approximately 80 per cent of revenue. It had a strong and growing brand presence in more than 65,000 traditional retail outlets in over 100 countries, as well as on hundreds of Web-based retail sites.[3]

Logitech had operating headquarters in Fremont, California, and a second head office in Romanel-sur-Morges, Switzerland, and regional headquarters in Taiwan and Hong Kong. It had manufacturing facilities in Suzhou, China, with contract manufacturing partners in China, Thailand, Hungary and Mexico. A Swiss public company, Logitech traded on the Swiss Stock Exchange and on the NASDAQ Exchange. Logitech was targeting US$75 million in net income in fiscal year 2002 with $944 million in revenues.

Logitech's Growth Strategies

The company's business model called for supplementing its internal engineering and manufacturing strength with additional products and technologies through a combination of strategic acquisitions and industry partnerships. Management believed that four strategic directions would result in continuing growth:

- Broadening the desktop presence: Logitech had already expanded beyond its traditional role as a provider of desktop pointing devices into a leading brand for cameras, keyboards, PC audio products and game controllers. It had the ability to introduce to the desktop an even greater number of essential interface devices that people touched and used everyday.
- Becoming a leader in media-rich Internet-enabled communication: Logitech continued to increase Internet functionality throughout all its products as it enhanced Web-based service offerings and

[1] Taken from Ivey case #9A92A012 "Logitech" by Brock Smith and Professor Adrian B. Ryans.

[2] www.hoovers.com accessed September 20, 2002.

[3] www.logitech.com accessed September 20, 2002.

explored additional new business models. The introduction of iTouch software to Logitech mice and keyboards and the creation of the SpotLife personal broadcasting initiatives were important steps in this direction. Additionally, the purchase of Labtec brought a broad range of Internet communication tools to the Logitech family, including voice-over Internet Protocol and voice chat.

- Expansion into additional computing platforms: Historically, the computing environment that Logitech served was centred on the desktop. But as the interface to the digital world moved beyond the desktop and beyond the PC—to the living room, to the kitchen, to wherever and however people wanted to access information, the need for an intuitive interface would remain. Logitech intended to continue providing this interface. Recently, for example, the company introduced its first product for the PlayStation 2.
- Broaden product portfolio in the mobile segments where the company intends to build on its brand and technologies. Logitech aims to launch personal digital assistant (PDA) peripherals and mobile phone accessories.

THE EMERGENCE OF PEN-BASED COMPUTING

In the 1990s, the hand-held computing industry grew out of a trend towards smaller and more portable computing devices. Beginning with the laptop computer, hand-held computing had progressed to its currently smallest form, a PDA.

PDAs became popular with the launch of the Palm Corporation's Palm Pilot 1000 in 1996. The Palm Pilot was a palm-sized device designed for portability. Below are some of the key features that led to the popularity of the Palm Pilot:

- Size—the Palm Pilot was small enough to be placed in one's pocket.
- Handwriting recognition—data could be entered into the Palm Pilot by writing directly on its surface using Graffiti, a proprietary handwriting-recognition program.
- Key programs—The Palm Pilot offered users basic—but important—programs such as a datebook/calendar, calculator, address book and a notepad.
- Portability—Powered by replaceable AAA batteries, Palm Pilots could outlast laptop computers (whose batteries lasted no longer than a few hours at best).

The same features which made the Palm Pilot successful also drew criticism from non-users: the screen was too small; users were unwilling to learn to use Graffiti; and functionality was limited.

Computer technology developers had been searching for a reliable and easy-to-use means to let people write on their hand-held computers as easily as they might type on them. This concept, pen-based computing, received widespread exposure in the mid-1990s with Apple's Newton computer—a pioneering hand-held computing device. Newton failed, as did several other later attempts including a pen-based IBM ThinkPad and a Sony Vaio desktop Pen Tablet. These computing devices were not well-accepted for note-taking for a number of reasons. They were too big, too heavy, and could not do enough. A liability had been handwriting recognition, which was necessary to turn scribbled writing into useful digital information. Industry experts suggested that Newton failed because its value proposition was handwriting recognition and it simply did not work.

Tablet PCs, an attempt to launch full-fledged PCs—where input was redesigned to support handwriting—began in 2001 with an announcement by Microsoft and its partners including Compaq Computer, Toshiba and Acer. At Comdex, a technology industry show, the consortium unveiled a series of pen-based, fully functional Tablet PCs slated to go on the market in November 2002. "Tablet

PCs will put an end to the pile management style of organizing pieces of paper," said Ted Clark, vice-president of Compaq's Tablet PC division.[4]

Microsoft was tackling the handwriting recognition challenge. At his Comdex keynote address, Chairman Bill Gates unveiled an application called Journal that turned handwritten cursive or block letters into editable text very efficiently. In development at Microsoft were other Tablet PC applications, such as extensions to the Outlook e-mail and Windows Messenger instant messaging programs. The applications would accept and display handwritten text when a person used a Tablet PC without a keyboard. Microsoft also planned to adapt its operating system, Office XP, to work with Tablet PCs. Michel Marriott, writing in the New York Times, commented: "How paradoxical, then, that in a time when handwriting is in such decline, the computer industry is making a new push to embrace it."[5]

LOGITECH AND ANOTO INTRODUCE IO

On March 19, 2002, David Henry, senior vice-president and general manager of Logitech's control devices business unit announced:

> We have seen intense interest and a great opportunity in the ability to align the computing experience with natural human behavior. This alliance (with Anoto) is a definite fit with Logitech's vision of extending the power of the PC beyond the desktop.[6]

Anoto AB (Anoto) was founded in Lund, Sweden, in 1999. It had licensed its digital pen technology to Logitech and was working with the company to develop io (see Exhibit 1). Key to io's uniqueness was the combination of a digital pen, digital paper technology and software. This combination, known as Anoto Functionality, had advantages versus computer mice and other competitive standalone digital pens. To understand one such advantage, *digital paper technology* had to be explained.

> Picture a geographic area the size of the United States covered by a single sheet of paper 2.5 million square kilometres in size. Now imagine that this entire sheet is covered by dots all located around the intersections of an imaginary grid, each dot having a pitch of 0.3 millimetre. Every collection of dots provides information about the absolute XY co-ordinates of the pen within the entire pattern space.
>
> When writing on digital paper, io's digital camera and embedded software "recognized" the positioning of the small dots relative to each other. This was the concept of digital paper technology (see Exhibit 2).

Anoto had already celebrated a key milestone with the recent launch of the Sony Ericsson CHA-30 Chat Pen (Chat Pen). Relying on Anoto Functionality, the Chat Pen had been launched in selected European markets including Sweden (with Vodaphone) and Denmark. Touted as a bridge between traditional and digital communication, the Chat Pen—which could be used only on two models of Ericsson mobile phones — included technology such as a camera, an image processor and Bluetooth[7] technology. It allowed users to write a message on Anoto's proprietary digital paper and send the message using their mobile phones by pressing a button on the pen. (The pen had to be within 10 metres of the phone.)

---

[4] Tom Spring, "Prototype Tablet PCs take Spotlight," *PCworld.com*, November 12, 2001.
[5] Michel Marriott, "Tablet PC Makers Embrace a Dying Art: Handwriting," *The New York Times*, August 1, 2002.
[6] Company press release, March 19, 2002.
[7] Bluetooth wireless technology was a worldwide specification for a small-form factor, low-cost radio solution that provided links between mobile computers, mobile phones, other portable handheld devices and connectivity to the Internet. The specification was developed, published and promoted by the Bluetooth Special Interest Group (SIG).

According to industry experts, there were various shortcomings to the Chat Pen including the use of graphic SMS[8] which was a poor application for graphics, and limitations to a user's mobility due to its reliance on a data transfer standard known as GPRS[9] which did not support mobile phone roaming.

Karcher explained the difference between io and other handwriting capture technologies:

> The main attribute of io is that it is the only untethered handwriting capture device — all other systems (tablets, triangulation pens) are tethered. The key is that io allows you to capture notes in an area where it is unsuitable or inconvenient to carry a laptop. Overwhelmingly, pen and paper continue to be the most convenient note-taking method.

Logitech's io had 1.3 megabytes of storage space, sufficient for 40 pages of text. To best explain its uniqueness, one could examine io's key advantages versus traditional mousing: Consider the use of a computer mouse to draw a series of pictures. If the user, while drawing, picked the mouse up (breaking contact with the surface-tracking function), moved the mouse five feet to his or her right, put the mouse back into contact with a flat surface and continued drawing, the mouse would not register that it had moved at all. Users could continue drawing where they left off. This was known as relative positioning.

Using io on several sheets of proprietary digital paper, the user could flip from page to page, drawing pictures and making notes at random, even returning to add to previous drawings and notes. Because of the unique properties of digital paper — each page being distinct from all others — the digital pen would always know on which page it was drawing or writing. This advantage, termed absolute positioning, was one of the unique features of io touted by Logitech.[10]

Anoto Functionality

Anoto Functionality depended on three component working together: digital pen technology, digital paper technology and software. The digital pen had the look and feel of an ordinary ballpoint pen and was used in the same way.

There were no keys to press and there was no display. The main parts of the digital pen included a digital camera, an advanced image-processing unit and a communication unit. Logitech io had a memory of more than one megabyte, sufficient to hold 40 full pages of text and drawings. As the user wrote, the built-in digital camera in the pen registered the pen's movements across digital paper. Then, a combination of digital image processing enabled information on pen movement and handling to be stored. When a user placed the digital pen in a cradle connected to a PC, the information contained within the pen would be saved through synchronization with the PC. What appeared on the PC screen was an exact facsimile of the image and words drawn by the user.

As indicated before, *digital paper* was created by printing a proprietary pattern of very small dots on ordinary paper that was perceived by the eye as a slightly off-white color. The dots had a nominal spacing of 0.3 millimetre. Each page was distinct from all others. Logitech had added several features to digital paper; one example was the e-mail feature (see Exhibit 3).

Users could write an e-mail address directly on the page and tick the box "e-mail." Upon synchronization with the PC, the software would recognize the e-mail address, reproduce drawings and notes in an e-mail message, and automatically send the e-mail to the target.

---

8 SMS is short messaging service, allowing mobile phones to send and receive short text messages.

9 General Packet Radio Service (GPRS) enabled networks to offer 'always-on,' higher capacity, Internet-based content and packet-based data services. This enabled services such as color Internet browsing, e-mail on the move, powerful visual communications, multimedia messages and location-based services.

10 If Logitech io was used on any other surface but digital paper, it would not be able to function properly. The pen would be a regular ball point pen in this case.

PC software was the last component that enabled the io system to function. According to Logitech, io software had no equivalent on the market. A Logitech manager proclaimed, "The software was not only a piece of code . . . but of a piece of paper as well!" The software integrated these four key features:

- Automatically place documents into folders on the PC's hard drive when the user synchronized the digital pen with a PC. A paper application definition (PAD) file contained the detailed description of the page (all fields and their location, type of service).
- Store and electronically search by keywords all handwritten notes. Keywords were written in special fields, like the title of the page. Only these fields would be fed into the handwriting recognition module.
- Write e-mails without a PC and send immediately upon synchronizing the digital pen with the PC.
- Cut and paste information contained in handwritten documents.
- Write a "to do" item or calendar entry without a PC and have them synchronized with popular organizer software.

For ease of use, io software interface was integrated into the Windows operating system. By 2002, Logitech had finalized its digital pen software and was in the final stages of manufacturing io for release.

POSITIONING RELATIVE TO COMPETITION

Logitech felt that io had significant advantages versus competitive devices. Table 1 describes io's positioning relative to competition:

With a target retail price of US$199, io was ontrack for its November 2002 launch in the United States and Germany. Logitech io would have a cradle, be USB-based, and would focus on advertising three features: organization, notes and e-mail. Included with the price of io would be several branded digital paper notebooks with organizer and e-mail integration.

An early estimate indicated that io had to achieve sales of 100,000 units in its first year in order for subsequent projects to take place. At this point, io was the number three priority in the control devices business unit. Logitech believed that initial customers w ould be mostly early adopters who would integrate io into their home and work lifestyle. Other target users included architects, engineers, marketers, salespeople and students. From internal studies, Logitech discovered that 43 per cent of surveyed engineers, architects, marketers and salespeople used drawings as part of their job. Of note, 98 per cent of engineers and architects used drawings daily. Additionally, half of those surveyed travelled as part of their jobs.

Table 1 Logitech io's positioning relative to competitive product categories

Product Category	Key Benefit	Logitech Pen Positioning
Tablet PCs (Toshiba Portégé, Compaq TC1000, Dell)	Pen input, inexpensive peripheral	portability, ink feedback
Laptops	Already use one regularly, can type very quickly, lighter weight models emerging	Augment laptop use, especially with drawings, use away from laptop
Triangulation Pens (Seiko InkLink)	Enables an ordinary pen and paper to become a computer input device for notes, diagrams and sketches	Untethered and unobtrusive portability as pen can be used away from laptop or pocket pc. Several documents or pages can be worked on at the same time.

MOVING TOWARDS LAUNCH

Christer Fåhraeus, chief executive officer of Anoto, was excited about the impending launch of io:

> The agreement with Logitech takes us from vision to actual implementation and implies that digital pens and paper . . . will reach an even wider field of applications and a larger number of users. By partnering with Logitech and thereby entering the PC market, we are on our way to achieving total coverage and establishing a de facto standard for paper-based digital communications.[11]

Karcher was cautiously optimistic. The majority of new product launches in high technology had failed to live up to their lofty expectations. His research and development team had high expectations for io — now it was up to them to articulate to potential users how io was to be used. Already, he was thinking about the next version of io — one such opportunity was the possibility of partnering with companies in the Tablet PC world to launch the next generation of io. A Logitech vice-president of strategic marketing once stated, "We are the most critical users of our products. Customer need recognition is limited by their understanding of technology — they don't know what is possible!"

Now as he began discussions with Etter on the development of the next generation product, Karcher needed several key questions answered. The overall question was whether there existed market demand for io sufficient to warrant further investment in research and development. Which target market would most likely purchase io? What were the features of io that appealed to them? For which applications would they use io? How likely would these users adopt io for consistent use? Most important of all, was there a "killer app" that would drive sales of io into the hundreds of thousands of units?

EXHIBIT 1 Logitech io

Pen

Pen in its cradle

Source: Logitech Web site.

---

[11] Anoto Press Release, March 14, 2002. Accessed September 5, 2002.

EXHIBIT 2 Digital Pen and Paper illustrating Anoto technology

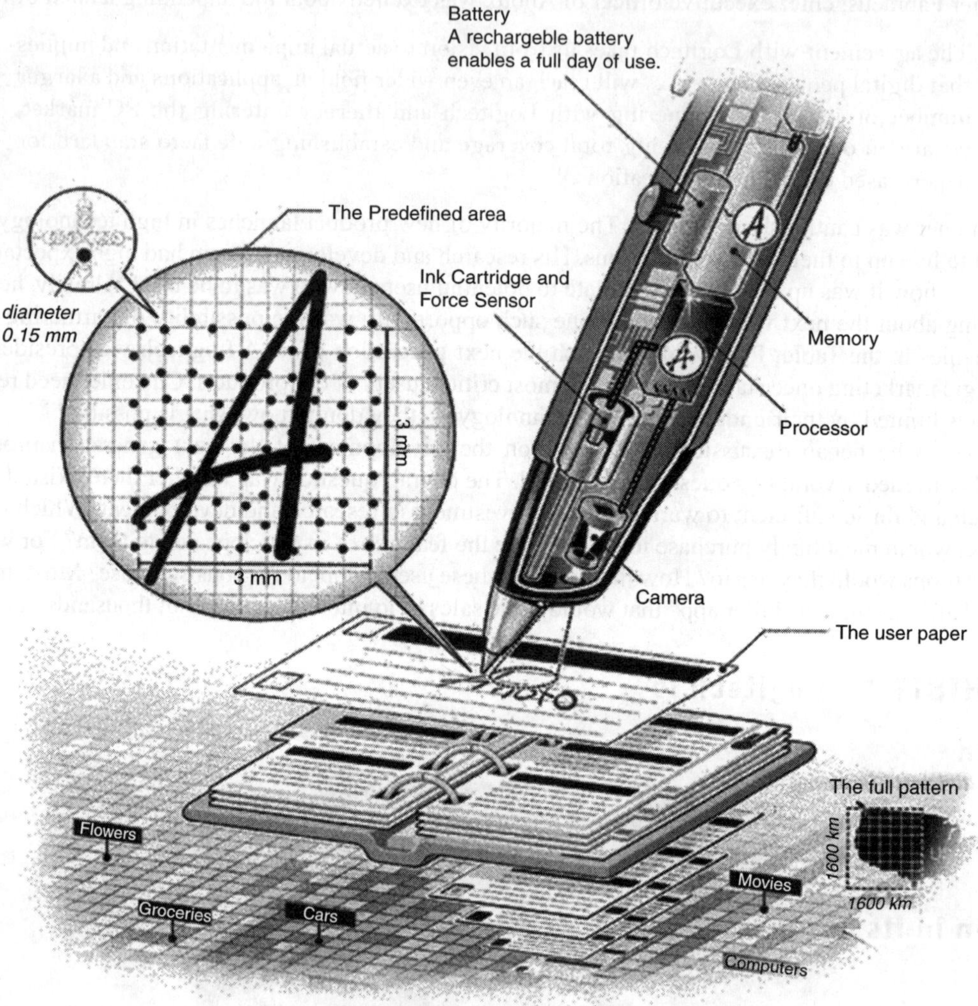

Source: Company files.

EXHIBIT 3 Sample Digital Paper features integrated with io software

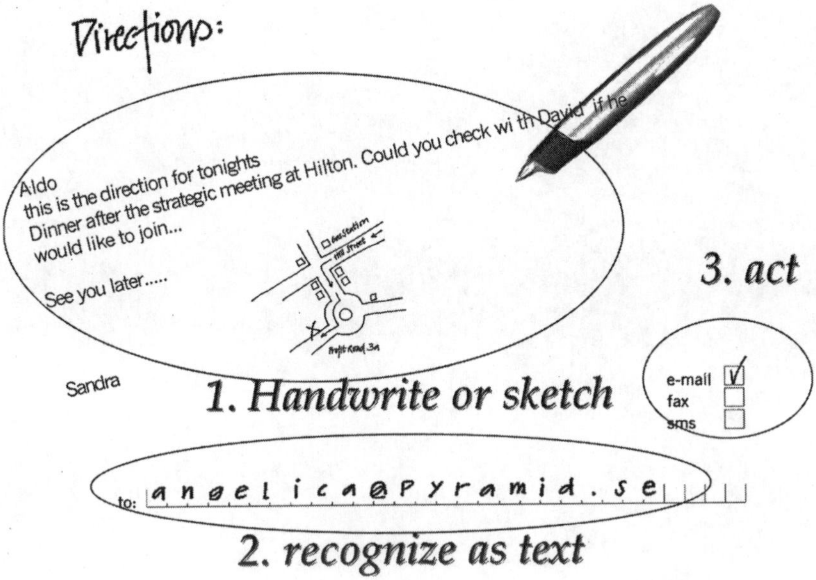

Source: Company files.

12

Global Branding of Stella Artois

Professors Paul W. Beamish and Anthony Goerzen prepared this case solely to provide material for class discussion. The authors do not intend to illustrate either effective or ineffective handling of a managerial situation. The authors may have disguised certain names and other identifying information to protect confidentiality.

In April 2000, Paul Cooke, chief marketing officer of Interbrew, the world's fourth largest brewer, contemplated the further development of their premium product, Stella Artois, as the company's flagship brand in key markets around the world. Although the long-range plan for 2000-2002 had been approved, there still remained some important strategic issues to resolve.

A BRIEF HISTORY OF INTERBREW

Interbrew traced its origins back to 1366 to a brewery called Den Hoorn, located in Leuven, a town just outside of Brussels. In 1717, when it was purchased by its master brewer, Sebastiaan Artois, the brewery changed its name to Artois.

The firm's expansion began when Artois acquired a major interest in the Leffe Brewery in Belgium in 1954, the Dommelsch Brewery in the Netherlands in 1968, and the Brassiere du Nord in France in 1970. In 1987, when Artois and another Belgian brewery called Piedboeuf came together, the merged company was named Interbrew. The new company soon acquired other Belgian specialty beer brewers, building up the Interbrew brand portfolio with the purchase of the Hoegaarden brewery in 1989 and the Belle-Vue Brewery in 1990.

Interbrew then entered into a phase of rapid growth. The company acquired breweries in Hungary in 1991, in Croatia and Romania in 1994, and in three plants in Bulgaria in 1995. Again in 1995, Interbrew completed an unexpected major acquisition by purchasing Labatt, a large Canadian brewer also with international interests. Labatt had operations in the United States, for example, with the Latrobe brewery, home of the Rolling Rock brand. Labatt also held a substantial minority stake in the second largest Mexican brewer, Femsa Cervesa, which produced Dos Equis, Sol, and Tecate brands. Following this major acquisition, Interbrew went on, in 1996, to buy a brewery in the Ukraine and engaged in a joint venture in the Dominican Republic. Subsequently, breweries were added in China in 1997, Montenegro and Russia in 1998, and another brewery in Bulgaria and one in Korea in 1999.

Thus, through acquisition expenditures of US$2.5 billion in the previous four years, Interbrew had transformed itself from a simple Belgian brewery into one of the largest beer companies in the world. By 1999, the company had become a brewer on a truly global scale that now derived more than 90 per cent of its volume from markets outside Belgium. It remained a privately held company, headquartered in Belgium, with subsidiaries and joint ventures in 23 countries across four continents.

THE INTERNATIONAL MARKET FOR BEER

In the 1990s, the world beer market was growing at an annual rate of one to two per cent. In 1998, beer consumption reached a total of 1.3 billion hectolitres (hls). There were, however, great regional differences in both market size and growth rates. Most industry analysts split the world market for beer between growth and mature markets. The mature markets were generally considered to be North America, Western Europe and Australasia. The growth markets included Latin America, Asia, Central and Eastern Europe including Russia. Although some felt that Africa had considerable potential, despite its low per capita beer consumption, the continent was not considered a viable market by many brewers because of its political and economic instability (see Exhibit 1).

Mature Markets

The North American beer market was virtually stagnant, although annual beer consumption per person was already at a sizeable 83 litres per capita (lpc). The Western European market had also reached maturity with consumption of 79 lpc. Some analysts believed that this consumption level was under considerable pressure, forecasting a decline to near 75 lpc over the medium term. Australia and New Zealand were also considered mature markets, with consumption at 93 lpc and 84 lpc, respectively. In fact, volumes in both markets, New Zealand in particular, had declined through the 1990s following tight social policies on alcohol consumption and the emergence of a wine culture.

Growth Markets

Given that average consumption in Eastern Europe was only 29 lpc, the region appeared to offer great potential. This consumption figure, however, was heavily influenced by Russia's very low level, and the future for the large Russian market was unclear. Further, some markets, such as the Czech Republic that consumed the most beer per person in the world at 163 lpc, appeared to have already reached maturity. Central and South America, on the other hand, were showing healthy growth and, with consumption at an average of 43 lpc, there was believed to be considerable upside. The most exciting growth rates, however, were in Asia. Despite the fact that the market in this region had grown by more than 30 per cent since 1995, consumption levels were still comparatively low. In China, the region's largest market, consumption was only 16 lpc and 20 to 25 lpc in Hong Kong and Taiwan. Although the 1997 Asian financial crisis did not immediately affect beer consumption (although company profits from the region were hit by currency translation), demand in some key markets, such as Indonesia, was reduced and in others growth slowed. The situation, however, was expected to improve upon economic recovery in the medium term.

BEER INDUSTRY STRUCTURE

The world beer industry was relatively fragmented with the top four players accounting for only 22 per cent of global volume — a relatively low figure as compared to 78 per cent in the soft drinks industry, 60 per cent in tobacco and 44 per cent in spirits. This suggested great opportunities for consolidation, a process that had already begun two decades prior. Many analysts, including those at Interbrew, expected that this process would probably accelerate in the future. The driver behind industry rationalization was the need to achieve economies of scale in production, advertising and distribution. It was widely recognized that the best profit margins were attained either by those with a commanding position in the market or those with a niche position. However, there were several factors that mitigated the trend towards rapid concentration of the brewing industry.

One factor that slowed the process of consolidation was that the ratio of fixed versus variable costs of beer production was relatively high. Essentially, this meant that there was a limited cost savings potential that could be achieved by bringing more operations under a common administration. Real cost savings could be generated by purchasing and then rationalizing operations through shifting production to more efficient (usually more modern) facilities. This approach, however, required large initial capital outlays. As a result, in some markets with "unstable" economies, it was desirable to spread out capital expenditures over a longer period of time to ensure appropriate profitability in the early stages. A second factor that may have had a dampening effect on the trend towards industry consolidation was that local tastes differed. In some cases, beer brands had hundreds of years of heritage behind them and had become such an integral part of everyday life that consumers were often fiercely loyal to their local brew. This appeared to be a fact in many markets around the world.

INTERBREW'S GLOBAL POSITION

Through Interbrew's acquisitions in the 1990s, the company had expanded rapidly. During this period, the company's total volumes had increased more than fourfold. These figures translated to total beer production of 57.5 million hls in 1998 (when including the volume of all affiliates), as compared to just 14.7 million hls in 1992. Volume growth had propelled the company into the number four position among the world's brewers.

Faced with a mature and dominant position in the declining Belgian domestic market, the company decided to focus on consolidating and developing key markets, namely Belgium, the Netherlands, France and North America, and expansion through acquisition in Central Europe, Asia and South America. Subsequently, Interbrew reduced its dependence on the Belgian market from 44 per cent in 1992 to less than 10 per cent by 1998 (total volumes including Mexico). Concurrently, a significant milestone for the company was achieved by 1999 when more than 50 per cent of its total volume was produced in growth markets (including Mexico). Interbrew had shifted its volume so that the Americas accounted for 61 per cent of its total volume, Europe added 35 per cent, and Asia Pacific the remaining four per cent.

Taken together, the top 10 markets for beer accounted for 86 per cent of Interbrew's total volume in 1998 (see Exhibit 2). The Mexican beer market alone accounted for 37 per cent of total volume in 1998. Canada, Belgium, the United States and the United Kingdom were the next most important markets. However, smaller, growing markets such as Hungary, Croatia, Bulgaria, and Romania had begun to increase in importance.

Adding to its existing breweries in Belgium, France and the Netherlands, Interbrew's expansion strategy in the 1990s had resulted in acquisitions in Bosnia-Herzegovina, Bulgaria, Canada, China, Croatia, Hungary, Korea, Montenegro, Romania, Russia, the Ukraine, the United States, in a joint venture in South Korea, and in minority equity positions in Mexico and Luxembourg. Through these breweries, in addition to those that were covered by licensing agreements in Australia, Italy, Sweden and the United Kingdom, Interbrew sold its beers in over 80 countries.

INTERBREW'S CORPORATE STRUCTURE

Following the acquisition of Labatt in 1995, Interbrew's corporate structure was divided into two geographic zones: the Americas and Europe/Asia/Africa. This structure was in place until September 1999 when Interbrew shifted to a fully integrated structure to consolidate its holdings in the face of industry globalization. Hugo Powell, formerly head of the Americas division, was appointed to the position of chief executive officer (CEO). The former head of the Europe/Africa/Asia division assumed the role of chief operating officer, but subsequently resigned and was not replaced, leaving Interbrew with a more conventional structure, with the five regional heads and the various corporate functional managers reporting directly to the CEO.

RECENT PERFORMANCE

1998 had been a good year for Interbrew in terms of volume in both mature and growth markets. Overall, sales volumes increased by 11.1 per cent as most of the company's international and local brands maintained or gained market share. In terms of the compounded annual growth rate, Interbrew outperformed all of its major competitors by a wide margin. While Interbrew's 1998 net sales were up 29 per cent, the best performing competitor achieved an increase of only 16 per cent. Of Interbrew's increased sales, 67 per cent was related to the new affiliates in China, Montenegro and Korea. The balance was the result of organic growth. Considerable volume increases were achieved also in Romania (72 per cent), Bulgaria (28 per cent), Croatia (13 per cent), and the United States (14 per cent). While volumes in Western Europe were flat, duty-free sales grew strongly. In the U.S. market, strong progress was made by Interbrew's Canadian and Mexican brands, and Latrobe's Rolling Rock was successfully relaunched. In Canada, performance was strong, fuelled by a two per cent increase in domestic consumption. Labatt's sales of Budweiser (produced under license from Anheuser Busch) also continued to grow rapidly.

Given that the premium and specialty beer markets were growing quickly, particularly those within the large, mature markets, Interbrew began to shift its product mix to take advantage of this trend and the superior margins it offered. A notable brand success was Stella Artois, for which total global sales volumes were up by 19.7 per cent. That growth came from sales generated by Whitbread in the United Kingdom, from exports, and from sales in Central Europe where Stella Artois volumes took off. The strong growth of Stella Artois was also notable in that it was sold in the premium lager segment. In Europe, Asia Pacific and Africa, Interbrew's premium and specialty beers, which generated a bigger margin, increased as a proportion of total sales from 31 per cent in 1997 to 33 per cent in 1998. This product mix shift was particularly important since intense competition in most markets inhibited real price increases.

Success was also achieved in the United States specialty beer segment where total volume had been growing at nine per cent annually in the 1990s. In 1998, Interbrew's share of this growing market segment had risen even faster as Labatt USA realized increased sales of 16 per cent. The other continuing development was the growth of the light beer segment, which had become over 40 per cent of the total sales. Sales of Labatt's Blue Light, for example, had increased and Labatt Blue had become the number three imported beer in the United States, with volumes up 18 per cent. Latrobe's Rolling Rock brand grew by four per cent, the first increase in four years. Interbrew's Mexican brands, Dos Equis, Tecate and Sol, were also up by 19 per cent.

Following solid volume growth in profitable market segments, good global results were realized in key financial areas. Net profit, having grown for each of the previous six consecutive years, was 7.7 billion Belgian francs (BEF) in 1998, up 43.7 per cent from the previous year. Operating profit also rose 7.9 per cent over 1997, from 14.3 to 15.4 BEF; in both the Europe/Asia/Africa region and the Americas, operating profit was up by 8.5 per cent and 4.9 per cent respectively. Further, Interbrew's EBIT margin was up 58.1 per cent as compared to the best performing competitor's figure of 17.0 per cent. However, having made several large investments in Korea and Russia, and exercising an option to increase its share of Femsa Cerveza in Mexico from 22 per cent to 30 per cent, Interbrew's debt-equity ratio increased from 1.04 to 1.35. As a result, interest payments rose accordingly.

Interbrew also enjoyed good results in volume sales in many of its markets in 1999. Although Canadian sales remained largely unchanged over 1998, Labatt USA experienced strong growth in 1999, with volumes up by 10 per cent. There was a positive evolution in Western European volumes as well, as overall sales were up by 6.5 per cent overall in Belgium, France and the Netherlands. Central European markets also grew with Hungary showing an increase of 9.6 per cent, Croatia up by 5.5 per cent, Romania by 18.9 per cent, Montenegro by 29 per cent, and Bulgaria with a rise of 3.6 per cent in terms of volume. Sales positions were also satisfactory in the Russian and Ukrainian markets. Further, while South Korean sales volume remained unchanged, volumes in China were 10 per cent higher, although this figure was still short of expectations.

INTERBREW CORPORATE STRATEGY

The three facets of Interbrew's corporate strategy, i.e., brands, markets and operations, were considered the "sides of the Interbrew triangle." Each of these aspects of corporate strategy was considered to be equally important in order to achieve the fundamental objective of increasing shareholder value. With a corporate focus entirely on beer, the underlying objectives of the company were to consolidate its positions in mature markets and improve margins through higher volumes of premium and specialty brands. Further, the company's emphasis on growth was driven by the belief that beer industry rationalization still had some way to go and that the majority of the world's major markets would each end up with just two or three major players.

Operations Strategy

Cross fertilization of best practices between sites was a central component of Interbrew's operations strategy. In the company's two main markets, Belgium and Canada, each brewery monitored its performance on 10 different dimensions against its peers. As a result, the gap between the best and the worst of Interbrew's operations had narrowed decisively since 1995. Employees continuously put forward propositions to improve processes. The program had resulted in significantly lower production costs, suggesting to Interbrew management that most improvements had more to do with employee motivation than with pure technical performance. In addition, capacity utilization and strategic sourcing had been identified as two areas of major opportunity.

Capacity Utilization

Given that brewing was a capital-intensive business, capacity utilization had a major influence on profitability. Since declining consumption in mature markets had generated excess capacity, several of Interbrew's old breweries and processing facilities were scheduled to be shut down. In contrast, in several growth markets such as Romania, Bulgaria, Croatia and Montenegro, the opposite problem existed, so facilities in other locations were used more fully until local capacities were increased.

Strategic Sourcing

Interbrew had begun to rationalize its supply base as well. By selecting a smaller number of its best suppliers and working more closely with them, Interbrew believed that innovative changes resulted, saving both parties considerable sums every year. For most of the major commodities, the company had gone to single suppliers and was planning to extend this approach to all operations worldwide.

Market Strategy

The underlying objectives of Interbrew's market strategy were to increase volume and to lessen its dependence on Belgium and Canada, its two traditional markets. Interbrew dichotomized its market strategy into the mature and growth market segments, although investments were considered wherever opportunities to generate sustainable profits existed. One of the key elements of Interbrew's market strategy was to establish and manage strong market platforms. It was believed that a brand strength was directly related to a competitive and dedicated market platform (i.e., sales and distribution, wholesaler networks, etc.) to support the brand. Further, Interbrew allowed individual country teams to manage their own affairs and many felt that the speed of success in many markets was related to this decentralized approach.

Mature markets

Interbrew's goals in its mature markets were to continue to build market share and to improve margins through greater efficiencies in production, distribution and marketing. At the same time, the company intended to exploit the growing trend in these markets towards premium and specialty products of which Interbrew already possessed an unrivalled portfolio. The key markets in which this strategy was being actively pursued were the United States, Canada, the United Kingdom, France, the Netherlands and Belgium.

Growth Markets

Based on the belief that the world's beer markets would undergo further consolidation, Interbrew's market strategy was to build significant positions in markets that had long-term volume growth potential. This goal led to a clear focus on Central and Eastern Europe and Asia, South Korea and China in particular. In China, for example, Interbrew had just completed an acquisition of a second brewery in Nanjing. The Yali brand was thereby added to the corporate portfolio and, together with its Jingling brand, Interbrew became the market leader in Nanjing, a city of six million people.

In Korea, Interbrew entered into a 50:50 joint venture with the Doosan Chaebol to operate the Oriental Brewery, producing the OB Lager and Cafri pilsener brands. With this move, Interbrew took the number two position in the Korean beer market with a 36 per cent share and sales of 5.1 million hls. The venture with Doosan was followed in December 1999 by the purchase of the Jinro Coors brewery. This added 2.5 million hls and increased Interbrew's market share to 50 per cent of total Korean volume. Thus, the Interbrew portfolio in Korea consisted of two mainstream pilsener brands, OB Lager and Cass, the two local premium brands, Cafri and Red Rock, and Budweiser, an international premium brand.

In Russia, Interbrew expanded its presence by taking a majority stake in the Rosar Brewery in Omsk, adding the BAG Bier and Sibirskaya Korona brands. Rosar was the leading brewer in Siberia with a 25 per cent regional market share, and held the number four position in Russia. New initiatives were also undertaken in Central Europe with acquisitions of a brewery in Montenegro and the Pleven brewery in Bulgaria, as well as the introduction of Interbrew products into the Yugoslavian market. Finally, although Interbrew had just increased its already significant investment in Mexico's second largest brewer from 22 per cent to 30 per cent, Latin America remained a region of great interest.

Brand Strategy

A central piece of Interbrew's traditional brand strategy had been to add to its portfolio of brands through acquisition of existing brewers, principally in growth markets. Since its goal was to have the number one or two brand in every market segment in which it operated, Interbrew concentrated on purchasing and developing strong local brands. As it moved into new territories, the company's first priority was to upgrade product quality and to improve the positioning of the acquired local core lager brands. In mature markets, it drew on the strength of the established brands such as Jupiler, Belgium's leading lager brand, Labatt Blue, the famous Canadian brand, and Dommelsch, an important brand in the Netherlands. In growth markets, Interbrew supported brands like Borsodi Sor in Hungary, Kamenitza in Bulgaria, Ozujsko in Croatia, Bergenbier in Romania, Jingling in China, and OB Lager in Korea. In addition, new products were launched such as Taller, a premium brand in the Ukraine, and Boomerang, an alternative malt-based drink in Canada.

A second facet of the company's brand strategy was to identify certain brands, typically specialty products, and to develop them on a regional basis across a group of markets. At the forefront of this strategy were the Abbaye de Leffe and Hoegaarden brands and, to a lesser extent, Belle-Vue. In fact, both Hoegaarden and Leffe achieved a leading position as the number one white beer and abbey beer in France and Holland. The Loburg premium pilsener brand also strengthened its position when it was relaunched in France. Further, in Canada, Interbrew created a dedicated organization for specialty beers called the Oland Specialty Beer Company. In its first year of operation, the brands marketed by Oland increased its volumes by over 40 per cent. More specifically, sales of the Alexander Keith's brand doubled and the negative volume trend of the John Labatt Classic brand was reversed. The underlying message promoted by Oland was the richness, mystique and heritage of beer.

To support the regional growth of specialty beers, Interbrew established a new type of café. The Belgian Beer Café, owned and run by independent operators, created an authentic Belgian atmosphere where customers sampled Interbrew's Belgian specialty beers. By 1999, Belgian Beer Cafés were open in the many of Interbrew's key markets, including top selling outlets in New York, Auckland, Zagreb and Budapest, to name a few. The business concept was that these cafés were to serve as an ambassador of the Belgian beer culture in foreign countries. They were intended to serve as vehicles to showcase Interbrew's specialty brands, benefiting from the international appeal of European styles and fashions. Although these cafés represented strong marketing tools for brand positioning, the key factors that led to the success of this concept were tied very closely to the individual establishments and the personnel running them. The bar staff, for example, had to be trained to serve the beer in the right branded glass, at the right temperature, and with a nice foamy head. It was anticipated that the concept of the specialty café would be used to support the brand development efforts of Interbrew's Belgian beers in all of its important markets.

The third facet of Interbrew's brand strategy was to identify a key corporate brand and to develop it as a global product. While the market segment for a global brand was currently relatively small, with the bulk of the beer demand still in local brands, the demand for international brands was expected to grow, as many consumers became increasingly attracted to the sophistication of premium and super-premium beers.

THE EVOLUTION OF INTERBREW'S GLOBAL BRAND STRATEGY

Until 1997, Interbrew's brand development strategy for international markets was largely *laissez faire*. Brands were introduced to new markets through licensing, export and local production when opportunities were uncovered. Stella Artois, Interbrew's most broadly available and oldest brand, received an important new thrust when it was launched through local production in three of the company's subsidiaries in Central Europe in 1997. This approach was consistent with the company's overall goals of building a complete portfolio in high growth potential markets.

By 1998, however, the executive management committee perceived the need to identify a brand from its wide portfolio to systematically develop into the company's global brand. Although the market for global brands was still small, there were some growing successes (e.g., Heineken, Corona, Fosters and Budweiser) and Interbrew believed that there were several basic global trends that would improve the viability of this class of product over the next couple of decades. First, while many consumers were seeking more variety, others were seeking lower prices. It appeared that the number of affluent and poor consumer segments would increase at the expense of the middle income segments. The upshot of this socioeconomic trend was that eventually all markets would likely evolve in such a way that demand for both premium and economy-priced beers would increase, squeezing the mainstream beers in the middle. A second trend was the internationalization of the beer business. As consumers travelled around the world, consuming global media (e.g., CNN, Eurosport, MTV, international magazines, etc.), global media were expected to become more effective for building brands. A global strategy could, therefore, lead to synergies in global advertising and sponsoring. In addition, the needs of consumers in many markets were expected to converge. As a result of these various factors, Interbrew believed that there would be an increasing interest in authentic, international brands in a growing number of countries. Interbrew had a wide portfolio of national brands that it could set on the international stage. The two most obvious candidates were Labatt Blue and Stella Artois.

The Labatt range of brands included Labatt Blue, Labatt Blue Light and Labatt Ice. To date, however, the exposure of these brands outside of North America had been extremely limited and they were not yet budding global brands. Of the total Labatt Blue volume in 1998, 85 per cent was derived from the Canadian domestic and U.S. markets, with the balance sold in the United Kingdom. The Labatt brands had been introduced to both France and Belgium, and production had been licensed in Italy, but these volumes were minimal. The only real export growth market for Labatt Blue appeared to be the United States, where the brand's volume in 1998 was some 23 per cent higher than in 1995, behind only Corona and Heineken in the imported brand segment. The Labatt Ice brand was also sold in a limited number of markets and, after the appeal of this Labatt innovation had peaked, its total volume had declined by more than 25 per cent since 1996. Total Labatt Ice volume worldwide was just 450,000 hls in 1998, of which 43 per cent was sold in Canada, 33 per cent in the United States, and 21 per cent in the United Kingdom.

STELLA ARTOIS AS INTERBREW'S INTERNATIONAL FLAGSHIP BRAND

The other potential brand that Interbrew could develop on a global scale was Stella Artois, a brand that could trace its roots back to 1366. The modern version of Stella Artois was launched in 1920 as a Christmas beer and had become a strong market leader in its home market of Belgium through the 1970s. By the 1990s, however, Stella's market position began to suffer from an image as a somewhat old-fashioned beer, and the brand began to experience persistent volume decline. Problems in the domestic market, however, appeared to be shared by a number of other prominent international brands. In fact, seven of the top 10 international brands had experienced declining sales in their home markets between 1995 and 1999 (see Exhibit 3).

Stella Artois had achieved great success in the United Kingdom through its licensee, Whitbread, where Stella Artois became the leading premium lager beer. Indeed, the United Kingdom was the largest market for Stella Artois, accounting for 49 per cent of total brand volume in 1998. Stella Artois volume in the U.K. market reached 2.8 million hls in 1998, a 7.6 per cent share of the lager market, and came close to 3.5 million hls in 1999, a 25 per cent increase over the previous year. By this time, over 32,000 outlets sold Stella Artois on draught.

Apart from the United Kingdom, the key markets for Stella Artois were France and Belgium, which together accounted for a further 31 per cent of total brand volume (see Exhibit 4). With these three markets accounting for 81 per cent of total Stella Artois volume in 1999, few other areas represented a significant volume base (see Exhibit 5). Beyond the top three markets, the largest market for Stella Artois was Italy, where the brand was produced under license by Heineken. Stella Artois volume in Italy had, however, declined slightly to 166,000 hls in 1998. Licensing agreements were also in place in Sweden and Australia, but volume was small.

Stella Artois was also produced in Interbrew's own breweries in Hungary, Croatia and Romania, with very pleasing 1998 volumes of 84,000 hls, 120,000 hls, and 60,000 hls, respectively. After only three years, the market share of Stella Artois in Croatia, for example, had reached four per cent — a significant result, given that the brand was a premium-priced product. In all Central European markets, Stella Artois was priced at a premium; in Hungary, however, that premium was lower than in Croatia and Romania where, on an index comparing Stella's price to that of core lagers, the indices by country were 140, 260 and 175 respectively.

Promising first results were also attained in Australia and New Zealand. Particularly in New Zealand, through a "seeding" approach, Interbrew and their local partner, Lion Nathan, had realized great success in the Belgian Beer Café in Auckland where the brands were showcased. After only two years of support, Stella Artois volume was up to 20,000 hls, and growing at 70 per cent annually, out of a total premium segment of 400,000 hls. Interbrew's market development plan limited distribution to top outlets in key metropolitan centres and priced Stella Artois significantly above competitors (e.g., 10 per cent over Heineken and 20 per cent over Steinlager, the leading domestic premium lager brand).

The evolution of the brand looked very positive as world volumes for Stella Artois continued to grow. In fact, Stella Artois volume had increased from 3.4 million hls in 1992 to a total of 6.7 million hls in 1999, a rise of 97 per cent. Ironically, the only market where the brand continued its steady decline was in its home base of Belgium. Analysts suggested a variety of reasons to explain this anomaly, including inconsistent sales and marketing support, particularly as the organization began to favor the rising Jupiler brand.

Overall, given Interbrew's large number of local brands, especially those in Mexico with very high volumes, total Stella Artois volume accounted for only 10 per cent of total Interbrew volume in 1999 (14 per cent if Femsa volumes are excluded). Interbrew's strategy of nurturing a wide portfolio of strong brands was very different as compared to some of its major competitors. For example, Anheuser-Busch, the world's largest brewer, focused its international strategy almost exclusively on the development of the Budweiser brand. Similarly, Heineken sought to centre its international business on the Heineken brand and, to a lesser extent, on Amstel. While the strategies of Anheuser-Busch and Heineken focused primarily on one brand, there were also great differences in the way these two brands were being managed. For example, Budweiser, the world's largest brand by volume, had the overwhelming bulk of its volume in its home U.S. market (see Exhibit 6). Sales of the Heineken brand, on the other hand, were widely distributed across markets around the world (see Exhibit 7). In this sense, Heineken's strategy was much more comparable to that of Interbrew's plans for Stella Artois. Other brands that were directly comparable to Stella Artois, in terms of total volume and importance of the brand to the overall sales of the company, were Carlsberg and Foster's with annual sales volumes in 1998 of 9.4 million hls and 7.1 million hls, respectively. While Foster's was successful in many international markets, there was a heavy focus on sales in the United Kingdom and the United States (see Exhibit 8). Carlsberg sales volume profile was different in that sales were more widely distributed across international markets (see Exhibit 9).

STELLA'S GLOBAL LAUNCH

In 1998, Interbrew's executive management committee settled on Stella Artois, positioned as the premium European lager, as the company's global flagship brand. In fact, the Interbrew management felt that stock analysts would be favorably disposed to Interbrew having an acknowledged global brand with the potential for a higher corporate valuation and price earnings (P/E) multiple.

As the global campaign got under way, it became clear that the organization needed time to adapt to centralized co-ordination and control of Stella Artois brand marketing. This was, perhaps, not unexpected given that Interbrew had until recently operated on a regional basis; the new centralized Stella brand management approach had been in place only since September 1998. In addition, there were often difficulties in convincing all parties to become part of a new global approach, particularly the international advertising campaign that was the backbone of the global plan for Stella

Artois. Belgium, for example, continued with a specific local advertising program that positioned Stella as a mainstream lager in its home market, and in the United Kingdom, Whitbread maintained its "reassuringly expensive" advertising slogan that had already proved to be so successful. For other less-established markets, a global advertising framework was created that included a television concept and a series of print and outdoor executions. This base advertising plan was rolled out in 1999 in 15 markets, including the United States, Canada, Italy, Hungary, Croatia, Bulgaria, Romania, New Zealand and France (with a slightly changed format) after research suggested that the campaign had the ability to cross borders. The objective of this campaign was to position Stella Artois as a sophisticated European lager. It was intended that Stella Artois should be perceived as a beer with an important brewing tradition and heritage but, at the same time, also as a contemporary beer (see Exhibit 10).

In 1998, an accelerated plan was devised to introduce Stella Artois to two key markets within the United States, utilizing both local and corporate funding. The U.S. market was believed to be key for the future development of the brand since it was the most developed specialty market in the world (12 per cent specialty market share, growing 10 per cent plus annually through the 1990s), and because of the strong influence on international trends. Thus, Stella Artois was launched in New York City and Boston and was well received by the demanding U.S. consumer and pub owner. Within 1999, over 200 pubs in Manhattan and 80 bars in Boston had begun to sell Stella Artois on tap. To support the heightened efforts to establish Stella Artois in these competitive urban markets, Interbrew's corporate marketing department added several million dollars to Labatt USA's budget for Stella Artois in 2000, with commitments to continue this additional funding in subsequent years.

CURRENT THINKING

Good progress had been made since 1998 when Stella Artois was established as Interbrew's global brand. However, management had revised its expectations for P/E leverage from having a global brand. The reality was that Interbrew would be rewarded only through cash benefits from operational leverage of a global brand. There would be no "free lunch" simply for being perceived as having a global brand. In addition, in an era of tight fiscal management, it was an ongoing challenge to maintain the funding levels required by the ambitious development plans for Stella Artois. As a result, in early 2000 the prevailing view at Interbrew began to shift, converging on a different long-range approach towards global branding. The emerging perspective emphasized a more balanced brand development program, focusing on the highest leverage opportunities.

The experience of other brewers that had established global brands offered an opportunity for Interbrew to learn from their successes and failures. Carlsberg and Heineken, for example, were two comparable global brands that were valued quite differently by the stock market. Both sold over 80 per cent of their total volumes outside their domestic market, and yet Heineken stock achieved a P/E ratio of 32.4 in 1999 versus Carlsberg's figure of only 17.1. According to industry analysts, the driving force behind this difference was that Heineken maintained a superior market distribution in terms of growth and margin (see Exhibit 11). The key lesson from examining these global brands appeared to be that great discipline must be applied to focus resources in the right places.

In line with this thinking, a long range marketing plan began to take shape that made use of a series of strategic filters to yield a focused set of attractive opportunities. The first filter that any potential market had to pass through was its long-term volume potential for Stella Artois. This volume had to trace back to a large and/or growing market, the current or potential sizeable premium lager segment (at least five per cent of the total market), and the possibility for Stella Artois to penetrate the top three brands. The second screen was the potential to achieve attractive margins after an initial starting period of approximately three years. The third filter was whether or not a committed local partner was available to provide the right quality of distribution and to co-invest in the brand. The final screen was the determination that success in the chosen focus markets should increase leverage in other local and regional markets. For example, the size and stature of Stella Artois in the United Kingdom was a significant factor in the easy sell-in of Stella Artois into New York in 1999.

Once filtered through these strategic market development screens, the global branding plans for Stella Artois began to take a different shape. Rather than focus on national markets, plans emerged with an emphasis on about 20 cities, some of which Interbrew was already present in (e.g., London, Brussels, New York, etc.). This approach suggested that the next moves should be in such potential markets as Moscow, Los Angeles and Hong Kong. Some existing cities would receive focused efforts only when distribution partner issues had been successfully resolved to solidify the bases for sustained long term growth. The major cities that fit these criteria provided the right concentration of affluent consumers, who would be attracted to Stella's positioning, thus providing scale for marketing and sales, investment leverage, as well as getting the attention and support of motivated wholesalers and initial retail customers. These venues would thereby become highly visible success stories that would be leveragable in the company's ongoing market development plans.

Thus, the evolving global branding development plan required careful planning on a city-by-city basis. Among the demands of this new approach were that marketing efforts and the funding to support them would have to be both centrally stewarded and locally tailored to reflect the unique local environments. A corporate marketing group was, therefore, established and was charged with the responsibility to identify top priority markets, develop core positioning and guidelines for local execution, assemble broadly based marketing programs (e.g., TV, print advertising, global sponsorships, beer.com content, etc.), and allocate resources to achieve the accelerated growth objectives in these targeted cities. To ensure an integrated development effort the company brought all pivotal resources together, under the leadership of a global brand development director. In addition to the brand management team, the group included regional sales managers who were responsible for licensed partner management, a customer services group, a Belgian beer café manager, and cruise business management group. Another significant challenge that faced the corporate marketing group was to ensure that all necessary groups were supportive of the new approach. This was a simpler undertaking among those business units that were wholly owned subsidiaries; it was a more delicate issue in the case of licensees and joint ventures. A key element of managing brands through a global organizational structure was that the head office team had to effectively build partnerships with local managers to ensure their commitment.

Fortunately, much of the initial effort to establish Stella Artois as a global brand had been done on a city-by-city basis and, as such, there was ample opportunity for Interbrew to learn from these experiences as the new global plan evolved. In the late 1990s, for example, Stella Artois was introduced to various Central European cities (e.g., Budapest, Zagreb, Bucharest and Sofia). In each of these cities, Interbrew's marketing efforts were launched when the targeted premium market was at an early stage of development. Further, distribution and promotion was strictly controlled (e.g., product quality, glassware, etc.) and the development initiatives were delivered in a concentrated manner (e.g., a media "blitz" in Budapest). In addition, results indicated that the presence of a Belgian Beer Café accelerated Interbrew's market development plans in these new areas. These early successes suggested that brand success could be derived from the careful and concentrated targeting of young adults living in urban centres, with subsequent pull from outlying areas following key city success.

The key lessons of these efforts in Central Europe proved to be very valuable in guiding the market development plan in New York City. In this key North American city, the rollout of Stella Artois was perceived by the analysts as "one of the most promising introductions in New York over the last 20 years" and had generated great wholesaler support and excitement. Among the tactics used to achieve this early success was selective distribution with targeted point of sale materials support. In addition, a selective media campaign was undertaken that included only prestigious outdoor advertising (e.g., a Times Square poster run through the Millennium celebrations). Similarly, the sponsoring strategy focused only on high-end celebrity events, Belgian food events, exclusive parties, fashion shows, etc. Finally, the price of Stella Artois was targeted at levels above Heineken, to reinforce its gold standard positioning. This concerted and consistent market push created an impact that resulted in the "easiest new brand sell" in years, according to wholesalers. The success of this launch also built brand and corporate credibility, paving the way to introductions in other U.S. cities as well as "opening the eyes" of other customers and distribution partners around the world.

To pursue this new global development plan over the next three years, a revised marketing budget was required. Given that the corporate marketing department was responsible for both the development of core programs as well as the selective support of local markets, the budget had to cover both of these key elements. To achieve these ends, total spending was expected to more than double over the next three years.

While great progress had been made on the global branding of Stella Artois, Cooke still ruminated on a variety of important interrelated issues. Among these issues was the situation of Stella Artois in Belgium — would it be possible to win in the "global game" without renewed growth in the home market? What specific aspirations should Interbrew set for Belgium over the next three years? Further, what expectations should Interbrew have of its global brand market development (e.g., volumes, profit levels, number of markets and cities, etc.)? How should global success be measured? With respect to Interbrew's promotional efforts, how likely would it be that a single global ad campaign could be successful for Stella Artois? Was there a particular sponsorship or promotion idea that could be singled out for global leverage? And what role should the Internet play in developing Stella Artois as a true global brand?

EXHIBIT 1 The World Beer Market in 1998

Region	% of Global Consumption	Growth Index ('98 Vs 92)	Per Capita Consumption
Americas	35.1%	112.6	57
Europe	32.8%	97.7	54
Asia Pacific	27.2%	146.2	11
Africa	4.6%	107.7	8
Middle East/Central Asia	0.4%	116.0	2

Source: Canadean Ltd.

EXHIBIT 2 Interbrew's 1998 Share of the World's Top 10 Markets

Rank	Country	Volume (000 HL)	Market Share
1	USA	3,768	1.6%
2	China	526	0.3%
3	Germany	-	-
4	Brazil	-	-
5	Japan	-	-
6	UK	3,335	5.5%
7	Mexico	21,269	45.0%
8	Spain	-	-
9	South Africa	-	-
10	France	1,915	8.4%
Total		30,813	3.6%

Source: Canadean Ltd.

EXHIBIT 3 Domestic Sales History of Major International Brands (million hectolitre)

	1995	1996	1997	1998
Budweiser (incl. Bud Light until '98)	69.48	71.10	72.43	40.00
Bud Light	n/a	n/a	n/a	30.00
Heineken	3.87	3.78	3.85	3.78
Becks	1.68	1.71	1.72	1.78
Carlsberg	1.47	1.39	1.31	1.22
Stella Artois	1.08	1.00	0.96	0.92
Fosters	1.48	1.11	1.40	1.43
Kronenbourg	5.65	5.53	5.35	5.60
Amstel	2.30	2.23	2.21	2.18
Corona	12.89	14.09	14.80	15.18

EXHIBIT 4 1999 World Sales Profile of Stella Artois

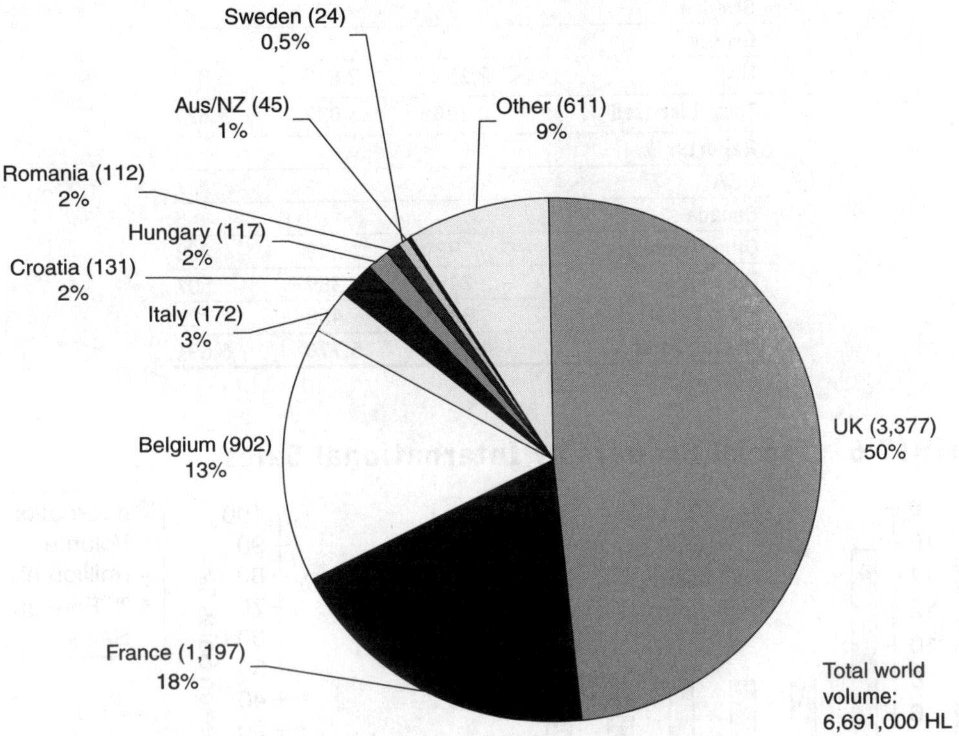

EXHIBIT 5 Stella Artois Sales Volume Summary (000 hectolitre)

	1997	1998	1999
Production:			
Belgium	965	921	902
France	1,028	1,110	1,074
Hungary	59	84	117
Croatia	54	120	133
Romania	17	60	112
Bulgaria	-	-	3
Bosnia-Herzegovina	-	-	2
Montenegro	-	-	0
Total Production	**2,123**	**2,295**	**2,343**
License Brewing:			
Italy	162	166	172
Australia	6	11	22
New Zealand	7	11	22

	1997	1998	1999
Sweden	29	27	24
Greece	7	7	10
UK	2,139	2,815	3,377
Total Licensed	**2,350**	**3,037**	**3,627**
Export:			
USA	-	-	7
Canada	-	-	5
Other Countries	92	49	202
Duty Free	245	389	507
Total Export	337	438	721
Overall Total	**4,810**	**5,770**	**6,691**

EXHIBIT 6 Top 10 Brewers by International Sales

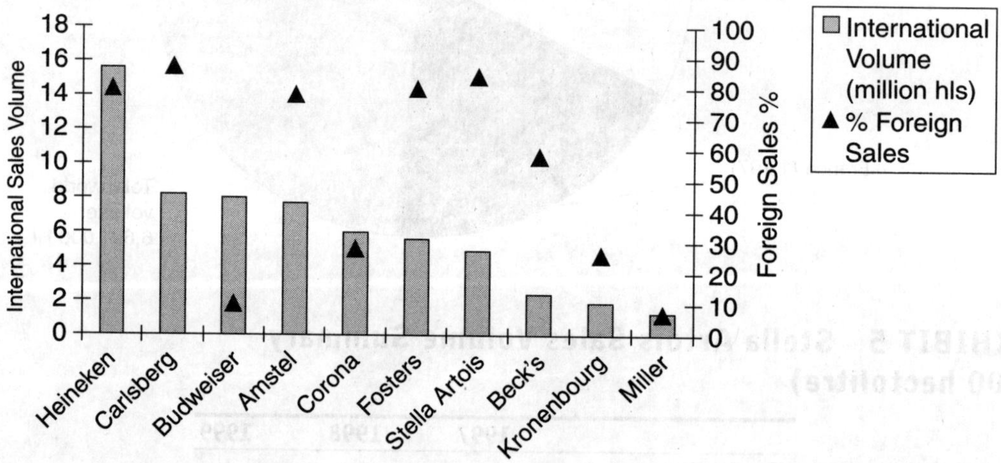

EXHIBIT 7 1998 Heineken World Sales Profile

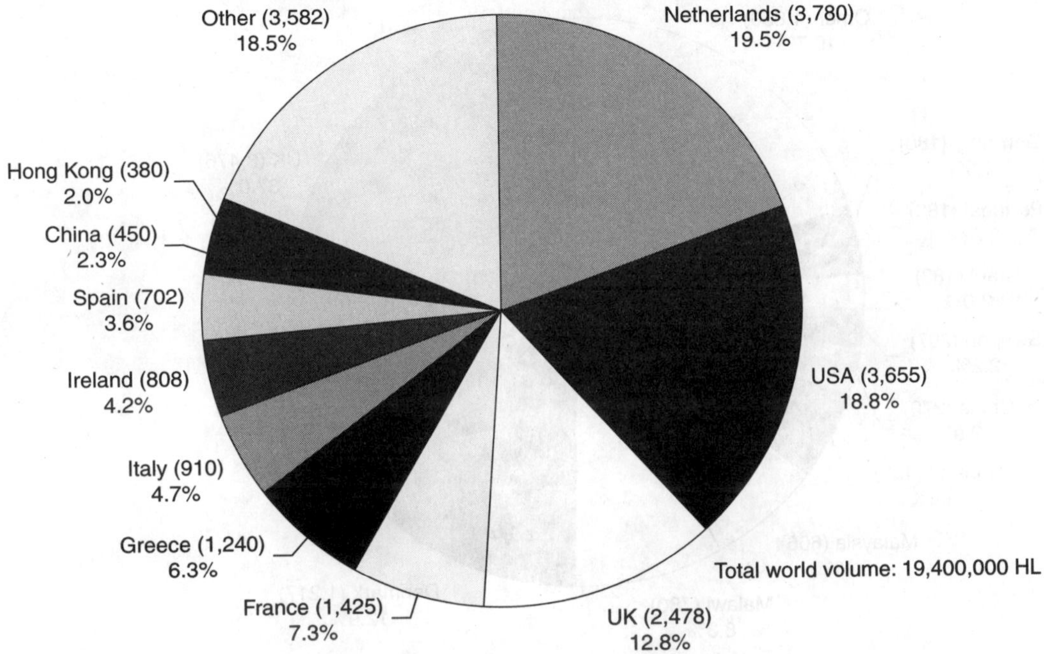

EXHIBIT 8 1998 Foster's World Sales Profile

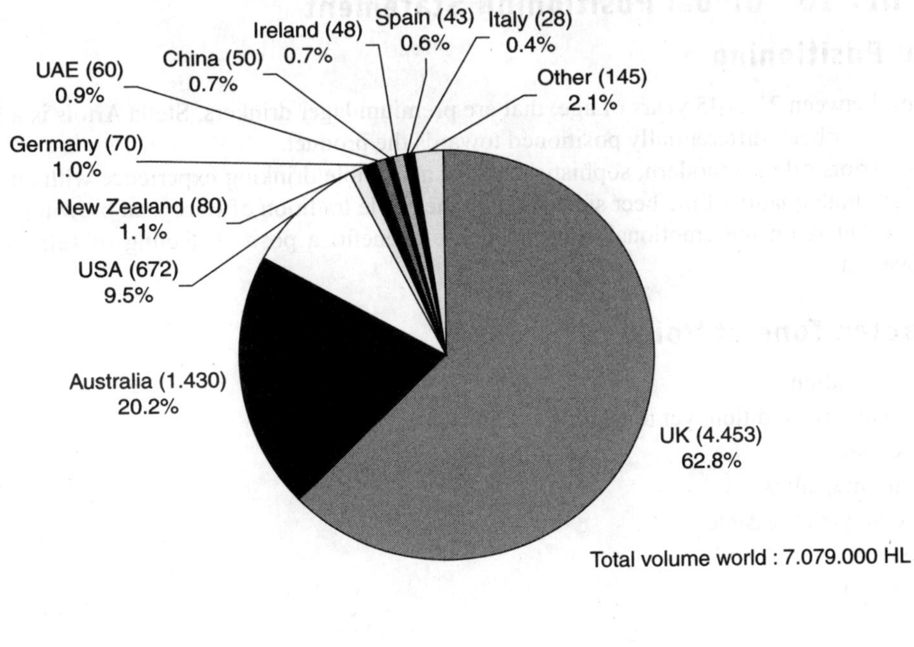

EXHIBIT 9 1998 Carlsberg World Sales Profile

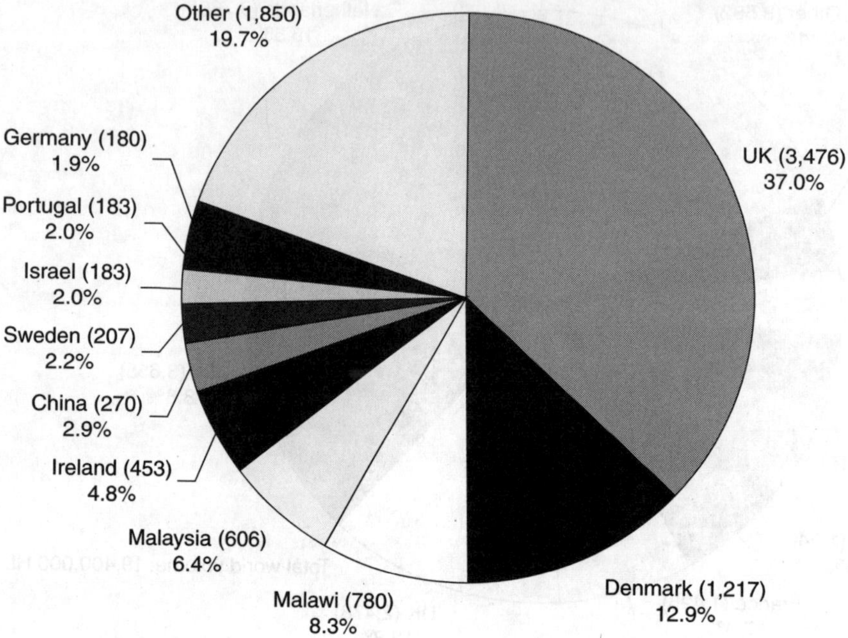

Total world volume: 9,405,000 HL

EXHIBIT 10 Global Positioning Statement

Brand Positioning

To males, between 21 to 45 years of age, that are premium lager drinkers, Stella Artois is a European premium lager beer, differentially positioned towards the product.

Stella Artois offers a modern, sophisticated, yet accessible drinking experience with an emphasis on the very high quality of the beer supported by the noble tradition of European brewing.

The accent is on the emotional consequence of benefit: a positive feeling of self esteem and sophistication.

Character, Tone of Voice

- Sophistication
- Authenticity, tradition, yet touch of modernity
- Timelessness
- Premium quality
- Special, yet accessible
- Mysticism
- European

EXHIBIT 11 A comparison of Carlsberg and Heineken

Profit Exposure by Market Type

Market Return \ Market Growth	Low	High
High	Carlsberg = 19% Heineken = 2%	Carlsberg = 22% Heineken = 46%
Low	Carlsberg = 56% Heineken = 2%	Carlsberg = 3% Heineken = 50%

13

The Home Depot Canada: Renovating Strategy

It was March 2005. It had been nine years since Annette Verschuren had been recruited as president of The Home Depot Canada (THDC), a subsidiary of U.S.-based The Home Depot Inc. (THDI). She was the first outsider to be named president, the first president without home-improvement industry experience and the first woman to be appointed president in the group. The Canadian division had grown, under her stewardship, from 19 to 123 stores, from 4,000 to 25,000 associates and from less than $1 billion to more than $5 billion in sales by 2005. THDC was the leader in Canadian home improvement with 14 per cent market share. But the market had become increasingly competitive: the U.S. major player Lowe's was planning a Canadian launch in 2007, and THDC's closest competitor on the home front, RONA, was planning to double its sales by that time. Sustaining leadership and growth momentum in a highly fragmented market was the new challenge before Verschuren who had recently articulated her own vision for THDC: to become Canada's top retailer (see Exhibits 1–4).

To achieve this goal, THDC would have to continue to evolve to meet the changing needs of its customer base. The do-it-yourself (DIY) segment, which THDC had nurtured, was giving way to a do-it-for-me (DIFM) segment. Attracting the female customer, a segment that the company had only recently turned its attention to, was critical to future growth. The big-box format, which THDI dominated, was approaching saturation in Canada's urban centers. THDC would have to look for growth from secondary, inner city markets, requiring stores with less square footage.[1] The balance of power in home improvement retailing, which had been favoring the large players, was changing. Suppliers could bypass THDC and establish their own e-commerce platforms, which allowed customers to interact with manufacturers directly.

A new retailing strategy was, therefore, in order.

Said Verschuren

> Growth in the home improvement market is limited, in a broader sense, only by the imagination of the customer. But it is necessary for us to anticipate customer requirements in advance. That is the only way to stay ahead. Clearly, the customer profile is changing in Canada. The Pro segment is growing. Color for the female customer used to be about what she wore, but today she is living in it. The growing trend towards energy usage efficiency means a demand for EcoOptions[2] in home improvement products. Is retailing at our company on track? That is the litmus test.

Annette Verschuren had joined THDC as president in February 1996, from Michael's of Canada, where she had been president since 1993. Prior to that, she had operated her own business, Verschuren Ventures. Verschuren held a Bachelor of Business Administration degree from St. Francis Xavier University.

THE HOME IMPROVEMENT MARKET

Definition

The Home Improvement Research Institute (HIRI) divided the home improvement market into 10 product categories: hardware, tools, lumber and building materials, plumbing supplies, electrical supplies, lawn and garden equipment and supplies, hard-surface floor coverings, soft-surface floor coverings, paints and preservatives, and major household appliances. Excluded from its definition were home furnishings, small appliances, sporting goods, auto supplies, cut flowers and indoor plants. Some of the latter were often considered by individual players, such as THDC, to be part of the home improvement market. The *Directory of Retail Chains in Canada* grouped all home improvement merchandise into five categories: houseware, furniture and décor, home appliance, building supply and hardware.

History

The retail hardware industry was, from the beginning, about supplying tools, materials and know-how to build, maintain, repair and improve homes. The booming post-World War II market was dominated by two major store formats: hardware stores (selling home maintenance and repair goods to consumers) and lumberyards (selling lumber and building materials to builders and contractors). As both sectors looked for expansion opportunities, they began to move toward each other. Hardware stores added building materials, and lumberyards added hardware. By the 1970s, a hybrid retail

[1] Richard Metters et al., "Welcome Back, Mom and Pop: Big Retailers Are Starting to Think Small Again," *Harvard Business Review*, May-June 2000, pp. 2–3.

[2] See Ivey Business School Case "The Home Depot Canada: EcoOptions" 2006.

format — known as the home center — had surfaced. By the 1990s, home improvement chains were at the forefront of industry expansion, opening stores of more than 100,000 square feet and moving beyond major population areas into smaller markets.

The market was fragmented on both the demand and supply sides. Hardware stores were primarily independent family-owned operations. Most were affiliated with wholesaler merchandising groups offering marketing programs. In general, these stores were no larger than 30,000 square feet and averaged annual sales of less than $1 million. They served homeowners in neighborhood markets and offered personalized customer service. In most cases, they were open late in the evenings and on weekends.

Lumberyards concentrated on contractors and builders for their business and started seeking consumers only as the DIY trend caught on. Averaging annual volumes of $5 million or more per store, their sales floors were less than 10,000 square feet with the majority of the merchandise stocked outside in the yard. The home improvement center segment was dominated by national chain operations, offering a mix of formats. They purchased most of their merchandise directly from manufacturers and rarely participated in wholesaler marketing programs.

Size

According to a forecast prepared for HIRI by Global Insight, home improvement product sales in 2004 totaled $271.4 billion in the United States, up 12.8 per cent over 2003. Growth over the next five years was expected to be slower at a rate of five per cent compound annual growth rate (CAGR), which motivated retailers to look for other ways to drive revenue expansion (see Exhibit 5).

THE HOME DEPOT INC.

Founded with two stores in June 1979, in Atlanta, Georgia, The Home Depot Inc. (THDI) had grown, by 2004, into 1,707 stores worldwide comprising 175 million square feet of selling space. With sales of $73.1 billion for the year ending January 2005, it was the second largest retailer in the United States, next to Wal-Mart, and the biggest home improvement chain in the world (see Exhibits 1 and 6).

Several factors had contributed to this spectacular growth during the company's formative years: the suburbanization of middle-class America, the real estate boom of the 1980s and the trend towards "nesting" among baby boomers. There were also more fundamental reasons. THDI gave people an opportunity to experience a sense of wonder similar to that of a child in a toy store. It tapped into the consumer's growing fascination with size, choice and bargains. It went against the prevailing wisdom that customers would prefer to pay someone else to renovate their homes. THDI targeted the DIY customer. By providing knowledge and confidence, in addition to the necessary tools and materials, the company empowered consumers to fix the furnace, paint the kitchen, or irrigate the garden on their own.

Since inception, THDI's operations were based on a decentralized business model. The responsibility for stocking and pricing had been given to employees that were close to the customer. However, this decentralization was no longer the case.[3] By 2001, merchandising, store planning and marketing functions had been centralized.

---

[3] Ram Charan, "Home Depot's Blueprint for Culture Change," *Harvard Business Review*, April 2006, pp. 61–70.

Said Verschuren

> THDI has articulated three clear business priorities: improving earnings growth, market share and stock price. These are best met by moving more products more quickly through more stores with fewer associates and lower overhead. The ability to do that hinges on operational efficiency. However, driving store efficiency does not always lead to an enhanced shopping experience for the customer. Striking the right balance between the two is a crucial component of managing the competitive retail environment. Retailing strategies that improve the bottom line and inspire investor confidence do not always generate customer satisfaction.

The company had followed a policy of "low day-in day-out pricing." Low prices prevailed throughout the year instead of being confined to sales events or seasonal promotions. The policy had been introduced in 1986 when the combined sales of the company's 60 stores crossed the $1 billion mark.

THDI had several exclusive private labels: Behr, Glacier Bay, Hampton Bay, Home Gardener, Husky, Scott's, Traffic Master and Workforce. Private-label merchandise provided an opportunity not only to increase sales but to improve margins.

OPERATIONS AND TECHNOLOGY

THDI had relied for many years on homegrown information systems. By building its own applications, it had preempted problems associated with buying and customizing off-the-shelf software. A standard database design and application architecture had enabled THDI to develop in-house solutions. An example was the company's mobile ordering system — a cart equipped with a computer and printer that store clerks could wheel around to reorder products and change prices.

In 2002, THDI announced a $1 billion overhaul of its information technology (IT) infrastructure. It was part of $7.7 billion modernization effort that included remodeling existing stores and opening new ones. The overhaul including replacing point-of-sale (POS) systems, installing self-checkout counters, upgrading local area networks, as well as substantial changes to critical systems software (including data warehousing, price optimization, SAP financial and PeopleSoft Enterprise Resource Planning software).

The change in technology focus was necessary because the company was growing in size. Building systems in-house was no longer cost-effective. Another reason was the need to close, or even leapfrog, the technology gap between THDI and other retailers, such as Wal-Mart and Target. The company was spearheading a range of new applications collectively known as FAST (front-end accuracy and service transformation) intended to enhance customer service.

The major goal of retail operations was to improve the quality of the shopping experience for customers. As part of the FAST initiative, the following measures were implemented:

Online Universal Product Code (UPC): This electronic catalog of products listed products that did not have barcodes on them (like nuts and bolts) and therefore could not be scanned at the POS. The electronic catalog made price determination on unmarked items easier.

Online receipt lookup: This function allowed customers to return an item without the original receipt if they had paid for merchandise using a credit card, debit card or check. When the customer's card was swiped, or the checking account number entered into the POS system, the application searched through 90 days of transactions to find an electronic copy of the customer's receipt. The receipt lookup helped THDI reduce the incidence of fraudulent returns.

Wireless scan guns: These scanners replaced corded scan guns. What made THDI's cordless scan guns different from those used by other retailers, such as Sam's Clubs, was their two-way communication feature that generated cross-selling opportunities. For example, when a cashier scanned the UPC for a barbecue grill, the gun transmitted the stock-keeping unit (SKU) number to the POS system, which identified the product. If the product required assembly, a message was sent to a small screen on the gun to prompt the cashier to ask whether the customer wanted the store to assemble the grill for an additional charge.

Web-based kiosks: In the paint department, these kiosks helped customers color-coordinate the rooms under decoration. Each kiosk contained a computer, a touch-screen monitor and a lens to scan fabric or wallpaper. Following prompts on the screen, the customer could print out a selection of coordinating paint colors. The store could then mix paints according to the color combinations chosen on the printout.

Back-end Automation and Receiving: This process was part of the new distribution initiative being implemented at THDI. Dubbed BEAR, it included certified receiving of inventory, with cordless scan guns, from approximately 80 current suppliers. With the truck already audited and sealed at the dispatch center, the need for checking at the store level was eliminated, which reduced the potential for shrinkage.

FORMAT

THDI had 1,890 stores in the United States and Puerto Rico, more than 123 stores in Canada and 47 stores in Mexico. It also had 34 EXPO Design Centers, five supply stores, 11 landscape supply stores and two floor stores.

The average THDI store was 192,750 square feet under one roof (see Exhibit 7), with an additional 20,000 to 28,000 square feet of garden center and storage space attached to the store. Each store stocked between 40,000 and 50,000 SKUs, including size and color variations. As a result, the company was able to offer a wide range of merchandise at multiple price points.

Each EXPO Design Center was about 100,000 square feet of selling space and housed eight showrooms under one roof, including kitchens, baths, carpet and rugs, lighting, patio and grills, tile and wood, window treatments and appliances. The EXPO Design Centers targeted affluent, buy-it-yourself customers interested in a total design package. THDI also had a number of "test" stores, including HD Supply (a specialized store for the professional customer), The Home Depot Urban Stores (currently with two locations in Manhattan and one in Vancouver, B.C.), The Home Depot Landscape Supply and The Home Depot Floor Store.

The company was planning smaller formats — at 60,000 square feet, about half the size of THDI regular store — in both the United States and Canada.

Said Verschuren

> We are beginning to open a number of 80,000 sq. ft. stores and a few 60,000 sq. ft. stores as well. We need to adjust to our communities. One size does not fit all. So it is important to produce concepts and distribution centres that fit the various regions and

demographics of Canada. We are also expanding the supply side of the business. For instance, we recently acquired Litemor, a Montréal-based commercial lighting company. That part of the business is very fragmented and we see enormous opportunities there.

ASSORTMENT AND MERCHANDISING

For many years, THDI's assortment had been product driven. However, with increasing emphasis on retailing complete "home improvement solutions," the company was adding a number of related services to its portfolio of offerings. These included installations by contractors who were on call across the country.

THDI's merchandising was currently being fine-tuned to attract not only the traditional DIY customer, but also the professional segment of customers. The company had rolled out a "Pro Initiative" in the Canadian market, with the aim of attracting building contractors. Designed to feel like a wholesale operation or lumberyard, it was a strategic move that had the potential to open new markets leveraging THDI's existing systems and corporate competencies.

Said Gino Digioacchino, director (merchandising), THDC

> There are four parameters that are used to evaluate merchandising efficiency: overall sales (broken down to division, district and department), average transaction size, the customer transaction report, and inventory position. The biggest challenge in merchandizing is in communicating, at the store level, the values that The Home Depot brand stands for.

STAFFING

The company had 299,000 employees, clad in construction-sign orange, in its stores worldwide. The small and medium players in the home improvement market usually relied on retired tradespeople to staff the stores. THDI had a full-fledged Web-based training course in place. In 2003, for instance, the company had delivered 23 million hours of Web-based courses to employees. The courses were delivered through dedicated computers located in stores. They helped employees acquire not only specialized product and brand knowledge but also basic sales and customer service skills.

THDI was running its stores with fewer staff than before. In 2000, there was an average of 200 associates per store. In 2003, there was an average of 175 associates per store. The company had created its first-ever sales goals in four departments: appliances, flooring, kitchen and millwork. The effects of this approach were already apparent in higher closure rates on appliances, as the company's market share improved from 7.6 per cent to 9.4 per cent between 2003 and 2004. Interestingly, no monetary compensation was involved; instead, the sales targets were used to identify associates who could benefit from further training.

Self-checkouts: Self-checkout registers had been installed in 1,029 stores by the end of 2004. Shoppers could scan items on their own and then pay by credit card with limited, if any, assistance from stores personnel. The system, which was similar to a bank's automated teller machine (ATM), included a central processing unit, a scanner, a touch-screen monitor, a keyboard, a receipt printer and a magnetic stripe reader. It also often included electronic tendering equipment to handle cash payments and a closed circuit television to deter theft. Self-checkouts had resulted in significant improvement in customer satisfaction scores, particularly among the professional segment. On average, the self-checkout initiative had reduced labour by about 40 to 60 hours (i.e. an associate and a half) per store per week. Once these registers were established in the store, 40 per cent of all transactions were accomplished through self-checkout. As a result, THDI was extending the project to all of its stores. To eliminate the need to have an associate present, the company was also testing call boxes and radios in self-service aisles where minimal assistance was required (e.g. in the household chemicals area).

DISTRIBUTION

The company had taken a Strategic Distribution Initiative (SDI) to improve inventory turns, in-stock levels, labor task-outs and transportation costs. This initiative had enabled THDI to expand into mid-sized markets within existing operating areas, as well as build on its fast-growing non-retail initiatives focused on the Pro customer. THDI could use more of the in-store square footage to stock a greater range of SKUs for direct store delivery. For instance, appliance buyers could immediately take their purchases home with them, rather than wait a few days for delivery.

INSTALLATION SERVICES

THDI estimated that the services market in North America was a US$200 billion opportunity, consisting of $90 billion in merchandise and $110 billion in labor, with an additional $55 billion in adjacent market opportunities. Services were targeted at DIFM customers who would select and purchase materials for a project, and then have the store arrange for professional installation. Developing an in-house services model had major challenges: creating, managing and maintaining an efficient and profitable on-demand labour force. THDI was outsourcing the labor component of the installation services to qualified contractors, focusing on what it knew best: retailing. However, to safeguard its brand equity, the company had added an administrative component between the customer and installer. By offering installation, even for goods that it did not sell, such as heating, ventilation and air-conditioning products, THDI was becoming the one-stop destination for its customers.

Execution was as critical to building a viable long-term platform for sustainable growth in services as it was in product retailing. THDI was making investments in infrastructure, technology and processes to provide an effective communications conduit among vendors, installers and customers of the services business. It had rolled out a special-order flooring system to reduce errors and free up associate selling time. It had centralized the customer service component of installations.

Said Roger Plamandon, regional VP (operations), THDC

> The installation part of the business has good potential in Canada because of the higher proportion of ageing but affluent consumers. The service segment is a powerful index of customer satisfaction. It provides extraordinary leveraging opportunities. Barriers to entry are high in services because of the limited number of installers in Canada.

HOME IMPROVEMENT MARKET IN CANADA

Size

The Canadian home improvement products market was estimated to be approximately $34 billion in 2004 (see Exhibit 8). It was projected to grow, in the next few years, at five to seven per cent per annum. A distinguishing feature of the Canadian retail market was its geographic diversity in sales. For example, the province of Ontario contributed 34.1 per cent of home improvement products sales in 2004 while the Northwest Territories contributed 0.8 per cent.

THE HOME DEPOT CANADA

THDC entered Canada in 1994 when it acquired a 75 per cent stake in Aikenhead's, a DIY chain. THDC had subsequently built a strong brand in Canada. Key to its success was the company's ability to secure prime geographic locations, including 30 stores in the tight Toronto market. THDI had announced plans to grow its Canadian presence to 137 stores in the next 14 months and more than 200 in the next three to five years. The Canadian arm of the company had developed an efficient supply chain model enabling it to profitably roll out smaller stores of between 60,000 and 80,000 square feet. The initiative was to be replicated in the United States. THDC was leading other group divisions in operating margins.

Customers

The customers of THDC fell into three categories: DIY (do-it-yourself), DIFM (do-it-for-me) and Pro (builders and contractors). DIYers were homeowners, eager and willing to complete projects and installations at home, on their own. THDC had consciously nurtured and developed DIYers by tapping on their innate enthusiasm. For example, it conducted a variety of "how-to" clinics in its stores. The DIFM segment bought all the requisite materials but contracted with others to do the work. THDC had contractors on call, who were authorized to provide services to such customers. The Pro segment comprised builders, professional remodelers, general contractors, repair persons and tradespeople. THDC was courting this group through credit facilities, convenient store hours and just-in-time delivery.

Home ownership was on a consistent rise, driven by a desire for equity, innovations in mortgage finance and rising average incomes. As the existing housing stock continued to age, routine maintenance and major repairs were required more frequently. There was a growing trend in renovation, which provided a supportive backdrop to expanding installation sales. Immigrants and minorities, a growing influence in the population mix, were also contributing to the demand for housing.

The cultural, demographic and market trends in Canada supported the DIFM category. The relatively large baby-boomer population was aging and, as a group, had more money, but less enthusiasm to fix things on their own.

Shopping Patterns

There were some recent changes in consumers' shopping patterns. They were bargain-hunting in several categories, to be able to trade up in other items. Opening price points were therefore very important in some categories, such as furnishings and home décor items. At the same time, premium products were experiencing strong demand, while mid-range sales were slowing. The frequency of shopping trips by customers was also declining, which was blamed on higher gas prices, less time to shop and the company's store cannibalization strategy. However, the decline in shopping frequency had resulted in, on average, a greater number of transactions per customer per trip, which was positive from an efficiency perspective and opened the door to increasing same-store sales.

Service

For years, customer service at the company's stores meant personal service — i.e., employees interacting with customers in store aisles. The definition of service had changed under the new management at THDI. It now meant self-service. Signage flourished in each store. Better signs were considered a cost-saving, non-labor-intensive way for the company to move customers in and out quickly. The signs were also meant to make the store space less overwhelming, particularly for female customers.

Said Verschuren

> For years, we thought we were a real guys' store, but research showed us that 80 per cent of home improvement decisions are influenced by women. So we found out what women wanted from our stores. We widened the aisles, shortened our racks and used brighter lights. We put the most popular departments closer together and created new ones such as home organization and design. There was some concern that we might scare off the male customers, but men too liked cleaner, brighter and better-organized stores. They just weren't as vocal about it.

Although self-service (including self-checkout) fit well with the profile of the DIY customer, it still had to be balanced with a personal touch, which was being provided through acts of courtesy, such as loading merchandise into a customer's car or hailing a cab.

Testing Ground

THDC had become a successful testing ground for new operating and merchandising initiatives that were being considered for subsequent roll out in the much larger U.S. market. Loyalty programs, for example, were currently being tested in Canada. The Canadian division was also the first to test the new Strategic Distribution Initiative. BEAR technology, which had saved labour hours in Canadian stores (hours that were reinvested in high-margin specialty merchandise), was now being replicated in the United States. Similarly, the separation of the selling function from project management in installation services was a successful Canadian initiative being tested in the United States. THDC was also currently testing a landscaping service. The division used outdoor special order sales display, for siding, fencing, decking and roofing products. It offered samples of the product categories on the outside wall of the store, where colors and finishes could be compared in natural light, similar to actual conditions of use. Other merchandising initiatives included bundling related products (such as a complete bathroom set or kitchen set with package discounts) and offering energy-efficient alternatives to more than 5,000 SKUs.

Prime Real Estate

As an entrenched player in Canada, the company had a major competitive advantage in prime real estate. With 20 per cent of Canada's population concentrated in major metro markets, THDC had cannibalized its own stores during from 1999 to 2001. It had thus captured valuable real estate locations in these areas. It had 30 stores in the greater Toronto area, compared to seven locations for RONA. The company was forward-looking in planning its real estate portfolio and had locked up a number of locations for potential future development.

E-Commerce Initiatives

Several of THDC's competitors had e-commerce platforms. Sears Canada and Canadian Tire, major players in the home improvement web space, were largely product-focused, while RONA's e-commerce platform was content-focused. THDC was seeking to differentiate itself by providing new functionalities, such as the ability to book services on-line. The purpose of e-commerce was not just to drive traffic into the store.

Said Simon Rodrigues, manager (e-commerce), THDC

> A survey has shown that 37 per cent of home improvement shoppers first research products and services online although they would not necessarily purchase online. We also know female customers are more inclined towards online shopping. We have thus incorporated new functionalities in the electronic medium to drive sales. This has been done at 25 per cent of the cost of opening a new store, and has generated returns approximately 3.5 times higher than in a physical store. The online platform is a wonderful opportunity to leverage equity established in the physical space.

COMPETITORS IN CANADA

Rona

A major player in Quebec for decades, RONA was in an expansion mode and was seeking a larger national presence. It had 530 stores whose formats ranged from small shops to big-box outlets. As a specialty retailer, RONA competed directly with THDC. The company sought differentiation with its balanced appeal to both men and women. It offered features such as decorator boutiques, displayed at the average woman's eye level. RONA's variety of formats had led to some brand confusion among consumers regarding what the company stood for.

Home Hardware Stores

Set up in 1964 with a view to match the buying power of the large national retail chains, Home Hardware Stores was a cooperative of 122 independent hardware dealers. It was Canada's largest hardware retail group with more than 1,000 independently operated hardware and building supply stores as its customers. Home Hardware Stores also sold more than 55,000 products online. However, the regional and rural focus was limiting future expansion and the diffuse ownership structure had led to a lack of consistency in product offerings.

Lowe's

A major competitor to THDI, Lowe's was the second largest home improvement chain in the United States. It had 930 superstores in 45 states, selling more than 40,000 products to do-it-yourselfers and professionals. Having established a strong base in small and medium-sized markets of the United States, Lowe's was now expanding into large urban centers. In April 2004, it opened its first predominantly urban-oriented store in Brooklyn. Like other players, Lowe's was moving into services. But unlike many, it had exclusive product arrangements with suppliers. It sought further differentiation through lighting, signage and store design. Lowe's was also a major player in the home appliance market. It had announced plans to enter Canada in 2007.

Canadian Tire

Home products were among the many items that Canadian Tire sold in its 450 stores run by a network of associate dealers. Its assortment included automotive, sports and leisure products. Canadian Tire was also the largest independent gasoline retailer in Canada. It offered branded credit cards and insurance products and provided a nationwide emergency roadside service. It also operated the Mark's Work Wearhouse chain of more than 300 corporate and franchised stores, selling work clothes as well as casual and business-casual attire. The company had launched an active e-commerce platform, marketing about 15,000 products online from a total portfolio of approximately 100,000.

A major component of Canadian Tire retailing was what it called Concept 20/20. It aimed to increase floor space by 20 per cent and simplify store designs, in order to make room for new categories of merchandise and services. Canadian Tire was retrofitting existing stores and constructing all new stores to conform to Concept 20/20 retailing. Canadian Tire was a powerful national brand; however, its product assortment was much broader than THDC and, as a result, its reputation was weaker in the home improvement market.

Sears Canada

The largest catalog business in Canada, Sears had 125 department stores selling home fashions, appliances and apparel. In addition to supplying home electronics, garden goods and appliances to independent stores, Sears Canada had 50 furniture and appliances stores of its own and more than 2,200 catalog pick-up locations.

Other Competition

A number of other Canadian retailers were pursuing the home improvement market. For example, Winners, the off-price clothing chain, was investing in its general merchandise counterpart, HomeSense. Less than a decade after its launch, Home Outfitters was the most lucrative part of the Hudson's Bay Co.'s group of companies.

Said Michael McLarney, publisher of Hardlines, a home improvement trade magazine

> Retailers from sectors like grocery are vying for a progressively bigger share of the kinds of hardlines and seasonal products they themselves sell. They provide tough competition to traditional home improvement retailers. In fact, home improvement retailers are under pressure to fight back and are therefore pushing their own assortment envelopes. Their offerings range from high-ticket items like heavy appliances and ready-to-assemble and finished furniture to low-value items like linen, soft goods, and even candles and massage oils. Lines are thus getting increasingly blurred in the Canadian home improvement market.

QUESTIONS ABOUT THE FUTURE OF THE HOME DEPOT CANADA

Verschuren was faced with a number of important developments in THDC's business. These included an evolving customer base, increasing competition, and a market that was nearing saturation for the traditional store format. Nevertheless, the stated goal for THDC was to become the top retailer in the country. Did THDC need a new retailing strategy? Verschuren wondered whether the strategy, which had been tried and tested, should be continued, tweaked or overhauled.

EXHIBIT 1 Top 20 Global Retailers 2003

Rank	Company	Country	Retail Sales (US$ Million)
1	Wal-Mart	USA	285,222
2	Carrefour	France	89,568
3	**The Home Depot**	**USA**	**73,094**
4	Metro	Germany	69,781
5	Tesco	UK	62,505
6	Kroger	USA	56,434
7	Costco	USA	47,146
8	Target	USA	45,682
9	Koninklijke Ahold	Netherlands	44,793
10	Aldi GmbH & Co.	Germany	42,906
11	Schwarz Unternehmens	Germany	42,793
12	Rewe-Zentral	Germany	42,782
13	Itermarche	France	41,721
14	Albertsons	USA	39,897
15	Walgreens	USA	37,508
16	Groupe Auchan	France	37,373
17	Lowe's	USA	36,464
18	AEON	Japan	36,345
19	Safeway	USA	35,823
20	Sears Roebuck	USA	35,718

Source: "2006 Global Powers of Retailing," *Deloitte Touche Tohmatsu*, February 15, 2006. http://www.deloitte.com/dtt/cda/doc/content/dtt_ConsumerBusiness_GlobalPowers_021006%281%29.pdf, accessed November 6, 2006.

EXHIBIT 2 Ranking of Canadian Retailers 2004

Rank	Company	Revenue	Assets	Profit
1	Loblaws	$ 26,209,000.00	$ 13,046,000.00	$ 968,000.00
2	Wal-Mart Canada Corp.	$ 12,500,000.00	na	na
3	Sobeys	$ 11,046,800.00	$ 3,274,700.00	$ 167,500.00
4	Costco Wholesale Canada Ltd.	$ 7,878,386.00	na	na
5	Canadian Tire Corp. Ltd.	$ 7,153,600.00	$ 5,218,600.00	$ 291,500.00
6	Hudson's Bay Co.	$ 7,069,736.00	$ 4,008,821.00	$ 59,738.00
7	The Katz Group	$ 6,500,000.00	na	na
8	Sears Canada Inc.	$ 6,230,500.00	$ 4,226,400.00	$ 128,700.00
9	Metro Inc. (Se05)	$ 5,998,900.00	$ 1,560,000.00	$ 168,800.00
10	Alimentation Couche-Tard (Ap05)	$ 5,872,394.00	$ 2,233,493.00	$ 79,505.00
11	Canada Safeway Ltd.	$ 5,681,400.00	$ 1,901,500.00	na
12	**Home Depot Canada**	**$ 5,000,000.00**	**na**	**na**
13	Shoppers Drug Mart Corp.	$ 4,723,119.00	$ 3,499,693.00	$ 725,000.00
14	The Great Atalantic & Pacific Co. of Canada Ltd.	$ 4,435,567.00	na	na
15	The Jean Coutu Group (PJC) Inc.	$ 4,096,138.00	$ 1,834,786.00	$ 176,923.00
16	Home Hardware Stores Ltd.	$ 3,800,000.00	na	na
17	Rona	$ 3,680,038.00	$ 1,336,745.00	$ 138,225.00
18	Liquor Control Board of Ontario	$ 3,320,681.00	$ 592,722.00	$1,045,428.00
19	Best Buy Canada Ltd.	$ 3,139,084.00	$ 1,513,955.00	$ (13,642.00)
20	Societe des alcools du Quebec	$ 2,070,100.00	$ 742,600.00	$ 570,800.00
21	Uniprix Inc.	$ 1,250,094.00	$ 338,350.00	$ 13,201.00
22	The Brick 2005*	$ 1,214,405.00		
23	The Forzani Group Ltd.	$ 985,054.00	$ 604,229.00	$ 21,545.00
24	Pharmasave Drugs (National) Ltd.	$ 928,437.00	na	na
25	Reitmans (Canada) Ltd.	$ 912,473.00	$ 467,059.00	$ 66,907.00
26	Indigo Books and Music Inc.	$ 805,716.00	$ 400,734.00	$ 4,346.00
27	North West Co. Fund	$ 782,720.00	$ 409,686.00	$ 35,730.00
28	Calgary Co-operative Association Ltd.	$ 751,998.00	$ 287,390.00	$ 3,029.00
29	Intertan Inc	$ 608,576.00	$ 224,211.00	$ 11,643.00
30	Hartco Corp.	$ 592,198.00	$ 139,141.00	$ 6,192.00

Source: "FP500 41st Edition," *National Post Business Magazine*, June 2005.

EXHIBIT 3 Retail Trade in Canada

	Operating Revenues	Operating Expenses	Gross Margin	Operating Profit	Operating Revenues 2003 to 2004
	$ Million				% Change
New car dealers	75,656	8,444	10,055	1,612	0.8
Used and recreational motor vehicles and parts dealers	16,050	3,166	3,685	519	1.7
Gasoline stations	35,681	4,559	6,985	2,426	10.7
Furniture stores	8,805	2,773	3,308	535	5.1
Home furnishings stores	5,278	1,713	1,976	263	11.6
Computer and software stores	2,213	523	557	34	–4.7
Home electronics and appliance stores	9,599	2,669	3,014	345	6.1
Home centres and hardware stores	17,232	3,896	5,147	1,251	10.2
Specialized building materials and garden stores	5,094	1,322	1,529	207	2.7
Supermarkets	58,670	11,767	14,444	2,677	3.5
Convenience and specialty food stores	13,674	2,933	3,375	443	5.1
Beer, wine and liquor stores	13,531	2,154	6,125	3,971	3.2
Pharmacies and personal care stores	24,295	6,319	7,416	1,097	5.4
Clothing stores	15,716	6,176	7,387	1,211	2.2
Shoe, clothing accessories and jewellery stores	5,122	2,085	2,395	310	0.4
General merchandise stores	42,339	8,920	11,278	2,358	4.0
Sporting goods, hobby, music and book stores	9,740	3,147	3,549	402	1.8
Miscellaneous store retailers	12,016	4,255	4,882	626	7.9
Totals	370,711	76,821	97,106	20,286	4.2

Source: "The Daily: Annual Retail Trade," Statistics Canada, Monday March 27, 2006 http://www.statcan.ca/Daily/English/060327/d060327a.htm, accessed November 6, 2006.

EXHIBIT 4 Market Shares of Canadian Home Improvement Retailers, 2004

Rank	Company	Market Share (%) 2003	2004
1	The Home Depot Canada	14.0	14.2
2	RONA Inc.	12.2	12.9
3	Home Hardware Stores	11.8	12.0
4	Canadian Tire Corp.	11.3	10.8
5	Sodisco-Howden	4.3	4.6
6	TruServ Canada	2.1	1.9
7	Alpa Lumber	1.5	1.6
8	Federated Co-op	1.3	1.2
9	Kent	0.9	1.0
10	UFA	0.8	0.7
11	Others	39.8	39.1
	Total	100	100

Source: "How Big is the Industry," Hardlines Quarterly Report Vol 3 2005.

EXHIBIT 5 U.S. Home Improvement Products Market: 2004–2009

	2004	2005	2006	2007	2008	2009
Billion $	271.4	280.9	288.1	299.2	313.4	329.1
% change	12.8	3.5	2.6	3.9	4.7	5.0

Source: "How Big is the Industry," Hardlines Quarterly Report Vol 3 2005.

Exhibit 6 The Home Depot Inc. Income Statement

Year Ending January in US $ Million	2005	2004	2003	2002
Revenue	73,094	64,816	58,247	53,553
Cost of Goods Sold	48,664	43,160	39,236	36,642
Gross Profit	24,430	21,656	19,011	16,911
Gen & Adm. Expenses	16,504	13,734	12,278	11,215
Operating Income	7,926	6,846	5,830	4,932
Net Income (after taxes)	5,001	4,304	3,664	3,044

Source: The Home Depot Annual Report 2004 and CIBC World Markets.

EXHIBIT 7 The Home Depot Inc – Sales Performance

Year Ending January	No. of Stores	Average Square Footage	Sales per Store: Average Store ($ mn)	Sales per Store: Average Sq Ft ($)	Inventory per Store: Average store ($ `000)	Inventory per Store: Foot ($)	Average Ticket Size ($)
2001	1,134	113,100	43.6	404.4	5,781	53.30	48.65
2002	1,333	137,725	42.4	388.8	5,045	46.06	48.64
2003	1,532	158,500	40.0	367.5	5,443	50.23	49.43
2004	1,707	175,250	39.7	369.8	5,317	49.60	51.15
2005	1,890	192,750	40.4	379.2	5,331	50.13	54.89

Source: CIBC World Markets Equity Research Report May 17, 2005.

EXHIBIT 8 Canadian Home Improvement Products Market: 2000–2004

	2000	2001	2002	2003	2004
Billion $	26.2	27.2	29.6	32.0	34.8
% Increase	-	3.9	8.8	8.2	8.9

Source: "How Big is the Industry," Hardlines Quarterly Report Vol 3 2005.

14

Molson Canada: Social Media Marketing[1]

Israr Qureshi wrote this case under the supervision of Professor Deborah Compeau solely to provide material for class discussion. The authors do not intend to illustrate either effective or ineffective handling of a managerial situation. The authors may have disguised certain names and other identifying information to protect confidentiality.

On November 23, 2007, the Molson brewing company pulled its promotion on Facebook, after numerous complaints that it promoted binge drinking. The promotion in question involved a photo contest targeting 19- to 24-year-old college and university students. The failure of this promotion on a social networking site forced Molson to think hard about its strategy vis-à-vis social media. What should be Molson's next move? How should it handle one of the fast emerging marketing channels? Should Molson use the social media for any commercial activities?

MOLSON COMPANY

The Molson Company was founded by John Molson in 1786, in Montreal. It was the second oldest company in Canada, preceded only by the Hudson's Bay Company. Molson Canada was part of the Molson Coors Brewing Company. At 41 per cent market share by volume in 2006, Molson was Canada's most preferred brand, slightly ahead of Labatt beer. Worldwide, Molson had 3.8 per cent

[1] This case has been written on the basis of published sources only. Consequently, the interpretation and perspectives presented in this case are not necessarily those of Molson Canada or any of its employees.

market share, placing it fourth behind InBev NV, Anheuser-Busch and SABMiller. Molson offered a range of brands in Canada, including Molson Canadian, Coors Light, Rickard's Red and Pilsner. Molson Canada also partnered with other leading brewers to offer such brands as Heineken and Miller Genuine Draft. Molson employed 3,000 Canadians and operated six breweries, including the boutique brewery in Creemore, Ontario.

Molson Canada invested in communities from coast to coast through its various charitable initiatives and through sports and entertainment sponsorships. It was proud to be a socially responsible company, which was reflected in its code of conduct:

> As a manufacturer of alcohol beverages, Molson Coors is committed to promoting legal and responsible decisions about drinking our products. In our sales and marketing practices, Molson Coors promotes the responsible use of our products by adults of legal drinking age. The Company makes every effort to avoid even the appearance of condoning underage drinking, drunk driving or other irresponsible activity involving consumption. When pursuing your work responsibilities or representing the Company, you should be aware that any inappropriate behaviour reflects negatively upon the Company's reputation and the equity of its brands. If you choose to consume alcohol beverages, you are expected to set a positive example of responsible alcohol consumption.[2]

Following what it espoused in its code of conduct, Molson organized annual awareness programs to encourage responsible drinking. In December 2007, Molson spent more than $100,000 to raise awareness and support communities across Canada in their efforts to encourage responsible drinking during the holiday season. Molson's sponsorship included complimentary New Year's Eve transit service in Ottawa and supporting Operation Red Nose in western and eastern Canada.

Elaborating on the company's efforts, Ferg Devins, vice-president Government and Public Affairs, Molson, explained:

> Community involvement is a major part of Molson heritage. Molson has long promoted responsible choices and this year's local initiatives across the country are consistent with how Molson has built its business in communities from coast to coast. This is our way of celebrating those who choose to make sure all their holiday memories are good ones.[3]

Over the years, the company had focused its efforts on brewing quality beers and taking social and community obligations seriously. The responsible drinking program was an example of Molson's commitment to consumers making responsible choices (see Exhibit 1). Because it was producer of alcohol, Molson directed its community investment donations to programs that encouraged adult audiences to make responsible decisions regarding drinking. Historically, Molson had focused most of its efforts on traditional marketing channels. However, since the beginning of 2007, Molson had started experimenting with social media and social marketing tools as means of targeting its potential young customers.

---

[2] Molson Coors Brewing Company, *Living Our Values*, p. 4, available online at http://www.molsoncoors.com/templates/molson_coors/pdf/Code_of_Business_Conduct.pdf, accessed May 10, 2008.

[3] Molson Coors Brewing Company, "Molson Celebrates Responsible Choices across Canada This Holiday Season," press release, December 19, 2007, available online at http://www.molsoncoors.com/newsroom/press-releases/2007, accessed February 17, 2008.

Social Media

Molson had already experimented with blogs and had tried having a static web presence at social networking sites. However, both these attempts had been at very early stages. Molson did not fully engage the social media (i.e. online technologies and practices used by people to share their experiences, opinions and perspectives others).

Like many other companies, Molson was still trying to make sense of how best to integrate its marketing efforts with various online activities that used technology for social interaction by integrating words, pictures and videos. Some examples were web content, such as blogs and wikis, created by individuals or a collaboration of individuals. Molson's executives found it intuitive that social media was a way of using the Internet to instantly collaborate, share information or have a conversation on anything — or everything. However, how to use these features to promote Molson products was a bit of intellectual exercise.

To make the matter more complex, in social media, anyone can be an expert, a poet, a musician, a photographer, a publisher or a reporter. Thus, how a potential community member would respond to content created by Molson and how much credence Molson should give to that response was very difficult to ascertain. This quandary was one of the primary reasons why many organizations had hesitated to enter the social media realm. In addition, in social media, the contents of one service could be mashed up with data from other services:

> Mashup is a web application that combines data from more than one source into a single integrated tool. An example is the use of cartographic data from Google Maps to add location information to real-estate data from Craigslist, thereby creating a new and distinct web service that was not originally provided by either source.[4]

Mashups led to issues of control and ownership. Content in social media could not be controlled by the individual who created it, especially in terms of how content could be used by others and the sorts of evolutionary trajectories they could take. Thus, nobody had complete control over social media content, which had great implications on how businesses could to use social media for promotion of their image and products.

Social media was characterized by such features as connectivity, community and inclusiveness that made it fundamentally different from traditional media, such as newspapers, television, books and radio. Exhibit 2 provides a partial list of social media characteristics. Primarily, these characteristics were related to interactions between people that were facilitated by the technology and design aspects of the social media websites. Companies tried to leverage one or more of these features of social media for building awareness and creating communities around their products.

For creating awareness about its product, Molson could choose from a variety of social media, such as blogs, forums, microblogging and news aggregation. To create communities, Molson could resort to sites that offered photo sharing, video sharing, social bookmarking and social networking. Some of the common categories of social media are described in the Exhibit 3. Based on the primary objectives of the social media sites, they could be classified into various communities that organized and shared particular kinds of content. Some of the most popular content communities tended to form around friendship (Facebook), photos (Flickr), bookmarked links (del.icio.us) and videos (YouTube).

---

[4] Wikipedia, available online at http://en.wikipedia.org/wiki/Mashup_(web_application_hybrid), accessed September 16, 2008.

Similar to other media, the type of social media and the features that were leveraged were determined by the target customers, the type of product and the marketing strategy.

Social Media Marketing

> Social networking sites like MySpace.com and Facebook attract large numbers of mostly young users who are eager to engage with their favorite brands. But most marketers use traditional marketing tactics like run-of-site advertising[5] and static microsites[6] to push messages into these networks. Instead, to realize the full value of marketing on social networking sites, marketers should be prepared to engage in a personal relationship with users by providing something of value. Promotions are good in this context, but even better are information or brand elements that users can pass on to their friends.[7]

Social Media Marketing (SMM) is a form of Internet marketing that utilizes social media to achieve branding and marketing communication goals. Social media sites, such as MySpace, Facebook, Bebo, YouTube, Digg, Flickr and Twitter, are used to communicate information about a company and its brand and products. Which social medium is most effective and how it can best be targeted depends in part on the goals of SMM campaign and the product offered by the company. In general, most campaigns involved propagating an idea, creating brand awareness, increasing visibility, encouraging brand feedback and dialogue and, in some cases, selling a product or service.

Social media marketers took advantage of the fact that average users of social networking sites were young. In a Forrester survey conducted in 2006, only 20 per cent of adults reported using social networking sites. In contrast, almost 47 per cent of teenagers and 69 per cent of young adults (ages 18 to 21) had a profile and had interacted with other users on social networking sites, such as MySpace and Facebook. Among the users of social networking sites, young adults' (18- to 21–year-olds) usage rate was higher compared with other groups, using social networking sites much more frequently (68 per cent reported making a daily visit) than 12- to 17-year-olds (60 per cent reported daily visits) or adult users (42 per cent reported daily visits).[8]

Another interesting aspect, from a social media marketer's perspective, was that social networking site users wanted to engage with their favorite brands. A Forrester survey found that the most common approach to marketing on social networking sites was to set up a profile for the brand, which members could then join, or "friend," as some social networking sites preferred to call it. For example, Molson's Facebook profile, Molson Canadian Nation, had more than 19,000 members (other Facebook users) as friends.[9] The Forrester survey also found that many social networking site users welcomed interactions with the brands that they loved: more than one-third of 18- to 26-year-old social networking users admitted that they would be interested in seeing a marketer's profile (see Exhibit 4).

---

[5] Run-of-site advertising is an advertisement buying option, in which advertisements can be placed on any pages of the target site. This option is usually inexpensive and hence advertisers generally give up their say over placement. Advertisements may be placed in the unsold, less valuable portions of the target site randomly.

[6] Static microsites are related pages on a website that have their own URL, which is not a derivative of home page. These websites are used for contextual advertisements or pay-per-click advertisements and are created with topic-specific, keyword-rich contents to attract web traffic; however, they are not dynamic and have very low customizability.

[7] Charlene Li, "Marketing on Social Networking Sites," Forrester Research Inc., Cambridge, MA, 2007.

[8] For more details on consumer usage of social networking sites, refer to Charlene Li, "How Consumers User Social Networks," Forrester Research Inc., Cambridge, MA, 2007.

[9] Molson Canadian Nation Facebook group had 19,063 members as of March 29, 2008.

Cold Shots Campus Challenge

In mid-October, on behalf of Molson Canada, Toronto-based ad agency Henderson Bas announced the launch of a campaign targeted at the 19- to 24-year-old demographic. The goal of this campaign was to use Facebook, a social networking site, to increase brand awareness of Molson products in Canada to reach Molson's "target demographics in most efficient manner."[10] The plan was to use the Molson Canadian Nation group profile on Facebook, which then had more than 17,500 members, to spread the word about Molson's products.

"Utilizing Facebook for this program made strategic sense," stated Heather Clark, creative strategy director at Henderson Bas, at the launch of the campaign.[11] The demographics present on most social network websites, including Facebook, were "ideal" for marketers such as Molson. Facebook, primarily created for college and university students, had a very young membership base. Moreover, these websites provided an environment where friends interacted in a trusted and open setting. Thus, social network websites presented opportunities to marketers to build their brands and promote their products through viral marketing as word of "mouse" spread among friends. These websites were a virtual space "where they hang out and it's a great opportunity to engage them in a dialogue. If you do it right, you can find yourself with a whole nation of brand ambassadors," claimed Heather Clark.[12] The campaign was planned to run from the end of October to the end of November, 2007.[13]

The *modus operandi* of the campaign was to have a virtual "dorm room" in the name of each university or college, where students from those institutions could post photos of themselves and their friends in full party mode. The school with the most photos would be awarded the title of number-one party school in Canada. The best photo, as determined by a panel of Molson judges, would win the Spring Break Trip Give Away Contest — a trip for the winner and three friends to Cancun, Mexico, for Spring Break 2008, sponsored by Breakaway Tours.[14] In addition, the Molson Canadian Nation group on Facebook would provide some features to attract members, including the Cold Shots Amped Up game, screen savers, wallpaper and MSN icons, the "Party Finder" section and customized searches for pictures and polls.

The students who were the target of this campaign grew up in the age of Internet and felt comfortable sharing their personal details in an online environment. They routinely upload their personal photos, shared their videos and spent more time on the social networking website than in a physical social space. Social networking sites such as Facebook were a common "hanging around place" for them. For these reasons, the contest became popular among students, particularly those from Memorial University of Newfoundland (MUN). By November 23, students from MUN had uploaded 67 photos, much ahead of University of Victoria, which was in second place with 26 photos. However, not all the students were proud of having their university "leading" this competition. Some argued that students in skimpy costumes who had consumed excess quantities of alcohol hardly matched their image of a wonderful time at university.

---

10 Marina Strauss, "Molson Photo Contest Brews up Anger," *Globe and Mail*, available at http://www.theglobeandmail.com/servlet/story/RTGAM.20071122.wmolsonface1122/BNStory/Technology, accessed January 6, 2008.

11 Kara Nicholson, "Molson Using Facebook to Engage Canadian Students," available at http://www.mediaincanada.com/articles/mic/20071122/molson.html, accessed January 6, 2008.

12 Ibid.

13 Karen Rouse, "Molson Ends Facebook 'Party School' Contest," *Denver Post*, November 26, 2007, available at http://www.denverpost.com/business/ci_7562948, accessed January 12, 2008.

14 Kara Nicholson, "Molson Using Facebook to Engage Canadian Students," available at http://www.mediaincanada.com/articles/mic/20071122/molson.html, accessed January 12, 2008.

Criticism of the Contest

Many students and administrators across the Canadian universities felt that Molson's "Cold Shot" was giving their school's image a bad reputation. They felt that the contest encouraged irresponsible behavior by inciting students to post their photos in outrageous situations. To get noticed, students who were posing for photos may have felt the need to present themselves in an extraordinary condition, which typically meant wearing skimpy costumes, behaving unusually and drinking more than what could be considered safe and responsible amounts of alcohol.

The non-participating students at the front-runner MUN felt this contest was giving their university image a "hangover." *The Muse*, a student-run newspaper at MUN, published an editorial bashing the competition. Editor Kerri Breen labeled the contest "really kind of lame." She criticized Molson's approach as inappropriate and stated "beer bongs and letterman's jackets, it's really not something MUN should strive to be associated with."[15] Another student at MUN found the contest frustrating because it gave an impression of the school that wasn't fair to students who attended MUN to study and achieved good grades. In her view, it was unfair "to have other people coming in, looking at the school as a whole and saying that we're a group of people who don't care about the academics, that we're just here to party."[16] Many students at MUN agreed that Molson's contest presented the wrong view about having a good experience at the university.

The University of Western Ontario (Western), which prided itself in providing best student experience wasn't amused with its eighth overall ranking (only 10 entries had been received by November 22) of "best party" school, which, according to Cynthea Galbraith, a Molson spokesperson, meant "the context of celebrating good times with friends after the academics are over for the day."[17] Students and officials at Western argued that if this was what "best party" school meant then Western should be at the top of the list and not at the eighth place:

> Party school is a very narrow definition of what we believe to be the best student experience in the country. When we talk to students, alumni and the public we emphasize [Western] has both an in-class component but also a great social experience . . . social experience means many different things. It means having great student government and opportunities to involve yourself in that, along with clubs, organizations, and the opportunity to involve yourself in varsity sport. It's the opportunity to build great networks because so many of our students live on campus. There are more important things to the student experience than just partying and drinking[18]

Responses from other universities also followed the same lines. Jason Laker, associate vice-principal and dean of Student Affairs at Queen's University, felt disgusted:

> Such an apparent and dangerous disregard . . . promotes an abusive use of alcohol . . . . In order for the photos to be eligible, to be notable, would require outrageous behaviour or profoundly dangerous levels of drinking, and of course the kind of decision making and behaviour that follow that. [Molson] are either unaware of it or simply placing profits above ethics.[19]

---

[15] "Molson's Facebook Contest Leaves Some MUN Students Frothing," CBC News, November 20, 2007.
[16] Ibid.
[17] Ken Meaney, "Anger Brews over Molson Contest," *Calgary Herald*, November 21, 2007, p. 5.
[18] Ted Garrard, vice-president external at Western, quoted in Mike Hayes, "Memorial Is the Number One Party School? Really?" *The Gazette*, November 15, 2007, pp. 1–2.
[19] Sarah Miller, "Molson Promo Challenged by Universities," *The Gazette*, November 28, 2007, p. 3.

Similar sentiments were expressed by Joe MacDonald, dean of Students Affairs at St. Francis Xavier University:

> These kinds of programs put added stress on our ability to ensure that students have a very positive, successful academic and non-academic development . . . . This is not something that is welcome within our campus community. It's cheap marketing, I'm concerned about Molson's lack of contrition[20].

Phil Wood, associate vice-president of student affairs at McMaster University agreed, "It is hard to believe that a leading corporation like Molson would stoop to such a . . . way of doing business."[21] He expressed his dismay especially because Molson Coors Brewing Co. was targeting students in residence even though many of them were too young to legally consume alcohol. Zach Churchill, national director of the Canadian Alliance of Student Associations, termed the Molson campaign as unfortunate because it stereotyped university students as being interested only in partying.[22]

However, the best articulation of universities' opposition to Molson contest came in the letter sent by Brenda Whiteside, chair of Ontario Committee on Student Affairs, the University of Guelph. In her letter to Molson she wrote:

> As professionals dealing with the transition of young students to university, we are continuously combating the stereotype of universities being places to party . . . . One of the risks of a "party university" culture is the increased potential for over consumption of alcohol by students with no previous experience. Each year we send a small but concerning number of students to hospital with alcohol poisoning. Some of us have had to deal with a student death due to over consumption. In addition, we continually struggle with the by-products of over consumption — vandalism, assault, sexual assault, and academic failure . . . we devote endless energy, resources and programming towards responsible drinking campaigns . . . . Imagine our dismay when we learned of this campaign — a competition for a party environment in residence. This campaign not only dismantles university efforts to create a culture of academics in residences, it also helps to establish an environment that could encourage irresponsible drinking. Our second concern with this campaign is the use of Facebook . . . . Facebook has the potential to be dangerous for students . . . . Of particular concern is students posting pictures of themselves in behaviour that could impact negatively on future careers or opportunities. There are numerous examples of students who have regretted the posting of such pictures. Thus, please understand again our dismay with a program that encourages students to potentially place such damaging photos on the internet . . . . This present campaign runs counter to Molson's commitment to responsible drinking. We hope that your company will be more thoughtful about possible risks of advertising campaigns prior to future launches.[23]

---

[20] Marina Strauss, "Molson Photo Contest Brews up Anger," *Globe and Mail*, available at http://www.theglobeandmail.com/servlet/story/RTGAM.20071122.wmolsonface1122/BNStory/Technology, accessed January 6, 2008.

[21] Ibid.

[22] Ibid.

[23] Brenda Whiteside "A Cold Shot to Responsible Drinking," available at www.macdrphil.wordpress.com/2007/11/27/a-cold-shot, accessed on January 27, 2008.

Her letter raised two critical aspects: 1) this contest was run against the often cited Molson virtue that it encourages responsible drinking and 2) this contest overlooked the privacy risk of sharing objectionable photos on a public website such as Facebook. Most of the objections from students and university administrators were around the first issue; however, some objections were raised about the second issue as well.

Administrators were of the view that Molson's Facebook initiative could jeopardize students' future career, especially those seeking jobs in near future, if potential employers stumble upon their not-so-graceful photos on Facebook. Phil Wood was concerned that some students' pictures may have been viewed by prospective employers or graduate schools, and these students could face biased treatment that could compromise their chances of landing a job or gaining admission to graduate school. He felt that encouraging students to post pictures of themselves engaging in excessive drinking or dangerous behavior was not a good idea in itself because students "don't understand the danger of the public-ness of Facebook. You're not anonymous."[24]

Because Facebook was a public virtual space, these photos were accessible to potential future employers, administrators and society at large. This exposure created a potential risk of students not being hired, being pre-judged if hired and being monitored in prejudiced way. Moreover, some students had become unconsenting participants. Not everyone who was partying and happened to be in photo wanted to be part of the contest, which had privacy implications. It was not clear whether Molson had any guidelines in place to ensure the consent of all those who appeared in the photographs was obtained before photo was uploaded for the contest. Many similar issues were raised regarding privacy and future implications of compromising this privacy.

One blogger's comment about Molson contest summed it up humorously:

Capturing these young heavy drinkers in Facebook is a great idea. We will have a vibrant montage of "before" pictures to mix with the "after" pictures of:

- people killed by drunk drivers
- students choking on their vomit
- students sexually assaulted or robbed while incapacitated (by heavy drinking)
- students later running for public office or other positions of trust etc.

> Then as the years go by, and Molson tracks their "best customers," we can see whether they reach their potential from a university degree, or struggle with alcoholism and its social and physical effects. Without using Facebook, we would never have such a well-organized audit trail, with poignant photographs, on which to base lawsuits for those who drink to tragic ends.[25]

The final proverbial straw in the coffin of Molson's photo contest came when administrators from four universities wrote letters to Molson and also expressed their opinions in the *Globe and Mail*, squarely criticizing the contest. They slammed Molson's contest saying it promoted irresponsible drinking and demanded immediate withdrawal of the contest. They argued that Molson should pull the campaign because it was inconsistent with the company's own promotion of safe and responsible drinking.

---

[24] Mary Jane Credeur, "Molson Coors Ends Facebook Contest after Complaints," available at http://www.bloomberg.com/apps/news?pid=newsarchive&sid=aFC76olDqrJQ, accessed January 9, 2008.

[25] Ziad Fazel, comments on the article "Molson Photo Contest Brews up Anger," available at http://www.theglobeandmail.com/servlet/story/RTGAM.20071122.wmolsonface1122/CommentStory/Technology, accessed January 11, 2008.

Molson's Response

Sensing the probable outrage from the academic community, Molson pulled its contest on November 23, almost a week before its scheduled end. Molson, however, argued that the contest was simply an effort to engage its target market with socially oriented advertising and should not be interpreted as any attempt to encourage irresponsible drinking. The company also initiated damage control by issuing public statements through various officials. Molson issued a public note on its Facebook page explaining why it withdrew the contest: "we promote responsible choices and wanted to be proactive in responding to concerns expressed from a number of different audiences."

However, Molson executives felt that the company's initiative had been misunderstood and misinterpreted as promoting irresponsible drinking. Ferg Devins, Molson's vice president, Government and Public Affairs, agreed that Molson had learned a lot from the contest:

> The whole realm of social media — there's lots to learn. It's really a new area. We're probably groundbreaking and leading in a lot of things we've been doing.[26]

Similar sentiments were expressed by Cynthea Galbraith, a spokeswoman for Molson: "Our take is that this whole social media realm is new. There's going to be some experimentation, there's going to be some learning." In spite of this failure, Galbraith was very positive about the future possibility of social media. She expressed cautious optimism:

> I don't know if surprised is the word, but we learn from these things. Our intention is to become a leader in that area and we'll go back and develop some new innovations in communications for next time.[27]

Like many others at Molson, Galbraith identified social media as one of the most important channels to communicate with the 19- to 24-year-old demographic. She observed "Social interaction is key with that [demographic], it seems to be all the rage right now." Ferg Devins was in total agreement: "We need to be communicating with our consumers because that's where our consumers are communicating among themselves . . . . We need to make sure we're in that relevant channel." Despite the setback to its contest, Molson planned to expand its social media marketing, and Devins highlighted the efforts Molson had initiated in terms of blogs and other social technologies.

With its marketing vision firmly rooted in the exploitation of social media, some Molson executives wondered whether they had really done the right thing by calling off the photo contest a week ahead of its scheduled conclusion. Had they given into unreasonable pressure or had they acted responsibly? Did they forgo the opportunity of using social media in its true sense by not taking the view of the participants of the contest into account? Should they continue to try to use social media as part of their marketing, and if so how? How would they combat the challenges they had encountered with the Facebook promotion, and what other challenges should they foresee?

Whether future attempts of Molson with social media would bear fruit would depend on how the company applied the lessons learned from the failure of the photo contest. How should Molson address the privacy issues? Should Molson include all the relevant stakeholders in the loop? And how could Molson best put the potential of social media to use?

---

26 "A Cold Shot to Responsible Drinking," available at www.macdrphil.wordpress.com/ 2007/11/27/a-cold-shot, accessed January 27, 2008.

27 Sarah Miller, "Molson Promo Challenged by Universities," The Gazette, November 28, 2007, p. 3.

EXHIBIT 1 Responsible Choices Campaign

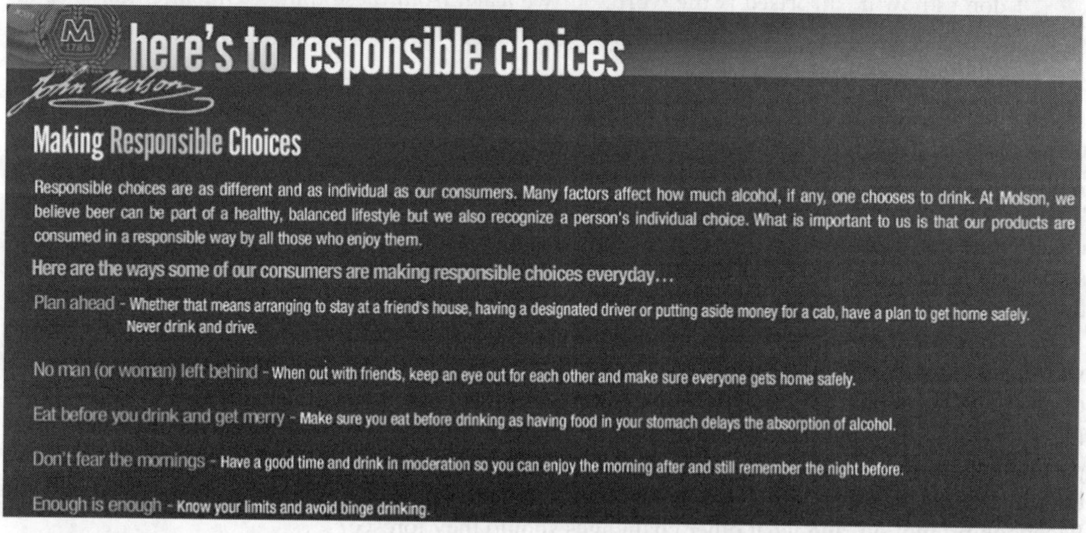

Source: Molson Canada, "Here's to Responsible Choices," http://www.responsiblechoices.ca/, accessed January 29, 2008.

EXHIBIT 2 Characteristics of Social Media

Archival and retrieval	In social media, all the events are automatically archived and normally available for retrieval to anyone who may have interest in looking them at later date. Retrieval of information in traditional media is not that easy
Community	Social media facilitates community building. It allows communities to form around a common interest, such as a favorite celebrity, a political issue, a sport, a hobby, etc.
Connectedness	Social media is also characterized by the endless possibility of connectedness, which may manifest itself in the form of links to other individuals, groups, forums or web resources.
Democratic	Most social media services are open to feedback and participation, which are actively encouraged. They also encourage discussion, voting, comments and at times some sort of ranking about shared information.
Dialogue	Traditional media, such as newspaper, radio and television, work on the principles of broadcast where readers, listeners and viewers are passive receivers. Social media is seen as a two-way conversation in which roles of "broadcasters" and "receivers" are continuously changed back and forth.
Dynamic	Traditional print media cannot be changed once it is off the press. Similarly, radio and TV programs once delivered are in the public domain without any possibility of revision. However, social media can be modified or corrected instantaneously. Moreover social media continuously evolves due to regular feedback and comments.
Inclusive	Contributions and feedback are encouraged from anyone who may be interested. No entry barriers exist. Digital divide issues may limit some people, but otherwise it is absolutely open.
Lack of control	In social media, the content of one service can be mashed up with data from other services. Thus, nobody has complete control over any content.
Real-time evaluation	It is very easy to evaluate the popularity of a social media service in real time, based on a site visit, comments left, growth of membership and number of links that the service solicits. Sites such as Wordpress (http://wordpress.org/) can identify how much traffic each blog receives. Visitors to Digg (http://digg.com/) can see voting on someone's blog items. In addition, sites such as TechMeme (http://www.techmeme.com/), provide statistics on which blog items received the most links in the past few hours. Traditional media provide some statistics on popularity but they are very coarse and available at the best in annual intervals and generally with the lag of one or two years.

Source: Compiled from various sources and authors own experiences. Sources include: What is Social Media? An e-book from iCrossing – available at www.icrossing.co.uk/ebooks, accessed January 15, 2008. What is Social Media? available at http://scobleizer.com/2007/02/16/what-is-social-media/, accessed on January 16, 2008.Social Media Sociology, available at http://social-media-sociology.com/, accessed on January 15, 2008.

EXHIBIT 3 Some Examples of Social Media

Blogs	Blogs are the most common form of social media. Blogs are online journals, with the most recent entries appearing first. These journal entries are available for other to read and comment on.
Forums	Forums are websites for online discussion, often around specific topics and interests. These online spaces provide an outlet for debates, arguments and counter-arguments.
Microblogging (Presence apps)	Microblogging is combination of social networking with bite-sized blogging, where micro blog-like posts, such as an announcement of what you are currently doing, are distributed online and through the mobile phone network. Twitter (http://twitter.com/) is a well-known example of microblogging website.
News aggregation	News aggregator websites provide a list of the latest news stories published by users from a range of different websites. Digg (http://digg.com) is one of the web's largest news aggregators.
Online gaming	Online gaming is often based around communities. World of Warcraft (http://www.worldofwarcraft.com/index.xml) is one of the popular examples of online gaming. Some aspects of Second Life (http://secondlife.com/) may also be included in online gaming.
Photo sharing	Photo-sharing sites facilitate uploading of pictures and images to a personal account, which can then be shared or viewed by web users the world over. A well-known example of a photo-sharing website is Flickr (http://www.flickr.com).
Social bookmarking	Social bookmarking sites allow users to publicly bookmark web pages they find valuable in order to share them with other Internet users. One famous example is del.icio.us (http://del.icio.us).
Social Networking sites	Social networking websites provide opportunities for individuals who either want to build online social networks to share their interests and activities or are interested in exploring the interests and activities of others. These sites allow people to build personal web pages and then connect with friends to communicate or share content. Some of the common social networking sites are Linkedin, MySpace, Facebook and Orkut.
Video sharing	Video-sharing sites facilitate the uploading and sharing of personal videos with the rest of the web community. A common example of a video-sharing website is YouTube (www.youtube.com).
Wikis	These websites allow people to add, edit, challenge or debate their content. The contents are collectively owned and act as a communal document or database. The best-known wiki is Wikipedia, the online encyclopedia, which has more than 2.3 million English language articles and more than 6.5 million articles in all the available languages (information as of March 29, 2008 on http://www.wikipedia.org)

Source: Compiled from various sources and authors own experiences. Sources include: What is Social Media? An e-book from iCrossing – available at www.icrossing.co.uk/ebooks, accessed January 15, 2008. What is Social Media? available at http://scobleizer.com/2007/02/16/what-is-social-media/, accessed on January 16, 2008. Social Media Sociology, available at http://social-media-sociology.com/, accessed on January 15, 2008.

EXHIBIT 4 Age and Frequency of Usagè (Indicators of Willingness to Engage with Favorite Bands)

4.1 By age

"How interested are you in social network profiles from a favorite marketer, retailer, or service provider?" [percent who answered 4 or 5 on a scale of 1 to 5]*

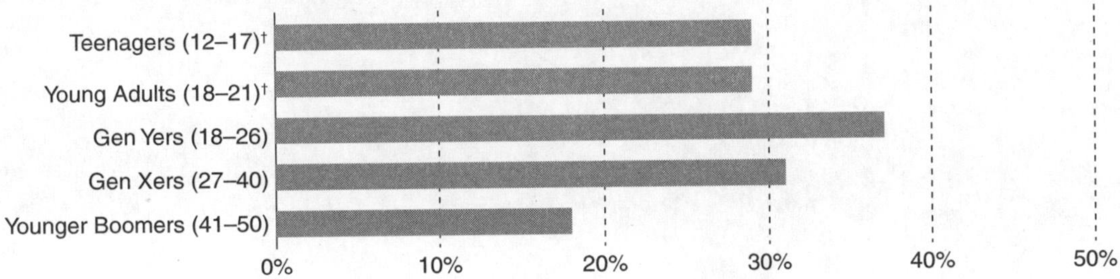

4.2 By usage

"How interested are you in social network profiles from a favorite marketer, retailer, or service provider?"

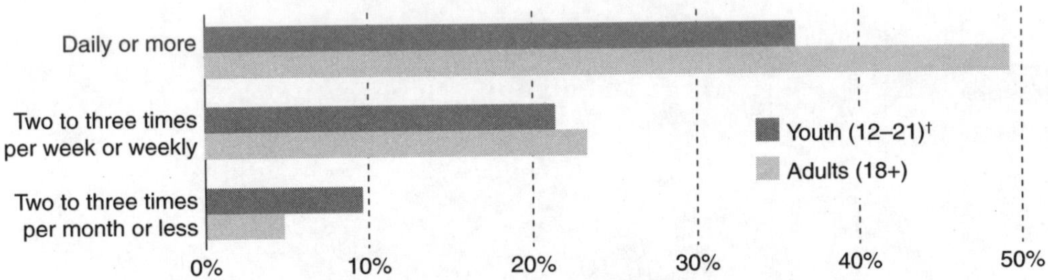

Base: US online social networking site users

Source: Forrester's NACTAS Q3 2006 Media & Marketing Online Survey
†Source: Forrester's NACTAS Q4 2006 Youth Media & Marketing And Finance Online Survey
*Note: Bases for Older Boomers (15–61) and Seniors (62+) were too small to report values

Source: Charlene Li, "Marketing on Social Networking Sites," Forrester Research Inc., Cambridge, MA, 2007.

15

jewellworld.com—Online Jewelry Shopping in China

In July 2004, Joseph Lee, the marketing manager of Jewellworld.com needed to consider how to expand the company's business in a saturated Hong Kong market. Not long before, Lee had a meeting with the marketing director, Derek Ling, who was responsible for the development of the Hong Kong and mainland Chinese jewelry markets.

One of the main topics of this meeting had been the expansion of the online shopping strategy into the business-to-consumer (B2C) area in mainland China. However, the staff of the marketing department held different views. The immediate question was whether Jewellworld.com should move into the B2C area at full speed or wait and see how other competitors fared in the mainland online market.

The other issue was the segmentation that Jewellworld.com should employ if it decided to enter the B2C market in mainland China. Luk Fook Jewellery, which, like Jewellworld.com, was a branch of the Luk Fook Group, had already established retail stores across the mainland. Lee needed to decide whether Jewellworld.com should aim to cover all market segments and product lines, like Luk Fook Jewellery, or whether it should target young people, among whom Internet use is the most popular.

The author appreciates the financial support of the Research Grants Council of the Hong Kong Special Administrative Region (Project No. HKU7213/03H).

HISTORY OF JEWELLWORLD.COM

Jewellworld.com was founded in May 2000, as a wholly owned subsidiary of Luk Fook Holdings (International) Ltd. (Luk Fook Holdings), and was wholly owned by the parent company. Initially, the portal was established to provide a business-to-business (B2B) platform for suppliers only, but following the company's initial success and praise from its suppliers, the executives at Jewellworld.com decided to enter the B2C market. In December 2002, the company set up another section on its website where the general public could purchase bracelets, earrings, rings, necklaces, pendants and mobile phone decorations in gold, karat gold, platinum and silver. The products were priced from a few hundred to a few thousand Hong Kong dollars.[1] Although some of Jewellworld.com's products overlapped with those of Luk Fook Jewellery, Jewellworld.com mainly focused on lower-priced products, and aimed its products locally at the younger generation, especially high school and university students and young white-collar workers. In addition to local customers, Jewellworld.com also had customers in Canada, Australia, the United Kingdom and the United States, to target people who had emigrated from Hong Kong in the past 15 years.

Luk Fook Holdings (International) Ltd.

Luk Fook Holdings was established in 1991 and was listed on the Hong Kong Stock Exchange in May 1997. The company handled all aspects of the manufacturing and distribution of its products, including procurement, logistics, management and marketing. Luk Fook Holdings had three fully owned subsidiaries: Luk Fook Jewellery, IceG and Jewellworld.com. Luk Fook Jewellery targeted mature customers aged 35 and older, and IceG targeted young female white-collar workers. The group offered products in pure gold, karat gold, gems, platinum, jade and diamonds. It operated factories and design houses in Hong Kong and mainland China. Currently, it operated 28 retail stores in Hong Kong, Macau and Canada, and expansion to the Chinese mainland had mainly occurred through franchising.

THE MACRO ENVIRONMENT

The Chinese Economic Environment in 2004

Since President Deng Xiao Ping introduced the "open market" policy in 1978, the Chinese economy has prospered. According to World Bank statistics, the annual growth of gross domestic product (GDP) in China in 2003 was 9.1 per cent, and in 2004, the mainland's GDP ranked seventh in the world. Although Chinese GDP is still at the developing country level, the GDP of the costal cities has grown rapidly in the past few years. Jewelry, which is considered in China to be a value reserve and a luxury product, has become more popular among consumers in China as their living standards have increased. The average spending on jewelry has remained at a high level over the past few years.

The Hong Kong Consumer Market

After 1997, Hong Kong entered a period of deflation, and the purchasing power of Hong Kong citizens dropped. Many retailers had to close down, and sales of jewelry, which was regarded as a luxury product, were badly affected. However, the increasing number of mainland travelers to Hong Kong had given some relief to the worsening retail business situation. According to figures from the Bank of

---

[1] US$1 = HK$7.8.

East Asia, the estimated number of mainland visitors to Hong Kong reached more than 8.5 million in 2003, which comprised almost 54.9 per cent of total Hong Kong tourist arrivals in that year. The introduction of visa-free individual travel to Hong Kong, in 2004, further improved the situation. Under this policy, the Chinese central government allowed many affluent cities, such as Guangzhou, Beijing and Shanghai, to lift restrictions on the travel of their citizens to Hong Kong. In 2003, mainland visitors spent an average US$723 per visit, which was more than the expenditures by visitors from the United States and Japan, and comprised about 64 per cent of the total expenditure of visitors to Hong Kong. Luk Fook estimated that each purchase of jewelry by mainland customers in retail stores was worth about HK$3,000 (US$385). According to the Hong Kong Tourism Board, jewelry was one of the most popular items among customers from the mainland, and 27.8 per cent (or HK$8.8 billion) of the shopping expenditure incurred by overnight visitors in 2003 was spent on garments, followed by jewelry (17.7 per cent) and watches (9.9 per cent).

The Hong Kong Jewelry Industry

Jewelry was one of Hong Kong's major exports. About 67 per cent of Hong Kong's jewelry output was exported to overseas markets at an annual value of billions of U.S. dollars. Traditional markets included the United States (44 per cent), followed by Japan, Germany, Switzerland, France and Singapore. Hong Kong's share of the mainland jewelry market was relatively small. Hong Kong was a leading processing center for jewelry in Asia, and was the most important distribution hub globally. In recent years, more suppliers had realized the huge potential of the mainland market as its spending power continued to rise, and the consumption pattern of the younger generation became more internationalized.

Hong Kong jewelry enjoyed brisk sales in the mainland market because of its design and quality. Under the Closer Economic Partnership Arrangement (CEPA), jewelry was entitled to zero tariffs, and there would thus be room for price reductions, which would benefit both consumers and suppliers.

CEPA

The Closer Economic Partnership Arrangement (CEPA) between Hong Kong and the Chinese mainland became effective in January 1, 2004, and provided Hong Kong manufacturers and service companies with preferential access to the mainland market. CEPA benefited Hong Kong companies that wanted to establish branches on the mainland by giving them "first mover" advantage. In the past, under the mandate of the Most Favored Nations (MFN) principles, international manufacturers and those from Hong Kong had to pay for tariffs on Hong Kong domestic exports to the mainland, and in the service sector, companies had to form joint ventures with local Chinese companies to open retail stores on the mainland. However, under CEPA, Hong Kong manufacturers could enjoy zero tariffs on 90 per cent of Hong Kong domestic exports (see Exhibit 1), and Hong Kong permanent residents were permitted to set up individually owned retail stores in Guangdong province. The launch of CEPA had further leveraged Hong Kong as a base for the distribution of international brands to the mainland, and had offered a great opportunity for foreign companies to move value-added research and development (R&D) facilities, procurement and assembly processes to Hong Kong to take advantage of Hong Kong's superior legal system and intellectual property protection. For local and foreign small and medium-sized enterprises (SMEs), CEPA had lowered the threshold to entry into the Chinese market. CEPA had also served to reinforce the relationship between Hong Kong and mainland China, and although the mainland would continue to be the "factory of the world," Hong Kong would focus on the value-added functions.

Since the introduction of CEPA, some international jewelry companies had moved their base to Hong Kong. Paspaley Peraling Company, an Australian pearl producer and distributor, recently shifted its base from Japan to Hong Kong, and the number of exhibitors at the four-day Hong Kong Jewelry Fair was up by 16 per cent from 2003.

THE MICRO ENVIRONMENT

The Chinese Internet Market

The Chinese Internet market had boomed in recent years. According to World Bank statistics, there were only 60,000 Internet users in mainland China in 1995, but by 2004, the number surpassed the 80 million mark, and there was an upward trend. Mainland China now ranks third in the world in the number of Internet users behind Japan and the United States. According to recent figures, the largest group to have access to the Internet in China is 18-to-24-year-olds with salaries of less than RMB1,000[2] (see Exhibit 2).

The Chinese Mode of Jewelry Distribution

Jewelry distribution in mainland China was different from the distribution in other places. In Hong Kong, companies purchased raw materials and design, manufactured, and then sold their products in their own stores, with the whole process being operated by a single company. On the mainland, domestic companies also designed and manufactured the majority of their own products, with a small proportion sourcing from other parts of the mainland. However, jewelry was mainly sold in department stores or shopping malls, and therefore, when customers entered a jewelry shop, they would be exposed to many brands, rather than a single brand. The centralization of retailers gave customers more choice in the same place, but also meant more competition.

Jewelry Competition in Mainland China

Statistics show that the mainland now ranks among the world's biggest jewelry markets, with annual sales exceeding US$10 billion and an annual gold consumption of more than 250 tonnes. In 2001, China consumed 42 tonnes of platinum, which accounted for 60 per cent of the world's total output, and the annual consumption of platinum now exceeds RMB10 billion. China is the world's largest market for jade, precious stones and platinum, and it is the fourth largest consumer of gold. It is also Asia's largest market for diamond jewelry. The mainland is projected to become a global jewelry center by 2010, as a result of high domestic demand, government encouragement to trade in gold, and the movement of gold working businesses to China. In 2002, sales of Hong Kong jewelry to mainland consumers registered an increase of 23 per cent.

As the Chinese market had so much potential, competition in the jewelry industry was intense. The competition could be classified into three categories: domestic brands, Hong Kong brands and international brands. Domestic brands, such as Laofengxiang and LaoMiao, had established a strong foothold in their "home" cities (different cities have their own batch of brands). They sold products to low- to middle-income customers. Compared with Hong Kong brands and international brands, they had less product variety, and sold their mainly karat gold and silver products in the range of a

[2] US$1 = RMB8.5

few hundred renminbi to RMB2,000. Hong Kong brands, such as Chow Tai Fook, Tse Sui Luen, J's, Luk Fook, King Fook and Chow Seng Seng, usually had better designs, a better reputation and better service. These brands charged a higher price and targeted the mid- to high-end market in more affluent cities, such as Beijing and Shanghai. They also sold a wider variety of products in more expensive materials, such as pure gold, karat gold, diamonds and platinum, priced between a few hundred renminbi and RMB10,000. International top-tier brands, including Cartier, Bvlgari and Tiffany & Co, charged a premium price and usually sold products with superior materials, such as karat gold, gold and diamonds, to target different customer categories. Prices range from a few thousand dollars to a few hundred thousand dollars. The following companies are the closest competitors to Jewellworld.com.

Laofengxiang

Laofengxiang was the best-known domestic jewelry maker on the mainland. It had more than 150 years of history and was headquartered in Shanghai. For five consecutive years, the company had been named as one of the top 100 companies in Shanghai. Currently, its distribution network spread across the mainland, with approximately 40 retail stores and more than 500 distribution centers. Laofenxiang was considered a pioneer in the mainland jewelry industry because of its wide variety of products. It offered products in pure gold, karat gold, silver and diamonds that ranged in price from a few hundred to a few thousand RMB. The targeted age group was those aged 30 and older.

LaoMiao

LaoMiao was established in 1982 and was headquartered in Shanghai. Currently, the company had assets of RMB160 million, 62 retail stores and distributors in Shanghai and more than 200 retail stores across the mainland. In 2001, the company's sales reached RMB1.3 billion. It sold necklaces, earrings, rings, bracelets and pendants in pure gold, karat gold, silver and diamonds to customers aged 35 and older. Prices ranged from a few hundred to a few thousand RMB.

Chow Tai Fook

Established in 1929, Chow Tai Fook was one of the largest jewelry retailers in Hong Kong. In 2002, the company was voted one of the most famous brands in Hong Kong. The company had retail stores in Hong Kong and the mainland, and offered a wide range of products in pure gold, diamonds, gemstones, pearl, jade, platinum and 18-karat gold. Products ranged in price from a few hundred to RMB10,000 and sold to customers aged 35 and older.

Luk Fook

Luk Fook was founded in 1991 and was listed on the Hong Kong Stock Exchange in 1997. The company currently had 28 retail stores in mainland China, Hong Kong, Macau and Canada whereas the number of licensee shops of Luk Fook Jewellery brand in mainland China had been rapidly grown to over 145. In 2004, Luk Fook was regarded as one of the best-known Hong Kong brands in mainland China. The company had a diversified business, and Jewellworld.com was one of its subsidiaries. The company sold products made from pure gold, diamonds, gemstones, pearl, jade, platinum and 18-karat gold. Prices ranged from a few hundred renminbi to RMB10,000, and customers were aged 35 and older. Over the years, Luk Fook had received many awards for innovative product design.

Other Mainland Online Jewelry Stores

In mainland China, many online jewelry stores had been set up in recent years as online shopping had grown. These online stores usually did not produce their own products, but instead acted as intermediaries and resold the jewelry of other retailers on their website. They were dispersed across the mainland in such places as Shandong, Shenzhen, Shanghai and Fujian province. Some of these companies offered online shopping and online catalogs, whereas others offered only online catalogs and accepted payment by mail, online payment or bank wiring (see Exhibit 3). Products ranged in price from as low as RMB10s to as much as a few thousand RMB, and included jade, silver, pearl and gold jewelry. In general, the products offered were priced lower than the Hong Kong and international brands, and were targeted at the low- to mid-end market.

The Purchasing Behavior of Consumers in China

According to a recent survey that was conducted by the Trade and Development Council of Hong Kong, different consumer groups, based on age and consumer preference, were gradually taking shape on the mainland, and were becoming increasingly distinct. On the whole, the buying habits of different consumer groups were quite similar, yet there were variations across different Chinese cities.

Products

Necklaces and rings were the most popular products, with platinum, diamond and gold being the most favored materials (see Exhibit 4). Consumer motivation included pleasing oneself and having an attractive style. There was a tendency towards impulse buying, which was particularly obvious among women. Male consumers mostly purchased jewelry to please others and to give as gifts. Goodwill, quality and price were the main considerations in purchasing jewelry. Hong Kong brands were by far the most popular, and were the top choice for mid-to-high range products.

Pricing

Consumers in China tended to choose low-price items, but their purchasing power was rather uneven. The median jewelry expenditure of respondents in the 12 months before the survey was RMB400. The majority of respondents found the pricing of jewelry to be reasonable, and were most willing to spend money on rings, followed by necklaces, pendants and bracelets, with the median spending ranging between RMB450 and RMB1,200 (see Exhibit 5).

Location

Consumers in China often visited jewelry shops, especially on holidays. The peak seasons occurred during the three "golden weeks" of the Chinese New Year (January 22 to 24, 2004), Labor Day (May 1 to 3, 2004) and National Day (October 1 to 3, 2004),[3] and there were usually large sales promotions

---

[3] The weekends (Saturday and Sunday) preceding and following these three-day holidays may be shifted toward the three-day block to give a continuous stretch of seven days off. Employees may end up having to work on Saturday or Sunday. The arrangement is usually finalized shortly before the holiday event.

around these holiday seasons. Counters at department stores were the most popular shopping spots (see Exhibit 6) for jewelry, but there were not many street-level jewelry shops, due to set-up difficulties. Mainland consumers were interested in buying jewelry products in Hong Kong because of the wider selection of designs, the reasonable prices and the guaranteed quality.

Consideration

When consumers in China chose jewelry, they regarded good design, goodwill and reliability as the three most important considerations (see Exhibit 7). Although customers also considered design and brand image when selecting jewelry, these factors were less important. Having been in the Chinese market for a couple of years, Hong Kong brands were considered by mainlanders to perform well in these areas.

Advertisement

TV commercials were the most influential marketing tool. Consumers mainly obtained information on jewelry trends from shopping malls and department stores, followed by TV commercials and the recommendations of friends and relatives. Consumer habits also varied from city to city. Residents of big cities tended to be more individualistic; they pursued fashion trends, styles and novelty and paid attention to company goodwill, brand image and product quality. These consumers also had higher purchasing power. In light of this, Hong Kong companies could benefit by launching products that suit local market needs.

The Purchasing Power of Consumers in China

According to the latest statistics from the National Bureau of Statistics of China, the annual disposable income per capita of city residents in 2002 was RMB7,703 (US$963) and of rural dwellers was RMB2,476 (US$310). The five highest spending regions were Shenzhen, Guangzhou, Beijing, Shanghai and Hangzhou (see Exhibit 8).

The official disposable income per capita was underestimated, because many Chinese people did not report their full income, and because the year-end bonuses and wages of rural workers who worked in cities were not reported to the Bureau of Statistics. Government subsidies also were not included in per capita disposable income figures.

Reasons for Consumers in China to Purchase Hong Kong Brand Names

Hong Kong brands, to a certain extent, had some advantages in mainland China over both Chinese local companies and foreign competitors. In Hong Kong, Chow Tai Fook, Tse Sui Luen and Luk Fook were the three major jewelry brands. These companies had been in the Chinese market for some time, and had built an awareness of their brands on the mainland. They focused on the mid- to high-end market, whereas local brands mainly targeted the low- to mid-end market (see Exhibit 9). By offering competitive pricing and designs that fit Chinese taste, Hong Kong brands had proved popular in the Chinese market. Good quality and a wide variety of styles and brands were the main reasons that mainland shoppers purchased Hong Kong jewelry (see Exhibit 10).

CHALLENGES AND CONTROVERSIES

Joseph Lee, who was responsible for the expansion of Jewellworld.com in the Greater China area, had proposed that Jewellworld.com should enter the mainland market. However, other Jewellworld.com executives were skeptical of the idea, because the scale in Hong Kong was still small and the Hong Kong market was still in its initial stages.

The most fundamental concern was the target segment of Jewellworld.com products. Although students who were aged 24 or younger were the biggest Internet users, their average salary was very low. The products of Jewellworld.com started at a few hundred RMB, and the price was still more than many of them could afford. However, Internet usage was not very popular among the richer 35 and older age group. Which market segment should Jewellworld.com enter? Or should Jewellworld.com adopt a mass-market strategy?

The second challenge for Jewellworld.com was the method of payment. Security was a large concern for customers who wanted to purchase online. With cyber crimes and stolen credit card information on the rise, potential online shoppers now regarded Internet security as one of the biggest concerns in purchasing online (see Exhibit 11). However, for those who did make purchases online, almost half paid by credit card followed by payment in cash upon arrival. Currently, Jewellworld.com only offered payment by cheque or bank deposit. Should Jewellworld.com also offer credit card payment? Managers had claimed that this option would significantly increase the maintenance cost of Jewellworld.com's website.

The third important issue that Jewellworld.com had to face was the delivery problem. Although there was a mail network on the Chinese mainland, the service was unreliable. If a parcel was mailed to certain rural areas, the delivery time varied and the parcel was hard to track. Furthermore, most customers preferred their items to be delivered by regular mail. If Jewellworld.com wanted to deliver its jewelry to customers, Express Mail Service (EMS) was the most preferable way of minimizing the risk of packages being lost, but this service would add to the cost of the jewelry.

Lee believed that if Jewellworld.com did not begin to sell its jewelry online in mainland China, other companies would take that initiative and they would provide strong competition, due to their first-mover advantage. Moreover, Chinese was getting richer, and in the near future, the purchasing of jewelry would become more common. The market had unlimited potential, and even if mainlanders did not want to purchase online, expansion into China would provide a means of increasing brand awareness of Jewellworld.com, especially among young customers, and could increase the number of overnight visitors who come to Hong Kong to purchase Jewellworld.com's products under the visa-free policy. However, some of Jewellworld.com's managers believed that it was too early to start conducting online business on the mainland, because online shopping was still in the early stages and there were so many uncertainties to be resolved, such as payment method and delivery problems. These managers suggested that the company should pursue a wait-and-see approach, and should seek other ways of doing business on the mainland, such as the establishment of specialty shops for young customers in major cities. Other managers had an even more conservative opinion about doing business on the mainland. They believed that the CEPA policy would generate enough business to offset expansion into the mainland. Lee needed to develop some marketing plans and set timelines for the future development of Jewellworld.com in mainland China.

EXHIBIT 1 Tariffs on Hong Kong Domestic Jewelry Exported to China (Rate %)

Description	2003 MFN	2004 CEPA
Unworked or simply worked non-industrial diamonds	3.0	-
Jewelry and parts of silver	26.7	-
Other articles of jewelry and parts of silver	26.7	-
Articles of jewelry and parts of gold inlaid with diamonds	26.7	-
Other articles of jewelry and parts of gold	26.7	-
Articles of jewelry and parts of other precious metal inlaid with diamonds	35.0	-
Other articles of jewelry and parts of other precious metal	35.0	-
Articles of jewelry and parts of base metal clad with precious metal and inlaid with diamonds	35.0	-
Other articles of jewelry and parts of base metal clad with precious metal	35.0	-
Articles of wares and parts of silver	35.0	-
Articles of wares and parts of other precious metal	35.0	-
Articles of goldsmiths' and silversmiths' wares and parts of base metal clad with precious metal	35.0	-
Articles of natural or cultured pearls	35.0	-
Articles of precious or semi-precious stones	35.0	-
Cuff-links and studs of base metal	35.0	-
Other imitation jewelry of base metal	24.7	-
Other imitation jewelry of materials not specified elsewhere	35.0	-

Note: On January 1, 2004, the Closer Economic Partnership Arrangement (CEPA) removed the tariffs that had previously been levied on Hong Kong domestic exports to China under the Most Favored Nations (MFN) mandate.

Source: The Hong Kong Trade Development Council.

EXHIBIT 2 Income and Age Distribution of Mainland China Internet Users 2004

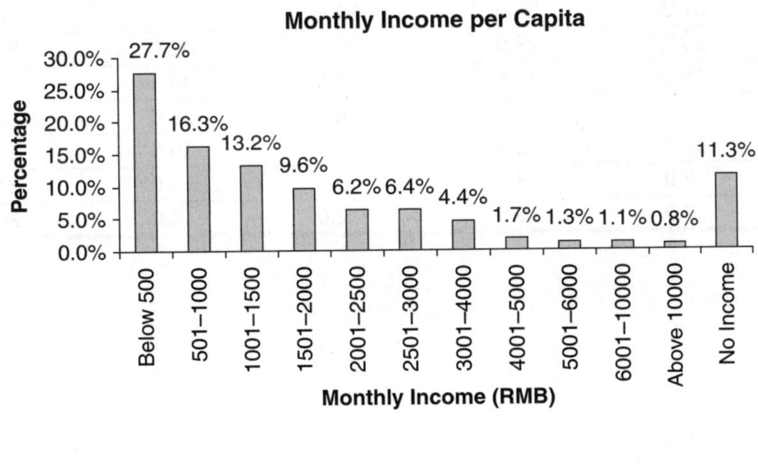

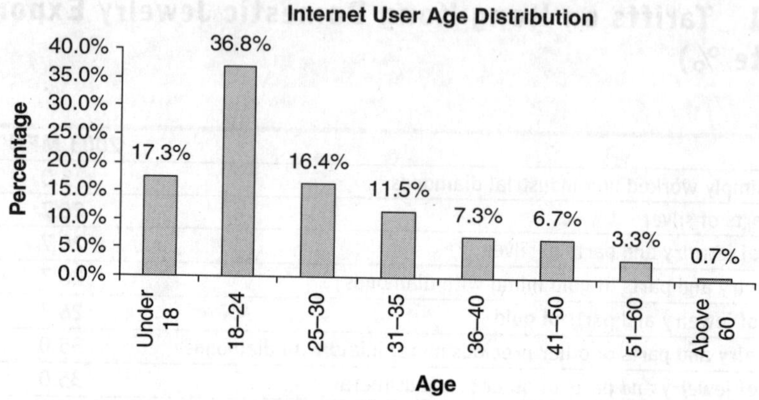

Source: The Chinese Internet Information Centre.

EXHIBIT 3 Online Jewelry Stores in Mainland China

Website Address	Online Function	Method of Payment
www.21gem.com	Online Shopping	Bank Wiring
www.cngem.net	Online Catalog	N/A
www.lanbaoshi.com	Online Shopping	Mail or Bank Wiring
www.wz-jewel.com	Online Shopping	Bank Wiring
www.pt990.net	Online Catalog	N/A

EXHIBIT 4 Most Popular Jewelry Materials in Mainland Chinese Cities 2003

(%)

	Eastern China			Southern China	
	Hangzhou	Nanjing	Ningbo	Fuchou	Shenzhen
Platinum	67.0	56.5	51.0	22.0	60.5
Diamond	33.5	29.0	29.5	36.0	59.5
Gold	15.0	22.5	5.5	34.5	35.0
Karat Gold	25.5	17.0	26.5	59.0	12.0
Gems	13.5	12.5	5.0	19.5	14.5
Silver	9.0	9.5	5.5	14.0	21.5
Pearl	7.0	10.5	2.0	9.0	28.5

	Central China		Western China		Northern China		
	Wuhan	Changxia	Chongqing	Xi'an	Tianjin	Shenyang	Harbin
Platinum	70.5	67.0	67.5	68.5	57.5	70.5	88.5
Diamond	32.5	43.5	17.5	30.0	26.5	22.5	44.5
Gold	15.5	16.5	27.0	20.5	27.5	38.0	59.5
Karat Gold	16.5	8.5	10.5	13.0	17.5	20.0	7.0
Gems	1.5	21.5	7.5	13.0	19.0	4.5	7.5
Silver	2.5	14.0	5.0	11.0	8.5	8.0	14.5
Pearl	3.5	14.0	5.0	9.0	9.5	3.5	2.0

Note: Interviewees were allowed to make more than one choice.
Source: The Hong Kong Trade Development Council.

EXHIBIT 5 Median Spending on Jewelry in Mainland Chinese Cities 2003

(%)

	Eastern China			Southern China	
	Hangzhou	Nanjing	Ningbo	Fuchou	Shenzhen
Rings	1,200	1,200	1,500	830	800
Necklaces	1,700	1,600	1,500	1,380	1,800
Earrings	500	500	550	300	500
Bracelets	1,300	1,000	1,000	800	880

	Central China		Western China		Northern China		
	Wuhan	Changxia	Chongqing	Xi'an	Tianjin	Shenyang	Harbin
Rings	1,000	1,000	650	1,000	860	1,400	1,000
Necklaces	1,800	1,000	1,100	1,380	1,000	1,700	1,500
Earrings	400	500	400	400	310	500	400
Bracelets	1,400	500	800	1,000	800	1,600	2,000

Note: US$1 = RMB8.5
Source: The Hong Kong Trade Development Council.

EXHIBIT 6 Preferred Jewelry Shopping Locations in Mainland Chinese Cities 2003

(%)

	Eastern China			Southern China	
	Hangzhou	Nanjing	Ningbo	Fuchou	Shenzhen
Department Stores	68.0	35.0	34.0	39.0	49.5
Street-Level Shops	17.0	44.0	41.5	43.5	18.0
Shopping Malls	14.5	21.0	24.0	16.5	27.0
Duty-Free Stores	0.5	-	0.5	1.0	5.0

	Central China		Western China		Northern China		
	Wuhan	Changxia	Chongqing	Xi'an	Tianjin	Shenyang	Harbin
Department Stores	54.5	55.0	70.0	44.0	49.0	44.0	24.5
Street-Level Shops	24.5	22.0	23.5	32.0	27.5	29.0	53.0
Shopping Malls	21.0	22.0	6.5	23.5	23.0	27.0	22.5
Duty-Free Stores	0.0	1.0	0.0	0.5	0.5	0.0	0.0

Note: Interviewees were allowed to make more than one choice.
Source: The Hong Kong Trade Development Council.

EXHIBIT 7 Decisive Factors for Purchasing Jewelry in Mainland Chinese Cities 2003

(%)

	Eastern China			Southern China	
	Hangzhou	Nanjing	Ningbo	Fuchou	Shenzhen
Good Design	87.5	85.0	80.0	88.5	94.5
Goodwill	86.0	88.5	87.0	90.0	94.5
Reliability	80.0	70.5	85.5	87.5	92.5
Reasonable Price	78.5	77.5	72.5	80.5	78.0
Good Reputation	78.5	72.5	71.5	75.0	89.5
Exact Price	74.0	75.0	75.5	80.5	85.0
Reasonable Finishing Price	78.0	72.0	79.0	81.0	74.5

	Central China		Western China		Northern China		
	Wuhan	Changxia	Chongqing	Xi'an	Tianjin	Shenyang	Harbin
Good Design	93.5	89.0	98.0	96.5	93.0	95.5	93.5
Goodwill	94.0	85.0	98.5	93.0	93.0	92.0	91.0
Reliability	92.5	85.0	95.5	93.5	90.0	95.0	93.0
Reasonable Price	85.5	82.0	93.0	94.0	84.0	88.0	91.5
Good Reputation	90.0	77.0	93.0	89.5	88.5	86.5	92.0
Exact Price	83.5	84.5	93.0	83.0	85.5	87.5	92.5
Reasonable Finishing Price	88.5	81.5	85.5	93.0	85.0	85.0	95.0

Source: The Hong Kong Trade Development Council.

EXHIBIT 8 Per Capita Monthly Income and Living Expenditures in 35 Chinese Cities August, 2004 (RMB)

Region	Per Capita Monthly Income	Per Capita Monthly Disposable Income	Per Capita Monthly Living Expenditure
Shenzhen	2,186	2,021	1,424
Guangzhou	1,542	1,317	1,185
Shanghai	1,521	1,375	979
Ningbo	1,435	1,263	891
Beijing	1,390	1,270	1,126
Xiamen	1,320	1,164	868
Hangzhou	1,237	1,109	945
Jinan	1,059	974	868
Dalian	1,031	927	741
Nanjing	970	904	697
Fuzhou	967	896	656
Qingdao	966	871	741
Tianjin	915	845	722
Hohhot	915	851	649
Changsha	907	836	719
Chongqing	849	803	659
Taiyuan	835	776	836
Wuhan	811	759	662
Harbin	806	788	673
Zhengzhou	799	760	596
Kunming	796	740	581
Urumqi	791	728	560
Nanning	786	714	593
Shenyang	769	696	614
Changchun	767	719	658
Chengdu	759	695	642
Shijiazhuang	755	696	538
Xi'an	735	691	597
Hefei	720	657	638
Haikou	717	686	561
Guiyang	707	684	588
Nanchang	660	631	438
Yinchuan	658	611	567
Lanzhou	657	602	498
Xining	624	595	496
Average	1,010	924	768

Note: US$1 = RMB8.5
Source: The Chinese Internet Information Center.

EXHIBIT 9 Mainland Jewelry Shoppers Brand Preferences by Market Segment 2003

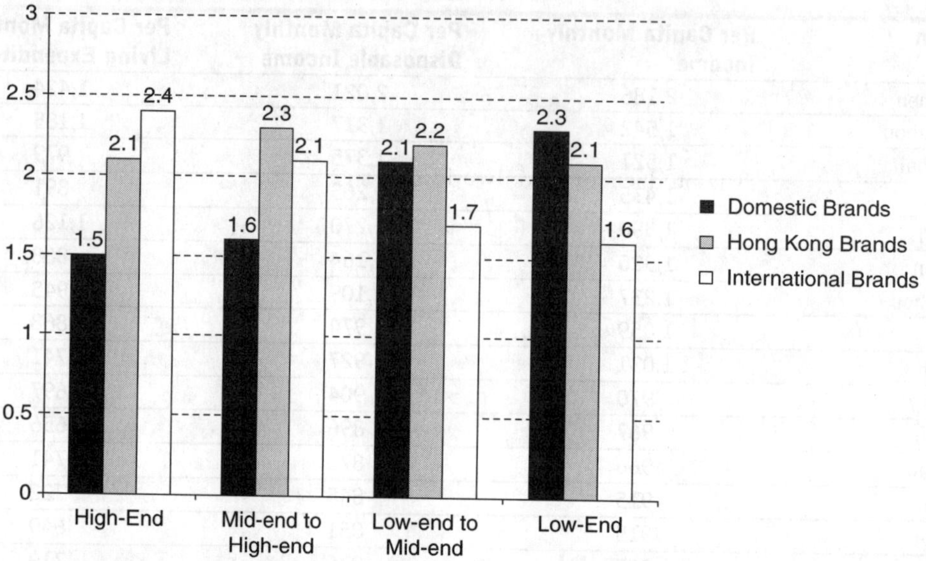

Note: The above figures are shown based on a scale of 3 (the most preferable).
Source: The Hong Kong Trade Development Council.

EXHIBIT 10 Reasons for Mainlanders Purchasing Jewelry in Hong Kong 2003

(%)

	Eastern China			Southern China	
	Hangzhou	Nanjing	Ningbo	Fuchou	Shenzhen
Lots of Styles	69.9	28.8	54.8	42.5	51.6
Lots of Brands	23.3	43.3	47.8	31.5	40.5
Quality Assurance	26.0	34.6	29.6	54.8	35.2
Reasonable Price	32.9	22.1	18.3	32.9	28.0
Travel Ban Relaxation	13.7	16.3	23.5	37.7	22.0
Good Reputation	8.2	17.3	12.2	53.4	21.3
Reliability	9.6	18.3	19.1	47.9	19.9
Tax-Free	16.4	26.9	13.0	22.6	17.7
Exact Price	5.5	5.8	12.2	28.8	11.1
Good After-Sales Service	4.1	2.9	8.7	25.3	9.6

	Central China		Western China		Northern China		
	Wuhan	Changxia	Chongqing	Xi'an	Tianjin	Shenyang	Harbin
Lots of Styles	43.9	44.6	80.0	56.7	51.9	64.9	46.0
Lots of Brands	37.9	43.4	57.0	38.1	27.3	32.4	37.0
Quality Assurance	22.7	33.7	40.0	29.9	22.1	24.3	50.0
Reasonable Price	22.7	34.9	38.0	33.0	20.8	27.0	17.0
Travel Ban Relaxation	30.3	20.5	24.0	14.4	26.0	18.9	19.0
Good Reputation	15.2	16.9	24.0	19.6	10.4	18.9	9.0
Reliability	9.1	15.7	19.0	12.4	7.8	16.2	23.0
Tax-Free	13.6	28.9	20.0	10.3	14.3	35.1	12.0
Exact Price	4.5	13.3	12.0	3.1	3.9	-	17.0
Good After-Sales Service	3.0	12.0	5.0	8.2	5.2	10.8	7.0

Note: Interviewees were allowed to make more than one choice.

EXHIBIT 11 Online Shopping Profile

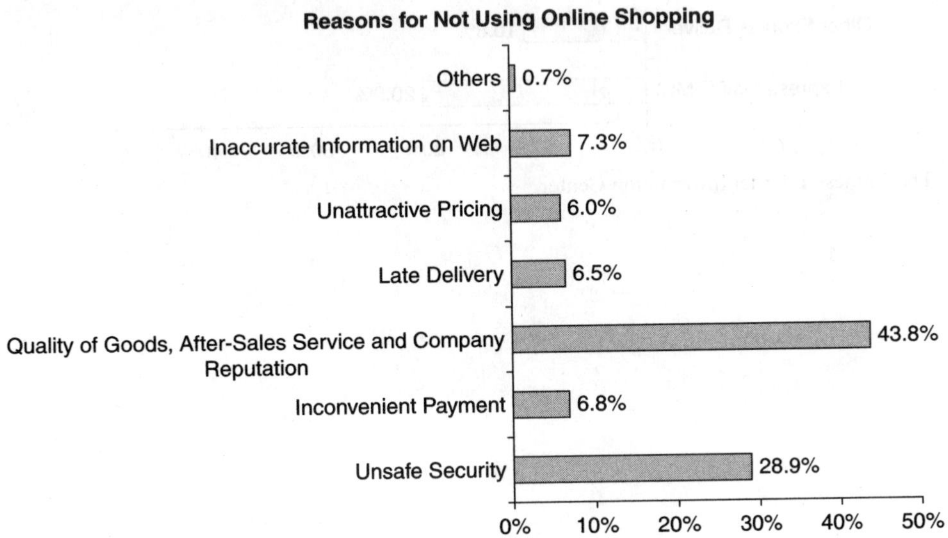

EXHIBIT 11 (Continued)

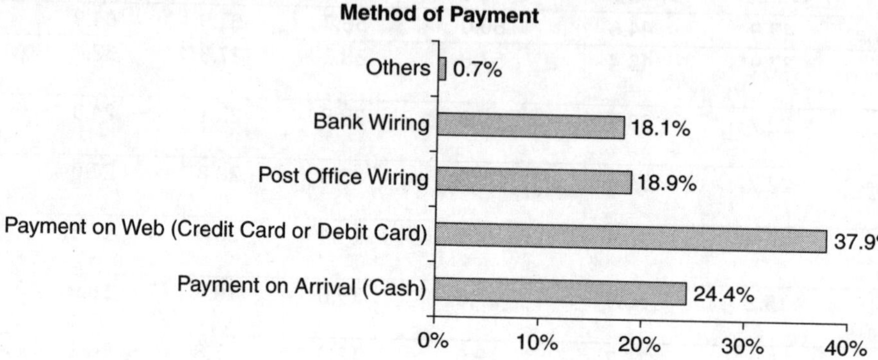

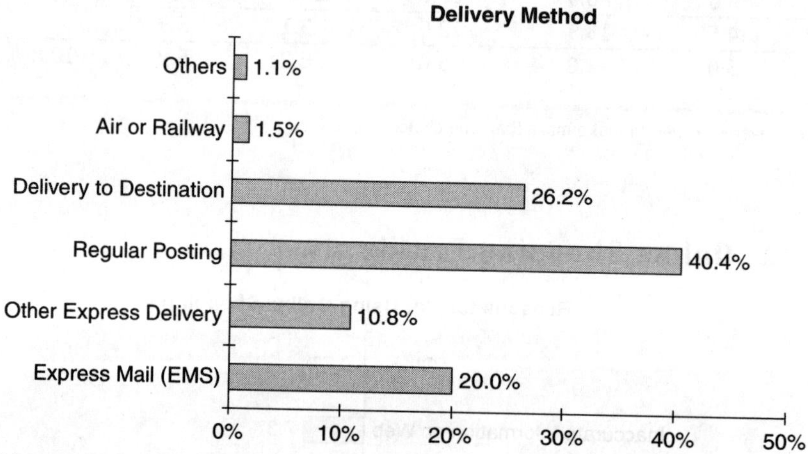

Source: The Chinese Internet Information Center.

16

Future Shop: Retail Customer Research[1]

Aly Alidina, Morley Ivers and Rachel Kay prepared this case under the supervision of Professor Michael R. Pearce solely to provide material for class discussion. The authors do not intend to illustrate either effective or ineffective handling of a managerial situation. The authors may have disguised certain names and other identifying information to protect confidentiality.

INTRODUCTION

In September 2000, three second-year honors business administration students at the Richard Ivey School of Business, Aly Alidina, Morley Ivers and Rachel Kay, met to discuss the customer research project for their retail marketing course. After lengthy discussions and copious amounts of Starbucks coffee, the threesome finalized their dialogue regarding areas of interest, marketplace dynamics and proposed timelines. The team unanimously chose to investigate the largest retail technology powerhouse in Canada: Future Shop Ltd. They knew their primary goal was to determine Future Shop's retail value proposition (RVP), but they faced a big challenge behind this investigation, which was determining what research design to use, how to implement the research and how to interpret the data that was collected.

[1] This case has been written on the basis of published sources only. Consequently, the interpretation and perspectives presented in this case are not necessarily those of the Future Shop or any of its employees.

During September and October, the team performed extensive research on Future Shop's overall business practices. In addition, they decided to conduct 48 customer surveys across the country (see Exhibit 1). Their goal was to determine if Future Shop was executing its strategies properly from the consumer's viewpoint and to provide their contact at Future Shop in London, Ontario, with recommendations for improving its retail value proposition.

BACKGROUND

To begin the research process, the team members split up their duties and spoke individually to company employees and customers at London, Ontario's south store and Toronto's Dundas store. They quickly discovered that Future Shop's mission was clearly communicated to all management and employees: "to create an advanced and cost-effective organization where every individual adds value." In addition to their field research, the group used the firm's 2000 annual report, which clearly communicated that Future Shop was Canada's largest, fastest growing national retailer and e-tailer of consumer electronic products for the digital age.

According to the data provided within the shareholder report, Future Shop operated 83 superstores, five Computer City stores and the nation's premier online electronics superstore, www.futureshop.ca. Sales totalled Cdn$1.7 billion for fiscal 2000, giving Future Shop a leading share of Canada's consumer electronics marketplace. Throughout the past several years, Future Shop had been committed to an aggressive growth plan through new store openings, relocations and upgrades in primary and secondary markets. It was currently in the process of enhancing market penetration in key product categories and was developing partnerships with leading global technology companies. Future Shop had 7,100 associates who were dedicated to providing Canadians with fast, friendly service, the latest digital products, such as DVD players, wireless devices and a wide selection of televisions, computers, music and appliances.

From a corporate standpoint, Future Shop had enjoyed exceptional performance in the past year. Sales rose approximately 16 per cent to $1.7 billion, setting a record for Canadian store sales. Net earnings reached $23.7 million or $1.50 per share, a record high for consolidated earnings. At the store level, Future Shop witnessed the highest annual sales increase since 1995, with growth of 10.7 per cent. In addition, Future Shop lowered its selling, general and administrative (SG&A) expenses to 20.4 per cent of sales.

This performance was achieved while going through the overhaul processes of relocating and upgrading seven stores, opening three additional outlets and financing the development of www.futureshop.ca. The strong growth reflected market share gains as well as more robust Canadian consumer spending. Pushing the upward trend in sales and market share were their internal initiatives to accelerate growth, improve service and expand margins. Future Shop expected to capture an increased share of the Canadian market, while ensuring that they remained the industry's lowest-cost player.

According to Future Shop, store associates played a major role in contributing to the improved results, which was a direct reflection of corporate emphasis on training and development programs. In the past year, employees had seen their selection training, compensation, recognition and rewards programs revamped, with clear performance benchmarks for store managers and sales associates.

The market had seen Future Shop re-engineer its supply chain and increase inventory turn to 6.25 from 5.75. The store's new advertising campaigns, such as "Fast Forward" and "We Sell Cool Stuff," were considered very successful. Future Shop's goal was to sharpen its focus on customer service through store redesigns, signage and changes to the incentive system for all 7,100 employees.

Future Shop's e-commerce business, www.futureshop.ca, established itself as Canada's premier e-tailer of consumer electronics products. This online business accounted for $25 million (or one per cent) of projected sales. This was expected to grow as internal Future Shop research indicated that 50 per cent of Canadians were aware of the site, up from five per cent in 1999.

The organization had not been successful in all of its ventures. In fiscal 1999, Future Shop decided to exit from the U.S. retail market, as it was unable to compete with major players like Best Buy, Computer City and Circuit City. In Canada, Future Shop was a power retailer with a superior value proposition. It was unable to develop this type of penetration in the United States, and thus exited the market with an invigorated refocus exclusively on its Canadian operations.

RESEARCH STRATEGY AND METHODOLOGY

Alidina, Ivers and Kay concluded that their retail marketing research could take several forms, and that the research could easily span across all facets of the company's operations. Ivers and Kay wanted to do something surrounding improving the customer service aspect because of their personal experiences of shopping at Future Shop. Alidina believed that the customer service was fine, and that they should instead look into the number of locations around the country and whether or not Future Shop was reaching all of its potentially profitable customers. To solve the problem of what specifically to research, the team decided to research consumers' impression of Future Shop's retail value proposition (RVP) in general. They looked at several aspects: whether Future Shop was meeting its objectives in terms of customer care, pricing strategies and selection segmentation from the customer's perspective.

As a starting point, the team decided to investigate the RVP of Future Shop — why do consumers go to Future Shop? Is there a single, most important factor that drives traffic to Future Shop, and if so, is it low prices, convenience of location, service or selection?

After determining Future Shop's RVP, the team planned on using surveys to establish an understanding of the organization's reputation in the marketplace from the consumer's vantage point. They were anxious to determine if this reputation was limited to a particular geographic area or if there was a general perception of Future Shop shared across the country.

More generally, the team also wanted to research the impact, if any, that the Internet has had on retailers such as Future Shop. Are Future Shop customers aware of the Future Shop Web site? Are they choosing to shop online in search of better prices or convenience, or are they simply wanting to avoid the Future Shop retail experience altogether?

In order to test their hypothesis, the three students carried out surveys of Future Shop customers in various regions. They knew that they could cover the London and Toronto areas with in-person surveys, and with such surveys, the team members would also be able to get valuable information through body language and record additional comments outside specific answers. It soon surfaced that Ivers was concerned that this would not be representative of Future Shop patrons across the country, since the store set-ups may differ and the customer service associates in certain locations may be more or less affective. Alidina then had the idea to e-mail consumers across the country to get their opinions as well, and in this way, the group gained additional data in very little time. Twelve surveys were conducted at Future Shop's location in London, Ontario, Wellington Road South. An additional 12 surveys were distributed at Future Shop's location in Toronto, Yonge and Dundas. Finally, 24 surveys were performed by e-mail, reaching Future Shop customers in Vancouver, Calgary, Oshawa, Kitchener, Windsor, Toronto and London.

KEY FINDINGS

Alidina, Ivers and Kay described their research:

> In the first question (see Exhibit 1 for questions), we asked the consumer how many times they had visited future shop in the last six months. Customers who visit Future Shop often (i.e., five or more visits in the last six months) would likely have stronger opinions than those who shop infrequently and would more accurately reflect Future Shop's reputation. One respondent, who had five visits to Future Shop in the last six months, said, "The only reason I ever go to Future Shop is to purchase an item." He also commented that the customer care was "terrible" but that he would return to Future Shop because of low prices and convenient store locations.

- 42 per cent of respondents had less than three visits to Future Shop in the last six months.
- 35 per cent had between three and five visits.
- 23 per cent had more than five visits.

Most questions were created to try to understand whether Everyday Low Pricing (EDLP) was the biggest motive for consumers to shop at Future Shop. The second question allowed us to gauge the price sensitivity of the Future Shop customer. By comparing prices, these customers who tend to shop around, prior to visiting Future Shop, were price sensitive consumers and thus likely attracted to Future Shop's "lowest price guarantee."

- 52 per cent compared prices.

Future Shop was known for its comprehensive flyers and extensive advertising. The third question allowed us to determine whether Future Shop's advertising drove traffic to the store.

- 50 per cent were attracted from advertising.

Questions 4 through 7 were created to determine if Future Shop was, in fact, a destination store for consumers.

- 43 per cent of respondents travelled less than 10 kilometres (km); 27 per cent travelled 10 km to 19.9 km; 30 per cent travelled more than 20 km.
- 19 per cent walked, 10 per cent took public transportation, 71 per cent travelled by car.
- 82 per cent intended to purchase (92 per cent of these respondents found what they were looking for).

Questions 8 through 12 were designed to explore why customers were shopping at Future Shop. These questions focused primarily on customers' areas of concentration — specifically, price and service.

People who considered Future Shop prices to be superior to other retailers generally rated price as an eight or higher. People who didn't consider Future Shop to offer better prices than competitors typically gave a rating of less than seven.

- 62 per cent rated price above average value (better bargains than competitors).

Survey respondents were advised that they should rate Future Shop as an eight or higher if they were pleased with the level of customer care. A rating of seven was considered average or that the consumer was indifferent about the level of service they had received. Ratings of six or lower indicated that the consumer was generally displeased with customer care. Ratings of less than four indicated that the consumer had a very negative shopping experience at Future Shop.

- 33 per cent rated service as 7 or higher.
- 42 per cent rated service between 4 and 6.
- 25 per cent rated service as 4 or lower.

Questions 10 and 11 gave the survey respondent the opportunity to express their favorite and least-favorite aspects about shopping at Future Shop. We believed that most consumers would express poor service or commission-based salespeople as their biggest complaints about Future Shop. With this in mind, question 12 was created to determine if the lack of customer care was a strong enough factor to deter consumers from patronizing Future Shop. This question was rephrased in question 19.

- Despite 94 per cent of customers having pet peeves about Future Shop, 70 per cent will not let their pet peeves keep them from coming back.
- Only one respondent said they would absolutely not return to Future Shop.

Question 13 allowed us to analyse the demographics of the survey respondents. We wanted to understand if a particular market segment was more sensitive to price or service than other segments.

- 73 per cent were single; 27 per cent were married.
- 19 per cent had children.
- Level of education: 19 per cent were high school graduates; 48 per cent had undergraduate degrees; 33 per cent had post-graduate degrees.
- Income level of consumers: 22 per cent less than $30,000 ; 24 per cent $30,000 to $49,999; 15 per cent $50,000 to $74,999; 13 per cent $75,000 to $99,999 ; 26 per cent were in the highest income bracket.

Questions 14 and 15 were created to gauge the impact of the Internet on retailing. People who shop on the Internet can compare prices easily — if they are still shopping at Future Shop, they had likely been unsuccessful at finding cheaper prices on the Internet. Future Shop advertises its Web site heavily on all flyers. Question 16 allowed us to observe whether, in fact, people are aware of Future Shop's e-commerce channel and whether they are switching in favor of the online experience.

- 63 per cent shop online.
- 31 per cent have visited FutureShop.ca.

Question 16 and 17 were again service-oriented questions. We wanted to understand whether having commission-based salespeople meant that customers were served promptly upon entering the store. We also wanted to evaluate opinions on the competence of salespeople at Future Shop.

- 63 per cent were approached in under two minutes, but 19 per cent weren't approached at all.

The last two questions were designed specifically to zero in on the single biggest factor drawing consumers to Future Shop. The factors that received the most votes can be interpreted as Future Shop's RVP.

- 35 per cent price, two per cent service, 57 per cent selection, six per cent location.

GROUP DISCUSSIONS

After performing the field research, Alidina, Ivers and Kay decided it was time to discuss some things they noticed when conducting the surveys.

Kay: "I noticed that there were a lot of comments such as " . . . there's no other game in town . . . I will go back — unfortunately".

Ivers: "I also noticed that although Future Shop emphasizes customer care in its in-store pamphlets and annual report, it's obvious that customer care is unsatisfactory in the eyes of many consumers."

Alinda: "I agree. People I spoke to commented that the salespeople were "pushy" or "aggressive."

Ivers: "It's actually unpredictable because the salespeople approach most customers in less than 10 minutes, while a large amount not at all!"

With all this research completed, the team pondered how to present the research in a valuable manner to their contact at Future Shop, and how to communicate the findings to Professor Pearce.

EXHIBIT 1 Retail Study

1. Approximately how many times have you visited Future Shop in the past six months?
2. Did you visit/compare any material of any competitors before shopping at Future Shop?
3. Were you attracted to Future Shop from advertising?
4. How far did you travel to get here?
5. What was your method of travel?
6. Did you intend to purchase something at Future Shop before arriving?
7. Did you find exactly what you were looking for?
8. On a scale of 1 to 10, how would you judge the prices at Future Shop?
9. On a scale of 1 to 10, how would you judge the service at Future Shop?
10. What is you favorite aspect about shopping at Future Shop?
11. If you have a "pet peeve" or severe dislike about Future Shop, what would it be?
12. Would this keep you from coming back to Future Shop in the future?
13. Please let us know a little more about your background: (check the ones that apply):

    ____ I am married ____ I have children ____ I am a high school graduate
    ____ I am a university graduate with an undergraduate degree
    ____ I am a university graduate with a post graduate degree

    What is your approximate household income?

    ____ Less than $30,000 ____ $30,000 to $49,999 ____ $50,000 to $74,999
    ____ $75,000 to $99,999 ____ More than $100,000
14. Do you shop on the Internet?
15. Have you visited www.futureshop.ca?
16. How long did it take for a salesperson to approach you after entering the store?
17. If you had one word to describe the performance of the salesperson in relation to their interaction with you, what would it be?
18. Will you return to Future Shop?
19. What was the Number 1 determining factor in your decision to visit Future Shop today?
20. Please circle ONE of the following that best describes Future Shop:

    a) low prices b) good service c) large selection d) good location

17

Exploring Category Benefits for Brand Building: Kaya and the Beauty Care Market[1]

Dr. S. Ramesh Kumar, Teja Ande and Syed Hussain.

India is an emerging market that is going through radical changes in lifestyles and spending patterns of consumers. Post liberalization after the early part of the nineties, urbanization has opened up many facets of lifestyles that have become a part of the consumer culture, especially in urban markets. While millions of consumers in the country were still grappling with the affordability to buy the essentials, there are several segments of consumers who indulge in discretionary spending on several categories of products associated with enhancing their self identity. These segments of consumers believe that these categories and brands would enable them to enhance their self concept. Beauty care categories are important for these consumers. Creams and lotions are "ready to apply" offerings with strong brands differentiating themselves in these categories with symbolic appeals that are directed to the self concept of consumers. Kaya is also a brand in the category of beauty care but the brand's offerings were associated with medically anchored services aimed at enhancing the looks of consumers. The brand opened up a new facet of offering beauty care services that were more associated with up market and state-of-the-art hospitals where consumers underwent these services through doctors who had specialized in cosmetic surgeries/interventions. The case dealt with insights from the beauty care services, specifically about the perception of beauty parlour consumers. The commonality of the benefits of beauty care delivered through a process by both beauty parlours and Kaya is the fundamental plane that was used to explore the usefulness of consumer response associated with beauty parlours. While Kaya attempted to draw consumers by appropriate positioning services, the insights from customers of beauty parlour were important for Kaya to build its brand by using loyalty as a differentiator in a market that is at a nascent stage. Would the differentiation between the first-time users of the beauty parlour and the loyal consumers of parlours offer insights to Kaya? Issues related to services management and, customer value and customer loyalty were relevant to the competitive strategies of Kaya.

[1] This case was written by Dr. S. Ramesh Kumar, Teja Ande and Syed Hussain. Teja Ande and Syed Hussain have completed their post graduation programmes in management from Indian Institute of Management Bangalore.

BEAUTY CARE INDUSTRY IN INDIA

Traditionally, beauty care products in Indian culture had been limited to herbs and homemade products. Only soaps, hair oil, shampoos and talcum powder from the organised industry had been able to penetrate the Indian consumer minds. However with the rise in awareness of hygiene and personal grooming across urban and rural India, several beauty and personal care categories had gained momentum. In India, marketing activities involved popular celebrities and have traditionally highlighted issues such as body odour, dandruff, oral health and spread of infection, further boosting the demand for beauty and personal care products.

The Indian beauty care industry had grown rapidly in the last few years with the penetration of premium beauty care products and services. The rising disposable income and changing lifestyles of the Indians had led to a boom in beauty and personal care industries. The Indian skin care industry, for example, was forecasted to grow at 9% CAGR during 2009-2014[2]. With an increase in the number of households who were willing to spend in upgrading to a higher consumption lifestyle, there was a huge growth happening in the Indian beauty care industry. Major FMCG brands like HUL, P&G, etc. had been aggressively expanding their product portfolios, distribution networks and marketing activities in this segment. With the proliferation of beauty and personal care categories and brands, consumer awareness of different types of products and brands increased.

The consumption of beauty products and services seemed to have experienced significant growth[3]. The emergence of brands such as Marico's Kaya Skin Clinic, Lakme Beauty Salon, VLCC, Shahnaz Husain Herbals, CavinCare's Limelite, Green Trends, Keune and Jawed Habib Hair & Beauty can be attributed to this trend, said observers. The boom was clearly evident from the fact that HUL was opening up a new Lakme salon almost every week and that Jawed Habib Hair & Beauty (JHHB) had grown from 37 parlours in 2006 to 225 by the end of 2010.The boom on the Indian beauty market had also been able to attract large multinationals like Jean Claude Biguine with annual revenues of 150 million Euros to set up parlours in India[4].

The predominantly unorganized, locally run beauty parlour market was now being replaced by the branded chains like Lakme, changing the landscape in the country. These branded beauty parlours were leading in a new era of trained parlour personnel, offering services based on global insights and professional products incorporated by latest international technologies.

The roughly Rs 7,000 crore organized and unorganized hair and beauty industry was growing at a CAGR of 35%. It was estimated to have a potential business of Rs 30,000 crore by 2015. Personal hygiene products (soaps and shower products) hair care, skincare, colour cosmetics and fragrances were the key segments in the Indian beauty care industry (Refer to Exhibit 1). The Skin care segment was relatively smaller compared to the personal care segment. The anti-ageing cream segment, which was only 2% of skincare market, alone, had been growing at a rate of 90% over the past few years. The rising number of educated and working women in the corporate world had been a major driver for this rapid growth. What made this industry more fascinating was that even with the high growth rate, the Indian market remained largely untapped as compared to other developing markets. In comparison (Refer to Exhibit 1), a developing country like China spent 10 times more on skincare, six times more on cosmetics

---

[2] Staying Ahead of the Game: How Companies are Adapting to the Changing Face of Beauty, Euro monitor November 2010.

[3] Beauty business set to boom, http://economictimes.indiatimes.com/news/news-by-industry/cons-products/fashion-/-cosmetics-/-jewellery/beauty-business-set-to-boom/articleshow/8921457.cms as accessed on July 12, 2011.

[4] Beauty's bet: JCB plans to set up shop in India, http://economictimes.indiatimes.com/beautys-bet-jcb-plans-to-set-up-shop-in-india/articleshow/1773980.cms as accessed on July 12, 2011.

and two times more on hair care on a per capita basis. It is also worth noting that Indians had the highest percentage of women in the 25–44 age groups, the key segment for the beauty industry[5]. These figures and facts indicated huge unrealized potential of the Indian market. Given the vast potential of beauty care services in the country, consumer perception on value with regard to the delivery of services, consumer loyalty and brand perception were important from the view point of any brand or unbranded offering in this category.

ABOUT KAYA SKIN CLINIC

In December 2002, after conducting extensive research, Marico identified an emerging need in the market in the form of an aspiration to look and feel good. On furthering this understanding with consumers, a more focused, yet still untapped need of having flawless skin that looks good naturally, was identified. The first Kaya Skin Clinic was thus launched with the single-minded objective of delivering flawless skin solutions customized to Indian skin, through the use of latest technology.

Today, Kaya has 81 clinics spread across 26 cities in India, 18 highly successful clinics in the Middle East and 2 clinics in Bangladesh at Dhaka. In May 2010, Kaya acquired the aesthetics business of the Singapore based Derma Rx Asia Pacific Pte. Ltd (Derma Rx). In the recent past, the company has launched more services like lip enhancement, fairness and hair removal services as part of its portfolio expansion. Kaya Skin Clinic now has a number of services and solutions for Skin Beauty, Skin Concerns, Laser Hair Reduction and Anti-Ageing. Their product range has over 40 products for skin, hair and body for both women and men.

Kaya offers 360-degree skin care solutions which include advice on proper diet and exercise regime. All the services offered at Kaya Skin Clinic are designed and supervised by a team of over 250 dermatologists and carried out by certified skin practitioners who have undergone more than 300 hours of training. The services are US FDA approved, tested in-house, and conform to the highest international quality standards. The services are competitively priced and start from Rs 1,250 onwards. Kaya has over 6,00,000 satisfied consumers.

Kaya had a slew of continuous in-house training programs for its skin practitioners and dermatologists. Once every six months, Kaya held training-cum-refresher courses for its staff to keep them up-to-date with the latest skin care techniques available internationally. Its team of dermatologists also participates in the in-house Continuing Medical Education (CME) program, where international doctors meet to discuss various trends in the skincare field.

Kaya, overall, is divided into six service verticals viz. Skin beauty, Skin concerns, Hair-free, Anti-ageing, Bridal and Kaya Men. Unlike other retailers, Kaya has not adopted the franchisee model. The company owns each of its clinics because Kaya Skin Clinic believes in providing consistent services across the country.

Philosophy of Kaya[6]

The philosophy at Kaya is governed by the single value of placing the consumer first at all times. The word Kaya in Sanskrit means 'body'. Kaya is all about personal confidence through expert skin care which seamlessly blends looking good with feeling good about our inner and outer selves at all times.

---

[5] Outlook for Personal Care Industry: An Indian Perspective , Tata Strategic Management Group http://www.tsmg.com/download/article/Personal_Care_Chemicals.pdf as accessed on 12/09/2011.

[6] Kaya Culture, Kaya Philosophy, www.kayaclinic.com accessed on September 13, 2011.
Note: Information on Kaya Skin Clinic was provided by Ms Garima Sharma, Ms Aditi Chada of Kaya Skin Clinic.

The emphasis, therefore, is on highly customized and personalized services most suited for Indian skin provided in a state-of-the-art clinic with a Zen-like ambience.

The core values of Kaya skin clinic were:

- **Customer First**: Spirit of Partnership – Keeping the consumer in focus, partnering to deliver skin care solutions. Doing what is in the best interest of the consumer, business interest will follow.
- **Openness**: Allowing diversity of opinion by listening to members without bias. Sharing information, both good and bad, and having a sense of trust and respect for each other.
- **Ownership**: 'My Kaya' mind-set. What would I do if I were the owner of the business? Displaying seamless behaviour across the organization rather than drawing boundaries of functions/grades when it is necessary in the interest of organization.

Kaya Skin Clinic can be called a chain of cosmetic dermatology clinics. It is a pioneer and thought leader in the skin care services space in the country. It offers its clients tailor-made, result-oriented, safe, non-surgical skin solutions with the latest and most suitable technology available in the world, which are completely administered by dermatologists. Any beauty or skincare brand/service could be a competitor to Kaya. One of their biggest competitors would be stand-alone doctors and dermatologists who offer one or two services as compared to them. It is in this context that Kaya was to use the commonality of category benefits to develop its brand, more so among loyal consumers.

METHODOLOGY OF STUDY

The objective of the study was to compare the value perception of first-time consumers and loyal consumers of beauty parlours in order to obtain category insights that Kaya could use. The value perception needed to be built around the consumers' experiences of the service at the service provider's premises. The questionnaire has a scale on several components of the service experience as shown in the three sections of Exhibit 2.

The responses were collected from the residents of cities viz. Bangalore, Hyderabad and Delhi. Data from 50 first-time consumers and 50 loyal consumers of beauty services was collected.

The list of items that reflect the dimensionality of value perception in the context of beauty services was developed from the academic literature: Millan et.al (2004)[7], Sweeney et.al (2001)[8], Jensen et.al (2007)[9], Sheth et.al (1991)[10], Huber et.al (2007)[11]. The responses were collected from 50 first-time consumers and 50 loyal consumers of beauty parlours. Loyal consumers of beauty parlours were those who had visited the same parlour more than three times (given the nature of the category as perceived by the authors, it was opined that a respondent who had visited a parlour more than three times would be good enough to be considered as a loyal consumer) .

---

[7] Angel Millan, Agueda Esteban, Development of a multiple-item scale for measuring consumer satisfaction in travel agencies services, Tourism Management, Volume 25, Issue 5, October 2004, Pages 533–546.

[8] Jillian C. Sweeney, Geoffrey N. Soutar, Consumer perceived value: The development of a multiple item scale, Journal of Retailing, 2001, Pages 203–220.

[9] Øystein Jensen, Kai Victor Hansen, Consumer values among restaurant consumers, Hospitality Management, Volume 26, 2007, Pages 603–622.

[10] Jagdish N. Sheth, Bruce I. Newman, Barbara L. Gross, Why we buy what we buy: A theory of consumption values, Journal of Business Research, Volume 22, Issue 2, March 1991, Pages 159–170.

[11] Frank Huber, Andreas Herrmann and Stephan C. Henneberg, Measuring customer value and satisfaction in services transactions, scale development, validation and cross-cultural comparison, International Journal of Consumer Studies, Vol. 31, 2007, Pages 554–564.

The respondents were drawn from the segments of students and working professionals. Likert scale was used for the purpose. The data collection was done at Bangalore in the months of June/July 2011.

Would differentiating between first-time consumers and loyal consumers be worthwhile for Kaya? Would the mechanism of studying consumer decision making be useful to the brand? Kaya had to decide on what kind of insights can be obtained from the data on beauty parlour consumers to develop itself in an emerging market in which the brand was required to diffuse itself.

Exhibit 3 captures some of the print advertisements carried out by Kaya. It gives an idea of how Kaya tried to differentiate itself from regular beauty parlours by consistently emphasizing its technology, expertise from dermatologists and skin experts, etc.

The authors would like to thank Garima Sharma, Aditi Chada, Executives of Kaya Skin Clinic and Deepa Rajaram who had earlier worked for the company for their sustained support towards this case initiative.

EXHIBIT 1 Market Share of Segments in the Indian Beauty Care Industry and Their Comparison with China[12]

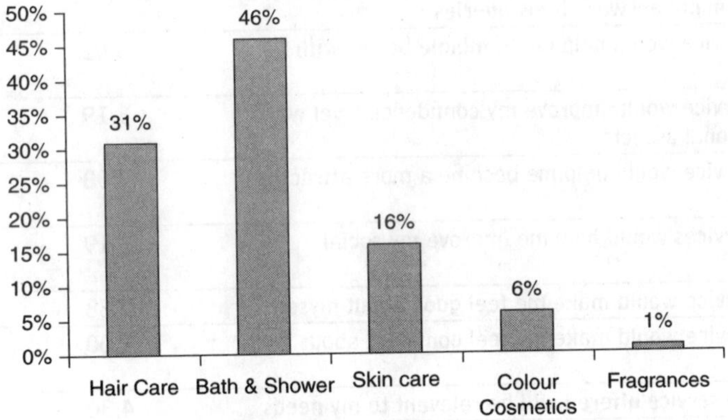

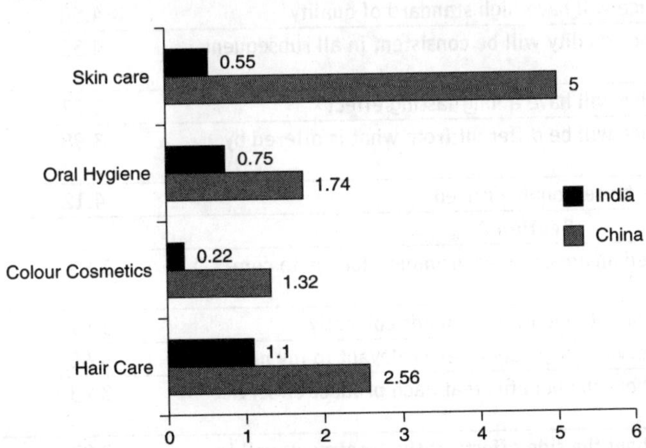

[12] Outlook for Personal Care Industry: An Indian Perspective , Tata Strategic Management Group http://www.tsmg.com/download/article/Personal_Care_Chemicals.pdf as accessed on 12/09/2011.

EXHIBIT 2 The Responses of Consumers of Beauty Parlours (First-Time Consumers vs. Loyal Consumers)

Item	Average of Responses Loyal Consumers	First-time Consumers
Section 1		
The ambience of the beauty parlour is expected to be attractive and comforting	4.21	4.27
The employees at the beauty parlour are expected to be well groomed	4.37	4.38
The employees at the beauty parlour are expected to be polite and friendly	4.56	4.43
The employees at the beauty parlour are expected to be willing to help me with initial queries regarding the products and services	4.47	4.19
The employees at the beauty parlour are expected to be dedicated and spend enough time to answer all my queries	3.74	3.62
I expect that the service would help me to mingle better with friends/people	3.02	2.84
I expect that the service would improve my confidence level with regards to interpersonal aspects	3.19	3.22
I expect that the service would help me become a more attractive person to others	2.98	2.97
I expect that the services would help me improve my social relations	3.19	3.14
I expect that the service would make me feel good about myself	3.88	4.00
I expect that the service would make me feel confident about myself	4.00	4.11
I expect the that the service offered will be relevant to my needs	4.30	4.32
I expect that the service will have high standard of quality	4.58	4.41
I expect that the service quality will be consistent in all subsequent visits	4.35	4.27
I expect that the service will have a long-lasting effect	3.77	3.84
I expect that the service will be different from what is offered by other Parlours	3.98	3.54
I expect the service to be reasonably priced	4.12	3.97
Section 2		
The beauticians created an amicable environment for me to communicate my needs	3.91	3.65
The beauticians were able to identify my needs correctly	3.67	3.27
All the products and services suggested were relevant to my needs	3.65	3.24
I was well informed about the benefits that each product or service would provide	3.23	3.14
I was well informed about the side effects of the treatment well in advance	3.07	3.19
The beauticians at the beauty parlour were punctual at keeping the appointments	3.88	3.70

The beauticians treated me well while conducting the sessions	3.70	3.73
The technology used in the treatments is the most advanced and offers the best results	3.70	3.49
Section 3		
I found the ambience of the beauty parlour to be attractive and comforting	4.00	3.86
I found the beauticians at the beauty parlour as well-groomed	4.00	3.89
I found the employees to be polite and friendly	3.98	3.76
I found the employees to be very helpful	3.79	3.65
I felt that the employees dedicated enough time in answering my queries	3.44	3.38
I feel that I have improved my confidence level with regard to interpersonal aspects	3.02	3.03
I feel that I became a more attractive person to others	3.09	3.14
I feel that I have improved my social relations	2.79	2.95
After using the services, I feel good about myself	3.79	3.78
After using the services, I feel more confident about myself	3.51	3.70
The services offered were relevant to my needs	3.88	3.70
The services offered were of high quality standards	3.65	3.73
The service quality was consistent throughout the course of the sessions	3.65	3.65
I feel that the beauty treatment will have a long-lasting effect	3.09	3.03
I found the services offered to be unique	2.77	2.84
The services offered were reasonably priced	3.21	3.05
I would recommend the service to those who seek my advice about such matters	3.77	3.59
I would encourage friends and relatives to use the service	3.81	3.70
I would post positive messages about the service on some Internet forums/social networking sites	3.19	2.95
I intend to continue to use the services of the beauty parlour	4.02	3.59

Source: Figures were derived from the field survey carried out by the authors.

EXHIBIT 3 Advertisements of Kaya Skin Clinic

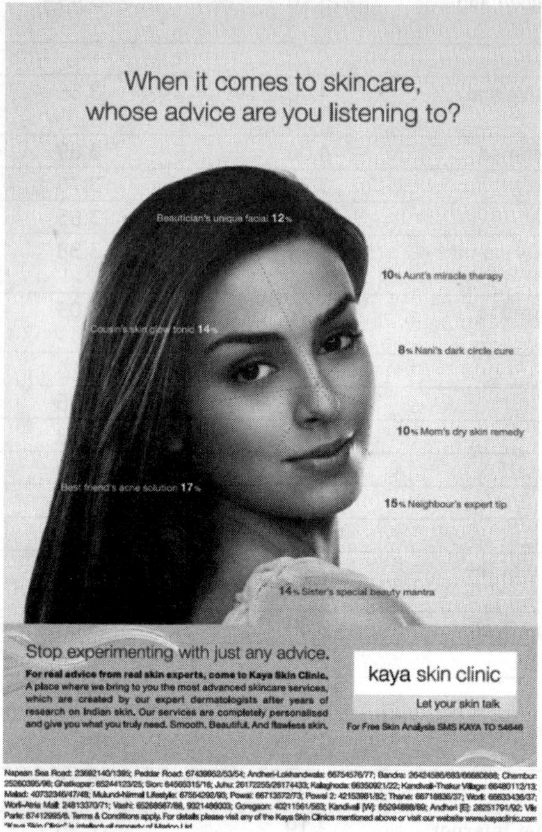